MUSIC IN AMERICAN LIFE

A list of books in the series Music in American Life appears at the back of this volume.

CHARLES MARTIN LOEFFLER

Ex Libris
Ch-Martin Loeffler

CHARLES MARTIN LOEFFLER

A Life Apart in American Music

ELLEN KNIGHT

UNIVERSITY OF ILLINOIS PRESS
Urbana and Chicago

Publication of this work was supported in part by a grant
from the Sonneck Society.

© copyright 1993 by the Board of Trustees of the University of Illinois
Manufactured in the United States of America
C 5 4 3 2 1

This book is printed on acid-free paper.

Loeffler's book plate, p. iii, designed by Frank Benson, courtesy of the Medfield
Historical Society, and the frontispiece, a charcoal drawing of Charles Martin
Loeffler by John Singer Sargent, bequest of Elise Fay Loeffler, courtesy Museum
of Fine Arts, Boston

Grateful acknowledgment is made for permission to quote "Violin Sonata by
Vincent d'Indy," from *The Complete Poetical Works of Amy Lowell.* Copyright
© 1955 by Houghton Mifflin Company. Copyright © 1983 renewed by
Houghton Mifflin Company, Brinton P. Roberts, and G. D'Andelot Belin, esq.
Reprinted by permission of Houghton Mifflin Company.

CONTENTS

ILLUSTRATIONS

(between pp. 242 and 243)

Loeffler at Age 16
Loeffler and Elise Fay, April 1886
Martin and Helene Loeffler, 1887
Erich Loeffler
Helene Loeffler
Denis Bunker's Drawing for the Cover of Loeffler's First
  String Quartet, 1889
The Boston Symphony Orchestra, 1891, conducted by
  Nikisch
The Kneisel Quartette during the 1890s
Sketch of Loeffler by Anders Zorn, February 1894
First Page of Loeffler's divertissement pour violon solo et
  grand orchestre, 1894
Loeffler in 1894
Loeffler's Apartment showing his Portrait by Léon Pourtau
The Music Room at Fenway Court
Vincent d'Indy in New York, in 1905, seated center with
  Loeffler and Franz Kneisel (front left), Arthur Whiting
  and Frank Damrosch (front right), members of the
  Kneisel Quartette, and others
Loeffler, Heinrich Gebhard, and Two Students, Misses
  Squires and Furlong
Loeffler with Irma Seydel
The Farmer of Medfield
Loeffler with His Dog
The Loeffler House after Restoration
The Loeffler Living Room
The Music Studio Exterior
The Music Studio Interior
Loeffler at the Window of his Music Studio, c. 1919
The American String Quartette

Loeffler in his Music Studio, c. 1930

The Yellow Room in the Isabella Stewart Gardner Museum; the Eberle viola d'amore is in the case far left, Loeffler memorabilia in the Musician's Case far right below the oil portrait of Loeffler by Sargent

Cast of Loeffler's hand, with other memorabilia, in the Musician's Case in the Yellow Room at the Gardner Museum

PREFACE

Charles Martin Loeffler belonged to a time described by music critic Lawrence Gilman as "golden legendary years when Boston was the musical Athens of America."[1] It was the era when Henry Higginson created the Boston Symphony Orchestra, when its concertmaster, Franz Kneisel, founded the premiere chamber music ensemble of the country; it was an era of unprecedented virtuosi, maestri, composers, critics, and patrons. It was a time when "a singular apparition"[2] in the person of Martin Loeffler appeared on the scene and became one of the most distinctive figures in American music. Part of Boston's culture for a half century and part of its pride, Loeffler was idolized by the Boston public and recognized internationally as one of the country's most important creative talents.

Part of a brilliant era, Loeffler also belonged to a critical one when America stood at a crossroads in its musical development. Long dominated by European culture, it sought its own identity and its own voice, quested after an elusive and uncertain goal. Loeffler moved into this setting as a creative artist unlike any America had ever experienced. Introducing repertoire hitherto unknown, creating in an eclectic style unfamiliar to American audiences, promoting an aesthetic that was controversial while yet compelling, Loeffler held, in the American musical scene, a position distinctive for its rarity and timeliness.

Loeffler first won his way as a violinist, a member and soloist of the Boston Symphony Orchestra, and had in the city a reputation equal to that of any visiting virtuoso. As a composer Loeffler earned equal respect and a reputation that extended throughout the country and to some European musical centers. His music was original, attractive, and, though often controversial for its modernity and Decadent qualities, popular. An eclectic, Loeffler was also the major (almost the only) representative of the French style, particularly of Symbolism or Impressionism, in America. Repeatedly his contemporaries hailed him as one of the most distinguished creative artists of his time. "There will not be another like him," it was written when he died. "No one in

America has approached him for individuality of style, perfection of craftsmanship, beauty of utterance, loftiness and subtlety of thought."[3]

Not only as an artist but also as a person whom some thought the embodiment of nobility of manner and character and of consummate artistic and intellectual refinement, Loeffler was valued highly by his contemporaries. In the city of Oliver Wendell Holmes, James Russell Lowell, the *Atlantic Monthly,* and the Saturday Club, Loeffler was acknowledged not only as a musician of the first rank but also as an intellectual of wit, charm, and fascination. He belonged to several of the foremost intellectual and artistic circles of the time and was adopted into that most exclusive of circles, Boston society. Indeed, according to critic Olin Downes, to have known Amy Lowell, John Singer Sargent, Charles Martin Loeffler, and certain others "was to be of the inner temple."[4] He was, in his own time, so distinguished that in 1931 Gilman wrote, "If Charles Martin Loeffler at seventy is not, musically speaking, the First Citizen of Massachusetts, at least he seems so to many among those who observe that Commonwealth from a distance."[5]

Yet for all that Loeffler suited Boston, in another sense he neither represented the city nor belonged to it. An American by citizenship and residency from the age of twenty, Loeffler had lived his first years in Europe—Germany, France, Hungary, Russia, Switzerland—all of which made their impression on him and his music. On the one hand a sober and staid New Englander, Loeffler was, on the other, a cosmopolitan, an exotic. Thus, while Loeffler's story is, in part, a story of Boston, in particular of its music and musicians, it is also part of the larger history of music in America and in Europe, particularly of France and Franco-American musical relationships, for Loeffler was a chevalier of the Legion of Honor, a correspondent of the French Academy of Fine Arts, a friend of many French musical figures, one of the most important links between French and American music of his time.

Primarily, however, Loeffler's biography is the story of a creative artist with a rare and individual talent and is the personal story, known only in small fragments to his contemporaries, of an unusual and complex man. A respected public figure for many years, Loeffler was yet a private person whose public appearance never revealed the whole man. He was a complicated person, described by his close friend Carl Engel as "a strange, a picturesque anomaly."[6]

Insights into Loeffler's private life are fascinating. He was a man who strove to adopt three different nationalities in preference to the one with which he was born, who prolonged for twenty-four years his engagement to a woman he faithfully loved, who suffered agonies of body, mind, and spirit and harbored deep, strong, sometimes violent passions while maintaining a stoical stance and a graciousness of manner. He was a man about whom there are still unanswered riddles and mysteries.

Loeffler intimated to Engel that he himself might write his "Recollections." He never did. "Seldom is Loeffler in a reminiscent mood," wrote Engel. "His memories do not gush forth as do those of so many musicians, lavish with anecdote and amiable chatter."[7] He rarely permitted interviews. The first biography of Loeffler was undertaken by Engel and published as an article in the *Musical Quarterly* in 1925. It was based on an interview granted by Loeffler to Engel, who had then been his friend for sixteen years, and it was reviewed (and censored) by Loeffler before publication.[8] After Loeffler's death, Engel revised the article for Thompson's *International Cyclopedia of Music and Musicians* (1936). These two articles have remained the basis for all subsequent biographical writings on Loeffler.

After Loeffler's death Engel continued pursuing Loeffler's biography. He gathered together what material he could, including the Loeffler correspondence collection now held at the Library of Congress (of whose Music Division Engel was chief). He visited Loeffler's sister Helene in Germany and spoke or corresponded with a few of Loeffler's early acquaintances. He did not write a fuller biography of Loeffler but left his notes on his researches as part of the Loeffler collection at the library. Any new biography of Loeffler, therefore, owes its first debt to Carl Engel. However, though his personal recollections, estimations, and criticisms remain of enduring value, his biographical work, as he himself admitted, was but a brief essay, a starting point for a fuller study.

Engel suggested that a full-length life of Loeffler would have to be a *vie imaginaire*, to add vividness, guess at the depths of his personality, and provide an intuitive and sympathetic understanding of his music.[9] Fortunately such a number of documents and other sources exist that imagination and guesswork need not be the biographer's major resource. While some speculation is unavoidable, the present volume intends to be, as far as possible, a *vie de documents*. To a great extent Loeffler has been allowed to speak for himself (retaining his stylistic peculiarities). Beyond that, as many primary sources as possible have been used.

In addition to being a biography of an artist, the present work is also a history of his work, but it is not a complete study of the music. New critical and analytical discussion of Loeffler's music is, indeed, needed but falls without the province of this volume. However, the present book does intend, by providing comprehensive historical information and a catalog of compositions, to serve as a foundation for this future work. Many historical commentaries on the music are quoted that evaluate Loeffler's music. Although nineteenth-century reviews were often printed anonymously, where possible the authors have been identified. The qualifications of some of these writers to review the music may be called into question; however, the reviews are quoted not to serve as adequate or valid musical critique but rather to record contemporary reaction to Loeffler's music.

Acknowledgements

The following libraries, archives, and organizations have made available materials relating to Loeffler studies: American Academy and Institute of Arts and Letters; Archives of American Art; Benediktiner-Abtei at Maria-Laach; Boston Public Library; Boston Symphony Orchestra; Eda Kuhn Loeb Library at Harvard University; Franklin Institute; Houghton Library at Harvard University; Isabella Stewart Gardner Museum; Library of Congress; Medfield Historical Society; National Archives; New England Conservatory; New York Public Library; Pierpont Morgan Library; St. Edward's Parish, Medfield; Tavern Club, Boston; and Yale University Library.

Vital records have been searched or made available by the Commonwealth of Massachusetts Vital Records Division, Evangelische Kirchengemeinde Alt-Schöneberg, Evangelisches Zentralarchiv in Berlin, Probate Court of Norfolk County, Southborough Massachusetts Rural Cemetery, and Ville de Mulhouse Archives Municipales. The Landeshauptarchiv Koblenz provided the information that records from Ehrenbreitstein were destroyed in October 1944.

School records were searched by Deutsches Demokratishes Republik Rat des Bezirkes Halle, Agrártudományi Egyetem Könyvtára in Debrecin, Hochschule der Künste Berlin, Ministère de la Culture et de la Communication in Paris, Bibliothèque du Conservatoire de Musique in Paris, and the Institut de France Archives.

Performance records have been provided by the Boston Symphony Orchestra, Harvard Musical Association, Cleveland Symphony, Philharmonic-Symphony Society of New York, Philadelphia Orchestra, Baltimore Symphony Orchestra, and Eastman School of Music.

In addition, personal recollections or private collections have been shared by several of Loeffler's friends and acquaintances or their families, including Olga Averino, Elizabeth Babcock, Francis Judd Cooke, Grace Deeran, Eleanor Diemer, Irene Forte, Samuel S. Gardner, Mr. and Mrs. Joel Goldthwaite, Katherine Griffin Hagar, Daniel

Hamant, George Jordan, Esther Peterson, Herman Silberman, Nicholas Slonimsky, Laura Smith, Alexander Steinert, and Kay Swift. Recollections of Heinrich Gebhard and Renée Longy were made available by tapes lent by Herbert Colvin. Assistance with photographic reproduction was provided by Amy Sweeney, Robert Hutchinson, and Christopher Greenleaf and was supported, in part, by the Massachusetts Arts Lottery, as administered by the Medfield Arts Lottery Council. A number of friends of the author have also lent assistance and support.

To all of the above the author expresses her appreciation.

CHARLES MARTIN LOEFFLER

1

Family and Country

"Not of his time was Charles Martin Tornov Loeffler," wrote one critic when Loeffler died, "yet he was not comprehensible in another age."[1] It may also be said, not of his nation was Martin Loeffler, yet he is not comprehensible without it. The life of Charles Martin Loeffler began in an era highly conscious of nationality. Nationality, in the nineteenth century, was one determinant of personal and cultural identity; the French character was quite distinct from the German character, and French art different from German art. In America, if the separate arts had not yet all found a distinctive national identity, a national awakening was occurring, and nationality was a force in the nation's development and thought.

Nationality played a profound, exceptional role in the life of Martin Loeffler. By birth he was German, but in taste and style he was French. By naturalization, therefore by choice, he was American. In addition, by virtue of an itinerant childhood and catholicity of interest and tastes, he was cosmopolitan. Yet, from another point of view, Loeffler belonged not to all countries, nor to any one, but to none.

In the beginning Loeffler belonged to Germany, but at an early age he developed a violent antipathy towards his homeland, repudiated his German birthright, and sought to identify himself with another country. To a large extent he succeeded. Americans thought him French; the French considered him American. But his roots remained German; his early training and the first foundation of his musical style were German. And Germany played a powerful, even severe, role in his family life and fortune that left a deep, permanent imprint on his mind and spirit.

Germany, inextricably part of the story of Loeffler's family, was in the nineteenth century a growing, changing, complex, and politically unsettled land. In 1821, when Loeffler's father was born, it was, in some ways, a new country, having been remodeled during the first two decades of the century first by Napoleon and then by the Congress of

Vienna. Loeffler's native state, Prussia, emerged from the Congress as a great power, doubled in size, and though still one of numerous German states, with the potential, later fulfilled, of becoming the ruling state. It was also a power ruling over the fortune and fate of the Loeffler family.

For at least two generations before Martin Loeffler was born, his family was centered in the capital of Prussia, Berlin. Loeffler's maternal grandfather, Carl Ludolph Schwerdtmann, was the owner of a carpet business in Berlin. He and his wife, Charlotte Wilhemine Schultz, lived on Leipziger Strasse, where their daughter, Julie Charlotte Helena, Loeffler's mother, was born on 25 March 1838.[2]

To judge by the affluence of Loeffler's maternal relations, the Schwerdtmann-Schultz family was prosperous. Loeffler had a number of these relatives, in whom he apparently had little interest but whom, upon his mother's suggestion, he visited in 1904 and described. His hostess was his aunt, Frau Geheime Commerzienräthin Kahlbaum. According to Loeffler, she was "enormously rich."

> At the station her footman received me and I drove to my aunts house in the swellest turnout I ever sat in. Imagine this old lady 78 years old and spryer than many a 40 year old one, living in their old home in the centre of this large city surrounded by a four acre park which leads to a lovely river [the Spree]. This estate is worth millions and millions on account of the value of the land alone. Their money was and is made in two enormous factories, one a scientifically chemical one, doing their business principally with American drugists, and one where pure alcohol is made. This aunt of mine has two sons—one who is professor of chemistry at the university of Basel (Suisse) and the other is also Commerzienrath like his father and runs the business part of the estate. He has a magnificent hunting castle about an hours ride from Berlin. He pays 28,000 marks a year for his hunting rights alone, which is let by the government. On the whole I did not know there were rich people like that in Germany.

His cousins, including also military officers, a musician, and a sculptor, "all seemed to want to know why we were not also very well off and what had become of my mothers inheritance of her mother, Oncle Jules's and so on and on. I of course knew nothing of it—, My mother herself only this much that of course she also had inherited like the rest of them but that the money was gone, disposed of by my father."[3]

Loeffler's father, Dr. Karl Löffler, was an extraordinary, well-educated, and accomplished man to whom Loeffler was evidently devoted and who provided much of his son's education, influenced his worldviews, and gave him an unusual home life. Except for music lessons and riding lessons given him by a former French cavalry officer,[4] Martin Loeffler claimed to have received his schooling in his own family. He left no detailed account of what that entailed but simply remarked that his mother was an assiduous reader, fond of poetry, and his father a scientist and writer. Given Löffler's diverse interests and studies and his son's development into an unusually educated, accomplished, and cultivated person, this home education was probably not inconsiderable. Martin Loeffler was said to have had a "razor-blade mind,"[5] keen critical insight, an insatiable intellectual curiosity, a versatility and breadth of interest and knowledge, and wit. An American friend, Olin Downes, referring to Loeffler's intellect, wrote, "it has been well said that he has looked on the other side of existence and taken notes."[6]

Yet, while his father's activities and ideas assuredly helped develop Loeffler's intellect, they also led to a spiritual crisis that almost destroyed him. Löffler's liberal views led to a political condemnation that altered the life of his young son from one of almost idyllic happiness to one where bitterness and melancholy dwelt almost incurably side by side with idealism and aesthetic sensitivity in the artist's soul.

Like his wife, Löffler was Berlin-born, the son of another Berliner, Konrad Adam Valentin Löffler. Loeffler's paternal grandfather, born in Berlin on 4 November 1782, was also an educated man who had attended the Gymnasium Berlin–Friedrich Wilhelm and the University of Halle, Tübingen.[7] In 1806 he was Kadettengouverneur in Küstrin and in that year married Christiane Renner. In the following year Konrad Löffler was ordained to the ministry, which took the Löffler family to Raduhn (1807), Brügge (1814), and back to Berlin (1820). While Konrad Löffler was minister at St. Gertraud in Berlin, his youngest son, Immanuel Karl Konrad Valentin, was born on 10 October 1821.[8] The Löffler family moved from Berlin in 1824 for what was to be the last ministry in Tornow bei Landsberg am Warthe, then a part of Brandenburg in Prussia (now part of Poland). At age fourteen, Karl returned to Berlin, according to an account in a literary lexicon, attended gymnasium, studied law, and began a career in the civil service which he abandoned in 1844.[9] At some point he acquired a doctor of philosophy degree.

Whatever the cause of Löffler's change of career, a contributing factor may have been friction with the state. Among Germany's intellectuals, of whom Löffler was one, disaffection was a common condition. The German political mood was a mixed one. Prussia was an authoritarian state whose authority was, on the one hand, being challenged and, on the other, championed. A growing number of liberals and nationalists were in favor of constitutional governments and the overthrow of noble control of the states, but there were also imperialists calling for a unified German nation. Löffler was, to judge by his son's statements, a liberal. "I am a true and good republican," wrote Martin Loeffler, "and furthermore there is nothing astonishing in that for I have it from my father, it is in the blood."[10] What precise sentiments Karl Löffler may have held or what actions taken are unknown. In 1848, when revolution broke out in Berlin, Löffler was there, though how involved or affected is unknown.

Löffler remained in Berlin and adopted a literary career. At first a contributor to existing literary papers, during the 1850s he also founded several new belletristic papers.[11] After about a decade, he left the publishing business but throughout his life continued to write stories, novels, plays, history books, and collections of poems and stories in Plattdeutsch. For some of these he used the pseudonyms Dr. Tornow, taken from his boyhood residence, or De olle Nümärker. He also wrote books relative to his third profession, agricultural and chemical science.

Precisely when or how Löffler acquired his expertise in agricultural science is not yet known. In an 1868 publication he claimed ten years of study and experience (in unspecified locations) as a practising sugar manufacturer, chemist, and agriculturalist and, in fact, began publishing in this field in 1859.[12] He held honorary and corresponding membership in learned societies of Paris, Marseilles, Agram, Turin, and Brandenburg[13] and received the distinctions of Knight of the Sachse-Ernestine Cross of Merit and Bearer of the Würtemberg Gold Medal for Merit in Science and Art. Though he wrote on a number of subjects ranging from silk to chicory to horses, his speciality was sugar production and manufacture. His expertise on the subject led to his employment in at least three, if not four, countries concerned with sugar manufacture. It also resulted in an itinerant style of life for himself and his young family.

Karl Löffler had married Helene Schwerdtmann at the Neue Kirche in Berlin on 6 December 1857 (by which time Carl Schwerdtmann had died, consent for the marriage being given by a guardian). At that time Löffler gave his profession as writer and his residence as Leipziger Strasse, where the Schwerdtmann family lived. Their first child, Gertrude, was born on 14 July 1859 in Schöneberg bei Berlin, and their first son, Martin Karl, was born on 30 January 1861. Five more children followed: Erich, born in Germany on 7 March 1863; Helene Alexandra, born on 12 March 1864, according to her own account, near Berlin; Jeannette, born, according to Helene, in Alsace; Marianne, again according to Helene, born in Kösen and, after dying of diphtheria, buried near the Rhine; and Raphael, born about 1880, died of typhus in 1895 in Marseilles. Only Martin, Erich, and Helene survived to adulthood.

After emigration to America, Martin Loeffler claimed to have been born in Mulhouse, Alsace, and has since repeatedly been called (and analyzed as) an Alsatian. Yet at the Archives Municipales in Mulhouse no record of his birth could be found. Loeffler also claimed to have been "born and reared in Alsace," suggesting that the major part of his childhood was spent in Alsace.[14] But, according to family, Erich and Helene were both born in Germany. If Martin Loeffler had been born in Mulhouse, the family must have returned to Germany soon thereafter. It is more probable that Martin Loeffler was not born in Alsace, though later the family probably did live there. On an appeal for a donation to support the University of Strasbourg, written to Loeffler in 1920, the phrases "votre naîssance alsacienne" (your Alsatian birth) and "votre origine mulhousienne" (your Mulhousian origin) are underscored with exclamation points placed in the margins (presumably by Loeffler). Were the phrases true, Loeffler would have had less reason for this private comment on them.

A record of students at the Hochschule für Musik in Berlin states that Martin Loeffler was born in Schöneberg bei Berlin. At some point, therefore, Loeffler or his mother attested, probably with documentation, to German birth for Martin Loeffler. In Schöneberg his elder sister had been born, and there the family had certainly lived. Loeffler's naturalization papers and death certificate both designate Germany as his birthplace. In any case, Loeffler was not Alsatian.

Not all the residences and travels of the Löffler family have been traced. Dr. Löffler could have visited France before as well as after his marriage. His 1859 book on Chinese kaolin displays a familiarity with French practices, and his 1863 book on French sugar production could also have been a product of first-hand observations.[15] Later visits to France are also possible, especially if Martin Loeffler did indeed spend part of his childhood there and if his sister Jeannette was born there.

Löffler's known journeys included trips to America and to the Orient during the mid-1860s. Between 1865 and 1866, the American Civil War having just concluded, he was a commissioner to a sorghum convention in Indiana (which provided material for yet another book).[16] If Löffler's family accompanied him, Martin Loeffler made no reference to it. The literary lexicon relates that Löffler went to New York, lectured at the Cooper Institute (of which the Institute has no record), and worked on a New Yorker Staatszeitung for three years, but to date there is no documentation. Between 1865 and 1867 Löffler was a directing expert of a commission sent to China and Japan, where they studied the sugar question and gathered seeds for experimental work.

In the spring of 1868 the Löfflers moved to Debrecin, Hungary. Löffler had been asked by the Royal Hungarian minister of agriculture to found a sugar factory that would be used as a teaching institute at the Agriculture Academy there. The institute advertised to open in September 1868 with Löffler offering his instruction in German, French, and English.[17] Martin Loeffler himself recalled that the academy lay outside the town on the road to vast open plains and that two or three inns stood directly opposite the academy buildings. Here gypsy caravans would occasionally stop, and their musicians would play. Here also, according to Loeffler, one of his sisters, also talented in music (perhaps Gertrude), died.[18]

Martin Loeffler remembered much more vividly living in Russia, to which the family next moved, Löffler having been asked by the Russian government to direct a sugar factory at Smela in the Ukraine.[19] The Löfflers lived in Smela from about 1869 to 1872. They moved there, Loeffler claimed, before the outbreak of the Franco-Prussian War (1870). He also recalled being there at about age eight, which age Loeffler turned in 1869.

Russia made a deep impression upon Martin Loeffler. He was happy there. In adult life he was always charmed to meet Russian people. Aside from the gypsy musicians in Hungary, his earliest remembered musical experiences were of Russian music. Repeatedly in his compositions written during the nineteenth century, he employed Russian themes, and later, in 1925, he recalled and paid homage to his Russian years in his tone poem, *Memories of My Childhood (Life in a Russian Village)*, which uses Russian melodies and depicts Russian scenes. The prefatory note that Loeffler wrote for the score emphasizes the fairy-tale and folklore aspects of the scenes and suggests that this was not simply a happy but almost enchanted time for Loeffler.

> Many years ago the composer spent more than three years of his boyhood in a Russian village near the small town of Smiela (Government of Kieff). He now seeks to express by the following music what still lives in his heart and memory of those happy days. He recalls, in the various strains of his music, Russian peasant songs, the Yourod's Litany-prayer, the happiest of days, fairy-tales and dance-songs. The closing movement of the Symphonic Poem commemorates the death of Vasinka, an elderly peasant, a Bayan or story-teller, singer, maker of

willow pipes on which he played tunes of weird intervals, and the companion-friend of the boy who now, later in life, notes down what he hopes these pages will tell.[20]

At about the age of eight, for Christmas, Loeffler received his first violin. He took his first lessons from a German member of the St. Petersburg orchestra who spent his summers in Smela. Loeffler's sister Helene thought that Martin received his first violin instruction while the family lived at Naumberg on the Saale,[21] which may be where the Löfflers lived upon returning to Germany.

The Löfflers also lived about one year at what Loeffler called his mother's "country seat," southeast of Berlin, which Loeffler described during a 1904 visit.

> While in Berlin I devoted one whole day to visiting my mothers old country seat, where I spent a year or so of my boyhood. I took a 7 a.m. train and arrived in a small town famous for the German Emperors hunting lodge. With great pains I at last found a horse and carriage to drive me to Prièros. We drove for 2 hours and a half through flat country and forests alive with deer. At 11 o'clock I arrived and saw the old place. It is thirty years ago since I had not seen it. The house is still there but the property has been cut up into house lots and therefore everything looked changed. It is right at the edge of the river Dahme. The trees had grown enormous since those early days and every body round there remembered Dr. Loeffler and his family. But my real fun I had in the village cross the river; there all the old peasants remembered "Martin L. on his little pony."[22]

Dr. Löffler also directed a sugar factory at Rothensee bei Magdeburg. The family could well have been living at Magdeburg while Loeffler himself was at school in Berlin during the mid-1870s.[23]

It is possible that the Löffler itineracy, begun in the 1860s when Bismark came to power, was influenced by political as well as professional reasons. In the 1870s the family did return to stay in Germany—though not Berlin, seat of Bismark and the emperor—but by the mid-1870s Löffler's difficulties with the government became serious. They caused traumatic change in the Löffler family life and cut short the happiness of Loeffler's childhood.

The exact nature and duration of Dr. Löffler's political problems and offenses cannot be determined but clearly revolved around the German chancellor and his imperial policies. The primary goal of Bismark's political career was the creation of a unified German state under Prussian leadership. He achieved this primarily through the manipulation of three wars—with Denmark in 1864, Austria in 1866, and France in 1870—by which he gradually bound the German states into political unity through joint military campaigns, secured for Germany new territory, and defeated its two major rival powers, France and Austria. While the war victories made Bismark popular with a great many Germans, they outraged others whose liberal ideals were opposed to his militarism and authoritarianism, the annexation of unwilling territories (especially Alsace and Lorraine), the fratricide (as some saw it) of the war with Austria, and the defeat of republican states. Löffler must have been one of those not only outraged but also outspoken in his criticism.

What little may be known about Löffler's case must be gleaned from the very few confidences Martin Loeffler put into letters, and from these the only detail revealed about his father's offense is an allusion to Alsace and Lorraine. In some way Löffler must have protested their annexation and angered the government. He was made a political prisoner; the date of the sentence is unknown. Loeffler was fourteen years old when he first learned that there was some serious trouble (1875); the imprisonment may have begun then, but, if not, probably by 1878. The place of imprisonment was the fortress at Ehrenbreitstein. This fortress was under the care of the military, whose archives were destroyed during World War II. Our sole source of information about the prison sentence is a letter written by Loeffler, then in Paris, to his best friend and confidant (later his wife), Elise Fay, in June 1884.

> Alas, many sad reasons have prevented me from writing. First I have been ill, and something sadder, I have received the news from home that my father is so ill that his death is expected any day. Probably I will leave Paris in a few days if I do not receive reassuring news on my father's condition. He is at the Ehrenbreitstein fortress to serve the rest of his sentence. For having said the truth about certain things about the Prussian government, the Hohenzollern family, and Prince Bismark, he had been sentenced several years ago, but since he was suffering the majority of the time he took so many leaves that the affair stretched out in a monstrous way. On the 26th of the month of June he would have been at the end of his pain, and it is in the last days that he fell so ill that his life was feared for. I am sure that it is grief and hate against Prussians and certain persons that have made him as ill as that. Finally, he would have been able to enjoy his freedom which he loved so much and today—who knows how many hours he still has to live.[24]

Dr. Löffler's political trouble was a great shock to the young Loeffler, who evidently adored his parents. It caused an abrupt change of fortune and bitter, life-long unhappiness. Loeffler never openly discussed the matter. When interviewed by Engel for a biographical article, he made no allusion to it, but after Engel wrote the following:

"The soul of a super-sensitive child, suddenly brought to maturity by a precocious shock and emotion of a powerful nature, might well be imagined to lie at the bottom of the exquisite sensibility, the penumbral delicateness, which one is ever aware of in Loeffler the man and musician,"[25] Loeffler commented to him:

> Here you have unbeknown hit on something which is true, although you cannot possibly guess, still less know, what it was that so utterly changed, changed and affected my soul and caracter after it became known to me. I became then very gravely ill. I was hardly at that time an adolescent, yet my heart and mind suffered then the most dire distress of my life. There was no shame connected with it to any of mine, do not think that, but it was so intensely and intimately concerning my beloved mother and me, that I have never even spoken of it to anybody, and there are today only two beings left that know about all this [presumably his sister and his wife], and they are unapproachable on the subject. I have hardly lived a day since without its still rising before me. It is my great faith in you that makes me even allude to it, for it concerns now only me. Even you . . . cannot ever hope to fathom what I shall not elucidate further at present. If it ever goes into my "Recollections," you shall be my editor-executor. Of interest it can only be to the extent of possibly revealing reasons why I am as I am and not otherwise. So much for my belief in you and that you will not ever allude to it to anybody nor to me.[26]

In 1889 Loeffler drafted a letter to a friend (identified only as "Henry") wherein he attempted to explain his discontent and why he felt "not destined to be very happy at this time." The draft was composed five years after his father's death.

> I know of no fellows life in which great happiness had changed so often with bad luck as in mine 28 years. In fact I am still under the influence of the different storms which blew through my father's life. This man who was by nationality ["birth" crossed out] and consequently by necessity one of the "uncontented" helped circumstances unintentionally to make me an other one for I, naturally resembling my mother, a German who was of sweetest temper and dowed with that almost proverbial endurance and patience which belongs to her nationality, in me the fact of Darwins observation is realized that "in countries where the foxes are hunted frequently and systematically their young breed are by far more careful and distrustful than elsewhere." When life steps on your toes brutally at boys age ["the age of 14 years" crossed out] and fortune leads you from better than well-to-do condition into worse than that—when you try in vain to learn by heart Caesars Bello gallicum by sentences because other sentences of that kind run constantly through your brain "avant d'annexer l'Alsace et La Lorraine on aurait dû

considerer quand même un peu si les Alsaciens voulaient être des Allemands ou des français" [Before the annexation of Alsace and Lorraine one would have had to consider, even though a little, if Alsacians wanted to be German or French.] etc. which cost your father some years "forteresse." Hélas! mon ami ["we are not all free in America and you know not what advantage it is" crossed out] how much misery can be told in few words I see now! I (a protestant) then went often with my Mother to the church of the Jesuits to pray with her and she good woman did the praying and I did the silent cursing! I do not deny that there were yet times of complete happiness now and then, but it changed often from good to bad and other ways, and human soul is like a rubber ball: it falls on earth, jumps up once, twice, perhaps three-four times each time with less and less strength, but finally titters [peters?] out—There are other strange things; one looks back in life and everything of which destiny, bad luck and human "Christians" have deprived you of seem ["just like a malediction" crossed out] 10 times as boy.[27]

Loeffler became not simply melancholic but also vehemently anti-pathetic towards Germany. In 1883, for example, he wrote a diatribe against the German character to a friend in America.

Although I am only 22 I have really had bad experiences because I have seen the world and people. . . . There is a *famous proverb in German* (I say "famous" because all that is infamous is called "famous") that says "Promises will be made, not to be kept." Is that not *infamous*? Let no one speak to me of *"deutsche* Ehrlichkeit" [*German* honesty], of *"deutsche* Treue" [faithfulness], or especially *"deutsche* Gemütligkeit [geniality]. I have really had some *famous* experiences with them. Even if it were true that they have fidelity, honesty, and geniality, what insolence to call that especially "German" as if all other nations were thieves, brigands, "Meineidige" [perjurers], etc. etc. I do not know if you have noticed that often Germans when they are very merry, drinking beer, sing "I do not know what it means, that I am so sad." I find more "Dummheit" [stupidity] than "Gemütligkeit" in that. Now, do not believe that I detest all Germans, far from it, I would be ashamed to say that of a nation which is also mine and which has had a Beethoven, Goethe, Schiller, Kant, Wagner, and thousands of others, only I want to say that the general character is insupportable. They criticize all, rarely become enthusiastic, "sind lau im Lob, scharf im Tadel" [are lukewarm in praise, sharp in censure]. That is what displeases me.[28]

In one more year, after Dr. Löffler suffered a stroke in prison, Loeffler would no longer admit that the German nation was his own.

He completely rejected his native land, as he wrote to Fay:

> I am unhappy, oh my God, unhappy to the point of despair. Oh if I could crush this filthy nation that I detest, that I hate, no, that I scorn. I have sworn to myself never more to be with or for them, these accursed Germans, who are cursed by all nations. These vows return what has been given me, do you understand? and I would kill anyone who would call me a German or a Prussian. If I could see it burn in hell! But, my poor father (who, if he actually succumbs, will be a martyr to freedom and who will die as a republican) was right when he told me "that they would be too bad, too wicked to be received even in hell, the Germans."[29]

"I have sworn to myself," Loeffler wrote, "never more to be with or for them, these accursed Germans." He kept his oath. Excepting his education at the Hochshcule für Musik in Berlin, he made no reference to any residence in Germany and claimed Alsatian birth. After leaving school, he returned to Germany as infrequently as possible, only to visit his family but never again to reside there.

The intense antipathy Loeffler felt towards Germany led to one of the major anomalies of his life. Essentially honest and of stern, upright moral character and integrity, Loeffler yet commenced a life-long deception, obscuring his true birth and affecting other nationalities by which he preferred to be known. These affectations, which began as soon as Loeffler left Germany, commenced with a claim to Russian ancestry. Like his father, Loeffler used the pseudonym Tornow (also spelled Tornov). Beyond its association with his father, Loeffler liked it, as suggested in a letter to Fay, because of its Russian sound. "I adore Russians, and for that, you understand, they also like me. Since the general [Davidoff] learned that one of my father's names is Russian (Tornow) he is perfectly enchanted with me."[30] The general issued Loeffler cards to the Cercle de l'union artistique in the names of "M. L-Tornov" and "Ch. Tornov."

Loeffler's first publication, *Berceuse* (Paris, 1884), was ascribed to M. Loeffler-Tornow, a name he used often (though not consistently) during the early 1880s. That he did not continue to use the name in his subsequent publications was due to the persuasions of Gustave Schirmer. However, although discontinuing the use of Loeffler-Tornov, Loeffler retained the occasional use of Tornov Loeffler. It appeared, among other places, on his citizenship papers, calling cards, wedding announcement, and his will.

Loeffler manifested his desire for Russian nationality also in 1909 when his brother Erich died and Loeffler designated Russia as their father's birthplace on the death certificate. Possibly Loeffler did not know his ancestry and, remembering Russia from his childhood, assumed a Russian background for his father. This hypothesis is supported by a comment written by Helene to her brother from Paris in 1888. "That I am German would unfortunately through my birth certificate be proved clearly, but that is now not to be changed. That Papa was Russian, I firmly believe; in my birth certificate it is stated that I am the daughter of Dr. C. Löffler but not from where, therefore they can still, however, always believe this, although it does not matter, generally noone believes it. I tell you, every German passes himself off for a Russian or Hungarian here."[31]

Loeffler laid only limited claim to Russian nationality. After moving to Paris to continue his education, Loeffler found his true spiritual homeland in France. He adopted French manners, tastes, and style, and, after immigration to the United States, changed his name Karl to the French form, Charles. After a few years in America he ceased to use the German language while increasingly using French, and after English became his principal language, he continued to riddle it with French expressions. His favorite poets, artists, and composers were French. His own musical style became modeled after that of France. After some years in America, he appeared to Americans as French.

Loeffler's emotional turmoil over his father affected more than his political and national outlook. There were also profound and enduring effects upon his personality, including an extreme reticence about his personal and family life; an austerity of manner with strangers; a reserved, even modest nature; a preference for privacy and seclusion; an abiding, though concealed, melancholia and occasional misanthropy. In public Loeffler's attitude, at least during his American years, was stoical. He buried his griefs deep inside, sharing them only with the closest of friends, and there thus developed a curious duality in the man between his public demeanor and certain inward feelings. Contemporary anecdotes repeatedly describe him as a delightful, genial, and charming companion—brilliant, witty, full of enthusiasms. In truth, Loeffler did enjoy good society, was befriended and widely admired, but privately he confessed to social malaise and fears of being unable to relate to others and to maintain friendships. He did, in fact, have fallings out with friends. Extremely sensitive and easily injured himself, he could be difficult, even acerbic, and often intolerant. He was not often at peace.

The family tragedy was also a powerful influence on Loeffler's music. Although Loeffler's hatred for Germany did not prevent his reverence for Bach, Brahms, Beethoven, Wagner, and even modern

German masters such as Richard Strauss, it influenced his moves to Paris and to America, each of which affected the development of his own style. As melancholy pervaded his life, the sorrow in his soul found frequent expression in his music. It may also have increased Loeffler's devotion to his art, for it was his great solace.

An immediate effect of the alteration of the family fortune was Loeffler's early realization of his need to seek and follow a profession. Loeffler may have already decided to study music intensively; his love and facility for music had manifested themselves years earlier. Albeit music was not a preferred profession among nineteenth-century parents, particularly impoverished parents, it was Loeffler's choice, one he was allowed to follow to the reversal of his own, if not his father's, fortune.

2

Education

Decided upon becoming a professional violinist, Martin Loeffler moved in 1874 to Berlin to study at the Hochschule für Musik. To him it was a practical decision—he had a natural facility for the violin, so he "decided to be a fiddler."[1] It was also, apparently, an uncontested decision. There is no suggestion that Loeffler's parents ever sought to bend their son to any other way of life. In fact, they fostered two other professional musicians—Erich, a cellist, and Helene, a harpist.

Loeffler may have received some early music training from his father, for Dr. Löffler played the piano and may have composed.[2] Loeffler received violin lessons in Smela and probably also in Naumberg. A classmate at the Hochschule, Sam Franko, stated that Gustav Hollaender (in Berlin) prepared Loeffler for entrance into the school.[3] Loeffler himself noted none of the names of his teachers before his study in Berlin.

Loeffler was taken to Berlin by his mother, but none of his family lived with him there. Loeffler boarded with the family of a Dr. Steinbeck. The Berlin to which Loeffler returned was changed from that which his father had known. The population had quadrupled since the time of Karl Löffler's birth and was close to a million. Its economy, stimulated by the French indemnity, had experienced a boom and attracted industrial enterprise and new labor. The city was steadily growing as an important world capital.

Life in Berlin, though clouded by family tragedy, must have been a musical awakening for Martin Loeffler. His brief recollections of music from his childhood were of folk music. Before Berlin his concert experience was probably very limited, but the Prussian capital (though overshadowed as a music center by Vienna, Weimar, and Leipzig) had an active musical life. There were concerts by Hochschule faculty and students, by the Royal Orchestra, the opera orchestra, and orchestras such as that of Benjamin Bilse, founded in 1867, devoted to more popular concerts. Many amateur singing groups existed, as well as the

Opera House and several private theaters. Wagner's operas were taking hold of the opera stages, and the controversy between the followers of Brahms and those of Wagner was in full heat; it was, in fact, the dominant musical issue of Loeffler's years in Berlin.

The Hochschule für Musik was not the only possibility open to Loeffler for his education, but probably it was the most attractive.[4] Founded in 1869 by the Akademie der Künste, it became known, under the leadership of Joseph Joachim, as one of the best in Germany.

School records from Loeffler's time, beyond a register of students, no longer exist. That register reads simply: "Martin Carl Loeffler, born Schöneberg bei Berlin from 1874 to October 1877 violin major." Loeffler's own brief record is that he studied violin with Eduard Rappoldi and Joseph Joachim, harmony with Friedrich Kiel, and Bach motets with Woldemar Bargiel.

Loeffler began his violin studies with Rappoldi, the official "preparer" for Joachim. A former orchestral violinist and opera conductor educated at the Vienna Conservatory, Rappoldi was, according to Loeffler's contemporary at the school, Sam Franko, "an excellent musician, a splendid pianist, but one of the driest and most pedantic teachers and violinists that can be imagined. I lost more than I gained by his instruction."[5]

Soon, however, Loeffler was studying with Joachim, popularly known as the "king of violinists," the most renowned violinist of his time in Germany. Educated in Pest and Vienna, Joachim began his brilliant concert career in 1843, playing primarily in Leipzig and London. In 1850 he moved to Weimar to be concertmaster under Liszt but after two years, as he was not in sympathy with Liszt, left to be concert director and solo violinist to the king of Hanover. In the fall of 1868 he went to Berlin to assume the directorship of the new Hochschule für Musik.

Joachim was an impressive figure and a personable one. Clayton Johns, a Boston friend of Loeffler's, described him: "Joachim was of large frame, had a big head and lots of hair and a heavy black beard. He invariably wore a black frock coat and a broadbrimmed black slouch hat. His face was serious but benign. He never seemed to be in a hurry, always having time to be kind."[6]

To Franko's mind, Joachim was not a great teacher. "Joachim the teacher was quite another being than Joachim the violinist. When teaching, he paid scarcely any attention to the technical side of violin-playing, made only general remarks about position, bowing, fingering, etc., and devoted his attention primarily to interpretation. But even there it was impossible to follow him unconditionally, for he would play a piece differently every time, following the inspiration of the moment. This is the explanation of the fact that his influence as a teacher was not of a practical nature, but due only to his inspiring personality. . . . I have a letter from him in which he acknowledges himself to be a poor pedagogue."[7] Others also considered Joachim less than the best teacher. Loeffler himself once commented, "Joachim's own [genius] had died, alas, under the weight of a pose purely academic."[8]

In chamber instruction, however, Joachim was, again in Franko's opinion, a superior instructor. "His quartet lessons were a source of pure joy. Here the full force of his genius unfolded itself and he was unsparing of wise and characteristic comment."[9] Joachim himself was a superb chamber violinist and his Joachim Quartet highly celebrated. Occasionally, when additional players were needed, as in octets or sextets, Loeffler was invited to Joachim's home to play second viola with the quartet.

Whatever his deficiencies as a teacher, Joachim did not want for students. Loeffler's fellow students included a number of outstanding violinists among whom Loeffler made friends, some remaining friends for many years, including Franko, Willy Hess, Johann Kruse, Eugen Huber, Henri Petri, Tivador Nachez, and Karl Halir—all of whom had distinguished careers as solo or orchestral violinists.

What sort of career Loeffler began while a violin student is not known. At the end of his life Loeffler told a student that he played in a concert in which Brahms, an early idol of his, also played. He related that hearing Brahms was "WILD—WONDERFUL."[10] The only other concert Loeffler is known to have mentioned was Joachim's conducting of Handel's *Alexander's Feast*.

One anecdote that may belong to this time is that told by Sam Franko about Berlin conductor Rudolf Bial, who asked Loeffler to substitute for Franko in his orchestra. After one performance Bial said to Franko: "Don't send that man back to me; he can't play." The cellist Emil Schenck said in explanation that Loeffler was too young.[11]

At the Hochschule Loeffler also studied composition. His teacher in harmony was Friedrich Kiel, himself a former student in Coburg of Kasper Krummer and in Berlin of Siegfried Wilhelm Dehn, the teacher of Rubinstein and Glinka. Clayton Johns recalled him as "a delightful old gentleman, I should think something like 'Papa Haydn.'. . . Joachim said, 'Nobody is as good as Kiel.'"[12] Loeffler also studied with Woldemar Bargiel, who, like Kiel, had been a student of Dehn but also a student at the Leipzig Conservatory of Hauptmann, Rietz, and

Gade. Loeffler claimed that, though he studied Bach's motets with Bargiel, he learned more from his own private discovery and study of Handel. As for Kiel, Louis Elson, who had apparently spoken to Loeffler on the subject, wrote that "Loeffler himself doubts, however, whether he ought to be called a pupil of Kiel, as his studies with him were interrupted and very brief."[13]

In 1877 Loeffler left the Hochschule. There were artistic reasons for his leaving. For one, the faculty was conservative, as Johns recounted: "Kiel, like all the members of the Hochschule faculty, was violently against Liszt and Wagner. They represented the modern school, while the attitude of the Hochschule was strictly classical. Kiel once said to me: 'It is a sin for you to go to hear a Wagner opera.' Think of that!"[14] Bargiel, a disciple of Schumann (his brother-in-law), also held moderate views, and Joachim, who later joined Brahms in attacking the "Music of the Future," was no more progressive.

Loeffler, however, had modern tastes in music and disliked the Berlin school's general intolerance for modern works. He also had different tastes in violin playing, not caring for the German method. He was said not to admire their bowing, and in later years was known to fume at "that damn German slow vibrato."[15] With Joachim himself Loeffler had an amicable relationship, but, discontented with the Hochschule in matters of performance and composition, Loeffler left Berlin.

Leaving the Hochschule could well have been a family decision. Whether his father's problems precipitated his entrance into the school is not known, but they doubtless influenced his decision to leave. Loeffler once referred to the time when he left Berlin as "when one wanted to make me leave Berlin."[16] Classmate Sam Franko was aware that something was wrong at home, later revealing that "Loeffler tried to cut his veins," suggesting that the initial shock may have occurred while Loeffler was at school.[17]

If fellow musician Gustave Strube's memories were correct, Loeffler did not go straight to Paris from Berlin (as he later indicated) but spent a short while at Dr. Brinkmeyer's Private School in Ballenstedt, where Strube declared they were "at the same school and in the same class." Strube said he did not know Loeffler well because the students from town did not mix well with the boarders, but as fellow violin students they became acquainted and compared the material they studied. According to Strube, Loeffler took violin lessons from a cellist of the disbanded Hoforchestra named Herrlitz.

Strube vaguely recalled Loeffler's saying that his home was Magdeburg, where his father was connected with a sugar factory. "There was a rumor that his father had some political trouble, but I was too young to understand that. I believe that Martin's hate for Germany and all the Germans was the result of that sad occurrence."[18]

Strube thought the date to have been probably 1877; however, Loeffler's name does not appear in the school's annual reports dating from February 1875. Supposing Loeffler to have been in Ballenstedt before Berlin presupposes Strube's memories to have been those of a six- or seven-year-old. The date could not have been later than 1878, at which time the family was domiciled in or near Coblenz and Loeffler moved to Paris.

To continue his musical studies, Loeffler, again on his own, went to France. It was a felicitous move. Loeffler loved Paris. Politically he was at ease there and in a letter written in 1884 declared: "it is a great nation. I have never refrained from admiring the nation that could have a revolution like that of 1789–93. After all that I have been able to do in the last years to learn, I have had to acknowledge that it is precisely this event, grandiose and at the same time tragic, that has inspired in me this admiration, this love for France and the French."[19]

Artistically also Loeffler admired Paris. Despite (or perhaps in defiance of) its defeat by the Prussians, Paris during the Third Republic was enjoying one of its most brilliant eras. One of the most spirited and attractive cities of Europe, where many artists and writers congregated, Paris was to Loeffler's mind the artistic center of Europe, and he himself became a Francophile in his musical, artistic, and literary tastes.

Visits to the bookstalls along the Seine were one of Loeffler's greatest pleasures in the city. Leading writers then included Flaubert (whose four-volume *Correspondence* Loeffler once said had been to him "an artists gospel"[20]), the brothers de Goncourt, Zola, and the early Huysmans. The early stages of Decadence (later Symbolism) had begun, the poetry of which, following the direction of such poets as Verlaine, Mallarmé, and Rimbaud, enchanted Loeffler. In Paris, too, he admired the pre-eminent modern artistic style, Impressionism.

Above all, Loeffler was attracted by the music. He arrived in Paris at a particularly opportune time to be influenced, and won over, by French music. The 1870s were a decade of new opportunities for French music and a new status for the French composer, especially in instrumental music. Earlier in the century music in Paris had been dominated by the opera, itself dominated by Italian music. Several chamber music groups did exist, as well as the popular Pasdeloup orchestra and the orchestra of the Conservatoire National de Musique et de Déclamation, the bastion of music education in France, but, though some French music was played, the staple of the instrumental repertoire was German and Viennese.

Following the Franco-Prussian War, French nationalism became revitalized. The Société Nationale de Musique Française was founded with the motto of "Ars gallica" and the purpose of promoting French music. Beginning in November 1871 the Société sponsored concerts devoted entirely to French music. In addition, orchestral and chamber music gained a better footing in France, in part due to the war indemnity and the great expense of opera. The orchestras of Edouard Colonne and Charles Lamoureux, founded in 1873 and 1881 respectively, gave Paris a new wealth of orchestral music, including music of modern French composers.

Paris offered Loeffler an abundance of new musical experiences, including the music of Saint-Saëns, Lalo, d'Indy, Bizet, Massanet, and other French composers. Although Loeffler always maintained the reverence for the Baroque and Classic masters which he had developed in Berlin, it was with the spirit of these modern French composers that his soul was particularly imbued. Loeffler was happier with his studies in Paris than he had been in Berlin. He always credited his French training above the German, to the point of whittling down his years in Berlin, in 1910 claiming, "I studied about a year and a half in Germany, but was educated chiefly in Paris."[21]

Loeffler's violin teacher was Lambert-Joseph Massart, a native of Liège and former student of Kreutzer. Formerly an outstanding concert violinist, for several years associated in concert with Liszt, he acquired such acclaim as a teacher that he received an appointment as professor of violin at the Conservatoire in 1843. Loeffler, who as a foreigner would have been refused admission to the Conservatoire, studied with him privately.

Massart's students included a number of concert violinists, among them Wieniawski, Marsick, and Sarasate, all of whom Loeffler admired. Of Sarasate Loeffler once said, "Sarasate has so much perfection in his playing *before the public* that I am dazzled by it each time that I hear him."[22] Loeffler's regard led him to dedicate his composition *Une nuit de mai*, as "Hommage à Pablo de Sarasate." A journalist reported in 1910 that Loeffler's "model was Sarasate in his earlier days."[23] Carl Engel, however, declared that "it was Wieniawski whom Loeffler regarded as the perfect model,"[24] and Loeffler himself wrote in 1922, "whosoever knew Wieniawski and heard him play Quartets, serious music and virtuoso stunts, could not help feeling that there was something and is something beyond natural charm. Even Joachim bowed before Wieniawski's genius."[25] Loeffler was well enough acquainted with Marsick (who had also been a student of both Joachim and Massart) that in 1891, after Loeffler had been in America for ten years, Marsick wrote to him for advice on the possibility of an American concert tour.

Loeffler studied composition with Ernest Guiraud, a conservatory-trained composer and winner of the Prix de Rome. A student of Halévy, a classmate and great friend of Bizet, he composed a series of operas which achieved moderate, fleeting success. He served on the committee of the Société Nationale and in 1876 joined the faculty of the Conservatoire. Though his own compositions were not modern, he was said to have been tolerant and broad-minded with students in whom he recognized promise. He is particularly remembered as having been the teacher of Claude Debussy.

Loeffler left no commentary on his composition studies in Paris. Music critic Louis Elson reported that "his chief studies of orchestration were made from the orchestra itself, or with men who (he says) are quite unknown to fame. His work with the Pasdeloup Orchestra, in Paris, and with other European orchestras, gave him a practical training that has been of the greatest value to him."[26]

The Pasdeloup Orchestra, for years offering the major alternative to the opera houses that dominated Parisian musical life, popularized orchestral concerts in France. Pasdeloup developed the Concerts populaires de musique classique in 1861 from the symphonic concerts of the Société des jeunes élèves du Conservatoire he had organized ten years earlier. His orchestra performed at the Cirque d'hiver. The concerts were popular—they were inexpensive and they introduced their audiences to music hardly known in Paris—and their popularity extended for over twenty years. In 1884, by which time rival orchestras founded by Colonne and Lamoureux had surpassed Pasdeloup's in popularity, the orchestra dissolved. A brief revival in 1886 died with Pasdeloup in 1887.

Pasdeloup's orchestra brought to the French public a great amount of orchestral music, primarily foreign. Pasdeloup's preference was for such composers as Haydn, Mozart, Beethoven, Schumann, and Wagner. Even in post-1870 Paris Pasdeloup performed Wagner, although it caused a tumult. Loeffler might have preferred a stronger French repertoire, since his tastes were inclining in that direction. Yet, with Pasdeloup, Loeffler was exposed to new music of some variety. At the first rehearsal on Monday, young soloists and new compositions were given a trial. On occasion the composers would direct the performances.

Loeffler himself left no impressions of Pasdeloup, beyond noting his old-fashioned habit of conducting with the violin bow. But his friend Franko, who moved to Paris at approximately the same time, did.

> Pasdeloup was a man of unpleasant personality, small and stocky, with a long, dark-yellow beard and small, restless eyes. He conducted with a violin bow, always keeping half a dozen in reserve to replace the broken ones. When his gestures became excited, you could hear the hairs of the bow whizzing through the air. . . . He was a mediocre conductor and musician, but he did a great service to music by presenting the classic works of the great masters, played by a first-class orchestra, to wide circles of the public at popular prices. . . .
>
> Pasdeloup paid the members of his orchestra fifteen francs for a concert with four rehearsals. Everyone who arrived late—which the long distances and bad connections made it very difficult to avoid—or, still worse, missed a rehearsal altogether, was punished by a deduction from his salary, so that one might easily be in a position of owing him money. He did not pay anyone till the end of the season.[27]

Loeffler spent only one season with the Pasdeloup orchestra.[28] He was next engaged to play in a private orchestra, an experience that far eclipsed the former with Pasdeloup in his recollections. It was, apparently, another almost enchanted period of Loeffler's youth. Between 1879 and 1881 he played under the patronage of the exceptionally wealthy Baron Paul von Derwies and lived at the baron's two estates, the Villa Valrose at Nice and the summer home, Chateau Trevano near Lake Lugano, which Loeffler once deemed "the most heavenly place in Europe to live in."[29]

Derwies was an extraordinary man. Of Dutch origin, he had emigrated to Russia during the reign of Peter the Great, where, in St. Petersburg, he gave piano lessons to a M. Mayer, who in return taught him the secrets of the banking business. Derwies attended law school and later served in the Russian ministry, worked as a draftsman and engineer, making his mark particularly in the area of Russian railroad line design. Eventually involved in industry, Derwies amassed an immense fortune and was ennobled by the Czar.[30] According to Loeffler, Derwies left some 150,000,000 roubles when he died. His household was of a size that required three special trains to move between the two estates: one for family (including his wife, Vera Nicolaiewna, and three children), guests, and tutors; a second for the servants and horses; and a third for the musicians.

The Derwies musical establishment was exceptional, producing opera, chapel music, orchestra concerts, and chamber music in which the family took part. Derwies maintained a chorus of about forty-six as well as an orchestra of about seventy. If additional personnel were needed, for example soloists for the opera, Derwies spared no expense to secure leading artists. Nor did he, in fact, spare expense in any aspect of staging the operas. According to Loeffler, Derwies spent 50,000 francs on bells alone for *A Life for the Tsar*. Loeffler's testimony to Derwies' grand manner is borne out by a remark by a fellow orchestra member, Victor Herbert: "That is the way those Russian millionaires do things. And our Fifth Avenue hostesses expect the whole country to gape if they engage Caruso and two horn players for a single night."[31]

According to Loeffler, Derwies had highly critical faculties. If no guests were present for the concerts, Derwies would form an audience of one, who might accelerate the performance with a "sans reprise s'il vous plaît [no repeats please]" or end the program with a courteous "Merci messieurs."

Derwies himself played the piano. Loeffler recalled his playing Weber and Mendelssohn with his orchestra. His sons played cello and violin.[32] Chamber music was part of the family activities, in which Loeffler, who enjoyed Derwies' personal friendship, sometimes participated. Occasionally, also, Loeffler had the opportunity to perform chamber music at soirées in Nice.

The repertoire throughout was, to judge from Loeffler's memories, varied and often modern. Among the composers and works Loeffler recalled were Schubert's Symphony in C Major, Wagner overtures, Berlioz, Saint-Saëns, Délibes, Liszt, Tchaikovsky, Bortniansky, and Dvořák (who dedicated one of his three *Slavonic Rapsodies,* op. 45, to Derwies). Among the operas, he recalled Glinka's *Russlan and Ludmilla, A Life for the Tsar,* and *Kamarinskaya;* Bizet's *Les pêcheurs de perles* and *L'arlésienne,* and Rossini's *Il barbiere di Siviglia.* The music in the chapel was that of the Russian liturgy, again exposing Loeffler to a national music he adored. The singers themselves were not Russian but a mixed chorus of Bohemians (who also formed the opera chorus) under the direction of the Czech conductor, Karl Bendl.

Loeffler joined the Derwies orchestra in 1879. He had obtained the position through Massart and had been signed by Karl Müller-Berghaus, the conductor of the orchestra and brother of Wilhelm Müller, whom Loeffler had known from the Joachim Quartet. Müller-Berghaus was with Derwies until early 1881, when he was succeeded by Hans Sitt. Loeffler signed his contract in February and joined the orchestra in Lugano in May. His six-month contract was repeatedly renewed, and his original salary of 190 francs per month increased to three hundred.

Sitting at the first stand next to the concertmaster, Loeffler rehearsed with the orchestra daily for two weekly concerts on Tuesday afternoons and Friday evenings. On occasion the orchestra gave special concerts. A program in the Loeffler collection, for example, states that on 26 March 1881 at the Grand-Hotel a concert was given by members of the Orchestre de Valrose, "graciously offered by M. le Baron von Derwies." Repeatedly Loeffler appeared as a soloist with the orchestra. One of his pieces was Müller-Berghaus's violin concerto.

Loeffler enjoyed his tenure with the Derwies orchestra. In addition to the musical and environmental advantages, he had opportunities to travel (for example, to Milan and Paris) and, again, to make friends. Foremost, Loeffler enjoyed the association of César Thomson, concertmaster of the orchestra and Loeffler's desk mate, who was one of the most influential personalities on Loeffler's career as a violinist.

Thomson, four years Loeffler's senior, was an extremely gifted violinist. Born in Liège, he attended the Liège Conservatory, where he took a gold medal at age eleven. He then studied with some of the brightest names in the field—Vieuxtemps, Léonard, Wieniawski, and Massart. Before joining the Derwies orchestra, he had already had successful concert tours to Spain and Italy. After Derwies's death he resumed his concert career, including visits to America. At these times and also during Loeffler's visits to Europe, Thomson and Loeffler renewed their friendship, which lasted throughout their lives.

Thomson was, in Loeffler's opinion, a technician *par excellence* to whom, in later years, he credited more of his own development as a violinist than to Massart or any other teacher. Fifty-three years after meeting Thomson, Loeffler wrote:

> I never even took a single lesson of him and yet I learned more from him (and through personal contact) in hearing him play in those glorious days of his and my youth in Lugano. He was a phenomenon, rare and unique. Speaking of technique, [Eugène] Ysaÿe used to say of him that "he surpassed Paganini, if we may judge by Paganini's compositions for we do not in this master's works encounter anything in difficulty like what César Thomson used to play." Ysaÿe himself learned *a lot of things* from M. Thomson; Ysaÿe used to say, "One can say of both of them: There was Paganini and—César Thomson!" One could furthermore say of Thomson: that his technique was so surprising, great and diabolical and inimitable, that it simply amounted to genius. With it he had the clearest, most seraphic tone imaginable. . . . As a man he is a great character, upright, manly and of great kindness.[33]

During this time, Loeffler also met Ysaÿe, who came as a visiting artist and became, like Thomson, one of Loeffler's great idols and life-long friends.[34]

Loeffler spent some of his time composing. By his own account, during the Derwies years he wrote a number of songs which he showed to Müller-Berghaus for criticism. The only surviving composition that may possibly be dated to Loeffler's years in Europe is a cadenza to Paganini's first violin concerto.

Loeffler would probably have remained in Europe with the Derwies orchestra were it not for the sudden and unexpected death of Derwies in June 1881. Since Derwies' widow then returned to Russia (his sons were still minors) and the orchestra was disbanded, Loeffler was suddenly unemployed. Although efforts were made to find him a position in Europe, he decided to try his luck in America.

Loeffler had already acquired an emigration permit in 1878. There and on his contract with Derwies his domicile was given as Coblenz, a town neighboring Ehrenbreitstein. It is probable that Loeffler's father was imprisoned when his son left Europe. Assuredly Loeffler was bearing the burden for the support of his family as well as himself when he sailed for New York. What might ordinarily have been a great adventure was also a great responsibility. Difficult as it must have been, the decision to emigrate was a good one. America was Loeffler's country. There he found the freedom to chose his identity and discard national boundaries in his art and in his personal life.

3

New York

In Europe America was advertised as the land of opportunity. For at least three years Loeffler contemplated the trip his father had made fifteen years earlier and about which he doubtless advised his son. Although first-class passage was considerably more expensive, Loeffler saved his money to avoid the overcrowded, underventilated steerage, and in 1881 he sailed, joining nearly 670,000 fellow emigrants to the United States.[1]

Loeffler sailed from Le Havre, departing on 16 July, on the French steamer *Le Canada* and, as he described to a fellow member of the Derwies orchestra, enjoyed the voyage: "The trip was very diverting. I had the opportunity to have a very fine time and with the exception of two days when I was seasick I amused myself very well. We saw many whales."[2] The ship docked in New York on 27 July. Among the first news that met the new arrivals was the shooting of President Garfield. Loeffler disembarked through Castle Garden, then the immigration receiving station, formerly a theater where Jenny Lind and other artists had performed. From there Loeffler entered the city in which he spent his first year in the United States.

Compared to his beloved Paris, New York no doubt presented a disenchanting aspect to Loeffler. Although the wealthy were raising mansions and there was evidence of the cultivation of the arts in the newly opened Metropolitan Museum of Art, the majority of New York's residents were poor and the city was crowded with slum buildings. Another musician, Georg Henschel (to be Loeffler's conductor in Boston), recorded his impression of the city, which he first saw two years before Loeffler, in 1879.

> It looked more like a huge village than an important town. Broadway, its main business street, was only partially paved. Of the unsightly telegraph poles alongside of it, placarded all over with advertisements, not two were standing upright . . . ; dirty little yellow cars, drawn by

small, bony horses, passed wearily along the row of warehouses between which there were still a goodly number of wooden shanties . . . ;
wooden planks still constituted here and there the side-walks; at nearly
every second corner there was a "saloon". . . . To this busy thorough-
fare the quiet dignity and elegance of "Fifth Avenue," with its brown-
stone-front houses, formed a remarkable contrast, and as to dear old
Washington Square, made immortal by Henry James' classical novel of
that name, it seemed a veritable patrician next to Broadway the plebian.
At 59th Street, the beginning of Central Park, the town practically
ended, and I remember a little hut among trees, and cows grazing before
it, on the site where now the Savoy Hotel stands.[3]

New York was on the verge of developing into a modern city; 1881
was the year before Edison opened the first electric plant and two
years before the opening of the Brooklyn Bridge. However, when
Loeffler arrived, farms still mingled with new city buildings along
Central Park, and the skyline of New York was still dominated by its
church towers. Loeffler's only known recorded impression of New
York, at this time, is extremely brief: "What a city New York is;
everyone works like madmen." Then Loeffler confessed, "I have not
yet found a position. Here one pays well 26 dollars a week, that is 500
francs a month, or if in the Italian opera, 35–40 dollars."[4]

Unlike the majority of immigrants, Loeffler was in a good position
to find work in New York. He was a professional (according to
immigration statistics, only 4 percent of immigrants in 1881 were
classified as professionals), and he belonged to a profession especially
favored for realizing the American dream—music.

Concert music in nineteenth-century America was, in general, anything but American music. The United States looked to Europe for its
artistic standards, its artists, and its art. European musicians filled the
majority of musical positions in America; every conductor under
whom Loeffler played in America was European born. Even American-born musicians were usually European trained and often adopted
European-sounding names to overcome American prejudice against
American artists.

It was a good time for Loeffler, not only because Americans thought
that the best in music had to be imported but also because American
pride ruled that America must have the best. Though early nineteenth-
century America had to depend to a large extent upon visiting traveling companies and virtuosi, generally from Europe, for its concert
music, by the 1880s a society had emerged in the cities that could
support resident artistic institutions and cultivate artistic attitudes.
During the latter part of the century the major cities began to establish

permanent, resident musical companies to be on a par with those of Europe—and to fill them with European musicians.

Much of the American public, however, was ignorant of European standards. America was the country where, earlier, Jenny Lind had been presented by P. T. Barnum and where orchestral audiences went to see entertainments such as those of Louis Antoine Jullien's popular traveling orchestra, whose performance of *The Fireman's Quadrille* was accompanied by fire bells and firemen to extinguish actual fire. The creators of America's new organizations, determined to improve the quality of American musical performance, had to set new standards of musical excellence in the country to educate the American public. Much of the progress made toward a maturity in musical performance and taste was made during the 1870s and 1880s.

In 1881, when Loeffler arrived in New York, he carried with him letters of recommendation to two men, Theodore Thomas and Leopold Damrosch, the leaders of orchestral music of the city, two of the major standard-setters in the country. Both were German immigrants; both were concerned with the quality of musical activities in the city. And they were bitter rivals as conductors.

Theodore Thomas, whom Loeffler deeply revered, came to America at age ten and became immediately involved in its musical life. He began his musical career as a violinist, playing concerts as a child prodigy and later playing in various theater and opera orchestras. In 1854 he was elected a member of the Philharmonic Society of New York (founded in 1842), which included the best musicians in New York. With William Mason he played in several seasons of chamber music concerts. He then began conducting.

In 1862 Thomas conducted the first concert of his own orchestra and in the following several years worked to establish it as a stable orchestra. The orchestra performed not only in New York but also, beginning in 1869, on tours, including a tour to the Pacific, which Loeffler joined, in 1883. The Thomas orchestra was a great success. It succeeded, as its founder intended, in improving the conditions of New York orchestras, set a standard for other cities, and promoted the spread of musical culture.

Thomas's major rival, Leopold Damrosch, arrived in New York in 1871. Behind him he had a distinguished career as a conductor in Europe. He began his American career as a choral conductor, then in 1876 was appointed conductor of the Philharmonic Society. Since its members were dependent upon additional means of income, the Philharmonic had been plagued with irregular attendance at both rehearsals and concerts. When Damrosch failed, after only one season, to rescue the orchestra from its already existing disastrous financial condition, the post was taken from him and offered to Thomas. Thomas accepted the position while continuing to conduct his own orchestra through its six winter concerts.

During the temporary absence of Thomas during the 1878–79 season, Damrosch formed his own orchestra, the New York Symphony Orchestra. It also was a success. After Thomas returned to New York, he, Damrosch, and their orchestras coexisted in the city.

"These men, Theodore Thomas and Dr. Damrosch, were the leading spirits of New York's concerts for many years," wrote Sam Franko. "There could scarcely be a greater contrast than the personalities of Thomas and of Damrosch: Damrosch, small and lively, didactic and talkative, given to enthusiasms, free and daring in his conceptions—semitic; Thomas, much taller, practical and matter of fact, taciturn, unimaginative, literal-minded—Nordic-Germanic. . . . Thomas and Damrosch were great rivals."[5]

Loeffler played at different times for both Thomas and Damrosch. He was first engaged by Damrosch, whose son Walter recalled that "Loeffler came to America in 1881, and presented to my father a letter of introduction from the great German violinist, Joachim, who had been Loeffler's master. My father was immediately strongly attracted by his high musical ability and an indescribable personal charm. He immediately took him into his orchestra."[6]

The Damrosch orchestra gave six concerts per season, each preceded by a public rehearsal, a much lighter schedule than Loeffler had known with Derwies. The conductor and most of the players being German, rehearsals were conducted in that language. Damrosch's orchestra performed in Steinway Hall; the Philharmonic Society used the Academy of Music. Like other orchestral musicians, Loeffler must have had to supplement his income with other employment; however, such employment during the regular orchestral concert season is unknown.

With Damrosch Loeffler also played chamber music, which Walter Damrosch also recalled. "Every Sunday afternoon during the winter he came to our house for afternoons of chamber music, playing the viola in a string quartet of which the other members were my father as first violin, Sam Franko as second and Karl Bergner as violoncello."[7] Franko also remembered the quartet.

Shortly after my arrival in New York, I called on Dr. Damrosch to bring him greetings from Madame Viardot-Garcia of Paris. On this occasion I asked him if he often played quartets, to which he replied: "Oh, if you only knew how hard it is to assemble four musicians in New York who want to play merely for the fun of it!" I thereupon offered to try to find them and he acquiesced gratefully but skeptically. It was not particularly difficult, for I found two extremely willing and excellent artists, Charles Martin Loeffler, a violinist I had known in Berlin, who had just arrived in America, and the first cellist of the Damrosch orchestra, Emil Schenk. We met regularly every Sunday afternoon that whole winter at Dr. Damrosch's hospitable home on East Forty-Seventh Street, and I count these musical afternoons among the most enjoyable events of my New York life.[8]

Franko claimed that "Dr. Damrosch was not so popular with his orchestra as Theodore Thomas. The musicians were easily disposed to criticize him, while they stood in awe of Thomas."[9] Loeffler also evidently preferred Thomas, for whom he did not play regularly but did join on special occasions. He mentioned to Engel playing in "various festivals under Theo. Thomas."[10] One he specifically recalled developed out of the Damrosch/Thomas rivalry. In 1881 Damrosch had conducted a "monster" music festival with an orchestra of 250 and a chorus of 1,200. It was so enthusiastically received (monster concerts being eminently suited to the taste of nineteenth-century Americans) that the next year Thomas staged an even larger, grander festival. Rehearsals were held in April and performances given 2–6 May at the Seventh Regiment Armory.

This time seven choruses combined to a total of three thousand singers; the orchestra numbered nearly three hundred. "It was," stated Thomas, "a great reunion, and there was much excitement and enthusiasm displayed at times." Loeffler was seated at the fifth stand of the first violin section. "The orchestra was placed," in Thomas's words, "on the stage so as to form a triple orchestra, similar to an organ with three manuals, which could be played on either singly or in combination, at the pleasure of the conductor."[11] It was a grand affair. The forces performed such compositions as Beethoven's *Missa Solemnis,* Handel's *Israel in Egypt,* Berlioz's *Fall of Troy,* Mozart's *Jupiter,* Schubert's C Major, and Beethoven's Fifth.

This concert took place after the regular concert season, when Loeffler was at liberty for the summer. In the fall he returned to regular orchestral playing but for the summer needed to secure other work. Like other New York musicians, he played in theater orchestras.

New York theaters hosted a number of opera companies, many imported but some based in New York. Among these latter was the short-lived Norcross Opera Company for whom Loeffler played briefly. "Norcross began in the spring of 1882 (?)," wrote Loeffler years later, "and did not last long without Stokes [the financier] who had made his outfit the finest legshow of the best looking girls then in New York." Loeffler's scanty information on Stokes includes only two short sentences hinting at some sordid notoriety: "Stokes who shot . . . whom? I have forgotten now."[12]

The company performed at the old Lester Wallack Theatre on Broadway, also called the Germania. It presented various operettas in English, including *The Mascotte, Patience, Olivette,* and *The Merry War,* the first and last of which Loeffler specifically recalled. The orchestra played under the direction of Ernst Catenhausen, formerly of the Thalia Theatre, for whom at times Loeffler substituted. Over forty years later Loeffler remembered the names of singers—W. T. Carleton, Pauline Hall, and Dick Golden—and the dancer Adele Cornalba.

The theater district at the time centered on 14th Street. Steinway Hall and the Academy of Music, where the Italian Opera would perform, were both located there. After concerts the gathering place for the musical elite was Lienau's (Luchow's) on 14th Street. Afternoons, a group of musicians gathered at the Café Fleischmann, at the corner of 10th Street and Broadway, next to Grace Church. Many visiting musicians, such as Eduard Remenyi, frequented the café, as did several residents including Loeffler and his friend Sam Franko.

Franko saw Loeffler frequently that year:

> Leopold Lichtenberg, Hermann Rietzel, and Loeffler came to my room nearly every day to try new music. We could never persuade Loeffler to take an active part in these intimate musical meetings. He was enthusiastic at the time over César Thomson, the famous Belgian violinist, with whom he had played in an orchestra in Nice. He never tired of telling us of Thomson's wonderful technique, and when Thomson at last came to America and did not meet with the anticipated success, Loeffler was quite nonplused. In order to tease him, Lichtenberg and I invented excercises which we called "Exercises Diaboliques à la Thomson"; they looked playable on paper, but were impossible of practical execution. We sent them anonymously to Loeffler and, although we met him every day, he never uttered a word about them. Many years later he confessed that he had received them, but in a fit of rage destroyed them, for which he was afterwards very sorry, as some of them were quite original and witty.[13]

In New York Loeffler continued to compose, but only one brief composition dated to the New York period survives, *Danse bizarre pour violon seul.*

Loeffler's residence in New York lasted one season. There are indications that he was still interested in a position in Europe. A friend from the Hochschule, Karl Halir, wrote to him in New York friendly letters with news on musical events, conductors, and performers, which Loeffler kept, perhaps with an interest in returning to that scene. J. J. Raff, a great friend of Joachim's, essayed to find a position for Loeffler. In April 1882 he wrote to report his lack of success. But in April 1882 Loeffler had no need to be concerned for his future as an orchestral musician if he remained in America. After his one season in New York, he was engaged to be the assistant concertmaster for the new Boston Symphony Orchestra. Before him lay a career that was to make him almost a cult figure in Boston.[14]

4

Boston

"How different the impression Boston made on me as compared to that of New York!" wrote Georg Henschel, first conductor of the Boston Symphony Orchestra, who, the year before Loeffler, came to Boston from New York. "In the first place the streets had names, not numbers. . . . And then the 'down-town,' i.e. business part of the city: narrow streets and crooked lanes, a dear old church with a beautiful portico, still called the 'King's Chapel,' the old Statehouse, with the Lion and the Unicorn still in its gable, the 'Old Corner Book-store,' and numerous other old-world landmarks—all this made me feel quite at home."[1]

In more than its physical aspect, Boston was closer to "old world" than much of the country. Called the "Athens of America," Boston had an established tradition of culture. By 1882 the area was long known as a literary center and seat of learning. Longfellow, Emerson, Dana (all three of whom died in 1882), Thoreau, and Hawthorne already belonged to its past. Lowell, Aldrich, Howells, Holmes, and many others were still active, as was the country's leading journal, the *Atlantic Monthly*.

Boston had a flourishing musical culture as well. There were many eminent and respected composers, including Paine, Foote, Beach, Chadwick, Converse, Parker, and MacDowell, who lived and worked in Boston during the 1880s and 1890s. Musical performances abounded, and several music journals co-existed, informing an ever growing Boston audience.

Boston also possessed a certain wealth of professional musicians and performing organizations. The oldest and most venerable was the Handel and Haydn Society, dedicated since its beginning in 1814 to the performance of music of the great masters. Other choral groups included the Cecilia Society, the Apollo Club, and the Boylston Club, all founded in the 1870s. Chamber music was presented by such groups as the Mendelssohn Quintette Club and the Beethoven Quintet Club and by a multitude of recitalists.

There were also orchestral concerts. Since 1809 enterprising Bostonians had been pulling together orchestras to perform symphonies. None of these was quite the professional organization that the Boston Symphony Orchestra (BSO) became, and the creation of the BSO to be different and the consequent changes in the orchestral climate were factors leading to Loeffler's own move to Boston.

The immediate forerunner of the BSO was the Orchestral Society of the Harvard Musical Association (HMA). The HMA itself had been formed in 1837 by a number of Harvard graduates to perform music among themselves and to encourage music at Harvard, which then had no music department. The association began with a series of "public benefits," i.e., lectures and concerts. Later they built the Boston Music Hall, and, finally, they founded and managed an orchestra. Conducted by Carl Zerrahn, the Orchestral Society gave its first performance in 1865 at the Music Hall. The concerts were popular and did a great service in putting the music of established masters before the Boston public. Yet, in the words of Arthur Foote, one of the committee that managed the HMA concerts, the visits of "Theodore Thomas, with more attractive programs and a far better orchestra, had shown us what first rate playing really was."[2]

That Boston should have its own first-rate resident orchestra was the ambition cherished by Major Henry Lee Higginson. "By common consent 'the Major' was the foremost citizen of Boston—the founder and sustainer of the Boston Symphony Orchestra, the princely benefactor of Harvard College, alive to every civic responsibility, a recognized leader in the financial, artistic, philanthropic, and social life of the community."[3] The Boston Symphony Orchestra was Higginson's gift to the city of Boston.

Higginson, a native of Boston and member of a socially prominent family, knew the cultural life of the city. From two trips to Europe made during his youth, he knew the possibilities of a symphony orchestra. Following the Civil War, he settled into his father's banking firm, where business success gave him the financial resources to realize his dream of a permanent resident orchestra of the highest excellence for Boston. Visits by the Thomas orchestra provided added inspiration. In 1881 he put his ideas into motion; he had found a conductor, Georg Henschel.

Henschel, who had come to America in 1879, had been asked to conduct the final concert of the HMA's 1880–81 season. Higginson, who had not felt inclined to entrust his project to any of the local men, saw his opportunity and asked Henschel to form the orchestra and be its conductor and music director. Henschel accepted a one-year appointment and within a short time proceeded to engage the musicians. In March 1881 Higginson announced the formation of the orchestra with a notice in the city's newspapers.

There was some feeling that, since Boston had the HMA Orchestral Society, there was no need for a new orchestra. To avoid antagonisms, Higginson and Henschel chose as many local men, including HMA musicians, as possible for their first season. But there were other targets for criticism, many centering on Henschel—his conducting, his tempi, his seating of the orchestra (equal division of strings to each side of the conductor), and his programming—especially his programming.

The Boston audience had, at this time, very conservative tastes in music, fostered to a great extent by John Sullivan Dwight, "the chief apostle of music in Boston,"[4] whose markedly classical views overspread Boston through his leadership position in the HMA and *Dwight's Journal of Music* (of which Loeffler himself had at least ten years of back issues). Though the journal was discontinued in 1881, Dwight's influence persisted for many years, and for many years there was much dissatisfaction with modernity in musical programs.

Yet there was an enthusiastic group that welcomed the idea of a permanent orchestra for the city. The opening season was a great success; the concerts and even Henschel himself gained an immediate and devoted following. When the second season arrived, the critics were no longer hostile, and the concerts were not just popular—they even became the fashion. Higginson and Henschel planned their second season.

In doing so, they created yet another controversy. At the end of the first season, Higginson produced new contracts for the musicians with the stipulation that on rehearsal and concert days "you will neither play in any other orchestra nor under any other conductor than Mr. Henschel, except if wanted in your leisure hours by the Handel and Haydn Society, nor will you play for dancing."[5] Before this time, required attendance at rehearsals and performances had not been a universally accepted practice. Substitution of players was quite common; Loeffler himself did some substitute playing. The ideals of Higginson and Henschel, however, demanded practices out of the ordinary by American standards. Thus the new contracts were unacceptable to some, and the end of the first season found both Higginson and Henschel scouting for new talent. They found several men in New York, where Loeffler was then playing.

Loeffler was recommended to Higginson, according to Loeffler, by Wilhelm Müller, who was then playing in the Thomas Orchestra in New York. Sam Franko also claimed credit for recommending him.[6] In the spring of 1882 Higginson traveled to New York. Highly impressed with Loeffler, he contracted him to be the assistant concertmaster, desk mate to concertmaster Bernhard Listemann. "As Higginson in later years remarked," wrote Carl Engel, "it was the only member of the orchestra whom he personally and independently hired, 'and it was the best.'"[7] Higginson also trusted Loeffler to recommend other personnel, a practice he continued throughout his life. Loeffler, like Franko, recommended Leopold Lichtenburg and also his brother Erich, who came to America in 1883 and joined the orchestra in mid-season. Higginson signed and dated Loeffler's contract on 10 April with the provision that Loeffler would "remove to said Boston some date before the first day of October, A.D. 1882."[8] Loeffler played his engagements with Thomas and the Norcross Opera Company that summer and moved to Boston in September.

Loeffler settled into an apartment on Charles Street. This street, by which the Charles River had originally run, had marked the westernmost part of the peninsular city before landfill created the Back Bay. In 1882 it lay at the west end of Beacon Hill and to the east of the Public Gardens. Loeffler moved into 128 Charles, later moving to 152.

During Loeffler's time many of the socially prominent moved to the Back Bay to build homes and new cultural buildings. Beacon Hill, however, remained a fashionable and culturally rich section of the city. A great number of men and women of letters had lived on Beacon Hill. Many were still there when Loeffler arrived: Francis Parkman, William Dean Howells, Louisa May and Bronson Alcott, Julia Ward Howe, Thomas Bailey Aldrich. Charles Street itself was the meeting place of a notable company of writers on account of the home of the publisher, editor, and writer James Fields at #148, where his widow, Annie, continued to receive local and European authors during Loeffler's time. Oliver Wendall Holmes had lived at 164 Charles until he moved in 1870 to nearby Beacon Street. Sarah Orne Jewett was another resident of the street. Henry James, who before expatriation had also lived on Beacon Hill, chose Charles Street as the setting for his fictional heroine Olive Chandler in *The Bostonians*. Loeffler, an avid reader, could not help but appreciate the milieu in which he found himself.

As a musician also he found himself well suited to Boston. Though very little recorded opinion survives from his first years in Boston, a letter to Sam Franko, written in 1882, reveals a mixed reaction.

Boston violinists, he wrote, were none as good as Lichtenburg. "He may not play solo here for to me unknown reasons and he is intelligent enough yet to know that he is the best here. . . . My dear Sam, if you would like to know how one really should not play the violin, then listen to different, or better, certain people here."[9] In particular he found a violinist in the orchestra, L. Schmidt, to be a simpleton and his cellist brother to be even more simple-minded. The playing of Listemann, the concertmaster, "who played an 'Allegro apathique,'" he thought to be "toneless." On the other hand, "we have better pianists in Boston. Sherwood, Perabo, Baermann, Lang, etc. are really true artists before whom one can with pleasure take off one's hat. Also the musicians in general are agreeable men." Evidently Loeffler liked the orchestra and Boston well enough. He himself quickly earned respect as an artist and soon became a favorite member with the public.

The routine of Loeffler's life for the next twenty-one years followed that of the orchestra. In the early years the orchestra played a twenty-six-week season, for which Loeffler was originally paid thirty-five dollars per week. Performances in the second season included twenty-six concerts in Boston, six at Sanders Theatre in Cambridge, and several in nine other New England towns. Performances in these latter towns were discontinued after a few years when the BSO began visiting New York, Philadelphia, and other more distant places.

Four days a week Loeffler would cross Boston Common to the Music Hall at Winter Street and Bumstead Place for a schedule of rehearsals every morning Wednesday through Saturday plus Wednesday and Thursday afternoons and of performances on Wednesday, Thursday, and Saturday nights and Friday afternoon. As required by contract, these four days were virtually given over to the orchestra.

Loeffler was conscientious to honor the rules of the orchestra. He was used to strict rules regarding attendance and punctuality from both the Pasdeloup and Derwies orchestras. He made a point of being punctual, once declining on a snowy evening the offer of a drive to Sanders Theatre at Harvard University in preference to going "by electrics" because, he wrote, "I do not wish to break my record by getting there too late tonight."[10]

Loeffler's time away from the orchestra was given over to various activities, including practice (it was his custom to practice at least five hours, if not six or seven, each day), teaching, composition, and playing in recitals and chamber ensembles. When Loeffler began taking students is unknown. Eventually he took a second place on Charles Street (112) as a teaching studio. In his first year, however, he could not have afforded a separate studio. The piano that he used for composition was either borrowed or rented, as indicated in a letter written in March 1883: "The piano will be taken back on the 27th of this month and before that I would much like to finish the accompaniment for the celebrated variations of N. Paganini [probably Capriccio 24]."[11]

Loeffler quickly found playing engagements outside of the orchestra, during the time not pledged by contract to the BSO. For example, as part of a concert on 5 February 1883, itself part of a recital series given by the Henschels, Loeffler and his deskmate Listemann performed a Godard composition for two violins accompanied on the piano by Henschel. That spring he was offered a place in the Beethoven Club.[12] Loeffler played in salons as well. Higginson invited him to play at his home, and other social leaders of the city invited Loeffler, among other local musicians, to perform for guests at their various parties and soirées. In the various homes of Boston and Cambridge to which he was invited, Loeffler met a variety of people with whom he shared interests in music, art, and literature, and he made friends.

Making friends and winning admirers began for Loeffler with his arrival in Boston. Loeffler suited Boston. In person, personality, character, and intellect he was, in the words of critic Olin Downes, "all that the elect of the city desired: a man of distinction, culture, cosmopolitan experience; as composer, a craftsman and stylist for the world to admire; an intellectual and a modernist, regarded with pleasing suspicion by the conservatives; a brilliant conversationalist, at ease and in place with the socially exalted, as John Sargent or Karl Muck were in place and on equal terms—really great artists, but, thank Heaven! not socially impossible!"[13] Loeffler might have been called a proper Bostonian. Yet, as Brookline-born, Harvard-educated Daniel Gregory Mason said, he was "something of an exotic in America."[14] In a society that recognized European supremacy in music and valued a display of cosmopolitan culture, Loeffler's exoticism added to his distinction and attraction.

Loeffler was, in fact, an attractive person—a fortunate asset in a society largely ruled by the ladies. He was slender and had fine features and clear blue eyes. In his youth he had fair blond hair and moustache; about 1891 he grew a Van Dyke beard. When Loeffler was in his sixties, his appearance was still such that a student described him as stunningly handsome—very erect and lean, with an excellent carriage and wonderful features, fair skin, and impressive light blue eyes that looked right at you and through you—like one's imaginary picture of a king.[15]

Loeffler's character also impressed people. To some he appeared distant and difficult. "If need be," wrote Engel, "his reserve can chill."[16] But those who knew him admired him greatly. "His bearing was aristocratic, sometimes even a little aloof," wrote Boston pianist Heinrich Gebhard, "yet under this exterior there was a warm heart."[17] Frank Benson, a Boston artist, declared: "Integrity and independence of thought were there without a shade of conceit, and, with all the rest, a generous appreciation of talent in others. . . . but, with all his splendid accomplishment, if you knew him well, you prized him as a man, an upstanding, steadfast friend, who, though he had more than a woman's tenderness of feeling, never yielded a point in the principles he believed in, or stood for anything but the highest and best."[18]

Walter Damrosch, who knew Loeffler for fifty years, said that he possessed "an indescribable personal charm."[19] "His personality was quite unique, for the most contrasting characteristics seemed to melt in him into complete harmony with each other. An aristocrat to his fingertips, he was democratic in his intercourse with others. His musical beliefs were very decided but he was always ready to acknowledge merit in his colleagues and to listen to their arguments. He loved to stress their good qualities and to ignore their failings. He always had a gentle and affectionate smile even when he maintained his views on a beloved or hated composer in some heated discussion with me or some other friends. He hated mediocrity and insincerity in Art and was quick to detect them, but he was always eager to discover and to proclaim real talent."[20]

His intellectuality was impressive. According to Olin Downes, he was "insatiably curious concerning life, art and the surrounding worlds." Downes remarked when Loeffler was forty-nine, "It seems that his peculiar eyes will always be peering, undismayed, into the indeterminate. A mind at once so nervous, so conscious, so perfectly poised, is the rarest of all things."[21] Gebhard said, "He had a marvelous mind, was well-read in English, French, and German literature, not only the classics but the newest books, including the so-called 'decadents.'"[22] "He was unique among composers," wrote fellow composer E. B. Hill, "in that he could drop music to talk of literature and painting with spontaneity and authority. He always had in mind some work of stylistic finesse and atmospheric charm to recommend whether it was Eckermann's *Conversations with Goethe,* Frazer's *Golden Bough,* or Gérard d'Houville's exotic picture of life in Martinique, *Le Séducteur.*"[23] Benson added, "If he had been reading something he liked, he must share it with another and must know if that other liked it too."[24]

Clara Rogers, an opera and concert singer, also enjoyed Loeffler's company. "Loeffler's companionship was always delightful because, apart from music, his intellectuality was of an unusually fine caliber. His ideals, his arguments and conclusions, were always more interesting, while his taste in poetry, literature, and other branches of Art, was invariably of the best. Conversations never fell into the commonplace when he was at our table, and though, happily, we did not always share the same opinions respecting other composers, we were entirely in sympathy about the basic principles—the essentials of true Art."[25]

Loeffler was possessed not only of eclectic but also discriminating tastes. He once wrote, "I ask so little of life, but that little is so fine, so exquisite that I hardly ever get it."[26] A student from his last years remarked that a favorite adjective of his was "choice."[27] Loeffler did have his opinions, and it was said that he did not suffer fools gladly. He could be sharp, even caustic, when faced with mediocrity or pretense. His wit could be sarcastic and his judgment acerbic. He was capable of referring to a composition as a "cod-livery emulsion" or an annoying accompanist as a "jelly-fish" and of making withering comments about musicians he thought incompetent.[28] He could be difficult and alienate people but could also radiate old-world charm.

Loeffler could hardly have been more respected in Boston. He achieved the rare distinction of being accepted into a proud and difficult society, of being listed in the social register with the Cabots and Lowells and others who did not make a custom of accepting immigrant musicians into their personal social circles. But these people (and others of Loeffler's friends who were not in the social register) could hardly say enough in his praise, for his love of beauty, his kind and warm appreciation of his friends and their work, the elegance, dignity, and graciousness of his manners, and the charm of his personality.

Unknown to most, however, behind Loeffler's outward demeanor there was, in addition, quite a different person. "God knows," he wrote in 1883, "from where comes to me sometimes this bad humor, this sadness; when I am really cheerful, I am frightened of myself, although I have a pure conscience up to now. Without being hypochondriac, I do not care at all to know many people."[29] He sometimes expressed wonder that certain people should esteem his friendship and, consequently, treasured those friendships that were his best, albeit he often felt insecure in them. A witness to his friendships, Carl Engel confirmed this insecurity when writing "Even the most loyal of his devotees, at some time or other, was apt to come under the suspicion of being his worst enemy. In cases of justified differences of opinion, one had to stand upon one's meager dignity and impose upon him an unalterable will not to budge from it. He respected sincerity, valued character; they were the essence of himself. And no sooner had calmer reason returned, when his affection and tenderness resurged with all the more force."[30]

Since Loeffler confided his personal life to few, not many of his friends knew the depths of his unhappiness, fears, and anxieties. Few knew much of the private man, either of his unhappiness or of his creative imaginings. "You have no idea," he wrote to a friend while discoursing on choosing a libretto, "how I live a double life—how my mind works and exists completely apart from that one knows of me."[31] His dark moods inevitably found expression in his music. A glimpse of the state of his soul can be seen, for example, in the text of *Rêverie,* one of his earliest extant songs, composed during these years.

> Leave me, my friends, leave me alone
> To surround myself with silence and shadow and mystery
> For my soul this evening, plaintive and contemplative
> Like a pale flower bending under the rain, needs to cry.
>
> Leave, I want to see again our poor cottage.
> The paths embalmed by the green hill
> And by the merry carillon, the dazzling spire,
> Which blends trembling sounds on Sunday at the whitening dawn.
>
> And then I will hear the plaintive harmony
> Of the silver-waved river
> Which at evening blends with distant lowings.
> Ah! Leave me to dream.

Beyond the hints left in his music, however, little would now be known of Loeffler's private melancholia and other aspects of his life and thoughts but for his friendship with Elise Fay and the letters that he wrote to this woman who became his confidant. Loeffler formed his long and significant friendship with the Fay family in 1882. This family consisted of Temple Fay, his sisters Theresa and Elise, and their widowed mother, Mary Nielson Fay. (There were other siblings, apparently with their own households, who were not close to Loeffler.) Temple Fay, who was sixteen years Loeffler's senior, was involved in the East India trade, with which Higginson also had once been involved. The family was one of the quieter members of Boston society.

The Fays were patrons of music in Boston. Temple and Elise were friends of the critic and composer Benjamin Edward Woolf, who dedicated compositions to each of them. Through Loeffler they formed further friendships, such as those with BSO members Franz Kneisel and Henry Eichheim, the latter of whom inscribed one of his scores to Elise Fay, "the most noble and charming woman in the world."[32]

Elise Fay was reputedly a fine pianist, a student of the concert pianist Ernst Perabo. Looking for someone with whom to play chamber music informally, she was introduced to Loeffler soon after his arrival in Boston. In 1884, writing a recommendation for Loeffler to Hubert Léonard in Paris, Fay wrote, "He came to us first professionally, over a year ago, being recommended as the finest violinist in Boston, and after playing with him, we were not slow to discover that he was an exception among artists and among men."[33]

The Fays helped the newcomer to settle and survive in Boston. They were probably responsible for his lodging in Charles Street, where they themselves lived. Loeffler soon became an intimate friend of the family. Fay, eight years Loeffler's senior, helped to manage Loeffler's business affairs—Loeffler once called her his "minister of finance"—and soon became Loeffler's most trusted friend. She was, Loeffler confessed, "the only one to whom I confide all my secrets."[34]

While away from Boston, Loeffler wrote frequently to Fay. On tour during the summer of 1883 he wrote several letters to her. That he had already grown attached to Boston was expressed in the first of these letters wherein Loeffler confessed to being "frightfully homesick for Boston." Further, he wrote that before leaving on that tour, a visit from Perabo made to assure Loeffler of his friendship particularly touched him. "I have had in Boston generally the luck to know endearing people who had shown me more goodness than I perhaps deserve, and there I must especially thank you and your dear family. And what can I do for you? Nothing else but strive every day to play better and better to the end that it makes friends for you."[35]

Yet simultaneously with securing a fine position and making good friends, Loeffler was experiencing an agonizing trial. In April 1883 he consulted Dr. Blake in Boston about ear trouble. In New York he consulted a specialist. He had an abscess in his left ear which, in that doctor's opinion, would scarcely heal. The specialist prescribed a treatment of spraying the ear with a mixture of warm water and Boric acid every evening. But although the pain stopped so that Loeffler could play without aversion, he could hardly hear with his left ear. Throughout the summer and the fall he was plagued by the problem. Nor did it end there; over a period of at least ten years Loeffler had trouble with his ear. In 1893 a perforated drum-membrane was diagnosed.

Despite this affliction, which sometimes made playing unbearable, Loeffler spent eleven weeks of the time he was at liberty from the BSO playing with the Theodore Thomas orchestra. Thomas had designed a festival tour, variously called the "March to the Sea" and "From Ocean to Ocean," which began in New York in mid-April, toured the East and South, then moved across the country to San Francisco and back to Chicago, where the tour ended in the Summer Night Season.[36] Loeffler joined Thomas in New York. In Philadelphia they presented an oratorio and two concerts, but in Baltimore the tour actually began. From there Loeffler wrote to Miss Fay the first of eight surviving letters from the tour.

The tour was, overall, not a happy experience for Loeffler. His ear plagued him and doubtless accentuated the other irritations. The trip was long and tedious, with most of the time spent on the train. There was little time to practice but many concerts to give. Although always booked into the best hotels, at times they were badly placed and fed. Loeffler summed it up in Memphis: "Work for a horse, heat for a dog, rubbish to eat."[37] In addition he missed Boston and his friends.

About the concerts themselves, after the first letter, he wrote nothing. At the first Baltimore rehearsal, he declared, all the singers sang too high and wrong. But in that letter he expressed his delight to be conducted by Thomas. "It seems to me that few conductors have their orchestras so in their power as Th. Thomas. I play with real pleasure under his direction."[38] Years later he said that after this tour "I knew Theodore Thomas like my left hand, admired and loved him."[39]

Aside from Thomas, Loeffler mentioned few of his fellow passengers. His best friend on the tour was an older (unnamed) man, also a former student of Joachim's. But, on the whole, he confided to Fay, he found it difficult to enjoy the society of the other men and wrote, "Monsieur Loeffler is out of tune like the violin of Monsieur Saint-Saëns [here quoting the opening two measures of *Danse macabre*]. At the end of July 'ça ira, ça ira' [it will be] better, I hope. I do not know myself at present."[40] ("Ça ira" is an allusion to a Parisian "chanson révolutionnaire," which he later quoted in his *La villanelle du Diable*.)

Expressions of isolation, disillusionment, bitterness, and even misanthropy (all stemming from the experiences of his youth) appear in his letters. He discovered that, had Thomas known Erich to have been in Boston, he might have invited him to join the tour; as it was *"both* idiots from S. Francisko," (the "simpleton" Schmidt brothers?) were playing in the orchestra and Thomas had constantly to ride on the cellist brother since "he is what your brother calls a 'Dead-head.'"[41]

What Loeffler particularly enjoyed was seeing the country. "If you could have seen the sublime landscapes that have passed before my eyes yesterday morning! It has been a long time since I have seen mountains, valleys, and forests as great as there are in Pennsylvania. I was so happy in seeing all that."[42] "I do not try to describe to you the magnificence of your country, or of the Mississippi of which I had a splendid view from my room, because I lack skill with the pen, but I tell you, since you have not traveled in the different states that you cannot imagine what a paradise America is."[43] "This America, that I would call: the garden of the good God, has always appeared to me as if God had made it for the unhappy, the poor, the oppressed . . . it is a real masterpiece." He was disappointed that some of his colleagues did not share his joy in the passing landscapes, but found that "happily there are also others who understand that America has other beautiful sides than dollars."[44]

Loeffler devoted the bulk of his letters not to the tour but to rhapsodizing on love and the fact that for "the first time I am really in love."[45] The object of his affections throughout these letters is unidentified—Loeffler referred to her only as "elle" ("her").

"It seems to me," he wrote, "that it is with her that my life began. . . . What an evening, when I spoke to her for the first time! We spoke very little together—of what could we speak? One is ashamed of one's own voice; one would like to develop a sumblime tone to unite in a celestial hymn. I no longer know if it was minutes or hours that I spoke with her, I only know that it was worth more than all the days of my life. . . . Since that concert where I spoke with her for the first time, my soul is like a fish cast from its element onto the shore. It wriggles and tosses until it is dried by the warmth of the day."[46]

"A few weeks before I left Boston," he also wrote, "I was not sure of myself, if I loved her truly and seriously or not, but I felt: if, if, if, if, if, if, if, if, if, if, if, if ever I loved her, it would be with a love as deep as true and certainly incurable, and that is dangerous, you know. But no, you do not know because you told me yourself, that you have never been in love and that you are not. Ah well, I wish that you will never be, and on the other hand I do wish it." And, "Her image never leaves me and often in dreams I see her before me, and I then read in her sad air: that she loves me. What sweet illusions! Perhaps she finds me detestable."[47]

Loeffler had a special reason for not declaring his love openly. "How often I have cursed this —— money. If she were from a respectable family but without means, I might have some chance because I would work so much, even if it cost ten years of my life, to be able to obtain a woman very suitable."[48] And later: "I had firmly resolved not to fall in love/not because I hate women, God forbid . . . because, as I said, I suffer a want of an abundance of money and one cannot live on love alone, and in consequence of this I cannot have a lass without money and may not have one with money, out of a sense of honor and other reasons."[49] Loeffler felt in honor bound not to try to claim a wealthy woman while their fortunes were so disparate. All things combined—including uncertainty of his beloved's reciprocity of feeling—Loeffler somewhat lamented being in love but at the same time lived most happily in thoughts of love and "her."

The final reference to this mysterious "her" occurred in September when Loeffler wrote a note of apology to Fay that he had not accompanied her to the railway station. He was sufficiently punished for it, he declared, for he did not see "her" again. That "she" may have been a veiled allusion to Fay herself is possible, although his wording in previous letters, such as "you . . . and the other young lady"[50] and an allusion in a letter from 1886 to "confidences of other times" (quoted in chapter 6), leaves the question open. For three years after this note not a further word of love, but only affection and friendship, occurred in Loeffler's letters.

After the tour Loeffler spent the rest of the summer in the country with the Fays, a custom he followed every summer that he spent in America. During a few summers he did return to Europe but not to resettle. In 1910 he said, "I came for the purpose of seeing your great country, and was so charmed with the outlook I decided to remain."[51] According to his friend Gebhard, "he adored America."[52] In two years Loeffler had seen the country, made a home for himself in a city for which after only one year he felt homesick when away, lost his heart to a young lady, secured a position that allowed him to support himself and his family and to save for the future, and made an honored place for himself in his profession with an organization he respected. In November he began citizenship proceedings. Loeffler had found his country.

5

The Henschel Years
(1883–1885)

Loeffler resumed his seat with the BSO in October 1883. It was Henschel's last season in Boston and Loeffler's first as a soloist with the orchestra. Loeffler's debut playing violin came on 16 November 1883. He chose to give the Boston premiere of Benjamin Godard's *Concerto romantique*. During November, December, and January the program was repeated in Fitchburg, Cambridge, Worcester, and New Bedford. His playing was enjoyed by the audience and praised in the papers (by unidentified critics):

Boston Traveller: "He made his first appearance in the city as a soloist, and made a good impression as a violinist, playing with much expression and fine execution. It is evident that he is a thoroughly accomplished violinist, and he will be a valuable addition to our solo talent."[1]

Boston Morning Journal: "[The concerto] was superbly played by Mr. Loeffler, who showed a broad and refined method, remarkable power of execution and unusual powers of expression. . . . he is undoubtedly a player of great ability, both in execution and expression."[2]

Boston Daily Advertiser: "Mr. Löffler's playing throughout was excellent; quaint and exquisite throughout."[3]

Boston Evening Transcript: "It was a very solid and praiseworthy performance and well merited the loud and persistent plaudits which the audience showered on the young artist."[4]

Loeffler was not a flamboyant musician; he indulged in no tricks or special effects of execution to startle an audience. His playing was considered "chaste" and, if occasionally (in the early years) found wanting in strength, was repeatedly described in the reviews as brilliant, exquisite, and elegant. Loeffler might well have had a career as a concert violinist, independent of his work in Boston. He reputedly developed into a "magnetic soloist of irresistible distinction"[5] and possessed "a tone like fine-spun silk yet rich, impeccable technic and intonation, and a style so elegant and polished that it could only be called aristocratic."[6]

With four exceptions, from 1883 to his retirement in 1903 Loeffler appeared each season as a soloist with the orchestra. The reviews, a sample of which are given below, were always complimentary, revealing that he had won his public.

1884—Lalo *Fantasie norvégienne* and Bruch Concerto in D Minor (*Boston Evening Transcript*): "Mr. Loeffler is a violinist well armed at all technical points. His tone is brilliant, his intonation is flawless, his phrasing artistic, often graceful. He plays with great musicianly feeling, and never for an instant descends to trickery. . . . Mr. Loeffler is so thorough an artist that he can afford to do without that diable-à-quatre dash with which some players can fiddle an audience into frenzy."[7]

1887—Lalo *Symphonie espagnole* (*Boston Transcript*): "Mr. Loeffler . . . played admirably at every point; with perfect technique, grace and security of phrasing and, especially in the final Rondo, with enchanting brilliancy and dash. He outdid himself, in a word."[8]

1888—Bruch *Scottish Fantasy* (*Boston Gazette*): "His playing throughout was exquisite in its purity of taste, its perfect intonation, the brilliancy, the precision and the fluency of its technique, and the grace and warmth of expression that characterized it. . . . He was applauded appreciatively and enthusiastically, and recalled again and again with the heartiest fervor."[9]

1890—Lalo *Symphonie espagnole* (*Boston Journal*): "The number was originally composed for Signor Sarasate, but we doubt if that brilliant artist could have given more pleasure to the audience than the deservedly popular violinist of last Saturday evening."[10]

1893—Saint-Saëns Concerto no. 1 (*Boston Gazette*): "Mr. Loeffler played the fine violin concerto with exquisite taste, perfect finish of style, purity and brilliancy of technique, and nobility of sentiment. The warm and graceful artistic feeling, and the conscientious devotion to the composer that always give a characteristic distinction to his playing, were manifested to their fullest, and proved a potent element in the pleasure that his performance afforded."[11]

Loeffler did not escape without some imperfections being noted. In the early years particularly it was said that he wanted strength or fullness of tone. In 1885 W. F. Apthorp commented, "He does not irradiate all the heat that is in him."[12] In time even that flaw disappeared. Apthorp (following other critics who had much earlier withdrawn the criticism) wrote of his performance of the Saint-Saëns *Concertpiece* in E minor: "The time is long since past for speaking of such matters as technique or intonation in connection with Mr. Loeffler; he has won his spurs and we take these things for granted in him. But last Saturday he played with a rich volume and warmth of tone which we had not associated with him before, with a penetrating sentiment and grace of phrasing that carried everything before them, and, in the Saint-Saëns piece, with immense brilliancy. . . . In a word, he was superb!"[13]

In short, Loeffler was "a thorough master of the violin." By 1894 it was claimed that Loeffler had "gained a recognition of his abilities as a soloist which has seldom been excelled in the appearance here of artists of world wide reputation."[14]

With respect to both technique and interpretation, Loeffler won praise from all quarters. At every performance he was recalled repeatedly. He was a great favorite with audiences both in and out of town. Another sample of reviews attest to his popularity with both his audiences and his colleagues. "There is no more popular man in the symphony orchestra than Mr. Loeffler, and this feeling of good will towards him is as pronounced among members of the orchestra as it is evident among patrons of these concerts." "During the ten years or more that he has been with the orchestra his unvarying courtesy has endeared him to all associates, and his uncommon talents as a musician have received full recognition from the patrons of the Symphony concerts." "Mr. Loeffler is a favorite with symphony audiences, and was heartily greeted as he left his desk in the orchestra, and again, after the concerto." "There is probably no more popular member of the Boston Symphony Orchestra than Mr. Loeffler."[15] He was admired by other violinists as well. Karl Halir, for example, was reported to consider Loeffler the greatest technician in America.[16]

Loeffler also attracted attention for his repertoire. He quickly made a reputation as a modernist, both for the music he chose to perform with the orchestra and for his recital pieces. A review of a Bruch premiere stated, "We have learned to look to Mr. Loeffler for a felicitous choice of new works, which he always selects from his repertoire, an example which other violinists might follow to their advantage."[17] Loeffler also became quickly known as a champion of the French school. He was, in fact, one of the few who presented French music, as noted in a review of the Lalo he premiered in 1887: "We have to thank [Mr. Loeffler] for almost all the chances we get nowadays of hearing French music."[18]

Although Loeffler had the talent to pursue a career as a concert soloist, he played outside Boston only when on tour with the BSO or when playing his own compositions (only once, however, with another orchestra). Much as he loved his art and worked at perfecting his playing, however, he discovered that he did not have the temperament for a soloist's career. "I know that the day when I have $10,000," he disclosed to Fay, "I will be heard no more in public and little will be lost. It is not part of my temperament to be 'public performer.' Kneisel told me yesterday that the day when he would have a certain sum of savings he would no longer perform in public because each time that he has to play a solo all his body and system is upset from anxiety for several days. At least he plays well before the world, but I never do myself justice, never! And I ask myself sometimes is it worth the pain to live with such a profession that makes you hate it."[19]

The public face that Loeffler wore, as a soloist, was that of a man who had mastered his art, performed with seeming ease, and accepted success with humility and dignity. Such success, however, was achieved through great industry and was complicated by tremendous strain, anxiety, illness, and an exacting nature that demanded excellence of himself and his art.

During the early 1880s Loeffler was at the beginning of his career. He threw his energies into it. He continued to appear in recitals as well as in symphony performances. In November 1883 he assisted Arthur Foote, a popular piano recitalist who was also a composer, by performing with him, Henry Hendl, and Wulf Fries the new Dvořák Quartet in D and the Brahms C Minor. Loeffler and Mrs. Henschel assisted at the first Boston recitals given by another performer-composer, Amy Marcy Cheney (later Mrs. H. H. A. Beach), in January and February of 1884. Loeffler and Cheney played Beethoven's Sonata op. 12, no. 3. Throughout the 1880s Loeffler would assist in similar recitals. While he did not give full-length public recitals himself, he did appear as a solo artist, as well as chamber musician, in private salon recitals and musicales.

In the salons Loeffler made friends in Boston. At a private concert in January 1884 Loeffler met Otto Grundmann, perhaps the first of Loeffler's good friends among Boston artists. Born in Dresden in 1848, Grundmann had come to Boston in December 1876. He became an instructor and director of the Boston Art Museum School of Drawing and Painting (which opened in 1877). In appearance, by virtue of "long hair, very wide-brimmed hat, flowing tie, and marked foreignness," he reputedly "conformed to the current stereotype of a painter."[20] Reputedly an excellent pedagogue, Grundmann was the teacher of others of Loeffler's painter friends, notably Frank Benson and Edmund Tarbell, leaders in the Boston art world and later also instructors at the Museum School. After the January concert,

Grundmann wrote Loeffler a note of appreciation about his playing and continued to take an interest in Loeffler and his career. He was one of the few to whom Loeffler confided his family grief, which worsened during the summer of 1884 when Loeffler returned to Europe.

Although achieving success as a violinist, Loeffler himself was not satisfied with his playing. He decided to return to Paris for further study. In January 1884 he wrote to Hubert Léonard to ask to be taken on as a student. Elise Fay also wrote to Léonard to recommend Loeffler as an exceptionally talented violinist: "His playing is strong and his intonation perfect,—he has a technique capable of anything, and plays with exquisite taste and sentiment—besides this, he has a remarkable memory which allows of his playing everything by heart. His solos are always received with enthusiasm. . . . You will find him very interesting personally, well educated, and charming manners."[21] Léonard accepted Loeffler as a student, and Loeffler sailed for Europe on March 26.

An item about his trip appeared in a Boston newspaper: "Mr. Martin Laeffler [*sic*], the well-known violinist, has sailed for Paris, where he is to continue his studies under the most eminent masters. This young musician has evidently a future before him, and does not propose to remain content with his present great success."[22] When Loeffler read this, he was not at all pleased. "I detest to be written about, no matter what. . . . I was perfectly furious with the journals that were sent me and the nonsense said in them. I absolutely do *not* want anyone to be interested in me; to be left completely undisturbed, that is what I want."[23] Loeffler never cared for notoriety, for attention from the press.

On his arrival in Paris, Loeffler visited Léonard at his home in Maisons-Laffitte and arranged to begin his studies after Holy Week. He spent the intervening time recovering his strength following a fever he had suffered during the crossing, finding lodging, renewing his acquaintance with the city, trying unsuccessfully to find a musician friend of his father's, Anthony Lamotte, and visiting musical establishments.

Loeffler was excited to be in Paris again. "Oh what a city! . . . Since I was here the last time it has not changed at all; however, I am almost blinded by the splendor."[24] Though he adored Paris, he also commented later, "Imagine, everyone takes me for an American and I am very content for Germans are hated here in an amazing way. Also Mons. Léonard believes that I am Amer. and I think that it is much better to leave them all with this idea. How happy I will be when I am really a citizen of the United States!"[25]

Loeffler's new teacher, Hubert Léonard, a native of Belgium, was a former orchestral violinist, soloist, and teacher at the Brussels Conservatory. Forced by ill health to give up his conservatory position in 1867, he returned to Paris, where he taught violin privately. Loeffler began his studies with Léonard by playing the Bruch concerto and Bach chaconne. "He told me," Loeffler wrote to Fay, "that I had much talent and that I played excessively well."[26] Then, with the Beethoven concerto, the lessons started in earnest.

Léonard invited Loeffler to join a musical evening with himself, Camillo Sivori, and a cellist named Brandoukoff. Loeffler played viola with them in the Brahms and Mendelssohn quartets. At the end of the summer Loeffler came to know Sivori better; at this time he was particularly taken with Brandoukoff "because he is first a charming boy, an artist of great talent, and he knows many of my friends in Russia and especially in Moskow."[27]

Loeffler met other Russians at a soirée given by Prince Davidoff, where he met also the General Davidoff who was particularly taken with Loeffler's Russian-sounding name, Tornov. Davidoff invited Loeffler to lunch and gave him cards to the Cercle de l'union artistique, Place Vendôme.

Loeffler's letters mention only a few others whom he met, for example, cellist Adolphe Fischer, who played an assortment of pieces for Loeffler, including Spanish dances by Sarasate. He also heard Ysaÿe play. Ysaÿe, he related, had once traveled with the conductor Bilse, who "the other day telegraphed him if he would accept an engagement to travel, with a salary of 1000 marks per month. Ysaÿe pretended to have responded: 'J'encule vos conditions,' and the other, who does not know a word of French and did not see the gag, replied: 'telegram incomprehensible.' 'J'encule vos conditions' means something like 'I give your terms a kick in the rear.' (I do beg your pardon!)"[28]

On May 2 Loeffler was introduced to Edouard Lalo. "I saw him several years ago; he then had black hair and a young air, today— white hair and beard, limping from paralysis, with an old and sick appearance. I could not prevent myself from giving him pleasure by telling the lie that I had played his 'Symphonie espagnol' with great success in America. This falsehood slipped out with good will! [and was one Loeffler later made good.] I will make him a visit one of these days."[29]

Loeffler's best friend during this time was Moritz Moszkowski, a concert pianist whom Loeffler had known previously, at least since 1879.[30] When Loeffler found lodging, he discovered that Moszkowski, though away at the time, was also living in the same building.

After Moszkowski returned to Paris, he and Loeffler often played together, including each other's compositions.

Loeffler lived simply and studied diligently. "In the morning I rise at 8; I have breakfast, I practice the violin until noon. Then I go out for lunch, after that I take a walk or go shopping or I go to the Louvre. At four o'clock I am home; I play the violin until about 7 o'clock. I go out to dine, and I go to the theatre or to a café-chantant [music hall] or a café(-simple) or to a soirée, oh well always somewhere."[31] He had saved two years for this trip and meant to live well and enjoy himself. He even declared that he was happy.

His lessons continued to go well. He played Paganini's *La clochette* and *Streghe*. He continued composing and saw the first publication of one of his compositions, a violin and piano piece entitled *Berceuse*. Because Léonard had recommended it for publication "and since he liked the piece so much," Loeffler wrote to Fay, "I saw myself obliged to dedicate it to him."[32] The publisher was J. Hamelle, the publisher of Fauré's *Berceuse*. As was the custom for a first publication, Loeffler paid the fee himself, fifty francs. The receipt was dated 30 Avril 1884; the music was issued in September.

Throughout the summer Loeffler was looking for a new violin. There was a Guarnerius he wanted; then he decided on a Vuillaume. Long discussions of his Parisian finances passed between Loeffler and Fay (true also of subsequent visits to Paris), including comments on Grundmann's offer to help Loeffler buy the Guarnerius. Loeffler protested that Grundmann did not know him if he thought he would accept. Yet he appreciated Grundmann's interest. "Grundm. is very good, but I could never make a practice of that. He has a lot of affection for me that I probably do not merit."[33] At some point, Loeffler did purchase a Vuillaume. In later years he may have purchased a second. Of other preferences in violins and equipment, it is known that he persuaded Hugo Schindler in Boston to manufacture 14K gold G strings, which he and Kreisler used but which were later discontinued after the use of cheaper gold brought them into disrepute.[34]

In May Loeffler visited his mother, sister, and brother in Homburg. It was a joyful reunion.

> My good mother, who loves me so much and whom I adore, only thinks of making me happy, then my sister, Helene,—I cannot express to you how I like her. She has a ravishing simplicity, a true little jewell. . . . And for a year she has played the harp . . . and she will be a great harpist because she has first a great talent, much energy, a love for work, etc. etc. Since she learned that my father was financially ruined, she took it

into her head to undertake something to be able to earn her living nicely and agreeably. She had a love for her instrument and for a year she took harp lessons while working nine to ten hours a day. Four weeks ago she played for the first time in public with *great success,* such that she was engaged to play solos during the summer at the Kur-Haus in Homburg, one of the largest watering-places in Germany. . . . I assure you, I am very pround of her.[35]

Back in Paris, Loeffler's life continued well. He was studying a Vieuxtemps concerto with Léonard, despite the latter's being afflicted with gout. And he continued playing with Moszkowski, who gave him copies of his *Ballade* and *Boléro,* which Loeffler found very pretty. Yet all was not well with Loeffler's spirit.

From his mother Loeffler had acquired a photo of himself taken at age sixteen. The photo brought back unhappy memories. "Dear friend," he wrote to Fay on his return to Paris, "I should truly be well satisfied and happy, since I am making progress, associating with charming artists, am personally liked, am busy with my talent more than duty, etc., etc. And yet! I am unhappy! I am entirely changed. Brilliant Paris has made me soft and melancholy. And my friend Moszkowsky who is an old dreamer of the first class is not the society to cure me (although he is the only friend I have in Paris). In sending you the enclosed photograph the saddest memories have come back to me. When this picture was taken I was sixteen years old, and you have no idea how I began already to be unhappy."[36]

Not much later Loeffler was not simply sad but desolate. Dr. Löffler, due to be released from prison on 26 June, had suffered a stroke. "I received news from home that my father was so ill that his death was expected daily. . . . Finally he would have been able to enjoy the freedom that he loved so much, and today—who knows how many hours he still has to live. . . . The whole family is in despair because we were awaiting the day of my father's liberation with impatience and joy, and now all is destroyed, perhaps forever."[37]

Loeffler plunged into deep depression. In his letters he vented his great hatred of the Prussian regime, his love for republican France, his great sorrow, and his pessimistic view of life. His thoughts became morbid, even suicidal. In early July Loeffler reported that his father's condition had improved. Yet he was still very ill, and Loeffler remained very depressed,

Never in my life have I had such a strong desire to die as today. I swear to you that if there were any war in Europe I would volunteer in order to find death. . . . Cholera is in France; if it wanted to trap me, I would be willing. . . . Death, is it not preferable to life? When all is withered in a sickly soul! The most extreme pain is to appear happy and to carry deadly griefs insíde. Believe me, dear friend, that grief is a living death! . . . I understand today that Alfred de Musset killed himself with absinth. The day before yesterday, for the first time in a long time, I drank absinth. It did not intoxicate me, rather it made me cry (behind a newspaper) like a child. . . . Destiny takes me as the whirlwind the leaf. Driven and driven away from valleys to mountains, from mountains to valleys.[38]

As every day he became more unhappy, Loeffler eventually sought the help of a doctor who predicted that his state, though at one time dangerous, would pass in time. Yet Loeffler's depression was deep-set, and his tone continued to be morbid. "It is said that not to want death is folly, to want it is a crime—it is thus that I try as long as possible to support this detestable life; perhaps it will finish itself sooner than I believe."[39]

Moszkowski left Paris in July; consequently, Loeffler spent much time alone, which he preferred to falling out with everyone on account of his depressed mood. Of particular comfort to him was the support of the Boston friends in whom he confided, Otto Grundmann and the Fays, particularly Elise. Before his father's stroke, Loeffler had commented on his friendship with Fay: "It is true that one can not be closer to me than you are and closer to you than I am. . . . there exists between us two, despite our great closeness, a little barrier, very agreeable and which we do not perceive. That comes from the formation of our characters which are, after all (and above all, mine) very reserved and can only open to others who are similar." And later: "Your affection and friendship are perfectly touching, and I can only say one thing, that they find their mirror and echo in me. We love each other without loving and yet we love each other." After the July tragedy, he leaned heavily on her moral support. "You cannot imagine what pleasure I see in each line that you are always the same, charming, and faithful friend."[40]

Dr. Löffler survived the summer; Loeffler survived his grief. In July Paris celebrated its national holiday. Loeffler found it "beautiful and grandiose," and it inspired him to write expressions of his republicanism, concluding, "I myself am a true and good republican . . . and I live in the greatest republic of the world, America. There are times when I am really homesick for Boston."[41]

Loeffler was encouraged by the success he was having with his violin studies. "Monsieur Léonard told me that if I were to continue to work for 3 or 4 more years I would play well, better than so and so

(I dare not say the names because they are famous violinists of today). He encouraged me enormously with that." Both were enjoying Loeffler's lessons, which could last two to three hours while Loeffler played Paganini, Beethoven, Wieniawski, Moszkowski. "Always when I leave he tells me the same thing 'perfect still a little, Loeffler, and you will arrive.'"[42]

Sivori also encouraged Loeffler. One day in August, when Léonard took Loeffler to Sivori's home, Sivori, who had been a student of Paganini, played some of Paganini's music for Loeffler. Afterwards Loeffler himself played. "Then Léonard said to him 'Isn't he on the way?' and Sivori replied 'Pardi, if he is going to continue like that.' So they said much about my tone and style, etc. but all very flattering."[43] Sivori impressed Loeffler deeply, as revealed in a letter written thirty-eight years later, in 1922, to Engel, then chief of the Music Division of the Library of Congress.

> I am very grateful to you for letting me see Paganini's Oeuvres posthumes. To one, who like myself up to the age of 25, played principally this grand old wizzards stuff, it brought a whiff of youth— my own—to me. Alas, "them days is gone forever!" Who knows today how P. played his music? César Thomson, but who else? When I lived in Paris, I used to play Quartets with my old teacher Léonard on Sundays, at Maison Lafitte. Sivori usually played first v. M. Léonard and I alternately 2d v. and viola and M. Bonjour violoncello. Although Sivori was not much of a musician, he interpreted intuitively the old masters, and even Brahms, most musicianly. His playing was besides, violinistically a delight. Sarasate had the same felicitous intuition in rendering all sorts of music delightfully. If he had kept his mouth shut, the world would never have suspected him of ignoring so much of what makes music an art. Both men phrased naturally and I believe (as I knew them) that they never put any intention or interpretation into their readings. Strange, isn't though? Through Sivori I learned a great deal of what was Paganini's manner and style: uncanny, fabulous mastery of left hand and bow arm, diabolic fire and that dose of exaggeration in expression which seems a caracteristic of all, even the most gifted Italian musicians. Neither Sivori (P.s pupil) nor Sarasate had this rather surprising failing, but neither did they have the above mentioned diabolic touch. They never strained themselves physically or mentally ("comme les éléphants pincent leurs fesses" [as elephants tighten up their rumps] when they have to cross a wooden bridge!) trying to express that which they could not feel. Both of them were delightful players with natural charm.[44]

Léonard encouraged Loeffler to continue composing, advising him to write a concerto and other pieces that he could play in concert.

Moszkowski also encouraged Loeffler to continue his composition studies. "He believes that I could compose very famous pieces."[45] Loeffler resolved, therefore, to study counterpoint on his return to Boston.

Before leaving Europe, Loeffler visited Homburg once more. In his letters he lapsed into silence on the subject of his father. At some point Dr. Löffler was transferred to a hospital in Coblenz, but Loeffler never mentioned seeing him again.

On 6 September Loeffler sailed on the *Canada* for Boston. He had not recovered from his depression but buried it deep inside. He looked forward to seeing Fay, playing his new music with her, and picking up his life in America. "Certainly it will be very painful to leave Paris," he confessed, "but since it is for Boston where I have friends like you and Grundmann and so many other pleasant acquaintances the pain must diminish to nothing."[46]

Loeffler had a new season to anticipate, with a new conductor who would form the Boston Symphony Orchestra into a truly great orchestra.

6

The Gericke Years
(1885–1889)

Despite his success with the Boston orchestra, Henschel had decided, at the beginning of his third season, to return to Europe in the spring of 1885 to continue his singing career. He had accomplished what Higginson had asked him to do: he had formed an orchestra to be a professional and permanent institution. In so doing he had earned the admiration of his orchestra and audience. At his final concert, when about to conduct the *Manfred* Overture, "I saw," he related, "as in a dream, the leader and, with him, the whole orchestra rise to their feet, and before I could realise what was happening, the familiar, affecting strain of 'Auld Lang Syne' filled the vast hall, played by those dear fellows of the orchestra and sung by the audience, which I noticed, in turning round bewildered and embarrassed, had risen too."[1]

There was then, as there always would be when a conductor left, great speculation and anticipation attending the arrival of the new conductor. Henschel's successor, Wilhelm Gericke, came to America from Vienna, where he had been Kapellmeister of the Vienna Court Opera and conductor of the Gesellschaft der Musikfreunde concerts and of the Singverein. Higginson, in Europe during a large portion of his orchestra's third season, approached Gericke after hearing a production of *Aida* by the Vienna opera. His offer came just at a time when Gericke was having difficulties with the director of the opera and, therefore, accepted Higginson's offer.

Gericke himself recounted his beginning with the orchestra: "In September, 1884, I went across the ocean to begin my new position as a Conductor of the Boston Symphony Orchestra. It would be untruthful to say that my beginning there was an easy one; for everything that Mr. Higginson felt years ago as an amateur about the difference of orchestras and artistic conditions, I felt ever so much more as a professional, and especially after having conducted the admirable orchestra of the Vienna Court Opera for ten years."[2]

Gericke was an experienced conductor and a strict one. Under his direction the orchestra developed into the organization that, after his second season, could go on tour to Philadelphia, New York, and other eastern cities and be recognized as a first-class orchestra. Yet it was a development not easily made.

"In my new work," admitted Gericke, "all sorts of troubles were going on during the first season. The members of the Orchestra were not accustomed to my way of rehearsing."[3] For example, Loeffler's friend Sam Franko, who joined the orchestra in 1884 and resigned after six weeks, could not abide Gericke's conducting. "The rehearsals were insufferably dull. The eternal interruptions and verbose explanations, illustrated by singing and playing on the piano, wearied the orchestra. It was only when we gave a concert that we had a chance to hear the composition as a whole. The performances were full of subtle nuances, finely balanced, but lacked spirit and life."[4] This opinion was not universal, but transformation of the BSO into a first-class orchestra was difficult for conductor and orchestra alike.

Gericke continued: "The audience did not like my programmes. Constant complaints were made about their being too heavy. . . . Mr. Higginson may have had a very hard time to defend my ideas against the many complaints and criticisms made to him about me; but in all that time, he stood most loyally by my side."[5] Henschel had been criticized for his preference for Brahms and for including Wagner on his programs. Gericke came in for even more criticism. At performances of not only Brahms but also Bruckner and the more modern Richard Strauss, audience members walked out in great numbers.

Loeffler had already learned of Gericke's tastes before his arrival in Boston. "Next winter," he wrote to Fay from Paris, "you will have Wagner and Liszt in mass because the Viennese artists have told me this Monsieur Gericke is a great Wagnerian. I have just read in a journal that he conducted the last Philharmonic Concert in Vienna and that he was given great ovations because of his coming departure for America."[6] At the time of Gericke's coming a few other changes in personnel occurred. Higginson turned to Loeffler for recommendations and dispatched him to New York to find new second violinists for the orchestra.

One new member of the orchestra, secured by Gericke himself, was Timothée Adamowski, ranked third in the violin section. Throughout their years together in the orchestra, Loeffler and Adamowski sustained a friendly rivalry. Both appeared as soloists with the orchestra, and apparently the number of appearances each had in a year became a competitive matter. A sense of the rivalry comes through a remark in a letter from Loeffler to Isabella Stewart Gardner, a Boston patroness who lent both her Stradivarius violin (purchased in 1894). "Tim Adams informed me some time ago with a curiously unfriendly polish(ed) glistening in his eye that: Mrs. Gardner was lending me the violin for only the year coming, on which remark I had to inform him that that was indeed much longer than I expected to have it." Loeffler also wrote to Gardner to reprimand "whomever will play on the violin" for the unclean condition in which it was returned.[7]

For Loeffler during the 1884–85 season, however, personnel matters were far overshadowed by personal problems. On 6 November Dr. Löffler died in the hospital at Coblenz. It was a difficult time for the entire family. Years later, Helene wrote, "For the funeral of our father, I had to make the trip all alone to Coblenz, and I alone was present there."[8] After the news reached Loeffler in Boston, his life was nearly shattered.

Although Loeffler attempted to adopt a stoical public attitude, he feared he had alienated everyone by his misery and coldness. Whether anyone beyond his closest friends—Grundmann, the Fays—knew the story or Loeffler's true feelings is unknown. Probably only to Elise Fay did he express such sentiments as "if it were not for my dear mother, sister, and you, I swear that I would voluntarily blow out my brains."[9]

It was a difficult time for both Loeffler and Fay. "Without doubt," he wrote to her in March, "you have been a little changed towards me, lately, a little fatigued. Perhaps I have let you see a little too much of my past life because with you I have been more frank than with anyone before. Also I have spoken or recounted many things about my family and my *late father* that you, as an American, have not been able to comprehend and which have given you wrong ideas about my family."[10] Loeffler wanted and needed her friendship—"Dear friend, stay my friend, for what would I become without you?"[11] he wrote elsewhere—and it may only be supposed that Fay bore with everything and, despite Loeffler's fears, never withdrew her friendship or affection.

Loeffler filled his time with work. In December he appeared as soloist with the orchestra to perform Lalo's *Fantasie norvégienne* and the Adagio of Bruch's Concerto in D Minor, op. 44, a program repeated in Salem in January and in Cambridge in March. Like the Godard of the last season, both selections were Boston premieres. According to the critics, this appearance was more impressive than the first. The *Boston Daily Advertiser* reported that "Mr. Loeffler played both selections well with better finish and secure ease than on his former appearance in one of these concerts. His technique was sufficient to accomplish all difficulties without betraying a consciousness of them." The *Boston Evening Transcript* declared that "he played the Bruch Adagio like a master."[12]

After Loeffler wrote to Léonard to inform him of his successes, Léonard replied, "You play very well—quite artistically—with an excellent style, and in all countries you will be recognized as a true artist. You can play anywhere with a certainty of success, and the only thing you should do is to play often and in every country."[13]

In 1885 Loeffler was playing also with another prestigious Boston group, the Mendelssohn Quintette Club, the creation of another European-born American, Wulf Fries, who had settled in Boston in 1847. In 1849 Fries formed this ensemble which, during its fifty years of existence, toured American cities with chamber music programs. The membership changed often. In 1885 the members were Loeffler, Max Klun, Thomas Ryan, Julius A. Kroyd, and Fritz Giese. Ryan and Giese were also then members of the BSO. Although Loeffler often played chamber music with Fries, his tenure with the Mendelssohn Club perhaps lasted only one year. As part of one program, in January 1885, Loeffler had the opportunity to play Paganini's *Witches' Dance*.

Loeffler also played rather frequently with pianist Carl Baermann. In February the two played at a benefit for a Free Hospital for Women; their selections included Beethoven's "Kreutzer" Sonata and Sarasate's *Danse espagnole*.

In March Loeffler performed at the HMA, which, though having discontinued its orchestral concerts, continued the chamber music concerts begun in 1844. On 18 March Loeffler performed the Bach Chaconne. Two days later, as part of the BSO's celebration of the Bach bicentennial, he played the same piece on a program devoted entirely to works by Bach. The highlight of the program, portions of the "Christmas" Oratorio, dominated the reviews, but Loeffler's performance was well reviewed, as, for example: "Mr. M. Loeffler played the Chaconne for violin in an artistic, earnest, and refined manner, and with that clean-cut technique and purity of taste that are always pleasing essentials in his playing."[14]

That same season Loeffler also played for a series of lectures presented by John Knowles Paine, Harvard University's first professor of music. At each of Paine's twenty-four public lectures on the history of music, given at Chickering Hall, a concert was given. Among those who performed were Perabo, Lang, and several BSO members—Listemann, Lichtenburg, and Loeffler.

Loeffler had thought, the summer before, of studying counterpoint with Paine. He did consult with Paine about his first orchestral work in 1890, but how much instruction he ever received from Paine is unknown. Loeffler did, at some point, study counterpoint and ever valued the study. In 1923 he advised a student that "though you may never wish to write a composition in fugue form, yet with the study of canon and fugue develop muscles in the musical lobes of your brain and form your style to write music with purity."[15]

During the summer of 1885 Loeffler remained in Massachusetts.[16] In June he spent some time in Gloucester, where he went sailing and swimming and where, for a change, "'Barnum's Show' came, and I saw the elephants."[17] Most of the summer Loeffler spent with the Fays, but he felt he made the time miserable for them. When the fall came Loeffler's routine began again. He continued to bury his grief inside and fill his life with activity.

The orchestra of 1885 was a different body from that of previous years. At the end of the 1884–85 season twenty members of the orchestra had been dismissed. After only two concerts into his first season Gericke had said to Higginson, "You have not an orchestra here. There are some musicians, but it is hardly an orchestra."[18] During the summer Gericke returned to Europe, where, particularly in Vienna, he engaged a new concertmaster and several other musicians. With a few more engagements made during the fall the orchestra was composed of about twenty-five percent new personnel.

At the time, changing orchestra players was an unpopular action. The dismissed members had admirers and friends, in and out of the orchestra, who resented the changes. And there was some feeling that the new personnel should have included more Americans. Sam Franko, one of the new members, himself an American, quoted Victor Herbert as calling Gericke's new orchestra the "Viennese Ladies Orchestra."[19] It was a difficult time for Gericke, as he admitted. "I was not popular in the Orchestra, especially as they did not yet understand why I should ask for better playing and more exact work than had been done heretofore."[20] In spite of the initial difficulties, however, with this and other changes Gericke eventually succeeded in creating what he could term an orchestra.

Loeffler's own feelings on the changes are unknown. The departure of the "simpleton" Schmidt brothers or of his desk mate, Listemann, would have caused him no grief. However, his friend Lichtenburg was also among those who left. But the changes brought to Boston a new concertmaster, Franz Kneisel, who became one of Loeffler's best lifelong friends.

Kneisel, four years Loeffler's junior, was, like Loeffler, a brilliant violinist with European orchestral experience behind him at the age of twenty. A graduate of the Vienna Conservatory, he had been concert-master of the Hofburg Theater Orchestra and had played with Bilse's Orchestra in Berlin. At his solo debut with the BSO in October 1885 he completely won over the orchestra and became, like Loeffler, a popular violinist. By the time he left the orchestra, he had played 103 solos, twice in double concertos with Loeffler.

Kneisel won prominence also as a chamber musician. During his first autumn in Boston, at Higginson's prompting, Kneisel formed the Kneisel Quartette from the orchestra's first chair string players—then Kneisel, Otto Roth, Louis Svecenski, and Fritz Giese. From its debut on 28 December in Chickering Hall, the quartet set a standard of excellence and elevated chamber music in America much as the early orchestra conductors—Thomas, Damrosch, Gericke—did the orchestra. American premieres of music of Dvořák and Brahms were entrusted by the composers to the Kneisel Quartette, which also premiered compositions by their friend Loeffler.

A month after Kneisel's debut, Loeffler again appeared as a soloist with the BSO. He played the Boston premiere of Bruch's Violin Concerto, no. 1, op. 26 and garnered renewed critical praise. The *Boston Evening Transcript* reported that "Mr. Loeffler's playing of the Max Bruch concerto was marked by all the fine qualities for which this young violinist is noted—precision, purity of intonation, intelligence and musicianly feeling." The *Boston Sunday Herald* stated, "His sterling worth as a musician was again shown in the intelligent and artistic finish of his work."[21]

Loeffler's reputation as an artist was enhanced by each of his performances. His personal position in the city also grew as his circle of friends and associates continuously expanded. During 1885 Loeffler joined the Tavern Club, organized the year before by a group of bachelors in artistic, literary, and scientific fields accustomed to dining together. They took rooms at 1 Park Place (moving in 1887 to 4 Boylston Place). Loeffler joined under the club's first president, William Dean Howells. Many other musicians, including the composers Chadwick, Foote, Johns, Converse, and Nevin, and several musicians of the BSO were members. All BSO conductors, if not members, were honored guests there, and Henry Higginson became the club's fourth president, succeeding Charles Eliot Norton. His vice-president was Oliver Wendell Holmes, Jr.

The club was a great meeting place for musicians. When Gericke first arrived in Boston, he was "most disagreeably homesick." "After a few days, however," he declared, "I was taken to the Tavern Club, which at this time was just founded by a number of young gentlemen—all nice and charming fellows. There I found kindred spirits, who did their best to help me over my first difficulties."[22] Clayton Johns described club life: "Every Saturday night all music lovers, members of the Tavern Club, used to come back after the Symphony Concert for supper at the Tavern. Mr. Higginson was always there. He and Gericke had much to talk over. Gericke was a bachelor, and we were all young, so we didn't care whether we went to bed early or not." Johns also related that "Paderewski spent much time there, playing billiards and the piano. The de Reszkes sang, Salvini and Coquelin dined, wined, and recited, and a host of other celebrities shared the club's hospitality. Even Lilli Lehmann ('no ladies permitted'), having said, 'I want to go to the Tavern Club,' went, sang, and (if I remember rightly) danced, taking with her a few choice spirits. The Tavern Club and the Boston Symphony were young in those days."[23]

Loeffler himself performed occasionally at the Tavern Club. One occasion was their New Year's celebration in December 1885. Gericke conducted a concert including the *Kindersymphonie* by Leopold Mozart (then attributed to Haydn), *Tavern Club March* and a waltz by Gericke, and *Kinder Symphonie* by Romberg. The orchestra consisted of Clayton Johns at the piano; Loeffler and Adamowski playing violins; J. Montgomery Sears (a great patron) on cello; Gericke himself playing tambour and dulcimer; while various other club members, including the artist Denis Bunker, played trumpet, bassoon, tambourine, cuckoo, triangle, flute, nightingale, canary, rattle, and four kazoos.

The club entertained frequently. "I shouldn't wonder," wrote John Jay Chapman, "if more unforgettable dinners have been given at the Tavern than in any other club in the world."[24] Honorary dinners were given for Henry Irving, Mark Twain, H. G. Wells, Galsworthy, Masefield, and Commander Byrd, to name only a few. Visiting musicians so honored included Sarasate, d'Albert, Paderewski, and d'Indy (Loeffler's own guest).

Among the Tavern Club's own members, the company (apart from its musicians) was illustrious, including T. B. Aldrich, E. F. Fenollosa, O. W. Holmes Sr. and Jr., W. D. Howells, and a number of men from Boston's prominent families—Gardners, Searses, Cabots, Lowells, and Peabodys.

Loeffler's own particular friends at the club included several artists and writers, for example, the poet Henry Copley Greene, the writers Owen Wister (who had studied to be a composer before he became a writer) and J. J. Chapman (then a student at Harvard), and the artists

Denis Bunker, Frank Benson, Edmund Tarbell, Howard Cushing, and John Singer Sargent. Outside the club as well, Loeffler gravitated to the company of artists and writers. The artists Dodge McKnight and Mabel Hunt Slater (daughter of William Morris Hunt) and several others were also Loeffler's friends.

Loeffler's most preferred company, however, was that of his new fiancée, Elise Fay. The engagement, evidently decided on 6 April 1886, was kept secret for a while. Fay feared three obstacles to their marriage: family obligations (concerning her brother, their mother having died in March), her age (she was eight years older than Martin), and her wealth. Loeffler would not, and did not, marry Fay for her money; he never allowed her to make gifts of money to him. He was determined to make his own way first. No immediate marriage plans were made.

Just after becoming engaged, Loeffler left Boston with the orchestra. Elise and Martin wrote nearly every day. On 7 April Loeffler wrote from Springfield: "Since I left you, I have done nothing but dream and think of you. I have repeated to myself every word from yesterday, the effect of which is that I love you more than ever. More and more each hour it seems to me however I loved you to distraction before yesterday. . . . Elise, with or without hope, you will be my ideal for life—you or noone." The very next day he declared, "If I could only see you for five minutes I would embrace your feet, your hands, your hair, your dear eyes and smother you with my kisses." Each subsequent letter was full of his joy. "I am so happy that I could hug everyone for joy. . . . It will be difficult when I return to Boston to treat you as a simple friend because of others, because this trip is oil on the fire of my love. I am yours, Elise, for this life and the next and nothing will change my adoration for you."[25]

Fay's letters are, like his, full of her love and of her joy in their new relationship. "What would I not give to draw you an instant in my arms and embrace you! I love you, Loeffler—that is all that I have to say to you. I love you and I will love you always." But they also express her concerns. "Do you have enough patience and friendship for me, to love me forever, in spite of all obstacles? and to help me do my duty to my brother [who never married but always lived with his sisters]. . . . If he knew at present how much I love you, he would be desolate." "Dear sweet Loeffler! as long as you love me I will be happy. My family knows that I miss you and I think one day will suspect that we are more than friends. . . . At present I prefer that our sentiments exist in secret between you and me, and you would want it, I am sure. Oh, Loeffler, if only I were younger!! Why was I born so early. It is not my fault but it is still a misfortune. It does not prevent my loving you but it is the largest obstacle to marrying you—greater than that of money, I assure you. . . . Adieu, my dear, be good, love me, and believe in my love, because I love you very, very much, and I embrace you with all my heart a thousand times."[26]

Loeffler's letters ignored any doubts or problems and simply concentrated on telling her how much he loved her. "Love is a curious thing. . . . Today it is incomprehensible to me that I did not feel sooner that you were for me the ideal. As for other little confidences of other times [the "elle" of Loeffler's 1883 letters?], do not think that I am light as to the question of love, because I have only truly loved you in my life, I assure you; and then I was at the age where one takes every emotion for love. But now it is different and you know it. Elise, I love you, I adore you to madness, my angel, and I will never differ on this subject. I am yours for life."[27]

As a result of this romance, Loeffler wrote little of the tour itself, which Gericke added to the BSO's regular schedule in 1886 as part of his renovation of the orchestra. Previously the symphony season had lasted six months, after which the orchestra disbanded and many players left Boston for six months, if not permanently. Gericke proposed a longer season that would include visits to other cities during the season and a longer tour at the end. This longer season plus the establishment of the summer Popular Concerts (Pops), in which Loeffler sometimes played, led to longer contracts for the musicians and a more stable orchestra.

In 1886 the orchestra made its first experiment with tours. It traveled to Springfield, Providence, Philadelphia, Washington, Columbus, Cincinnati, and Chicago. Loeffler performed the Bruch concerto in Washington, Cincinnati, and Chicago, and commented only that he hoped to play well in Cincinnati because Henry Schradieck and Simon Jacobsen, two good violinists, and other professors of the College of Music were coming to the performance. But he wrote no post-concert report.

The added expense of the tour to Higginson was considerable, yet it brought a great change to the orchestra. "The musicians," related Gericke, "began to understand what the hard work and earnest study had meant, and what results were reached by it; it opened their eyes and gave them a feeling of pride and satisfaction with themselves." The experiment being a success, he decided to continue. Especially encouraged by their reception in Philadelphia, Gericke then particularly wanted a success in New York, which was used to high standards from the Thomas and Damrosch orchestras. After canceling the first date, he trained the orchestra until it was ready—and had his success. It was, in Gericke's own estimation, important for the orchestra. "There is no doubt that this first success in New York affected the Boston audience; from that moment, the Boston Symphony Orchestra began to stand on solid ground. The members of the Orchestra began to feel that they belonged to an artistic corporation of first rank—and in the same measure as the success increased, they took more pride and satisfaction in their own work."[28]

After completing the 1886 tour, Loeffler passed the summer, as usual, in the country. During his summers he liked to leave the city for a quiet country retreat and devote most of his time to working on his music. In various years he visited Gloucester, Bridgewater, Worcester, Lexington, Newburyport, and Wayland but usually summered in a boarding house in Dover or Medfield. At whatever country retreat, Loeffler usually escaped from public playing, though occasionally he gave lessons or performed at musicales. His favorite companions were Elise and Temple Fay. A new friendship began at the end of this summer when he performed in Worcester and met Harold Bauer, at this time a violinist, later a concert pianist. They renewed their friendship on many occasions, including Bauer's frequent solo appearances with the BSO.

Loeffler began his fourth season as a soloist with the orchestra in the fall of 1886 with Mendelssohn's Violin Concerto. The critics, given a chance to judge Loeffler in a piece already known (though only twice performed previously by the Boston orchestra), again rendered enthusiastic reviews. The *Gazette* declared that Loeffler played "with exquisite purity and finish of style, grace of expression and of sentiment. We cannot remember that we have ever heard this work more chastely interpreted, or with a feeling more in harmony with the spirit of Mendelssohn." The *Courier* concurred. "We have never heard the performance of last night excelled." Loeffler received, it was reported, "the unusual compliment of a triple recall,"[29] actually not untypical of Loeffler's career.

Encouraged by the success of the 1886 tour, the BSO inaugurated in 1887 its annual spring tours, taking place in April and May. The itinerary, in the first years, generally included New Haven, New York, Baltimore, Philadelphia, Washington, and occasionally Providence. The entire orchestra did not always go. "Because of the 'Interstate Commerce Law,'" Loeffler wrote to Fay in April 1887, "M. Higginson is going to send only a small orchestra on the trip, which is very disagreeable to M. Gericke."[30] This did not exclude Loeffler, who, though not keen on traveling, found himself often on tour.

Loeffler played the Mendelssohn concerto on tour in Pittsburgh, St. Louis, Chicago, and Troy. Once again his letters do not give much of a view of the tour. His surviving out-of-town letters for 1887 include only one from New York, where he again visited Barnum's circus, and two from Philadelphia, where the orchestra was once more well received. He wrote from Philadelphia: "Our last concert yesterday evening was an unparalleled success. The great 'Academie of Music' was packed and the public was more than enthusiastic. Mr. and Mrs. Higginson were here. But despite all that we didn't play as well as many other times in *my* opinion. . . . It seems that Mr. Higginson is a little grieved at enormous expenses that the maintenance of the orchestra costs. He told Gericke (but don't tell anyone) that the season of the year past with the voyage to the west cost 50,000$ out of his pocket."[31]

Following the 1887 tour Loeffler went to Europe for the summer. This time he could be taken in all accuracy as an American; his citizenship was granted on 23 May. Loeffler had written to Léonard to ask to be taken on once again as a student, but Léonard, ailing from gout, was unable to teach. Loeffler, therefore, spent most of his time with his family in Homburg.

Besides visiting his family, Loeffler saw, by chance, two friends from his student days, Johann Kruse and Tivador Nachez. "[Kruse] has stayed all this time in Berlin and today is professor of violin at the same school where M. Joachim is director. I played for him yesterday morning some different things, and I assure you he was very astonished and enchanted. He told me that if I were to go once more to M. Joachim I would have the best time in the world because for 8 to 10 years he no longer has had students as in my time."[32]

Loeffler himself was rather astonished by his meeting with Nachez. "Imagine, who did I meet at the café yesterday afternoon? Tivador Nachez, my comrade from my youth and study with Joachim. There remains very little of the old 'Theodor Naschütz.' First he has the air of a Parisian celebrity, he has been decorated by the king of Italy, the king of Sweden, and the Duke of this and that, etc. and he has made progress in vanity and other things of that sort."[33]

Though Loeffler liked Nachez personally and admitted his talent, he deplored his manner of playing. "Nachez plays . . . to please the public without thinking for an instant of his artistic confrères." However, Loeffler thought Nachez a better violinist than Kruse, who, though more serious, had neither Nachez's technique nor tone. The two violinists, Loeffler confessed to Fay, "amused me enormously with their hate one for the other."[34]

Loeffler did not take Kruse's advice and visit Berlin but before returning to Boston visited Paris briefly. There he paid an advance on Higginson's behalf to the orchestra's new oboist, Sautet, visited Léonard, and visited the Maison Erard to buy a harp for Helene. On the sixth of August, Loeffler left Le Havre on *Le Bourgogne* for America.

Back in Boston for the 1887–88 season, Loeffler made good his fib to Lalo by performing the *Symphonie espagnole,* in Boston in November and in Cambridge the next February, with, as he had claimed before the fact, great success. The *Gazette* observed that "Mr. Loeffler played his part beautifully. . . . It was fine, honorable art of bow and finger, enlightened and enhanced in worth by thoughtfulness, consideration and high-minded sympathy." The *Post* concluded, "It will be sufficient praise of Mr. Löffler to say that we have never heard him play so well."[35]

After the Boston performance, Loeffler met John Singer Sargent, who was passing his first year in Boston. Loeffler himself described their meeting.

> He came to the Artists room that evening and with that irresistible charm of his said a few words which made one rise in one's self esteem and then arranged for our meeting a few days later at dinner in a mutual friends house. On this delightful occasion Sargent played with me "en petit Comité" the *Symphonie Espagnole* in which he revealed himself as the admirable musician which he innately was. He was quite amazing in accompanying The 3rd Movement ("Intermède") a quite splended piece of music with rather complicated rhythms in 5/8 time, which he played with complete musical and rhythmical understanding, verve and spirit. In his luminously intelligent manner he spoke of the various characteristics of Spanish rhythms in music, quite in the manner in which M. Eduoard Lalo had expounded these intricacies to me in prior years. That same evening we also played the first Sonata by Gabriel Fauré for whose music Sargent had a strong predilection which I ever sincerely shared. Sargent had the insinuating and consummate art of initiating music lovers and musicians as well, to the hidden charms, harmonic innovations and the felicitous melodic lessons (?) in the works of this unassuming composer of genius. . . . he was in music as in all things "frightfully" intelligent, not merely glib or clever.[36]

Several points of similarity existed between Loeffler and Sargent. Both had been born and raised in Europe in itinerant families; both had lived and worked in Paris, where each was influenced by modern French art. Both appeared somewhat austere and were reticent about their personal lives, but they got on tremendously well, each admiring the other enormously. Many years later Loeffler wrote to Sargent,

"Everything that counts, is essential, is always there in whatever you touch or undertake, and out of that 'essential' grows so naturally all that grace and charm that makes you just what you not seem but are to us. If you had chosen, you would have written the best books of our time or given us the best music. One does not meet all that much in one man but once in a lifetime."[37]

The mutual friend at whose house they met to play Lalo's music was Isabella Stewart Gardner, to whom afterwards Loeffler wrote, "You don't owe me anything at all and you must accept my having played for you as an homage to you and Mr. Sargent. Since you enjoyed it I am fully rewarded."[38]

Belle (Mrs. Jack) Gardner, one of Boston's leading ladies and leading patrons, was Loeffler's greatest patroness, as well as lifelong personal friend. Her reputation—she was literally a legend in her own time—rested upon her strong personality, her audacity and knack for startling Boston, and the entourage of famous and talented people she kept about her. Clayton Johns described Gardner's charm: "She had no beauty of face, but a wonderful and illuminating personality which drew about her all sorts and conditions of men and women. She was interested in everything that was interesting and in everybody who interested her. She had the power of getting the best out of each thing and person. She had a marvelous determination about anything she wanted to do. When she broke her ankle, years ago, she was carried up in a hammock by her servants to the balcony in the old Music Hall, where she appeared at every concert. She knew no obstacle; in fact, obstacles were to her an inspiration. Her own charm, with her beautiful surroundings, formed an unforgettable atmosphere of music, flowers, and art."[39]

Gardner's enduring fame rests upon her patronage of the arts. In 1879, under the influence of Charles Eliot Norton, she began collecting rare books and manuscripts and later collected art treasures and built a museum. She also helped individual artists. A personal friend of Henry Higginson, Gardner was a staunch supporter of the BSO. When rehearsal tickets were put up for public auction, she outbid everyone. If possible she never missed a performance of the Pops. She was a great friend of Gericke, who brought the orchestra to play at her entertainments several times. In 1898 she donated the grounds of Green Hill, her summer home, for a symphony benefit concert for Carney Hospital. Gardner held frequent musical parties at her Boston home, 152 Beacon Street. In her music room, white-walled and adorned with plaster casts of della Robbia's angels and boys singing and playing instruments, large enough for private concerts and alleged to have wonderful acoustics, many musicians performed. Often the performers were students, many from the New England Conservatory; others were members of the symphony and some her own protégés. Gardner's most sensational engagement was that of Paderewski in 1891 to play for her alone for a fee of $1,000.

Loeffler met Gardner within the first few years after his arrival in Boston. His relationship with her was one of mutual respect which supported a life-long friendship. Loeffler once wrote to Gardner, "I know you often wish me different on many points, dear Mrs. Gardner, but as to you, I would not have you changed an atom."[40] Loeffler was frequently invited to the Gardner home and met many of the eminent people whom Gardner gathered around her. Loeffler and Gardner exchanged, on birthdays and Christmases, a number of gifts, carefully chosen, such as antique books, autograph poems and letters, and musical instruments.

Loeffler often played for Gardner, accompanied in the early years by either of her favorite pianists, George Proctor or Clayton Johns. Johns, who had studied in Boston and in Berlin, returned to Boston to follow his career in 1885. Recalling his Boston years, he wrote: "I continued to give a recital nearly every year for more than twenty years, for the sake of introducing my new songs. I hated playing in public. I never got over a temperamental nervousness. Nevertheless, I played from time to time in chamber concerts. Mrs. Gardner invited me and Charles M. Loeffler to play the whole range of piano and violin sonatas in her music room before about twenty-five people each time. Bach, Mozart, Beethoven, Schumann, and Brahms—the series lasted through four years."[41]

Johns and Loeffler had other opportunities to play together, in salons, in recitals, and at benefits such as the December 1888 benefit concert for the Massachusetts Indian Association. Johns must have admired Loeffler's playing greatly; in 1888 he dedicated his *Quatre Morceaux* for violin and piano to Loeffler. That same year the two played again at the Gardner home when Gardner hosted the first performance of the Manuscript Club. Formed in 1888 under the direction of Evelyn Ames, this club was founded to offer local composers the opportunity to hear their works performed before an intelligent audience. At the first meeting the program consisted of music by Clara Rogers, Clayton Johns, Owen Wister, Margaret Lang, and Arthur Foote. Loeffler played Rogers's *Sonata Dramatico,* op. 25, and Johns's

Petite Suite for piano and violin, in each case with the composer at the piano.

The club unfortunately had a brief existence, not surviving its second year under different management; however, it did bring together Loeffler and Rogers, who struck up an immediate friendship. Under the name Clara Doria, Rogers had had a successful career as a singer. In Boston she taught voice and composed. With her husband, Henry K. Rogers, she held Saturday (later Friday) evening musicals every week to which many musical artists were invited, including B. J. Lang, Edward MacDowell, J. Eichberg, George W. Chadwick, Arthur Foote, various critics, and the BSO conductors.

Of Loeffler she wrote in her memoirs: "Another friendship was that of Martin Loeffler, who, in those distant days when Franz Kneisel and he led our Symphony Orchestra, was frequently present in our music room. At first, ostensibly because he had taken upon himself the infliction of playing with me my Sonata for piano and violin at the first concert of the Manuscript Club, to be held in the music room of the John L. Gardners. This brought us together for rehearsals which invariably merged into a musical orgy of one kind or another. Such orgies oft recurring, as time went on, were the means of making me first acquainted with Loeffler's genius for composition."[42]

Rogers's memoirs disclose that Loeffler also played at the home of Sarah Bull, widow of the violin showman, Ole Bull. Mrs. Bull spent her widowhood in Cambridge where the lustre of her husband's fame gave her a leading position in music society of the Boston area.

Loeffler was among those invited to her home and allowed to play her husband's violin. Rogers recalled being there in 1892 when Loeffler and Wulf Fries were to play some trios. Bull invited Rogers to play her own violin sonata with Loeffler: "Accordingly, armed with my Sonata, we arrived at the house of Mrs. Bull and listened attentively to a trio of Beethoven, after which I expected my turn to come. But not at all! Instead of that Mrs. Bull played another long trio, and after that went on playing this and that until tea was served. No allusion whatever was made to my Sonata, either then or at any future time! Mrs. Bull had evidently forgotten all about her desire to hear it! We had a good laugh over it with the [Childe] Hassams, who thought it was quite a good joke on me."[43]

Loeffler was often in demand to play in the salons of Boston. It became the vogue to include a music room in the houses erected in the Back Bay. Henry Higginson himself added a music room to his Commonwealth Avenue apartment to which he and Mrs. Higginson (daughter of the scientist Louis Agassiz), another Boston salon hostess, invited Loeffler and others for private performances.

Another music room was constructed for the home of Mr. and Mrs. J. Montgomery Sears, both great friends of Loeffler's. Their house, at 12 Arlington Street, had first contained a "moderately large music room dominated by a dignified pipe-organ," where, said Rogers, "many a cosy evening of music did they enjoy there with Gericke, a few members of his orchestra, and a handful of friends."[44] The Searses later added a banqueting hall and a music room large enough to accommodate instrumentalists and singers from the Cecilia Society for a private performance of one of Loeffler's choral works in 1902.

The Searses were charming people who possessed a love for beauty and good company. Clayton Johns wrote:

> Mr. and Mrs. Montgomery Sears gave wonderful musical parties. One in particular was in honor of Mr. Sears's birthday. Paderewski was in Portland but expected to arrive in Boston in plenty of time for the party. An unexpected blizzard held up all trains. Paderewski, being determined not to disappoint Mr. Sears chartered a single locomotive without cars, in which he was carried from Portland to Boston, and in which he arrived just in time to play for the guests already assembled.
>
> . . . Mr. and Mrs. Sears entertained so lavishly. They had a big house and a big music room. Melba, Plançon, and any number of other guest artists sang and played there. Mr. and Mrs. Sears loved entertaining as much as their guests loved to be entertained, while the artists loved to sing and play because the host and hostess and guests loved to hear them.[45]

The Searses were fond of Loeffler. Sarah Sears, an artist, once wrote to Loeffler, after he had been sent away because she had asked not to be disturbed while working in her studio, that she would always see him. When Loeffler made his next trip to Europe, Montgomery Sears was able to provide Loeffler with letters of introduction to his musical friends there.

Loeffler enjoyed playing for those who appreciated good music. But he did not always like to play, especially if it meant playing with dilettantes. During the summer of 1888, for example, he wrote to Fay from Newburyport: "It is a malediction to be a violinist because everyone expects you to play for them. But if I were a dentist I would not at all be asked to fill their teeth or if one did ask me how I could revenge myself at least! . . . But Musician! . . . For example, Mme. S. is charming, good, etc. But when I am her host [guest], it is necessary to play with: C. Johns, Mme. S., her daughter, her niece, give a daily lesson to her son, etc. It is too much, it is tiring to the last degree. One would never dare ask that of anyone but a musician."[46] It was not that Loeffler objected to playing for friends, as he continued in the same letter: "Yesterday was charming. There was a banjo here and I played to them, in what way you know, and then I played the violin alone without Miss S. something of Bach. That pleased me because I like to play for my friends and then alone I could make better music."

For the 1888–89 season, Loeffler introduced another new composition, Bruch's *Scottish Fantasy,* to symphony audiences. It was yet another triumph. According to the *Transcript,* "The part bristles with difficulties, and it takes a virtuoso to play it. . . . Mr. Loeffler played it exquisitely. His technique and intonation can now go without saying; both were flawless." The *Herald* reported, "He commanded the most rapt attention of the audience throughout the fantasie and gained a great and well-merited ovation at its conclusion, being recalled again and again to recognize the applause which rewarded his effort." The *Traveller* asserted that "Boston owes Mr. Loeffler much for again introducing a new and lovely work."[47]

BSO soloists did not always fare as well as Loeffler himself. In December 1888 Loeffler wrote to Fay from New York about a disastrous solo appearance: "The program was perfectly ridiculous. Concerto Spohr (Violin) Conc. Brahms (Piano) Eroica! Adamowski played poker all night!" "You missed something by not having heard the 'violinist'!!! [Madge Wickham] It was beastly. *Woman, beautiful,* with a lovely instrument, a good even beautiful figure, and plenty of aplomb—however she was not a success. For diverse reasons she played false, false! She scraped, scraped!! abominably. Then she paints her eyes and brows black and lips and cheeks red. She is a pretty woman aged 17–18, and it is a pity she is what she is. Gericke was furious because of her. But the Eroica was a *great* success!"[48]

This New York concert took place during the winter rather than the spring, the BSO schedule having been rearranged once again. Beginning in 1889 and continuing for about ten years, the orchestra made its visits to New York, Philadelphia, Baltimore, and Washington during the regular season, for an eight-day period in each month from November to March. Thus, beginning in 1889, the spring tour was extended to include cities further south and west—Richmond, Louisville, Chicago, Cincinnati, Detroit, Cleveland, Grand Rapids, and several others. In the spring of 1889 Loeffler took the *Scottish Fantasy* on tour, performing it in Buffalo, Chicago, Cincinnati, Pittsburgh, and Washington.

Loeffler's letters beginning with 1889 give more information on the tours themselves than previous out-of-town letters. However, these letters, taken as a whole, give a distorted picture of the tours. Usually he had a cold or some other illness and consequently complained about bad health, as well as the weather, accommodations, and food. While many of his fellow musicians played cards to pass the time, he did not and on the trains felt isolated. Often he wrote upon arrival at his hotel or after a long day of rehearsal and performance and so wrote about the tedium of traveling and how tired he was.

That Loeffler did not enjoy the tours is made quite clear in a letter from April 1892: "To go on a journey in my condition [cold, headache, sore throat, ear trouble], doing the work for another better paid man [Kneisel not having gone], with such an arrangement of spending nights in sleeping cars, days in cold hotel rooms, with all the changes of climate (going from a warm part of the country into a cold one in this time of the year anyhow), going actually to pieces as a violinist, musician, and as a man. And yet there is nothing else to do when one is poor."[49]

His infrequent comments on performances were usually about the disasters. For example, in New York in March 1889, the orchestra had "the worst concert that I have ever played with Gericke. The house was only a third full, and Kneisel played as if he were playing the Mendelssohn for the 1st time in his life. . . . And then in the Scherzo (Queen Mab) of Berlioz, we had the greatest catastrophe in the world. Reiter's music fell to the floor just at the moment where his solo began, and nothing was there! Then 50 measures later, at the most difficult and complicated place, the clarinet missed his entrance and consequently for 70–80 measures the orchestra played real cacophony, and it was not until the last great *ff* that we found one another again and finally *finished together*." Fortunately, at the succeeding concert in New York, "the house was actually full and the public very enthusiastic. The orchestra played superbly well."[50] After the concert, Loeffler, Adamowski, and two friends dined with Gericke at Delmonico's, where Gericke treated them to champagne.

The 1889 spring tour began badly for Loeffler, who had a cold and found the traveling as usual tiring and trying. In Detroit, however, the weather was good, and Loeffler was refreshed by a day spent boating at Belle Isle. The orchestra had particularly good accommodations in Detroit. The hotel manager asked for their autographs, "and, after having played a little for him, he sent up chilled champagne and treated us pleasantly." The orchestra had some trouble, however, in Detroit, "on account of the guarantee given by a rich piano merchant. He refused to pay because the contract said that we were going to furnish 'first-class soloists' and he did not consider as first rank neither

M. nor Mme. H[enschel] nor Giese nor Adamowsky."[51] Gericke and Higginson, however, who regularly used as soloists their own players—Kneisel, Loeffler, Adamowski, Giese, and others—considered that they were "first-class."

The tour took a turn for the worse for Loeffler in Chicago, "the city par excellence for filth and smoke."[52] Not only was the air bad and weather again unpleasant—infernally hot until a great thunder and hail storm—but also Loeffler's ear was again giving him great pain. "I am almost at the point of committing suicide," he wrote from Milwaukee. "For the past hour my ear has troubled me so that I cannot bear it. With each note that I hear or that I play myself, I hear another note nearly a quarter tone lower, which means that each note of music beats unmercifully on my ears to the highest degree." He went to see a specialist in Chicago and another in St. Louis. "But the sole effect that I feel at present from their treatment is that I am ten dollars poorer." Loeffler tried to be optimistic, but the agonizing pain caused great anguish of spirit. "I recall that Wieniawski had this during 8 months or a year without being able to play the violin during that time. But what if it remains always like this? What then?"[53] Unhappily the condition lasted the summer.

Despite this Loeffler played well and was recalled four times in Chicago, "and everyone has been saying that I have never played better. But my ear is in such a state that I do not even know if my violin is in tune! My fingers, which are naturally still habituated to playing in tune, have pulled me through the affair."[54] Loeffler also received encouragement from Georg Henschel, who was traveling with the orchestra as a soloist. "Henschel told me that I have made much progress in 5 years, that if I wanted to play the Fantasia, no matter when, in London with his orchestra, he would give me the chance.... He told me that if ever I wanted to establish myself in London, he would present me to . . . everyone whom it is necessary to know to have a career in England." Loeffler continued this letter with remarks on Adamowski, with whom his rivalry appeared to be strong in 1889. "He [Henschel] says that no one knows Ad. in London, that he only played at very minor concerts. He tried (Henschel) one time last winter with Ad. to play a sonata of Brahms but he played so like an amateur (Ad.) and so falsely that he never again invited him to his home!—Ad. told me that Henschel does not like him, but I know better: Henschel is too good an artist to like such amateurs."[55]

Evidently Loeffler had had some complaint with Gericke (and Adamowski) about the past season, possibly the distribution of solos. On the tour he had the chance to settle matters, which proved doubly helpful since "without these two I would have been more ill," both men having helped Loeffler protect himself during his cold. Gericke, however, dismissed Loeffler's ear trouble as a passing consequence of his cold, "but his opinion," Loeffler commented, "counts for nothing because he does not know me."[56]

In St. Louis Loeffler had the opportunity to meet and converse with Lilli Lehmann and Paul Kalisch. However, he wrote at more length of a meeting in Milwaukee between BSO member Xavier Reiter and a brother who had emigrated to America before Xavier had been born and who had been believed dead for forty years. Loeffler, who hardly knew his own younger brother in Europe, was touched by the meeting. Reiter did not long remain with the orchestra; he came to the performance in Cincinnati intoxicated and received a scathing letter from Gericke "such as R. never before received in his life. He told him in this letter that he always had the highest opinion of him as a man and artist but he saw that that was only another disappointment. That he had spoiled the Beethoven Symphony in C. as well as the whole concert and that his manners approached those of a 'zaloppe' and not those of a gentleman. That M. Higginson had founded this institution for art, for music, but not to educate drunkards. That he would inform Mr. H of what had happened and that he R. must bear the consequences."[57] Reiter left the orchestra in 1890.

Later Gericke's wrath was directed at Giese, who performed his last solo of the tour intoxicated. "He came 3/4 of an hour late to the concert—happily full of beer and whiskey, and could not keep his eyes open, but played nevertheless very well. Gericke made a scene."[58] It was Giese's last season with the orchestra.

In Pittsburgh Loeffler had problems of his own, though not of his own making. As the weather was quite warm, Loeffler had been worried about his strings and his fingers, as well as his ear. To make matters worse, "All the windows of the hall were open and there was a dissonant noise and scandal that came from the street. Towards the end of my last movement (very *p* you will remember) a negro band with drums and fifes crossed the street so that we had to stop for 3 minutes and then I *re*commenced the last two pages."[59]

Upon the orchestra's return to Boston, the BSO performed a farewell concert for their conductor. According to Higginson, "his [Gericke's] contract had been made for five years, and at the end of that time he had a trouble with his throat, and, to our great regret, left the town. Everything had gone smoothly, and everybody was very sorry to lose him."[60] Higginson exaggerated. Gericke's years with the orchestra had been trying. He had had difficult relations with the musicians and much criticism from the press. He confided to Rogers: "It would be impossible for me to stay any longer—I could not bear it. A man cannot stand more than five years of hard work with no encouragement. His spirit dies!"[61] Yet Gericke had had a large amount of support in Boston, much of which he was not fully aware of until he left. His final concert began and ended with standing ovations. He was treated to farewell parties and tributes, including an album, conceived by Sarah Bull, full of pages of tributes written by Boston friends and musicians. There were many who recognized what he had made of the BSO.

Gericke would return to Boston after nine years. During those years Loeffler remained one of the orchestra's most popular soloists, in fact, enjoyed his greatest triumphs as a violinist. But when Gericke returned he would find that Loeffler had emerged as a respected and equally popular composer.

7

The Nikisch Years
(1889–1891)

Before rejoining the orchestra under new leadership, Loeffler took his annual vacation from orchestral playing during the summer of 1889 in Medfield with the Fays. "These summers are something charming for me—" Loeffler wrote to Elise Fay while on tour in 1889, "all alone in the country, living only for one another"—always, of course, accompanied by Temple Fay.[1]

This summer they were joined by Denis Bunker, one of the most talented of Boston's artists. Temperamentally very similar, Loeffler and Bunker had met in 1885, the year Bunker came to Boston. A native of New York, Bunker had been a student in New York and Paris and in Boston worked at the new Cowles Art School. Like Loeffler, Bunker was a member of the Tavern Club, and both performed there in Gericke's 1885 New Year's concert. Bunker inscribed a painting titled *Yellow Roses* to Loeffler in 1886 and a nude study in 1888, and did a painting of Loeffler's violin in 1887. Occasional references to Loeffler in Bunker's correspondence relate that they went to dine together or that Loeffler and Sargent were in his studio banging the piano or even once that Kenneth Cranford tried—unsuccessfully—to hypnotize Loeffler "with a small looking glass and a fierce look."[2] Sargent told Clayton Johns "that he did not know that he had ever been fonder of anyone than he had been of Denis Bunker."[3]

Loeffler was also very fond of Bunker. That they spent this particular summer together itself attests to their friendship, since Loeffler had written to Fay that he wanted them to spend that summer absolutely alone. He had asked her to dissuade Clayton Johns from joining them as Johns had wished. "I think," wrote Loeffler, "that you, Temple, and I are enough company for one another. Occasional visits from one or another of your or my friends will occur and pass again but for 2 months! No."[4] Loeffler was ill and had been out of sympathy with Johns that winter. "Why would it be necessary to continue *that* during the summer?" he continued. "'His fancies' his

opinions etc. In short *this 'jelly-fish'* will not do for *one week*!" He did
not want the pianist's company, but a summer with Denis Bunker
(who ironically had occasion later to complain to his own fiancée of
Loeffler's manner of considering himself the only being of importance
on the earth) was another matter.

The Fays, Loeffler, and Bunker boarded at Miss Alice Sewell's that
summer. In July Bunker described their life to Gardner: "I get up at
six—this statement I know will be promptly disbelieved, but you can
ask Loeffler—he always tells the truth. . . . Loeffler writes music and
plays it—and practices on his violin, and Miss Fay practices also and
behold! even your slave practices with a bit more method than in the
old days owing to the presence of real musicians in the house." A week
later he wrote again: "I hear Loeffler downstairs working—working
over his composition, going over one phrase, hundreds of times and
days at a time—a most wonderful patient—slow—courageous work.
I wonder if people know what a labor it is—but they can't." And later:
"How fast the summer is slipping by us. . . . Nothing seems to have
changed here—I even hear Loeffler working down stairs on the same
phrase that he began two months ago."[5]

Unfortunately, Loeffler still suffered ill health, as Bunker wrote to
Gardner: "He is in such a mess of work that he can't go anywheres
even if he were well—and he is far from it—his ear has begun to
trouble him again and I am afraid it is more serious than he thought it
was. . . . I hate to leave Loeffler who is melancholy and unwell and
dreadfully nervous."[6]

The two continued together working through to the end of the
summer. When not working, they enjoyed quiet pleasures. Bunker felt
as Loeffler did about country living. "The calmness of everything
here—its roughness and simplicity is to me the most charming and
restful—and I feel more happy and in better courage than in the hurry
and countless duties of winter life."[7] They both enjoyed reading and
walking in the countryside. Sometimes they played tennis.

Part of Bunker's work that summer was a portrait of Loeffler. "He
is half-length—standing—with his violin and bow, flannel shirt and
grey coat, a lovely head and hands to paint. I am enjoying it immensely."[8] Bunker also designed a title page for the composition on
which Loeffler worked all summer, his Quatuor pour deux violons,
alto, et violoncelle.

In many respects the summer of 1889 was typical of Loeffler's
summers. Whether in Massachusetts or abroad, Loeffler used his
summers principally for composing. During the 1880s he composed a
number of short violin pieces, all of which, with the exception of

Berceuse, remained in manuscript and never figured in any of Loeffler's public performances. These early violin works include *Airs tziganes; Barcarolle (d'après des mélodies arabes); Capriccio russe,* dedicated to Leopold Lichtenburg; *Requiem/Variations diaboliques sur le thème "Dies irae, dies illa"; Romance russe; Spring dance (Danse norvégienne),* dedicated to César Thomson; and *Tarantella.* Some of these may have been those that he played with Moszkowski in Paris in 1884.

When Loeffler met Kruse in Homburg in 1887, the latter suggested Loeffler send Joachim his sonata, a piece to which Loeffler also referred in an 1886 letter[9] and with which Loeffler was credited in the program accompanying his first orchestral performance. However, no violin sonata, so titled, survives. The only multimovement composition among the above-named is his *Airs tziganes* in three movements.

A letter Loeffler wrote from Washington in 1888 refers to a performance (probably at the home of a friend) of some songs in Philadelphia: "Mlle. E. sang my songs delightfully and advised me with good sense."[10] Neither singer nor music were further identified. The songs, or romances, were probably the set including *Marie* (text by Alfred de Musset), *Madrigal* (Paul Bourget), *Les hirondelles* (A. d'Hotelier), and *Rêverie* (unidentified). Loeffler never published nor, evidently, performed them in public.

An undated letter (probably from 1885) refers to a sextet, doubtless that premiered in 1893. In another letter, written in 1888, a fantasia is mentioned. Loeffler gave its title in Russian and mentioned its hair-curling harmonies. In May 1890 Loeffler again made a passing reference to a Russian fantasy, not yet finished, leading to identification of the piece as *Les veillées de l'Ukraine,* performed in 1891.[11]

In later years Loeffler overlooked all his early small violin pieces and songs when listing his compositions. They were youthful works in which he was no longer interested. Clara Rogers, at whose home Loeffler would sometimes play his compositions privately, observed this as characteristic of Loeffler.

> Loeffler himself could not fail to get inspiration and stimulus from our sympathetic appreciation; moreover he needed that sort of stimulus more almost than any other composer I have known; as, after the first heat of creation was over, a fit of depreciation of his own work was quite apt to set in.
>
> In fact, at that period of his career, he seemed incapable of harbouring lasting enthusiasm for any composition or for any composer. He saw things each day from a different angle, and it was always the *new* vista which held him enthralled to the exclusion of any other.[12]

A simple look at the titles of Loeffler's early works reveals some of the variety of the vistas that interested him. There are works colored by the national musics of Hungary, Russia, Arabia, Norway, Italy, as well as songs written to texts from yet another country, France.

Although diverse in color and material, Loeffler's early works exhibit certain common traits. When compared to later works, they reveal a simplicity of construction in their texture, classically composed and ordered melodies, straightforward meter and rhythmic patterns, and diatonic harmonies. They are marked especially by melodic charm; the songs have a delicate prettiness. Though some anticipate his use of chromatics as a color element, especially in the fluctuation between parallel major and minor at particularly affecting moments, he employed chromaticism sparingly in these works. Yet, though conservative, these works hint at what would become a special preoccupation in Loeffler's compositional process, the evocation of sentiment through precisely colored moments.

Another fundamental trait of Loeffler's compositional work, as revealed in Bunker's letters, was his meticulousness. Loeffler was his own most severe critic. He labored over his compositions, rewriting and revising them often. Finally, however, with his quartet, Loeffler allowed a public hearing. But it was not a Boston premiere. Rather, the performance took place while the BSO was out of town during its first season under its new conductor, Artur Nikisch.

To fill the conductor's position, Higginson had looked again, as always, to Europe. On the recommendation of several friends, he engaged Artur Nikisch. Born in Hungary, trained at the Vienna Conservatory in composition and violin, Nikisch came to Boston after having conducted at the Leipzig Stadt Theater.

Nikisch's style differed from Gericke's. Gericke had trained the orchestra in technique; Nikisch is reported to have said, "All I have to do is poetize!"[13] He had a pronounced poetic quality in his personality and a corresponding romantic element in his conducting. Clara Rogers characterized Nikisch's style and described the response of the musicians. "Gericke's successor, Artur Nikisch, was of an entirely different makeup:—gentle and persuasive rather than authoritative, he was beautifully tender of other people's feelings. A consummate artist, full of sentiment and poetry, most affectionate and very lovable. Happening to fall in with a few members of the orchestra after his first rehearsal, I asked how they liked their new conductor. The reply was, 'We have heard today words that we did not hear in five years.' 'What words?' I asked. 'Sehr gut, meine Herren!' (Very good, gentlemen.)"[14]

Nikisch introduced no major changes in the orchestra, either in personnel or routine. With Nikisch the BSO sustained its popularity in Boston and established an even greater reputation outside its home city.

Under Nikisch Loeffler continued to appear as a soloist. During the 1889–90 season he played the Lalo *Symphonie espagnole,* which he had first played in 1887. According to the local critics, he played with similar success. The *Boston Gazette* reported that "his elegant and sympathetic rendering of the work excited a storm of enthusiasm, and he was recalled three or four times with some of the most hearty applause that has been given at these concerts this season." The *Beacon* judged that "he played it all so exquisitely that none could have desired to transfer it to Sarasate, for whom it was written, and unstinted applause rewarded the movement."[15]

Loeffler appeared during this season in more recitals and special concerts. Performing Sarasate's *Romanza Andalouza* and Lalo's Rondo for Violin, he was a featured artist at a Grand Miscellaneous Concert for Artists' Night at Mechanics Hall in Worcester. He also assisted Carl Baermann in concerts at Union Hall (December) and Clayton Johns in a concert at Steinert Hall (February 1890). In April, with Perabo and Leo Schulz, he performed a Beethoven trio at the Harvard Musical Association.

During this same season (1889–90), Loeffler debuted in public as a composer with the help of the Adamowski Quartette. This quartet, organized in 1888, gave about thirty concerts annually both in and out of Boston. In Philadelphia, Adamowski included the Minuette from Loeffler's string quartet on a quartet program. In an undated letter from Philadelphia, Loeffler wrote, "My piece went well, as everyone has been telling me, and I had much success at last."[16] Since Loeffler performed a solo with the BSO in Philadelphia in this year, "my piece" could well refer to the Lalo solo, not his quartet. In either case, the debut of the composition was a quiet one, and Loeffler continued to be known publicly, for a while longer, only as a violinist.

The tour of 1890, according to Loeffler, was a great success for the orchestra. Loeffler himself was again a soloist; he played the Lalo *Symphonie espagnole* in Columbus, Minneapolis, and Albany. He thought he played "abominably" in Columbus, although the soloist with real problems was Mme. Steinbach-Zahns. "Mme Steinbach sings worse and worse and since she had not been a success she is becoming very nervous, and this morning she asked M. Nikisch to give her a rest for today because she could not sing again in Cincinnati for she was a fiasco yesterday night. . . . The orchestra in general is indignant and Comee [assistant manager] thinks that Nikisch himself is mortified by his error."[17] Otherwise, he reported that the tour, before Cincinnati, was a success.

The most enjoyable part of the tour was Loeffler's stay in Washington. It was a city he generally liked. "Since my childhood," he reported to Fay in 1888, "I have had a preference for southern countries, and I can not but regret that Boston is not on the same longitude [latitude] as Washington."[18] During this 1890 visit he met several interesting people. He had breakfast with Henry Adams, whom he found "amiable and interesting," and his secretary, Mr. Dwight. Through Dwight he met Charles Warren Stoddard, professor of literature at Catholic University, "one of the most interesting men I have met in America."[19] With Stoddard he conversed about the Belgian missionary Father Damien, who had worked in leper colonies and had recently died. Stoddard presented Loeffler with a sketchbook about Stoddard's visit to Father Damien.

In Washington Loeffler also met an (unnamed) attaché to the Russian embassy at lunch with Nikisch and Adamowski. "After lunch Nikisch played a Fantasia by Schumann and the Russian played wonderfully on the piano pieces by Schumann and Rubinstein. That one is an artist! He was in Petersburg a student of A. Rubinstein and plays excellently. Afterwards I went with the Russian in a party to Col. Hays where Adamowski played with his Quartette. Col. Hay is very rich and has a wonderful house. He is as Dwight said: 'a very distinguished literary man and one of the most brilliant men in America.' Through him I met the Russian minister who invited me to the legation for the evening. There I played with the attaché the Kreutzer Sonata, the G Major of Brahms, and the G Major sonata of Beethoven."[20]

Unfortunately after Washington the tour became less and less agreeable. The most distressing event was an accident in Prescott, Wisconsin, on May 11. Loeffler happened to be in conversation with the conductor of the train when the train whistle blew a warning and the train suddenly stopped. The two left the train. "The conductor ran towards the engine but I through instinct ran toward the other direction where to my horror I found three workingmen laying near the track, two of them dead and frightfully mutilated and the third one stunned and one arm broken. . . . it was a terrible shock to all of us. For ten minutes I was unable to speak a word—for if I had done so I feel I should have collapsed and fainted."[21] Their train, a special one not on the regular schedule, had collided with a handcar taken by three men for a trip to town, from which they were returning intoxicated. The members of the orchestra took up a collection for the injured man, whom they took to his family. Headlines in Boston read, "Boston Musicians Just Escape Death," but the orchestra escaped injury entirely.

Soon afterwards Loeffler suffered ill health again, having contracted a cold that produced severe headaches. He yearned for "the d... old bore of a journey" to be over and for a peaceful and quiet summer in the country.[22]

That summer he and the Fays went to Wayland. He also spent a short time in Readville, where he saw his first polo game. Loeffler wrote to Gardner, who had gone to Venice, expressing regret that he too could not have gone abroad "but I had too much work at hand. For a violinist there seems hardly to be any rest from hard work." He also wrote to her, "as I have lived very secludedly in the quietest of country, my life has been very uneventful. With one exception though: the death of dear Mr. Dresel."[23]

Otto Dresel had been a friend to Loeffler, although Dresel, like J. S. Dwight, had been an arch conservative and Loeffler a modernist. Their difference in taste has been illustrated by Clara Rogers.

> Dresel frequented our Saturday evening musicales, much to the mental discomfort of certain of the performers, who dreaded his alleged hypercriticism, and not altogether without reason, for, when some of these had acquitted themselves triumphantly of their chosen selections, Dresel would approach me with that cold expression we all knew so well, and say dryly, "Come, now let us have some *music!*" After that, no one presumed to sing or play anything more modern than Schumann or Franz! After one of these dry reflections I sought to pacify him—as in promise of something particularly worthwhile—by saying, "Martin Loeffler is going to play to us now." But he only responded with a weary expression, remarking hopelessly, "He—will—play some-thing by Lalo!"
>
> It was a difficult task to get Dresel interested in anyone of whom he suspected ultra-modern tendencies. At the period of which I am writing, Loeffler had not yet revealed himself as a composer but was only known as an admirable violin virtuoso and a musician, but some years later, when his compositions were beginning to win fame for him, I said to Dresel one day, "I wish you would make yourself acquainted with some of Loeffler's works. As a musician you could not fail to find real merit in them, provided you would not expect them to be on any beaten track, but would accept them as free imaginative creations." The suggestion was coldly received but I argued the matter further, dwelling on Loeffler's masterly part-writing and unsurpassed knowledge of the best effects to be produced by all the different instruments of an orchestra. This elicited a mocking laugh and the remark—in a slow, deliberate

falsetto, "You might as well extoll a fish for being acquainted with water!"[24]

Loeffler, however, admired Dresel and expressed this to Gardner: "In him the best of musicians in America I have lost a very kind friend, one to whom I always looked up with deep reverence. You hardly know what a help he was and could be to young musicians. Though very acid in his criticisms on one's compositions he would also help to *better* matters. It has often been said of him that he was intolerant in regard to new compositions and composers, yet would it be wiser to say that he was most loyal to the best of music such as Bach's, Händel's, Beethoven's, Schubert's, Mendelssohn's. After all *they,* his gods, have not been surpassed nor even equalled. You and I have lost in Dresel an illustrious friend[;] *others* have lost an enemi."[25] In October when the BSO held a memorial concert to the memory of Dresel, Loeffler and Kneisel performed Bach's Double Concerto in D Minor.

Dresel was not the only friend Loeffler lost that year. Hubert Léonard had died in May, and Otto Grundmann, on leave from the Museum School for reasons of his health, died in August in Dresden.

The most difficult loss, however, came at the end of the year, following a festive event, Bunker's wedding. In September Loeffler had written to Gardner: "Perhaps you already know that I am going to be his best man. You know how much I care for Bunker and you can imagine how proud I am that he should have chosen me out of his friends. But I am scared to death about the ceremony etc. however not any more than he."[26] Early in October Bunker married Eleanor Hardy in Emmanual Church in Boston. The Bunkers settled in New York, where Loeffler visited them when the orchestra visited that city in November. He reported that "they are marvellously well, are perfectly happy and with the exception perhaps of a little money lack nothing."[27] But in December Bunker died from pneumonia. It was a great shock to all of his friends, including Loeffler, who cared deeply for Bunker.

Soon after, Loeffler also became ill. In January he appeared once again with the BSO, performing the Godard *Concerto romantique.* Then he succumbed to what the reviews next year referred to as a "long grave illness." His season ended early while he remained ill for some months.

In April Loeffler went to Southborough as a guest of J. Montgomery Sears at his farm. Temple Fay also spent some time there with him. From there he reported, "I am in splendid health."[28] During the summer he went to Portsmouth, where he enjoyed a seaside vacation, yachting and fishing. He was introduced to Francis Parkman, who took Loeffler fishing, "only I am afraid he will go a little too far out to sea and you know I am not a very good sailor."[29]

During the summer of 1891 Loeffler put finishing touches on his orchestral suite, *Les veillées de l'Ukraine,* which had been the major work of the previous summer in Wayland. He had worked on it some years and had consulted J. K. Paine about it in 1890.[30] Finally he showed it to Nikisch, who decided to premiere it in Boston.

Clara Rogers's comments on Dresel and Loeffler suggest that Loeffler was becoming known as a composer by 1890 when Dresel died. But it was only in the homes of his friends that Loeffler's compositions had been heard. The general public did not yet know Loeffler as a composer. In 1891 this situation changed when the BSO presented his first orchestral composition. Then Loeffler, already lionized as a musician, was to earn equal acclaim as a composer.

8

Debut of the Composer
(1891–1894)

The Gilded Age was a golden age for music in Boston. It was an era of great, even brilliant, activity from its resident organizations—the BSO, Handel and Haydn Society, Kneisel Quartette, Adamowski Quartette, Mendelssohn Quintette, Cecilia Society, Apollo Club—and resident artists like Kneisel, Loeffler, Adamowski, Johns, Proctor, Perabo, as well as a host of stellar visitors like Paderewski and Melba who made dazzling appearances in Boston's recital halls and salons.

During this time a great deal of new music was imported from Europe, including the music of such composers as Grieg, Tchaikovsky, Dvořák, Bruch, Strauss, Elgar, Saint-Saëns, Sibelius, Franck, and Raff, and it was received with a new spirit. With more exposure to new music, Boston was becoming more appreciative of modern composition. Originally suspicious of new works, Boston audiences increasingly looked forward to the novelties on the programs. Gericke, who like Henschel had endured much contention over his programs during his first term, concluded during his second (1898–1906) that his audiences wanted to hear modern works, including those of young Americans.[1]

For American composers the Gilded Age was an important time. The character and direction of American music had become an issue, particularly among nationalists. "It is perhaps difficult now to realize," composer E. B. Hill wrote in 1949, "the extent to which composers in the 'Gay Nineties' were at the crossroads in determining their creative future."[2] Perhaps nowhere in the country as in Boston, because of its large number of composers (including George W. Chadwick, Arthur Foote, J. K. Paine, Arthur Whiting, Edward MacDowell, Amy Beach, Frederick S. Converse, Clayton Johns, Margaret Lang, Horatio Parker, and others), was the course of American composition a more important issue.

The 1890s were a particularly good time for Loeffler's music to appear. In retrospect, critic Olin Downes stated, "Loeffler was symbolic in his presence here of the stage of American music that he knew."[3] Since Americans still recognized European supremacy in musical composition, Loeffler had the advantage of having been born and trained in Europe. But since he was about to present a compositional style unfamiliar to Boston, he was an object of interest to Americans looking for innovation. From every country and culture experienced in his youth, Loeffler had formed his tastes, acquired material, and learned his art. Since many of the influences he favored, principally those that were French, Slavic, and Russian, were unfamiliar to most Americans, when Loeffler appeared in America as a composer, it was as "a singular apparition in music."[4]

Interest also attended Loeffler's appearance as a composer locally because he was already a popular figure. Among symphony personnel, Henschel and Gericke had been heard as composers, but never yet had a player in the orchestra been presented as the composer of his own solo composition. Loeffler's following as a violinist was so strong that the announcement of an original composition of his to be performed doubtless created some excitement and an atmosphere of anticipation among BSO patrons.

The date of the premiere was 20 November 1891, during the BSO's tenth season. The composition was *Les veillées de l'Ukraine*, a suite for violin and orchestra. Loeffler himself played the solo part. As he stepped on stage, it was reported that he received "an amazingly ardent reception—a welcome after his long grave illness of last season" and that "the spontaneous outburst of appreciation that welcomed him when he mounted the platform was proof positive of the numberless admirers and friends he has in our musical community."[5]

The suite was composed of four movements—*Pastoral, Rune, Dumka, Finale*—individual tone poems based on stories by Gogol. There was some feeling that the work was over-long, that perhaps the second and third movements were too similar, but there was no question of its success. Every paper contained an accolade. The *Boston Transcript*: "This suite is remarkable, both for the inherent charm of its themes and the excellence of its musical workmanship. The handling of the orchestra, too, is admirable. . . . Composition and performance were equally, and highly, enjoyable. Bravissimo!" The *Beacon*: "It is thoroughly and elegantly written and there is a good deal of 'meat' in its material—such a work as would have been written by none but a sensitive spirit speaking through a rich musical vocabulary." The *Boston Home Journal*: "'Les Veillées de l'Ukraine' is a wholly delightful work abounding in weird Russian melodies, which the composer has most skillfully woven together and ingeniously elaborated upon."[6]

The *Boston Gazette*: "From beginning to end Mr. Loeffler has shown unerring artistic taste, and the work gives him a prominent place among the best of our young resident composers. It is the achievement of a thorough musician, and the same refined judgement that is manifested in the rest of the suite is shown in the writing of the solo part, which is not given up to deliberate virtuoso display, but takes its place in preserving the due balance of the whole." The *Boston Courier:* "Mr. Loeffler is not only a player of unusual ability, but the possessor of creative talent of an equally exceptional nature. . . . Mr. Loeffler's music is exceedingly attractive. There is plentiful evidence of inventive and constructive skill, and the orchestration displays a sure hand." The *Boston Musical Herald:* "His composition is convincing testimony of a fine musical mind drilled in technical points, and a faculty in instrumentation which presages marked results in the future."[7]

Differences of opinion always attended performances of Loeffler's works, but in the first reviews and in those of subsequent performances certain features were repeatedly marked: melodic beauty, ingenious orchestration (which later earned him the appellation from Louis Elson as a "modern Berlioz"), original and effective—though often controversial—harmony, technical skill, and individuality of talent.[8] It was not that Boston critics were easily swayed. Boston had barely accepted Brahms and was having great difficulties with Richard Strauss. Critics in Boston were a discerning and opinionated group. Loeffler well earned his plaudits—and came in for his fair share of resistance.

The most criticized feature of *Veillées,* besides its length, seemed to be that as a showpiece for solo violin it was rather disappointing. Albeit he had not made his own part as dazzling as possible, Loeffler, who had had a sympathetic audience before the performance, had now secured them. The judgement that "he gained as favorable an endorsement for his suite as he had formerly received in these concerts as a player" was no modest praise.[9] Loeffler was Boston's own, and they were proud of it. From this point Boston rarely went a season without a Loeffler performance and Loeffler accolades. His music became a part of Boston's culture for about a half century.

Loeffler performed his suite again in Cambridge in December and, in January, played Mozart's Sinfonia concertante for violin and viola with Kneisel. Just as Kneisel and Loeffler individually had each received copious acclaim, together the situation was no different. Their "merits are so nearly equal," claimed one reviewer, and another that they played "with rare taste, perfect mechanism and absolute sympathy."[10]

A few days following, the orchestra left for its January New York–

to–Washington visits. Taking the same train was Sarah Bernhardt on her Grand World Tour. Loeffler or Fay evidently admired the actress (a photo of her survived in the Loeffler estate), but as she had a private car, the musicians may not have had an opportunity to meet her.

That January Loeffler was again traveling with a cold and experiencing trouble with his ear. He felt particularly bitter about having to make this trip but saw no way out. "Of course if I go home now that K. is sick on Monday next I dare say that Nikisch would take somebody else for next season from his beloved Leipzig."[11]

At home, Loeffler had more recital work—with the Kneisel Quartette playing the Svendson Octet, with the Baermann recitals, with Faelton and Schulz playing Beethoven at the HMA. In addition Loeffler appeared again as a composer when, in April, the Adamowski Quartette performed the second and third movements of his quartet at Union Hall. The consensus of the reviewers' opinions was that it was a well-constructed work. The *Boston Post* remarked that "Loeffler's quartet is clever, exceedingly clever, and one could but regret its brevity. It is well built, and repeats the good points of his suite heard here earlier in the season." The *Boston Transcript* decided that "Mr. Loeffler's two movements . . . made one wish to hear the whole quartet; in these movements, as in his 'Veillées de l'Ukraine,' Mr. Loeffler shows that he knows how to unite grace with solidity of writing."[12]

As with the suite, there were some reservations. For example, the reviewer of the *Herald* wrote: "The first movement is the work of an accomplished musician rather than that of an inspired composer, the graceful phrases which form its basis being worked out, elaborated and ornamented with the skill of a master, but with all this it fails to leave much satisfaction because of its fragmentary characteristics." He did, however, conclude, "The two examples created, on the whole, an excellent impression and a desire to hear the completed work."[13]

Philip Hale, writing for the *Boston Journal,* also liked the composition, but with reservations. "The andante and the variations show scholarship and fine taste. The theme is of the character of plain-song; the variations suggest the thought that they were written when the composer had not entirely escaped from contrapuntal studies on a cantus firmus in one of the old modes. They are exercises, in a certain sense, and exercises that are creditable to the author."[14]

Loeffler's quartet was indeed done at a time when he had been studying counterpoint, evidenced clearly by the motivic melodic writing and the pervasive, recurrent imitative texture, including fugal sections in the first movement, the canon in the second, and imitative contrapuntal variation and development in the Andante assai and

Rondo pastorale movements. The third movement is perhaps the most striking for its theme, composed, as indicated on the manuscript parts, "in medieval folksong style." The quartet gives barely a hint of the style rich in mood and atmosphere that Loeffler was to create for himself, yet it does again reveal his eclecticism—in a quartet that is essentially an essay in Baroque counterpoint, with a passing nod to Classic forms, he found place for medieval modality.

Loeffler affected disdain for critical opinion. "If my music is bad my friends won't save it; if it is good my enemies won't kill it," he said in 1910.[15] In fact, he was very sensitive to criticism. He set aside the quartet, which was never performed in public as a complete work. The suite he subjected to revision. Its length having been a major criticism, he dropped one movement (in some manuscripts the second; in others the third). Eventually he extracted the second movement as a separate composition, *Une nuit de Mai,* which, as such, was never performed. The revised suite came onto the BSO schedule again in 1899.

During the 1892–93 season Loeffler continued his work as a violinist, assisting Carl Baermann and Arthur Whiting in recital and, of course, playing in the BSO. The orchestra had a full season, including extra performances in New York. As a substitute for the lack of opera that year, Mr. H. LeGrand Cannon organized four special concerts by the Boston orchestra, one given in each month from December to March, in private homes. The subscribers included the Astors, Vanderbilts, and others of New York society. Loeffler's letters from New York, however, did not mention any performances but merely expressed again his desire to leave public performance for composition. "I contemplate my life with horror to be sure! How I kill my talent, scraping in the orchestra—how I assassinate it giving so many lessons. I have done nothing for some years but smother what is most important in me—my talent for music. I have become bourgeois as an artist and musician clearly in order to earn a lot of money."[16]

The same letter reveals a quite different reason why Loeffler felt he should quit appearing as a soloist with the orchestra. "Quite frankly when I contemplate myself in the mirror there is no way to have success putting oneself in front of a large audience with a bald skull such as mine. Decidedly, more is necessary than to play the violin well. When a man no longer interests the women in the audience, it is necessary to renounce success."

Loeffler's ambitions increasingly became centered on composing. He looked for a libretto for an opéra comique. In Philadelphia he was visited by Owen Wister and wrote to Fay, "I believe he is the man to write me a libretto for an opéra comique."[17] The opera would have been based on the life of François Villon, but the collaboration never took place.

In February the Kneisel Quartette premiered Loeffler's Sextuor, upon which he had been working for several years. This work was scored for two violins, two violas, and two cellos, in three movements. The composition was dedicated to Franz Kneisel "in friendship and veneration"; the second movement, based on the Russian *Volga Boatmen* theme, bore a subdedication to the memory of Denis Bunker. Assisted by Max Zach and Leo Schulz (both of the BSO), the Kneisel Quartette performed the complete sextet in Chickering Hall.

The sextet was another critical success. The *Boston Daily Advertiser* announced, "It is by far the best work which the talented violinist has yet given to the public. Founded on folk themes, it has a degree of development that is not in the earlier works of the composer, and the leading of the voices is easy and masterly everywhere." The *Boston Transcript* agreed: "In Mr. Loeffler's new sextet we hail a work that can be musically and unreservedly enjoyed from beginning to end. . . . We know of no sextet for strings in which the almost unavoidable thickness of tone resulting from the preponderance of instruments of low register has been so triumphantly overcome as in this one. The 'instrumentation' of the work is simply masterly. And how fresh, vital, naturally musical its themes are! The first movement is a dream of beauty, of grace, of outline and sensuous wealth. . . . There is an immense amount of elaborate work in the sextet, and carried through with a very sure hand. . . the whole is strong, coherent, and full of meaning. It is a work for Boston to be proud of."[18]

Elements of Loeffler's modernity were remarked upon but recognized as deliberate, not consequent of a lack of skill. The *Boston Journal* observed, "On the whole, this sextet . . . is written with infinite care. The development often appears to be a procession of spontaneous thought. The very passages that appear needlessly, cruelly harsh, as well as certain hair raising harmonies, are evidently the matured purpose of the composer."[19]

Loeffler enjoyed his success. "What the journalists and Kneisel have cost me since the Sextet made its appearance is really tragicomic. . . . First a bottle of champagne here and a bottle there, to celebrate 'the 6tet' and then 'the future of the composer' and then 'to the symphony to be written' and then 'to the cello concerto to be written' etc. etc. etc."[20]

Later that same month Loeffler played the solo part of the Saint-Saëns Concerto in A. The cadenza was his own. His performance was judged "simply exquisite," and the cadenza, a "distinctly traceable and logical use of the thematic materials derived from the main body of the work," was pronounced "brilliant," "masterly," "a masterpiece."[21]

That spring Loeffler took the Saint-Saëns and his cadenza on his last tour, the 1893 spring tour. Kneisel conducted the tour since Nikisch had left the orchestra early to assume a position in Europe. Loeffler reported that "the concerts in Buffalo, Cleveland, and Louisville have been a fiasco as far as receipts go because we have had empty houses. But the musical success has been good everywhere, and the journals have not been flattering to Nikisch, I guarantee you. This stupid fellow has not had much luck lately, for we learned yesterday that he had to change his travel plans because of an illness in the family. . . . Without wishing him ill, I have, however, little sympathy for him."[22]

The highlight of the 1893 tour was Chicago, which was hosting the quadricentennial of Columbus's discovery of the New World. The exposition in many ways was quite marvelous. Frederick Law Olmstead, America's premier landscape architect, had transformed a lakeside marsh into the exposition grounds. Architects such as Richard Morris Hunt and the firm of McKim, Mead and White designed the buildings in the style of the castle-like mansions they built for the Vanderbilts and their social peers. Augustus Saint-Gaudens was in charge of the sculpture. Loeffler was quite taken by the spectacle. "The exposition itself is indescribably beautiful. . . . the buildings are incredibly beautiful but—it is all half finished. More than three quarters of the foreign exhibits have not yet been unpacked and great disorder reigns in the buildings. *Nothing* is finished or complete. But what there is is the most imposing, the most grandiose, the most beautiful that one could see."[23]

The music of the exposition was under the direction of Theodore Thomas. Orchestras, bands, and choral societies of several cities had been invited to give concerts. The BSO and Kneisel Quartette both performed. The BSO concert was an ill-attended success. According to Loeffler, "The audiences are very small because the world is too occupied seeing the buildings or rather the edifices of the exposition." There were other problems. When the orchestra arrived in mid-May, workmen were still at work on the hall, and although they were persuaded to stop for rehearsal, the building was not finished, and it was cold. It remained cold throughout the performance. Nevertheless, Loeffler was warmly applauded, and "the journals spoke very well of me and also of Kneisel."[24]

More important to Loeffler was Thomas's reaction. "Thomas invited us after the concert (Kneisel Quartette, Ellis, and me) to drink a glass of champagne with him. Thomas complimented me sincerely on my playing and told me that I had developed into a first rate artist. Thomas and his entire orchestra were present for my solo, and the orchestra was very enthusiastic over me."[25] Loeffler, no doubt, hoped that Thomas might accept the conductorship of the BSO, left vacant after Nikisch's abrupt departure. Thomas, however, remained with his orchestra in Chicago and the position was filled by Emil Paur, who had been Nikisch's successor at the Leipzig Stadt Theater.

Paur was impressed with the Boston orchestra. "Great was my delighted surprise and astonishment when I heard the Boston men at my first rehearsal! I found an excellent assembly of musicians of the first rank who did not play only to do their duty to satisfy the conductor and audience; they played in the heart and soul, joy and enthusiasm, inclined always to give their very best and cooperate with the conductor to reach the highest possible perfection. It is the best orchestra in the world, that was my conviction which I had when I started my work in Boston, and which conviction has not changed since then."[26]

Paur remained with the orchestra five years. During that time, because of financial difficulties (1893 having been the year of a national depression), the western tours were abandoned and plans to build a new music hall delayed.

Loeffler then had a respite from much of the traveling he had had to undertake. Increasingly he also gave up playing in recital halls. One of the more unusual events in which he did participate, however, was the appearance of French pantomimists, Mme. Pilar Morin and M. Aimé Lachaume on 1 December 1893. The music for their pantomime "Pitou Soldat," composed by M. Lachaume, was performed by Loeffler, Adamowski, and other members of the BSO.

The majority of Loeffler's non-orchestral playing, however, was done in salons. In January 1894, for example, Loeffler and Ferrucio Busoni performed Fauré and Bach at one of Gardner's musicales and returned the next month to play for a birthday party given for the artist Anders Zorn, whom Gardner had met at the Chicago Exposition the summer before. Zorn presented Gardner with a pencil drawing of Busoni, made on the back of a calling card, and a pen-and-ink sketch of Loeffler.

Loeffler continued working assiduously on his compositions. During 1893 he borrowed from Gardner collected poems by his favorite poet, Paul Verlaine, and set seven to music—*La chanson des Ingénues, Sérénade, Le son du cor s'afflige vers les bois, Le rossignol, Rêverie en sourdine, Dansons la gigue!* and *La lune blanche.* For the last he reworked his earlier song, *Les hirondelles.* About the same time, probably in the next year or two, he also set two poems by Charles

Baudelaire, *Harmonie du soir* and *La cloche fêlée*. All nine songs were scored for voice, viola, and piano.

Loeffler presented a copy of five of these songs to Gardner in London in 1894. At that time he revealed his characteristic reservations about his work to her. "They are entirely yours only some day if convenient to you I should like to have a copy to—perhaps burn in case of course I should replace the compositions with some better ones to you."[27]

The viola songs were performed at the Gardners', as well as the Rogers' salon and probably others. Since one song (*Le rossignol*) is dedicated to Mrs. Henschel, it is probable that she sang this song, if not others, on one of her visits to Boston. The first public performance of any of the songs did not occur until 1897. At some point (before 1897) Loeffler orchestrated *La cloche fêlée* and *Sérénade*, never performed.

Also during the summer of 1893, Loeffler finished writing a cello concerto, about which he again revealed his doubts to Gardner. "At present I am working on a 'morceau de fantasie' for Violoncello and orchestra which will be or very good or very crazy I do really not know. Certain days it seems like a good thing on others again I suspect the author to be ripe for the lunatic asylum. However the thing is in such an embryo state that one does not quite know if it is going to be a frog or a bird."[28]

On 16 February 1894 Paur conducted Loeffler's *Morceau fantastique* for violoncello and orchestra. The concert opened with Beethoven's Eighth Symphony, but, according to the *Boston Courier,* "the audience at the 111th Symphony concert evidently found its chief satisfaction in Mr. C. M. Loeffler's new composition for violoncello and orchestra, entitled by him 'Fantastic Concerto.'"[29] Alwin Schroeder, principal cellist and member of the Kneisel Quartette since 1891, played the cello part. Composed of five continuous movements, the concerto again manifested Loeffler's predilection for Russian themes. (The music is now lost.)

The performance was occasion again for Boston to rejoice in its own. The *Boston Sunday Herald* asserted that "Mr. Loeffler is a capital musician, with a thorough knowledge of the art of composition, possessed of good taste in the choice of forms, and a master of orchestration. All these characteristics are shown in his concerto of last evening, and its merits were quickly received both by the audience and his fellow-players in the orchestra." The *Boston Courier* concurred: "Mr. Loeffler gave an intimation last winter, in the string sextet which the Kneisel Quartette played, that he is a man who has something to say and knows how to say it. This concerto enforced that affirmation. It is music of the time in its diversity of treatment . . . Yet it does not seem eccentric, extravagant or far fetched. . . . Mr. Loeffler's [instrumentation] is natural, fluent, and emerges from the instruments with the suggestion that each odd little bit is just where it ought to be, can be found without anxiety and presented with facility."[30]

Echoes were heard in New York. The *Musical and Dramatic Word* commented: "I cannot speak in too high enthusiastic praise of Mr. Loeffler's 'cello concerto, or of Mr. Schroeder's great performance of it. As much as I have always admired Mr. Loeffler both as a violinist and composer, I was quite unprepared for such masterly skill, such wealth of invention as this work evinced."[31]

The *Boston Transcript,* like several others, considered Loeffler's talent to be established. "He is a composer to the manner born; he has abundantly proved this before."[32] Yet Loeffler's critics began to divide into two groups. Loeffler's modernity was becoming more pronounced with each composition and earning him some critical disapproval. Among the censorious was Louis Elson, critic with the *Boston Daily Advertiser,* who wrote: "There is a constant boldness in the treatment and modulation that causes the auditor mental effort at every turn; it is too modern in its progressions and some of its orchestral combinations are experimental. . . . The work at first seemed too improvisational in flavor, it left the impression of being disjointed and spasmodic, its ideas seemed loosely strung together. The Russian finale reminded the reviewer of how much better the composer had done in his sextette, a composition which greatly overshadows this work."[33]

When the *Morceau fantastique* was taken to Washington in March, it shared a program with Beethoven, Berlioz, Liszt, and Wagner. Loeffler's music was there in the company with which it would be classed for years to come—the nontraditionalists, the avant-garde.

Charges of being too modern, of breaking rules, did not disturb Loeffler. In discussing the music of Bach, Loeffler said: "We hear Bach's modernism, his chromatic progressions spoken of. We should go farther. Bach broke all the rules. . . . Bach wrote music to be alive, not to follow rules."[34] Loeffler's music was also alive, and it continued a success with the public. His concerto was heartily applauded.

Then, hard upon this victory, Loeffler appeared to rave reviews as soloist playing Bruch's Romanza in A Minor and the Saint-Saëns Concert Piece in E Minor. These were the last solos that Loeffler was to play with the orchestra of music other than his own. His playing was judged by one critic to have been the "greatest triumph of his entire artistic career." Another said he played "seemingly without a flaw." In the Saint-Saëns he again used his own cadenza, "bristling with terrible but not repellent tests of technique," which "may stand as the last word of violin virtuosity up to date." He was recalled four times, and "his fellow-musicians vied with the members of the audience in expressing their delight at the good playing they had listened to." "In a word, he was superb!"[35]

Boston could hardly heap enough laurels upon his head. It was thus, with his success both as a violinist and composer firmly established, that he returned to Europe for the summer of 1894.

9

Decadence

In May 1894 Loeffler made his first visit to England. His ship, the S.S. *Columbia,* docked in Southampton, and "for 3 hours we travelled through the most enchanting country I ever saw. The country of England seems to be one great garden. Of London I am disppointed. It is great, smoky, cloudy, black, rainy. The people seem to be dumb. Of course from a historical point of view it is *unequalled.* There are as you know magnificent buildings here but give me *Boston,* that is all I can say." As for music there: "London is a hard place for musicians or virtuosi. *Everybody* is here but nobody has a chance to play—if they do it costs from 100 guineas upwards for the privilege. Paderewsky is the only one who makes money in London."[1]

In London Loeffler lunched and dined with Hans Richter, having "a splendid time," and watched him conduct. "There is no mistake about his being the best of conductors. His orchestra is not good but in spite of it you could see what his intentions were even if the musicians did not carry them out. . . . Then he does look so splendid when he conducts, and everything goes by heart with him."[2] At the concert Loeffler saw Henschel, Sir Frederic Leighton, Josef Hofmann, and Tivador Nachez.

Loeffler also attended a concert given by Cécile Chaminade of her own compositions, including a "perfectly splendid song and wonderfully sung by Miss [Camille] Landhi," who was the original dedicatee of his own song, *Dansons la gigue.*[3]

Loeffler was able to visit John Sargent's studio, where, with "immense pleasure," he saw the new decorations for the Boston Public Library.[4] He dined with the J. M. Searses at the Berkeley Hotel, "*the* finest and swellest place in London"—"swellest," he explained, because the Prince of Wales' set frequented it. But Loeffler's reaction to this glamor was: "I am glad when I am out of this, also glad when I am back with you in Medfield."[5]

From England Loeffler went, in June, to Liège, where he visited his old friend from the Derwies orchestra, César Thomson. "He is still as he was and as to his playing—it is incredible. He played part of the Brahms Concerto today and it was grand. . . . I can say I thank God that I once knew him for my playing has been much influenced by him all these last 15 years."[6]

Loeffler spent the bulk of the summer in Paris. His mother and sister were living in Enghien, twenty-five minutes outside of Paris by railroad. Helene had been studying harp with Hasselmann of the Conservatoire, and Loeffler reported that "my sister is the best harpist that I have ever heard. Even her celebrated professor has told her that she has a tremendous technique and that she has more sound than anyone in Paris, which is a lot."[7] She also had, Loeffler declared, great personal charm and related that "Mme. Kraus of the grand opera likes her very much, as well as Ernest Reyer, the famous composer of the opera 'Sigurd' and of 'Salammbô.' She receives very kind letters from all these celebrated people."[8]

Loeffler's brother Raphael was given a week's leave from his school in Marseilles to visit his brother from America. After Raphael's return to school, the family moved to Paris. There Loeffler rented a piano in order to work on his compositions. He sketched a new suite for violin and orchestra in three movements. He outlined the work, which he expected to be "a piece of effect," to Fay.[9] When he finished the work back in America, he did not adhere to this original orchestration plan but did, in the second movement, omit the violins to give the solo instrument added prominence.

A highlight of this Paris visit was Loeffler's meeting with Gabriel Fauré, whom he approached with a letter of introduction from Sargent and met on the fourth of July. "He was perfectly charming and gave me the best welcome in the world and asked me to come again next week which I will do without any doubt."[10] Fauré liked Loeffler, and during Loeffler's subsequent visits to France their friendship deepened and strengthened. Although Sears had given Loeffler letters of introduction to Massanet and Widor, neither was in the city during Loeffler's time there.

In both London and Paris Loeffler looked for a new violin. The best ones, which were in London, were too expensive; however, in Paris he found a viola d'amore from the time of Louis XIV, which he bought for sixty dollars. Loeffler was enchanted with the instrument and set about learning to play it. "The viole d'amour [spelled variously in different sources] has a special charm that does not at all resemble other instruments of the same family," he wrote to Fay, to whom, as usual, he reported his financial, musical, and personal affairs.[11]

The first of his American friends to whom he showed his purchase was Belle Gardner, whom Loeffler saw in late July on his return to England. The Gardners themselves had just purchased a Stradivarius, for which Loeffler advised them on the purchase of a case. Loeffler also showed off his purchase in America. "On certain occasions," related Rogers, "Loeffler brought with him a *viol d'amor* which he had unearthed in Paris, and in which he revelled as does a child with his first electric railway. And how we loved to listen to its mysterious tones—as of passion unrevealed—of love unconsciously brooded."[12] He talked Rogers into writing a piece for the instrument and wrote for it himself. Later, in 1900, he sold this instrument (for $200) but owned at least three other violas d'amore.

Loeffler returned to America in late July. As usual he was sad to leave his family. "I must tell you that I have a heavy heart at leaving my good mother and Helene. Two beings more sweet and gentle there could not be."[13] But he experienced less regret about leaving Paris than he might have anticipated. The city itself, though at the height of La Belle Epoque, had been disappointing.

> Paris has a completely different aspect than before for me. First, I am older, more serious, then Paris itself is not the same thing. It has appeared to me more vulgar, less original. The women dress in the English style, and under the republic the people seem to me to have become bourgeois. They lack aristocracy, distinction, and above all morals. All is in decadence, and one can easily foresee the next downfall, the final collapse of the nation. It seems to me to be among those who are mistaken about what they believe or do, who are in error in all serious matters, political or business. It is too bad all the same—because this was a great nation. Their literature, painting, music itself seems to be infected with this immoral illness. You read the newspapers, even the best lack seriousness, are always seasoned with humbug. The compositions, for example, for piano are always in the genre of ballet music, their songs in the genre of ditties from the music halls, violin pieces in the genre of berceuse or bourgeois dance badly imitated. It is deplorable. The violin class at the Conservatoire (Professor Marsick) plays badly with the banal pursuit of wanting to please the gallery. It is deplorable. One is ignorant everywhere of what concerns foreign countries. They are mistaken about everything. America has opened my eyes about all countries; America is good enough for me thank you and as to Americans I only need to think of you, chérie, to be completely happy with my lot![14]

It was ironic that Loeffler should condemn what he disliked about Paris as decadent, for that term would often be applied to his own aesthetic—though in a much different sense. *Decadence* is a word of varied usage. In a general way it has been applied to the last two decades of the century, the era of Impressionism, Symbolism, and the English Aesthetic Movement. It was, more specifically, a term applied to the literary movement that was the immediate forerunner of Symbolism, sometimes treated synonymously with Symbolism. As a literary term, it was first used in reference to Baudelaire to refer to the beauties of past and exotic civilizations in decline.

The word acquired a number of connotations: languor, ennui, repletion, cultivated sensuousness, exquisite refinement, a penchant for the colorful and exotic, for the esoteric or extraordinary, for the grotesque and bizarre, inquietude, nostalgia for the past (a dying past, a hedonist past, a splendid, passionate, or dramatic past). Since it also implied corruption, debility, and often eroticism and since these poets did not see their art as a degradation or decline but rather possessed of a new sensibility, a turning away from the bourgeois (the brutal and materialistic) to the exquisite and unworldly, the literary movement in France assumed, about 1885, the name Symbolism.

The term *Symbolism* added even more meaning to the concept of this style, particularly the aspect of mystery or mysticism. Symbolists used symbol and suggestion to convey meaning and held freedom of form to be fundamental to freedom of expression. Poetry, they maintained, should be like music and suggest or evoke feelings.

Symbolists found kindred spirits in other cultures and other arts. Loeffler was a kindred spirit in music. His favorite poets were Decadents or Symbolists—Verlaine, Kahn, Mallarmé, LaForgue, Huysmans, Maeterlinck—or similar poets such as Poe, Rossetti, and Yeats who were, in Gilman's words, "as bone of his bone, flesh of his flesh."[15] In the early years, Loeffler was often compared with such poets, rarely with composers. A New York paper, in fact, called him "the blond musical Verlaine of Boston."[16]

Although his readings were diverse and the programs for his musical compositions ranged from Virgil to Walt Whitman to Okakura Kakuzo, Loeffler frequently founds his texts or inspiration in some Symbolist reading. His music was further allied to Symbolism in that the spirit of his music had an affinity to that of the literature. Loeffler's music was Symbolist in its emphasis on color, nuance, emotional expression, and the evocation of atmosphere and mood. Like the poets, Loeffler was attracted to the exotic, extraordinary, and exquisite, to enchantment, to moods of longing and melancholy, and frequently to the macabre.

Loeffler's music was Symbolist not only for the subjects of his music, but also for its style. Though Loeffler did make use of use traditional forms, his music was often programmatic or through-composed, the freedom of form allowing freedom of imagination. He composed program music not to tell stories but to evoke moods and images, to stimulate fantasy and imagination. As one critic put it, "He does not pre-determine to express or depict in his music some particular fact, but he rather insists on the hint being born of the mysteries of his harmonies."[17]

Loeffler experimented with harmony and orchestration to create, either subtly or strikingly, novel and colorful effects and kaleidoscopic visions. His harmony is tonal, but expanded. His horizontal harmonies use chromatic, whole-tone, and modal patterns. His vertical harmonies include frequent chromatics, unresolved dissonances, added tones, and altered chords within both major and minor. He did not bind his modulations by any set key relationships and frequently obscured his tonality.

In the realm of tone color, Loeffler displayed particular imagination. In several scores, he employed instruments not commonly used in symphony orchestras, such as the viola d'amore, saxophone, harmonica, and mandolin. He composed a chamber work for the perhaps unique combination of saxophone, viola d'amore, and piano. But, in addition to the use of unusual sounds, his distinction as a coloristic rests upon his imaginative flair for tonal combinations, constant experimentation, and attention to detail.

Like harmony and tone color, Loeffler treated melody and rhythm in a free manner, suiting the musical elements to each moment. Loeffler's melodies are fluid, usually composed of small intervals, often motivic, unbound by regular lengths. His equally fluid rhythms are marked often by meter changes, use of different meter in different parts, cross rhythms, and frequent fluctuation between duple and triple meters.

Loeffler employed all the elements of music carefully for effect. His scores are replete with meticulous expressive markings, and many scores reveal, through revisions, the attention Loeffler gave to each moment. Loeffler once said of Verlaine and Baudelaire. "Of course, having a horror of the obvious, they changed a word or phrase a dozen times, that they might produce a beauty before unknown."[18] Loeffler, himself a tone poet, was possessed of just such finical meticulousness. H. T. Parker, Boston critic, wrote: "Sit over the printed score of one of Mr. Loeffler's compositions in the smaller forms, and it seems a thing of minute poetic impressions and implications in tones. Not a harmony, not a modulation—the reader persuades himself—but has some subtle purpose to which it has been duly wrought."[19] Fellow composer

E. B. Hill wrote that, whatever verses he chose to set, Loeffler "always found the precise equivalent."[20]

A few times Loeffler's music was called Impressionistic. Some compositions, usually those with macabre or morbid subjects, were called Decadent. His aesthetic was most frequently called Symbolist for its affinity with the literary movement. For the exquisitely crafted moods of his music—whether darkly brooding or delicately iridescent—as well as for a measure of exoticism, he was called a mystic or visionary. In later years he was termed an "ivory tower" composer for caring more for unworldly enchantment than modern industrial realism.

Lawrence Gilman, who several times wrote eloquently on the subject, described Loeffler's mysticism:

> *Au fond* he is a mystic, a dreamer, a visionary. A mystic: for Loeffler has the mystic's bias toward that which transcends the immediate and the tangible phases of experience, his serene conviction of the reality of the extra-sensational. His imagination ranges most freely and familiarly in that psychic borderland where the emotions become indescribably rarefied and subtly heightened—where they become more the echo and reverberation of emotions than emotions themselves, yet gain rather than lose in intensity by the process of alembication. He is of the order of mystics whose thought, while it has the penetrative power of all mystical thought, is saturated with a quality of feeling that springs from an exquisite and supersensitive intuition of the human heart."[21]

Symbolism was not what Loeffler deplored about Parisian decadence. What he disliked was that which he found trivial and trifling. He decried the suborning of the arts to popular tastes, the vision of art as mere embellishment. The entertainment of a pleasure-seeking, frivolous public was never important or amusing to Loeffler. As a composer, he declared to Gardner, "I write for the few, almost 'en une de quelqu'un.'"[22] Loeffler would never be bourgeois. Highly sensitive to the beautiful, he disdained mediocrity and was meticulous, even fastidious, about his own compositions. What he sought for his creations was acknowledged by many to be there—fineness of construction, choiceness of material, splendor of effect. Yet his aesthetic was not universal. His music became controversial among the critics, and principally it was on his Symbolist nature that the controversy focused.

Loeffler's Symbolism was not as striking in his first works as it was in those beginning with the cello concerto. In that work a multiplicity of influences was still recognized. "If his enthusiasm for Brahms leads him in the direction of solidarity of workmanship, his admiration for the French and Slavic composers leads him quite as naturally toward brilliance, piquancy and the highly-spiced and charming in general. He has much of the characteristically French lightness of touch, of their instinctive knowledge when they have said enough, while his German side saves him from their too frequent contentment with half-expressed ideas, with mere clever innuendoes."[23]

Assimilation was, in fact, one of Loeffler's declared ideals in art, and eclecticism always characterized his style. In 1910 a critic remarked: "Mr. Loeffler's compositions have at different periods reflected the influences of Brahms and Wagner, and, later, of Debussy and other moderns. His eclecticism and breadth of horizon are almost unparalleled among his colleagues, and are only less remarkable than the patience and persistence with which he has planned and evolved his own distinctive style."[24] Others also recognized the variety of influences in Loeffler's music.

However, Loeffler's affinity with the French and particularly with Symbolism was undeniable. It was also novel and even confusing, since Symbolism in music was unknown on the American concert stage before Loeffler. However, Philip Hale was able to identify Loeffler's dominant aesthetic in another review of the cello concerto when he remarked: "Mr. Loeffler here seems to me to be a symbolist." Other critics then discussed Loeffler as a Symbolist or a Decadent. In New York he was called, in fact, "a decadent of the decadents."[25]

While some music critics used the term *decadence* simply to designate the kinship of Loeffler's music with the French literary movement, others used it in a pejorative sense to deplore Loeffler's departure from tradition into a vague, disturbing new realm. Although critics in Boston had already experienced challenges to classical tradition with the music of Liszt and Wagner, its accommodation had been difficult for many. In addition, Boston was not used to French music, excepting some opera. "Musical Boston was, in effect," wrote composer Arthur Shepherd, "an outpost of German musical culture."[26] Modern French music—Loeffler's music—presented yet another affront to the conservatives. And, standing in opposition to the Germanic hold that had gripped American concert music, Loeffler stood virtually alone.

Controversy over Loeffler's aesthetic began with the *Morceau fantastique*. Though Philip Hale was intrigued, some others were not impressed. After the concerto's presentation in New York in 1895, the critic of the *Times* objected that it had "no form . . . no thematic development. It is an impressionistic picture in tones. It is splendidly scored, and it has warmth, body, élan, spirit. But it is inchoate. It is not without fascination, but it is the fascination of a disembodied spirit.

Mr. Loeffler has no business to introduce Maeterlinckism into music."[27]

Doubts and displeasure, as well as enthusiasm from the progressive camp, attended his next orchestra work, that begun in Paris during the summer of 1894, entitled *Divertissement en trois parties pour violon et grand orchestre*, op. 1, first performed in Boston in January 1895.[28] The movements include *Préambule, Eclogue,* and *Le Carnaval des morts,* the last being variations on the *Dies irae* from the Requiem Mass, dedicated to the memory of Franz Liszt. As a piece for solo violin, the virtuosity of the *Divertissement,* whose solo part resembles nonstop violin exercises, quite made up for any disappointment created by the restraint of *Les veillées de l'Ukraine.* Using the Gardner Stradivarius, Loeffler gave a dazzling performance, playing with what Hale called "an air of provoking ease." It was such a tour de force that Higginson granted Loeffler the salary raise he had requested unsuccessfully the year before.

In his review of this work Hale again discussed Loeffler's aesthetic. "Mr. Loeffler is a decadent. He believes in tonal impressions rather than in thematic development. How fastidious he is in the search after the proper, the one, the felicitous word! . . . he has the delicate sentiment, the curiosity of the hunter after nuances, the love of the macabre, the cool fire that consumes and is more deadly than fierce, panting flame. Mr. Loeffler is more than an experimenter in color. He is a man of refined and fantastic imagination." After a later performance, Hale wrote: "Fancy a Paganini who has read Maeterlinck; fancy an imagination fantastic and slightly strained in the path of the morbid; fancy perfect musicianship, a delicate sense of color, values, and a sense of the grotesque; fancy all these things and you have not yet grasped the half of Loeffler's music."[29]

The piece was, for the most part, well received, though its modernity was well recognized, as Loeffler himself expected. "No conventionality need be looked for in the piece," he wrote to Gardner. "It may stir your imagination by astonishing your ears for I believe in tone coloring lies principally the possibility for future compositions. The orchestration therefore I have given great thought and there is many a new effect in the score I am sure."[30] The score reveals Loeffler's increasing departure from harmonic conventionality. For example, whereas Loeffler opened *Veillées* by establishing a basic tonic-dominant relationship, at the beginning of this work he quickly moved from his tonic chord through a series of full-diminished seventh chords, maintaining the tonal center by an underlying pedal.

In the program notes William Apthorp pointed out another of the work's major departures from convention. "It makes no pretensions to strict form, which indeed, would not be in keeping with the character of the work," which he described as "a study in tonal color." Without conventional form, however, some critics were baffled. They criticized the composition for having "little meaning or form," for lacking "pleasing harmonies" and for containing "very little inspiration."[31] The critic for the *Transcript* found the *Divertissement* too shifting, vague, and indistinct of purpose.

To other critics the composition's modernity was not at all distasteful. The *Boston Sunday Herald* stated, "It is a credit to his brilliant musicianship, the purity of his taste and the skill with which he departs from set forms and takes refuge in the bizarre without becoming merely eccentric." The *Boston Traveler* observed, "Its very uniqueness, doubtless, is a shock to the ultra-classical, who believe that composition ceased with Mendelssohn, but in the fresh breeze of its inspiration the moderns can find a deal of reviving force."[32]

On the whole the piece had more supporters than not. Loeffler revealed to Gardner the true success of the first performance. "I played a new thing of mine which may be termed a success artistically as well as popularily (is there such a word?). Indeed a petition was sent to M. Paur asking for a repetition of the work signed by some of the best musicians in Boston."[33] The petition was successful. When, in 1897, the BSO performed the composition again, critical reaction was more solidly behind the composer. The *Gazette* praised it as his "most musicianly work . . . brilliant, richly colored work in the impressionistic style; indistinct in outline and in meaning but impressive from its technical skill, its daring and bold artistic dash." Even the *Transcript* was now "in doubt whether to call Mr. Loeffler's divertimento his best thing, or only one of his best."[34]

Loeffler himself thought it his best, as he so wrote when he offered the dedication, with "embarrassed squirming," to Gardner. "I offer it to you, not because I feel so sure that it is beautiful (for you may be bitterly disappointed) but because I think it is original and the best I have done. The sentiments that go with it towards which you shall not be told of now for the music must do there its mission. I will only say, that it is the hommage of a friend."[35] The homage was entirely acceptable to Gardner.

The premiere of Loeffler's *Divertissement* occurred during the same season that both Thomson and Ysaÿe visited Boston, but whether either heard him play it is unknown. Ysaÿe later asked to look at the score but returned it as "too hard for his hands."[36]

While Thomson was in Boston, both he and Loeffler were guests of the Searses, and Loeffler recommended his company to Gardner. "Thomson you ought to know for he is the best talker and the most original of beings. His mind (while at times going the crooked direction) is most extraordinary to watch. You can take him either way: consider him sane and he is at times bewildering to talk with, consider him insane and he is the most amusing of all artists."[37]

Neither violinist had the success in Boston that Loeffler wished. "Ysaÿe and Thomson," he continued to Gardner, "have been disappointments to me. Neither have advanced any in their art in many respects they have both seen their best days. If Ysaÿe loses yet a little more of his technique he will stand par with Reményi. Thomson disappointed me a little musically but he is the better violinist of the two (to a violinist). . . . The concerts here go along with a bourgeois-every-day-trot and Boston likes it. Few know and feel that the best concerts were given long ago, Alas!"

In February 1895 the *Morceau fantastique* was performed in New York. Impressions of this work in its second year were much like the first. Reviews ranged from the condemnation of Maeterlinckism in music quoted above to the following review in the *New York Herald*.

> Beethoven, Mozart, Handel and Dvořák figured on the programme of the Boston Symphony Orchestra's concert at the Metropolitan Opera House last evening, yet it was Loeffler's music (a cello concerto) which many people had come to hear.
>
> Think of it!
>
> Beethoven, Mozart, Handel, Dvořák and—Loeffler.
>
> Who is Loeffler?
>
> Echo answered Who, until a tall, blond and embarrassed young man rose from the ranks of the orchestra and timidly bowed his acknowledgement of much applause.
>
> A violinist, then, and, well—decidedly not without talent. He calls it a fantastic concerto, this cello composition of his. A good title, too, because it is in a sense rather formless. But there is music in what he says, particularly in the first half—the cadenza later on is really hideous—and the young man is uncannily precocious in his knowledge of orchestration. Loeffler sounded decidedly more imposing after Mr. Schroeder had spoken for him than it did before the concert.[38]

Later that same month (18 February) Loeffler's Quintet in One Movement for Three Violins, Viola, and Violoncello was performed by the Kneisel Quartette, assisted by William Kraft. Clearly textured, regularly phrased, and tonally conservative, styled similarly to his works from the previous decade, the quintet is music of brightness and charm, as indicated by the original title, *Spring Music*. Loeffler described the form of the piece to Richard Aldrich: "The Quintette is in one movement Allegro commodo . . . with a first and second theme which leads up to a slavonic episode Allegretto 3/4 (I herein used a motiv belonging to a russian folksong suggested to me by friend Krehbiel) through an Allegro I then drift back to the first theme (Allegro commodo)—2d theme coda—finis."[39]

Little controversy attended the performance. The critic of the *Daily Advertiser,* perhaps reacting to the *Divertissement,* claimed that Loeffler was "at his best in chamber music." The critic of the *Transcript* declared, "it was perhaps the most exquisite piece of string-writing, as such, that we had ever heard." Still, at least one critic found this an occasion to lament that "Mr. Loeffler has a poetic imagination and rare ingenuity in discovering novel instrumental effects, but he has a horror of form and rules generally. He is a worker in dainty mosaics, although he has nothing to tell; he uses the little fragments of glass for their color, and the finished work is color without form, beautiful in effect, charming in harmonies and in contrasts, but with a great deal that must be taken for granted." However, he admitted, "Mr. Loeffler's quintet is charming; it is unlike everything but the other compositions of Mr. Loeffler."[40]

In 1920 Loeffler's music still encountered some of the same criticism—color but no form or body. Paul Rosenfeld wrote:

> For Loeffler is one of those exquisites whose refinement is unfortunately accompanied by sterility, perhaps even results from it. . . . One finds in him almost typically the sensibility to the essences and colors rather more than to the spectacle, the movement, the adventure of things. . . . The gems and gold thread and filigree with which this work is sewn tarnish in the gloom. Something is there, we perceive, something that moves and sways and rises and ebbs fitfully in the dim light. But it is a wraithlike thing, and undulates and falls before our eyes like flames that have neither redness nor heat. . . . All his energy, one senses, has gone into the cutting and polishing and shining up and setting of little brightly colored bits of music, little sharp, intense moments. . . . But though in result of all the chasing and hammering on gold, the filing and polishing, the vessel of his art has perhaps become richer and finer, it has not become any fuller.[41]

On the other hand, David Ewen, also using the jewel image, held that "exquisitely refined and rarified though it is, this music has a very definite muscle and sinew, a perceptible spine, a solidity and depth. . . . His music is very much like a precious gem that has found a setting of equal perfection."[42]

However the critics reacted to Loeffler's music, they generally did agree that Loeffler was original. "He reminds you of no one but Loeffler," wrote Hale.[43] And each new composition by Loeffler was recognized as an individual creation. Thus, critics who did not care for one composition might hear another Loeffler work with which they were thoroughly enchanted.

Yet the 1890s were a decade in which Loeffler established a reputation as a composer of a particular type of music—that based on morbid, dark, and brooding subjects. It was a decade when his enduring private melancholy found frequent expression in his music. A motto for this time could be said to have been the *Dies irae* from the Requiem Mass. It ran almost like a motif through many compositions of these years, including the third movement of his *Divertissement,* several viola songs, and later the *Rapsodies* and *L'archet.* It appeared also on a portrait of Loeffler painted in 1896 by Loeffler's friend Léon Pourtau, a clarinettist in the BSO. Pourtau depicted Loeffler's head in a monk's cowl and painted the incipit of the *Dies irae* at the bottom. It was appropriate; it suited Loeffler's temperament.

Many found these *Dies irae* compositions beautiful and moving. Gilman wrote: "Even when Loeffler is most eloquently sinister, most disquietingly baleful, a rare tact, an unerring sense of measure and balance, a prophylactic humor, save him from extravagance and turgidity. . . . He is capable of making us dream of black stars, and at times there is gall and wormwood in his music; but there is no decay and no squalor in it. With all his passion for the bizarre and the umbrageous and the grotesque, we are never in doubt as to the essential dignity, the essential purity and nobility of his spirit."[44] However, several critics heartily disapproved of his penchant for sombre moods and fantastic subjects so frequent in his compositions of the 1890s. In 1902, in fact, a New York critic wrote that "Mr. Loeffler ought to cheer up."[45]

It would be several years before Loeffler would "cheer up" in his music. The 1890s were a time when his melancholy was renewed by further family loss. In February 1895 Raphael Löffler, then fifteen, contracted typhoid fever and died. It was a great blow to Martin, who had barely begun to know his brother the summer before and had been planning to bring him to America. Loeffler was also concerned about his mother and sister. Not only grief stricken, they were soon experiencing further troubles. Frau Löffler and Helene had been living in Marseilles, where Helene had been harpist of the Concerts Classiques. Because of some problem with a M. Lecoq, Helene left the orchestra and returned to Paris with her mother. She had difficulty finding work and during the winter of 1895–96 suffered from articular rheumatism and later from an infected finger, which prevented her playing. During this discouraging time for Helene, Martin and Erich sent money for support and medical bills. By April she was playing but declared that it was to Martin especially that they owed the fact that they had been able to live well that year.

During the 1895–96 season Loeffler continued playing with the BSO and assisted the Kneisel Quartette in a performance of Handel's Concerto Grosso for Strings. He did not appear as a soloist, although two more friends from Europe, Halir and Marsick, did, giving Loeffler further opportunity to stay informed on the progress and news of friends from his student years.

Halir returned to Europe not only with news of Loeffler but also with his music. On 23 November 1897 he performed Loeffler's *Divertissement* at a Gürzenich concert in Cologne. "Halir," Engel wrote, "in spite of his technical facility, could not do all the notes that were on paper; the composer himself had tossed them off brilliantly at Boston, in 1895."[46] Later Halir also played the piece in Berlin, Leipzig, and Breslau.

During the 1896–97 season, the BSO itself repeated Loeffler's *Divertissement*. New works were also heard in Boston. For Kneisel's performance of the Brahms concerto on 12 February 1897, Loeffler wrote a cadenza described by C. L. Capen of the *Boston Journal* as "an episode of no inconsiderable charm."[47] Three days later, at Association Hall, the Kneisel Quartette, assisted by Pourtau and three others, premiered Loeffler's new Octette for two clarinets, harp, string quartet, and contrabass.

Although Apthorp in the *Transcript* wrote, "Of Mr. Loeffler's new octet one can hardly say enough. The work took nearly everyone by storm," several other critics, including Hale, expressed disappointment.[48] The criticisms were familiar—vague form and meaning, harsh dissonances, as well as excess complexity. These critics felt that, although the Octette did have moments of beauty, warmth, and color, Loeffler had done better. Loeffler did not have it performed again. Twenty-eight years later he wrote, "The work, belonging to my earliest years, contained very modern symptoms not in use during the XIXth century and which were therefore severely condemned by Ben. Woolf, Howard Ticknor and some other d..f..! of the Press."[49]

One of the more familiar Loefflerian elements in this octet is that found in the third movement, Andante—Allegro alla Zingara. Though not as frequent as his musical references to Russia, memories of the gypsies he had heard in Hungary recur in several early compositions, in two violin compositions, *Airs tziganes* and *Divigations sur des airs tziganes,* and his song *Rêverie en sourdine,* noted as being "a little in the Hungarian manner."

At the end of 1897, four of Loeffler's viola songs (those with texts by Verlaine and Baudelaire) were first performed in public. On 30 November Lena Little, Loeffler, and Mrs. Emil Paur (wife of the BSO conductor) performed *Harmonie du soir, Dansons la gigue!, La cloche fêlée,* and *Sérénade* in recital at Steinert Hall. Lena Little, a member of the Cecilia Society, a Boston recitalist, and a favorite of Gardner's, made a felicitous choice with Loeffler's songs.

"The interest of the evening," wrote the *Transcript* critic, "centered in the four songs by Mr. Loeffler," and they were a success. "In these four songs Mr. Loeffler evinces a quality which, to our mind, is the quality of all others for the song-writer to possess: the power of musical crystallization. Like Handel, he seizes upon one particular word or phrase in his text, and makes this the keynote of the musical character of his song. . . . This is song-writing in its purest estate." Philip Hale declared, with good reason, that "they are not songs. They are musical paraphrases of the poems—pieces for three instruments." The songs might more accurately be called tone poems. Later, W. J. Henderson reported from New York that the songs were "far and away finer than many of those which are sung year in and year out by singers who are wise, perhaps, after all, in their choice. Mr. Loeffler's songs are not for the ordinary salon singer, but for the vocalist who possesses deep musical insight and the art of conveying the inner content of songs to the audience."[50]

All of the viola songs are Symbolist pieces, evocative of atmosphere and mood, each in its own distinctive way. *Harmonie du soir,* for example, is a song of lyrical arpeggiated charm. *La chanson des ingénues* is also graceful, despite its ironical text, but is composed in the form of a canon (the same canon as in the second movement of his quartet). Several songs exhibit Loeffler at his most Decadent (in the macabre sense). The texts contain such images as a soul like a cracked bell, a serenade sung as though from the depths of a grave, and the plaintive visions that begin *Le son du cor:*

> The sound of the horn grieves near the woods
> With a sadness one wants to believe of an orphan
> Coming to die at the foot of the hill
> Amid the breeze straying in short gusts.
>
> The soul of the wolf cries in that voice
> Rising with the sun that sets,
> With an agony one wants to believe caressing
> And that enraptures and rends the heart at the same time.

All the images of these songs found expression in Loeffler's music in moods melancholy, poignant, pungent, and bittersweet and in music much richer and more complex than in his first songs. His instrumental figures and textures are here more widely varied and expressive, his forms freer and more complex, his harmonic writing more advanced, revealing his developing tendency to obscure tonality through the liberal use of chromaticism and more complex chord structures, including the pandiatonic and pentatonic moments that color *The Sound of the Horn.*

Loeffler continued to compose in the same decadent vein in his next orchestral work, *La mort de Tintagiles,* inspired by the marionette drama of the same title written by Maurice Maeterlinck and completed during the summer of 1897. Early in 1895 Loeffler had become acquainted with the play, the story of a young boy, Tintagiles, imprisoned in a gloomy castle and, despite desperate efforts made by his sister Ygraine to save him, killed by his grandmother, a wicked queen. Soon after Loeffler first read the play, his brother Raphael died. The character Tintagiles then became intertwined with Raphael in Loeffler's imagination and inspired the music of the tone poem.

Loeffler did not set the story but rather expressed the moods of the drama.

My music starts in at the opening lines of the play. What, therafter, becomes of the play in my score? I do not know, and I believe it a good thing that I don't. Nobody can read the play without having his soul stirred, a mood created. My music was my mood then; and that is as far as the score is related to the actual events of the play, until towards the end, where the last act made me take up the thread of the drama again, and I endeavored to become dramatic in my expression. The epilogue to it all is not in the book, but in the "scena dolente" of my score beginning thus ["lento molto dolente" theme quoted]. I chose my themes in accordance with the play—in fact, I thought of the Evil Queen as typified by the menacing chief theme of the piece. I thought of the viole d'amour as the only instrument capable of expressing the spirit and mood of the doomed. I meant to have my music pervaded by the sadness and inevitableness of the play—all this is true. But I did not mean to . . . keep step with the scenes, or, still less, with the lines, of the play.[51]

It was generally agreed that Loeffler did indeed capture the mood. "It is the drama of the soul, wherein lurks strange terrifying shapes, monstrous nightmares and sounds heard before dawn. It is all atmosphere, suggestion and shiver." "Mr. Loeffler does not beat about the bush; he plunges bodily into the brambles of the modern path. He begins with a dissonance that makes the first chord of the finale of Beethoven's Ninth Symphony seem sweet by comparison, and, once launched, there are no stopping-places, no cadences of repose—all is restless, agonizes, sorrowing."[52]

Many of the composition's effects were harmonic. Loeffler used progressions that Hale claimed were "sometimes jarring, almost disconcerting, but deliberately contrived, effective, eminently Loefflerian."[53] His harmony, in regard to tonality, was puzzling to some. *Tintagiles,* for example, opens in the key of two sharps, on an E minor seventh chord (which he later revealed to a student was borrowed from a factory whistle[54]) that immediately goes through several inversions and fluctuations between natural and altered forms. Tonally based, Loeffler's harmony yet incorporated an increasing number of devices to obscure the tonal center and allow his harmonies to follow his imagination rather than a conventional pattern or progression. Puzzling or not, as a color element Loeffler's harmony was effective.

The "brilliancy and masterful skill of its orchestration"[55] was a second major factor in the composition's effectiveness. "The odd effects produced upon the cymbals (not unlike Wagner's rattling in the Venus-scene in 'Tannhäuser'), the impressive tolling of midnight upon the harps (Berlioz and St. Saëns may stand sponsors for this), the bold use of bass drum and of percussion generally, the muted horns, the 'ponticello' work of the strings, the short trumpet-blasts, the mournful organ-point against the viols d'amore, these, and a host of other striking touches might be mentioned to prove what a master of scoring we have in Mr. Loeffler."[56] The most arresting orchestral effect was the use of two violas d'amore to represent Tintagiles and Ygraine. Loeffler and Kneisel played the solo parts, using the instrument that Loeffler bought in Paris in 1894 and a second instrument Loeffler secured for the performance from Arthur Hill in London in the fall of 1897.

Many were quite won by the new composition. "But there can be no doubt as to the new and striking revelations which this score makes of his originality of fancy, his mastery of form, his bold, independent, masterful orchestration, his clear perception of the line which bounds the weird from the melodramatic, his distinction of the complex from the obscure, his potential directness of appeal."[57] But this composition was terribly Decadent. Certainly it abounded in color, effect, and beautiful moments, but to some its meaning was vague and comprehension difficult. "The subject of the picture does not come out clearly; it is overly impressionistic." "It leaves you in the dark, all the time."[58]

Some of the bemused were looking for a clear story in Loeffler's tone poem, which, as critic Henry Krehbiel correctly explained in a review of a later performance, was not Loeffler's intent. "Moods, not incidents, though these are not wholly overlooked, are the subjects of Mr. Loeffler's music, which, after a fourth hearing, we are still able and more willing than ever, to characterize as strikingly beautiful music, profoundly beautiful music—music of high imagination, distinguished far beyond the general of modern works." Still, to some, whether the subject be a story or mood, *Tintagiles* was simply thought inappropriate for musical setting. Louis Elson complained, "He has given us a *carnaval des morts*, and has revelled in the verjuice of Verlaine, and now he plunges into the still deeper gloom of Maeterlinck."[59]

Philip Hale defended *Tintagiles*. "It would be easy for such a man [a declaimer of Decadence] to listen to Mr. Loeffler's symphonic poem, call him a decadent, and then betake himself cheerfully to bed, sustained and soothed by the reflection that he had done society a service. Mr. Loeffler, however, is no more to be snuffed out by such orthodox breath than is Verlaine or Maeterlinck. Whether he is or is not a decadent is not the question; the question is this: Is the music good or bad?"[60] Hale thought it was good.

Several other critics who were not sure expressed a desire to hear the piece again, to learn if a second hearing would clarify their understanding of the music. In response, two months later (March 1898) the BSO performed *Tintagiles* again, twice in Boston and once more later in Cambridge. More than one critic agreed that it "brought into a clearer light much that seemed vague and bizarre on the previous occasion."[61] The only persistent criticism was that the two violas d'amore—though in tone suited to their roles—became monotonous. Whether for this reason or another, when Loeffler revised the score a few years later, he deleted one of the solo violas.

The season that saw the premiere of *Tintagiles*, 1897–98, was a busy one for Loeffler as a composer. The viola songs and *Tintagiles* were premiered; the *Divertissement* and *Morceau fantastique* were both repeated by the BSO in Boston and out of town. Then during his summer vacation Loeffler began new works.

The summer of 1898 found Loeffler once again in Medfield. Bad health from overwork had prevented his going abroad. It was fortunate that he did not travel with three other members of the BSO who embarked for Europe on *Le Bourgogne* in early July, because the ship was sunk, causing the deaths of Léon Jacquet (flute), Albert Weiss (oboe), and Léon Pourtau. Loeffler was especially distressed over the death of Pourtau, his friend. Loeffler had been composing a work for him that very summer, as he explained to Gardner:

> I have written at a good many things this summer but have finished so far only three Rapsodies for voice (baryton), Viola, Clarinette, and Piano. The words are by Maurice Rolinat "L'étang," "La cornemuse," "La villanelle du Diable." With dear old Pourtau at the Clarinette there might have shone some beauty out of them but now—I am discouraged. We shall not hear another artist like him in our days. What a catastrophe it all was and what a loss! I was truly fond of him. . . . He was an excellent companion, well read in what is interesting and not so at all in what the average fellow considers one ought to read or have read. A curious coincidence was his great liking for two poésies by Rollinat one "L'étang" the other "La rivière dormante" to the point of knowing them by heart. Hélas—and now—it's where he found his grave.[62]

Loeffler dedicated his *Rapsodies* to Pourtau's memory. Though Loeffler asked Gardner if she would like to hear them, no performance is known. Three years later he revised the works, rescoring the first two for oboe, viola, and piano and the third for orchestra. The texts of the *Rapsodies* were poems by Maurice Rollinat from *Les névroses.* Among the most eerie and sinister of the texts used by Loeffler, the subjects of the poems are an ancient pool full of blind fish, revealed through the noise of consumptive toads, used as a mirror by a spectral moon (an excerpt of which is quoted in chapter 10); the haunting music of a dead bagpipe player; and the devil's nocturnal perambulations.

Further change in BSO personnel occurred in 1898, when Paur resigned and Gericke was contracted to return for a second term as conductor. To celebrate his return, Gardner, a friend of Gericke's, held a party on her birthday in April that included a burlesque orchestra in which Loeffler played autoharp.

Gardner continued to be one of Loeffler's most ardent supporters. In 1899 her efforts in his behalf assumed a new dimension when she endeavored to help him publish his music. Gardner, widowed in 1898, was at the time building Fenway Court to be her home and a museum in Back Bay. In July 1899 she sailed to Europe for additional architectural materials. Before she sailed, Loeffler entrusted to her the score of his *Divertissement* with the request that she show it to two publishers in Paris. The score, however, was not published.

In 1899 other compositions occupied Loeffler's attention. During the summer he revised *Les veillées de l'Ukraine,* three movements of which the BSO performed in November and December 1899. With Kneisel playing the solo part, once again the piece was well received.

Elson considered it "the best of Mr. Loeffler's compositions," and Apthorp wrote, "The thing seems to me a work of genius from beginning to end."[63] The BSO performed the work in Boston, Cambridge, Baltimore, New York, and Philadelphia. Outside Boston, as well as in, the work was, on the whole, judged to be clever, charming, spontaneous, and particularly well orchestrated.

Also during 1899 Loeffler composed another set of songs to texts by another Symbolist poet, Gustave Kahn, from his collection *Les palais nomades,* first published in 1877. Like the poems of Rollinat, they reveal Loeffler's more erudite interest in contemporary French poetry. Kahn would not have been known to Americans of Loeffler's own time, and hardly another American but Loeffler, well versed in French literature, would have attempted to set such obscure poetry, "which, we are told," wrote the critic of the *Boston Transcript,* "very intelligent French people cannot fathom."[64] In 1900 Loeffler, undaunted by the poet's abstruseness, set yet another Kahn text, titling the song *Boléro triste.* With Kahn, as with other Symbolist poets, Loeffler responded not only to the moods but also to the imagery of the poetry, such as that in "Timbres oubliés."

> Forgotten sounds, lost lifeless sounds . . .
> Silvery sounds of distant Thules,
> Violet sounds of consoling voices
> Scattering solemn benedictions,
> Blue sounds of peris in fairy-land,
> Sounds of gold from Mongolian jewelry
> And old gold of ancient nations!

The original four Kahn songs, collectively titled *Quatre mélodies,* were performed at Gardner's summer home, Green Hill, by Julia Heinrich and George Proctor on 10 May 1900. After publication in 1903, they were often performed in recital, frequently in combination with the viola songs. Subsequent reviews thus often refer to both sets of songs. The reviews of Lawrence Gilman are perhaps the most rhapsodic as he sought to describe Loeffler's style. "He is a seeker after the realities of shadowy and dim illusions, a painter of grays and greens and subtle golds. . . . Loeffler is, primarily, a creator of atmosphere, a weaver of evanescent and slender arabesques. His music has the subdued and elusive beauty of antique tapestries. He reminds one, at times, of Brahms in his more ascetic moods; yet, he has a concentrated intensity, a veiled yet stinging poignancy, and sensuousness of mood, quite foreign to the frankly Teutonic temperament of that master."[65]

None of the criticisms or reservations about Decadence in Loeffler's music ever attached to Loeffler himself. In some respects his temperament could be described as Symbolist: he had been disillusioned with the state of society and experienced disaffection with his own culture; he retreated into the arts and nature, turning away from the world of politics and bourgeois utilitarian endeavors; he was acutely sensitive to beauty and to suffering; he became a retiring, very private person; he leaned, as did some others, towards the Catholic faith in seeking spiritual peace and understanding—Loeffler was eminently suited to be a Symbolist.

In outward appearance, however, he was no Decadent. He adopted no extravagances or eccentricities of dress or Bohemian habits; he was always socially correct. He was industrious and of a sober and frugal disposition. There was no question of his moral uprightness. To his audiences he appeared modest and unassuming, and to his social contacts and friends he was charming and delightful company.

What Loeffler had become in outward appearance was French. During the twentieth century he struck people as actually being French by nationality. His music's alliance with the French became well established. His Russianisms decreased, and the Germanic element of his music was all but forgotten.

Loeffler's compositional palette had, nevertheless, many colors. Just as critics became accustomed to Loeffler's mode of composition, a new succession of original compositions emanated from his fertile creative imagination through the next thirty-five years.

10

End of an Era

The turn of the century brought Loeffler to the beginning of his fortieth year. Significant changes would come into his life; however, he began the new century continuing in his routine, established for eighteen years, of playing in the orchestra, teaching, and composing. During the summer of 1900 he returned to Europe.

As in 1894, Loeffler sailed to England in May on the S.S. *Columbia*. "To my great surprise," he wrote to Fay, "the following friends and personages are on the same ship: Ben Davies (singer), an Englishman by the name of Maxwell which I knew in N. York, then Krehbiel and wife, Mme. Nordica, Mme. Sembrich, and then old Doctor Greenough formerly of Charles Street."[1]

Loeffler spent May in England. He admitted that he disliked London more than ever but still found the countryside "adorable." As he traveled to other parts of Europe, he related to Fay that "of the sentiment in Belgium, Germany, and France à propos of England against the Boers you have no idea. To say that all Europe despises the attitude of England is to say nothing."[2]

By chance Loeffler encountered Ysaÿe at a dinner party in London and subsequently met him often. "Tonight I dined with him," he wrote to Fay, "then by appointment we played through my divertimento which he read admirably. This has upset my plans about Sarasate, who everybody tells me is getting old and not enterprising about new pieces. Ysaÿe was very enthusiastic about my piece, and he will play it next season here, Brussels, etc. etc. He played it wonderfully well—the cantilenas were simply heavenly. He is the only fiddler who can sing and has temperament. Then he insisted on my playing my last songs on G. Kahn's (an old friend of his) poetry. He was crazy over them, thought them wonderful."[3] The news about Sarasate combined with Loeffler's renewed delight with Ysaÿe may be the reason that, while the orchestral manuscript of Loeffler's *Une nuit de Mai* bears the phrase "Hommage à Pablo Sarasate," the piano transcription is inscribed "A Eugène Ysaÿe en profonde admiration."

In London Loeffler also met Sargent. "I received from this busy, great artist a line to come to lunch today. I fetched him at his house—then we went out to lunch—from there to his great studio where he paints for the B.P. Library. It was a treat. Conversation: Fauré, Fauré, Fauré! . . . He was kind, charming, and interesting. . . . Tomorrow he fetches me to dinner—then we go to his house to play and sing. . . . He is absolutely now on the top of the ladder—his success at the Roy. Academy Exhibition this year is the talk of the season—day before yesterday he dined with the Prince of Wales."[4] Sargent gave Loeffler a copy of his portrait of Fauré.

On route to Homburg, Loeffler passed three days with the Ysaÿes in Brussels. He found the Ysaÿe home to be superb, "the home of a great artist with much taste. As to his family it would be necessary to invent superlatives in elegies to do them justice."[5]

Loeffler then traveled to Cologne, where he visited the cathedral, then to his mother's and sister's home in Homburg. As Loeffler described it, "Homburg is naturally a very chic watering-place—but happily we are a little off the first street where there are only princes, dukes, lords, etc. etc. and millionaires. But the beautiful forest and the nice villages are only frequented by us three and a few simple people like us. . . . The German court arrived yesterday in the afternoon—the Emperor, Empress, and their children with a lot of grandees from all countries. . . . Consequently the town is decorated from one end to the other."[6] (The Löfflers' former home, Enghien, was also a watering-place. Loeffler described his sister on separate visits as being delicate and from Enghien wrote that she drank the waters.)

Although with his family, Loeffler expressed "the sensation of being expatriated," out of sympathy with "this old hovel of Europe with which I am profoundly broken off."[7] Similarly, about this time, he confessed to Lawrence Gilman to feeling "somewhat of a foreigner" visiting Germany or France.[8]

However, the company of his mother and sister was a joy, and Loeffler wrote with special delight about his sister. "You have no idea how kind and amusing this girl is. She is really droll, with an energy, in a little frail body, that must be called extraordinary. As to her harp playing, she is really one of the most skillful, most artistic whom I have ever heard." Loeffler described their daily life: "A routine has already been established among us. We breakfast at about 8 o'clock and at 9 o'clock my sister begins to practice her harp, and I go to write for several hours in the room that I rented nearby where I have a piano.

. . . Then we lunch, then in the afternoon we go on excursions into the neighboring villages. . . . Then after our return we dine between 7–8 o'clock, then we talk until 10–11 o'clock. The next day repeats. How life is all simplicity and unnaturally happy."[9]

The compositions that Loeffler worked on were revisions to *Tintagiles* and to the second movement of his Sextuor—which he gave the title *Le passeur d'eau*—and a new work, *Divertissement espagnole* for saxophone and orchestra.

Loeffler admired little in Germany beyond the forests and the horses. But for his family Loeffler would not have stayed there. In order to prolong his visit with them, he changed his plans to visit Paris, despite the lure of the Exposition.

Loeffler did return to London. He visited Sargent, Mme. Wieniawski (for whom he played), Percy Pitt (an English conductor), Andreas Dippel (tenor), and Tivador Nachez, whom he described this time as a "mediocre violinist but a good child and friend of my youth." He went with Paur to see Puccini's new opera *La Tosca* and commented, "How horrible the drama is for a musical setting but as orchestration and harmonization it is interesting." With Dippel he attended a vaudeville, *Kitty Grey*, which he deemed "not bad."[10] Loeffler purchased a Vuillaume violin, which he had had on loan throughout this European visit and which Ysaÿe "who is very difficult and skeptical about violins" advised him to buy.[11] He left for America at the end of July and spent the remainder of the summer in Medfield.

The Boston to which Loeffler returned in 1900 wore a different aspect from the city Loeffler had first known. Throughout the late nineteenth century Boston had been gradually expanding westward into the Back Bay, where an increasing number of new cultural buildings were erected. Some, such as the Museum of Natural History and the Massachusetts Institute of Technology in the Copley Square area, were built there as early as the 1860s. The Museum of Fine Arts (built in 1876), Harvard Medical School (1883), and the Boston Public Library (1895) were also built in Copley Square. In the twentieth century construction moved further west, especially along Huntington Avenue. In the first decade of the century the Massachusetts Horticultural Society, the new Chickering Hall, the New England Conservatory, the Boston Opera House, and Symphony Hall rose there. Further west the Gardner Museum and the new Museum of Fine Arts were constructed.

In 1900 the building most eagerly awaited was Symphony Hall. It was built at the corner of Massachusetts Avenue and Huntington Avenue by the firm of McKim, Mead and White, who "spared no pains to make it one of their many masterpieces."[12] The design was based on the Leipzig Gewandhaus and used the researches of a Harvard professor of physics to produce excellent acoustics. In Symphony Hall Loeffler played his last three seasons with the orchestra, appearing as a soloist only in performances of *Tintagiles*. Twentieth-century symphony audiences would know Loeffler more as a composer than as a violinist.

Loeffler wrote also at this time for another Boston orchestra, the Orchestral Club of Boston. This group had been organized in 1884 for the purpose stated in its program: "This Club has been started as a means whereby amateur musicians and professional students may obtain orchestral practice, both ladies and gentlemen being admitted as members, and has been arranged on the plan adopted in the best English amateur orchestras." A large number of the players (for example, seventeen of the first violins) were women. The club's conductors were Bernhard Listemann (1884–87), George W. Chadwick (1888–91), and Georges Longy (1899–1911). During its second period (after a few years of inactivity), under Longy, the orchestra presented a more challenging repertoire, including several first performances of French compositions.

The club had many sponsors, including Belle Gardner, who served as a vice-president during Longy's years. An active member of the club was Mrs. R. J. (Elise Coolidge) Hall. Born in France, married in New York, widowed in California, Hall came as a widow to Boston. As a member of the Orchestral Club she was not only a performer but also committee member, chairman, and eventually (from 1904) president. Her instrument was the saxophone.

Since the saxophone was not a regular orchestra instrument, Hall had to commission many of the pieces she performed with the club. As Carl Engel put it: "If a musicologist of the year 2000 should shake his head in wonder over the remarkable fact that every French composer of note who was living in the first decade of the twentieth century— Debussy, d'Indy not excepted—as well as Martin Loeffler, wrote one composition for the saxophone, let him look to Boston and Mrs. R. J. Hall for the answer."[13] The composers whose works she performed while a member of the club included Longy, d'Indy, Caplet, L. Moreau, and H. Woolett. She commissioned a piece from Debussy but never received it. Loeffler composed his *Divertissement espagnole* for Hall during the summer of 1900. She performed it with the Orchestral Club in January 1901, on the day before Loeffler's fortieth birthday. A second performance occurred in April 1902.

The composition was out of the ordinary both for the orchestral repertoire and for Loeffler. The saxophone was not generally endorsed or used as a symphonic instrument, although Loeffler himself was particularly keen on the instrument and produced, for the time, surprising results. One review read: "Mr. Loeffler shows that he has endowed the orchestra with a really new voice, a new timbre, at once individual and profitable. One would hardly have thought that that chilly, lack-lustre tone could be made to blend so well with the other warmer voices of the woodwinds and horns; but Mr. Loeffler has so exploited it as to show it to be of real value."[14]

The composition differed from Loeffler's other orchestral works in that it was "written in a genial vein," in the style of a Pops piece.[15] Highly colored by a Spanish sound, it is a very episodic piece composed of a succession of sections in differing moods, concluding in march and waltz tempi, loosely bound by irregularly recurring themes. It is very much in the character of an operetta overture. "In feeling and style it is, as usual with the composer, the last word of modernness; but the writing is clear as crystal, and shows throughout a keen sense for musical beauty. The coloring, the orchestration, is simply superb; the whole work sparkles and scintillates, has an enormous dash and go to it, yet with occasional moments of entrancing tenderness and subtle charm."[16] It was undeniably Loefflerian but cut from another cloth than, for example, *Tintagiles*. The audience response was so enthusiastic that the orchestra played the piece twice.

In February the BSO presented, in Boston, Philadelphia, and New York, the revision of *Tintagiles* upon which Loeffler had worked in Homburg. This new score, featuring only one viola d'amore, was reviewed much like the original; to some it was still difficult to comprehend, but to others it was strikingly beautiful. The following month another of Loeffler's compositions featuring the viola d'amore, *L'archet,* was presented in Boston. Probably composed soon after *Tintagiles, L'archet* was scored for soprano solo, women's chorus, viola d'amore, and piano. B. J. Lang conducted the Cecilia Society and soloists Julia Wyman, Loeffler, and Heinrich Gebhard in its first performance on 5 March 1901 at the Searses' home.

The text of *L'archet,* from a poem by Charles Cros, is based on a medieval legend of enchantment. It tells of a troubadour who strung his bow with the hair of his dead beloved and of a queen who, charmed by the music, ran away with him, only to die with him at the next sound of the music. When the Cecilia Society presented *L'archet* in public the next year, the story was called "quaint, sad, strange" and "weird and eerie."[17] Judgments of the music were similar. "It is a curious, weird, remote, perplexing music, yet not altogether gloomy or uncanny, and sometimes purely and sweetly beautiful." "The weird, picturesque spirit of this ballad Mr. Loeffler has retained with wonderful sympathy. . . . It is a question if the music to this ballad can be called beautiful, but in its picturesqueness, its poetical fancy, its vivid illumining of the text, and in its strange emotional power of making one sad, it is not short of great."[18]

L'archet is, to use Gilman's term, one of Loeffler's "antique tapestries," music of an exquisite poignancy and bewitching beauty. As the soprano tells the story, enhanced at the most fateful parts by the chorus (including an ethereal Agnus Dei and tolling amens), the viola d'amore is woven in to represent the troubadour's own instrument, while the piano accompaniment throughout reiterates a motive representing the bow, binding all the pieces together. "This music haunts the memory," wrote Philip Hale, "as a whole how exquisite this ballad is! It is one of the finest, most poetically musical works of a composer who combines the rare fancy of uncommon skill in workmanship and the keenest appreciation of nuances of color."[19]

In 1901 Loeffler revised his vocal rhapsodies, originally written in 1898, into purely instrumental tone poems. Inspired by the artistry of Georges Longy, oboist of the BSO (successor to Weiss, who went down with Pourtau on *Le Bourgogne*), he rescored the first two pieces for oboe, viola, and piano and titled them *Deux Rapsodies*. Their texts were as begloomed with lurking horror as *Tintagiles,* displaying the most deplored aspects of Decadence, as, for example, in the first two stanzas of *L'étang*.

> Full of very old fish struck by blindness,
> The pond, under a low sky rolling with dull thunder,
> Displays between its rushes several hundred years old
> The lapping horror of its opacity.
>
> Over yonder, hobgoblins serve as lights
> To more than one black bog, sinister and dreaded;
> But the pond only reveals itself in this deserted place
> By its hideous noises of consumptive toads.

The poignant and plaintive music of *L'étang* and *La cornemuse,* some of Loeffler's most chromatic and rhythmically complex music, was judged to be beautiful. The *Boston Transcript* declared, "For mere beauty of sound, anything more striking has not been heard here in years; the combination of oboe and viola formed a mass of tone the strange loveliness of which can only be described as haunting." The *Boston Journal* claimed that "no sensitive hearer could have failed to recognize the presence of something rare and wildly beautiful."[20]

The *Rapsodies* were first performed on 16 December 1901 at the first concert of the second season of the Longy Club, a wind instrument ensemble formed by Georges Longy. Longy, Loeffler, and Heinrich Gebhard performed the premiere and thereafter played the *Rapsodies* several times. These two pieces became the favorites of Loeffler's chamber compositions.

In February 1902 a new choral work by Loeffler was premiered, *Psalm 137,* a four-part women's chorus with accompaniment of organ, harp, two flutes, and cello. The first performance took place in the Church of the Messiah as part of the first concert given by the Choral Art Society, directed by Wallace Goodrich. Although set to a sorrowful text ("By the Rivers of Babylon"), the music was thought neither "perplexing" nor "uncanny" as *L'archet* was and is, in fact, exquisitely lush and sensuous.

Another choral composition, a setting of the *Sermon on the Mount,* was probably also written about this same time. It was never performed, may not even have been completed.[21] Like the *Psalm,* it is scored for four-part women's chorus with an unusual accompaniment: two violas d'amore, viola da gamba, harp, and organ. In April a new song by Loeffler, a setting of Baudelaire's "Le flambeau vivant," was first heard, performed by Lena Little. (The music has since been lost.)

With some of these new compositions and with others produced in the first few years of the new century, Loeffler's critics and public began to regard Loeffler anew and to realize how rich his musical palette could be. Although no radical changes, no volte-face occurred, the part of Loeffler's public that had come to expect that the bizarre and macabre were inextricably part of Loeffler's music—despite such compositions as the quartet and quintet, which are devoid of menacing gloom, of weird or unearthly imagery—were to be surprised.

Symphony audiences heard a change in Loeffler's music in April 1902, when the BSO premiered Loeffler's two new symphonic tone poems. Originally paired under the title, *Deux poèmes pour grand orchestre,* they became better known as individual pieces, *La villanelle du Diable* and *La bonne chanson* (later retitled *Poem*). The former was an orchestral revision of the third vocal rhapsody of 1898 and gave audiences, to judge from the reviews, no surprise for its tone or theme. It had a fantastic subject and a grim sort of humor—its two refrains were based on the lines "Hell's a burning, burning, burning" and "The devil is prowling and moving about"—and it was replete with energetic and colorful flights of musical fancy, which Loeffler's audience had come to expect from him.

However, it was *La bonne chanson,* newly composed in 1901, that particularly caught the critics' notice. Loeffler, ever reticent about the evolution of his music, simply remarked in the printed score that "the music was suggested to the composer after reading the fifth poem in Paul Verlaine's *La bonne chanson.*" The music was originally titled after that poem, "Avant que tu ne t'en ailles." The work, as Loeffler wrote to Walter Damrosch, is formed of a theme and variations (free canonic imitation, inversion, return) with diverse lyrical episodes, interruptions suggested by the poem.[22] The majority of critics were delighted with *La bonne chanson* for its happy subject, its charm, and graceful beauty. There was no *Dies irae,* no devil, no Maeterlinckan gloom. The music was not controversial at all; it was "exquisitely lovely . . . beautiful, beautiful indeed."[23]

New compositions continued to flow from Loeffler's imagination. In 1902 he finished two chamber works, *Ballade carnavalesque,* not performed until 1904, and *Poème paien,* which evolved into one of Loeffler's most important and popular works, *A Pagan Poem* for orchestra. Inspired by the Eighth Eclogue of Virgil's *Pharmaceutria* (the Sorceress), Loeffler originally called the composition *Poème antique* but changed it because he said, "I love the word 'pagan' connected with the ancients."[24] (The English title is often used for the work in any form.)

After the orchestral version of the work became popular, Loeffler was often asked about the composition and the program. Revealing details of the compositional process, however, was something Loeffler never did. "When I am ready to write," he explained, "the ideas are likely to be clear in my head. More often than not they come from something that I have read, some impression received, perhaps from a single line. With the exception of the tone-poem 'The Death of Tintagiles,' which was imagined with the drama in mind, my orchestral music is what has been thus wakened in me. For example, 'A Pagan Poem' was the result of the chant of the sorceress as recited in Virgil's Eclogue. From that the rest grew."[25]

Poème paien's most ardent champion was Heinrich Gebhard, one of Boston's leading pianists. A student of Clayton Johns, Gebhard gave his first concert, arranged by Johns and sponsored by Gardner, in April 1896. After study in Vienna, Gebhard returned to Boston in 1899. Johns introduced Gebhard to Gericke, who engaged Gebhard to play with the orchestra in February 1901. He played with the orchestra nearly every year for twenty-five years. Through this association he met Kneisel, Longy, and Loeffler, with whom he became great friends. Gebhard's opinion of Loeffler was succinctly put: "As a man, he was one of the most distinguished persons in this country."[26]

Gebhard was invited to play with the Longy Club and with the Kneisel Quartette. He played the *Deux rapsodies* with Longy and Loeffler several times and often accompanied performances of Loeffler's songs—a special tribute, for Gebhard claimed, "I have never played accompaniments publicly except in my own songs and in Mr. Loeffler's songs. The piano parts of his songs are really beautiful fantasies interwoven with the voice part." Gebhard participated in nearly every performance of *A Pagan Poem* in all its forms and wrote about the history of the composition.

> I had the grand good fortune to watch Mr. Loeffler create this master-piece from its earliest inception to the final completion. He began it in 1902, and it went through two metamorphoses before its final stage. First, it was composed as a chamber music piece for piano, two flutes, oboe, clarinet, two horns, viola, double bass, an important English horn solo (specially for Mr. Longy) and three trumpets obligato behind the scenes. It was fine and we played it, [the piece was announced for the March 1903 concert of Longy Club but was cancelled] but Mr. Loeffler found that as a chamber work it was rather unwieldy, and he rewrote the piece (with some changes) for two pianos and three trumpets behind the stage. Mrs. Jack Gardner engaged George Proctor and myself to play the piano parts and also the three first trumpets of the Boston Symphony Orchestra for the obligato, and in this form we played it in 1903 at Fenway Court.[27]

Fenway Court was Belle Gardner's masterwork. After the size of her art collection had forced the decision to leave Beacon Street, Gardner planned a new home that would also be a museum. She had it built, after her childhood ambition to live in a palace, in the style of an Italian Renaissance palazzo. It was named Fenway Court from its location on Boston's Fenway. The entire building and collection reflected Gardner's own taste and judgement. She had advisors—Bernard Berenson in Europe located many of her treasures—but she supervised the entire operation. She was as careful with her art collection and museum as Loeffler was with his compositions—both had to be exactly right.

Loeffler was one privileged to see the building before its official opening. "That revelation of Dec 25th I shall not forget as long as I can think. I seemed to have dropped out of the clouds when I reached Huntington Avenue," he declared to her.[28]

Fenway Court was indeed fabulous. At its center was an enclosed indoor garden, surrounded by a cloister walk, where flowers bloomed all year long. The rooms opening off the cloister were filled with art and literary treasures of all eras and genres. Along one side was a spacious music room. Gardner's entertainments at her palace were famous for their brilliance and lavishness.

The opening of Fenway Court occurred on 1 January 1903. Gardner invited a company of one hundred and fifty friends. The music was provided by fifty members of the BSO, conducted by Gardner's friend Gericke. The program included music of Bach, Mozart, Chausson, and Schubert. The new music room, almost entirely white, was of simple design and decor but of excellent acoustics. Critic William Apthorp wrote, "Listening to music in such a hall, you feel as if you were inside of some musical instrument, indeed, such a hall is a musical instrument in itself."[29] "How the music did sound," Loeffler himself wrote, "What acoustics!"[30]

For her birthday celebration during the first year in her new home, Gardner planned three successive concerts. The first, on April 13, the day before her birthday, was devoted entirely to Loeffler's music. The program included six songs, sung by Susan Metcalfe, accompanied by Loeffler and B. J. Lang; *L'archet,* performed by the Cecilia Society, Metcalfe, and Loeffler; and *Poème paien.* Gebhard described the rehearsals for the *Poème.*

> Those were the early days of Fenway Court, when the ground floor of this heavenly place was a huge, beautiful music room with high ceiling. The five or six rehearsals for this performance were rare events. They were all in the evening from 8:00 till 11:00 o'clock. Mrs. Gardner, at the height of her powers, was always present, and there were four or five distinguished guests present each time, while Mr. Loeffler presided over the rehearsing. John Singer Sargent was in America at that time, doing a lot of portraits. And Okakura, the great Japanese connoisseur of art, was here supervising the wonderful new Japanese collection in our Art Museum. Sargent and Okakura were with us at these thrilling evenings, and everybody was much excited over the trying out of the trumpets in various parts of the Palace.
>
> The "Pagan Poem" is of about twenty minutes' duration. In the course of this the trumpets are heard at three different intervals; the first two times playing a hauntingly exotic theme from the distance, and the third time triumphant fanfares close by. Trying these wonderful passages with the three trumpeters far behind the stage, also below the stage in the basement, and finally above the beautiful courtyard from the high balcony, made these evenings most exciting. After each rehearsal Mrs. Gardner regaled us with a late supper in the Gothic Room, and how unforgettable this was in these marvelous surroundings, with the brilliant conversation between Sargent, Loeffler, and Okakura, and Mrs. Gardner's great charm of personality, her delicious speaking voice, and her unequalled talent of narrating. The performance before a brilliant audience of high Boston society was a tremendous success."[31]

Poème paien was a sensation. The trumpets were positioned along the balcony at the back of the hall by the windows overlooking the court. The effect was thrilling. Two years later, Gebhard called the performance one of the most wonderful events of his life, indeed one of the most extraordinary musical events of the age.[32]

The following day was Gardner's birthday. Loeffler sent her a viola d'amore for the occasion. Made by Tomaso Eberle of Naples in the eighteenth century, this was the second instrument used in the original performance of *Tintagiles*. Gardner placed it in a glass case in her Yellow Room, where she also hung Sargent's oil portrait of Loeffler, painted during this same time as a gift for Gardner.

For Loeffler himself the occasion of his concert was all the better for the presence of Theodore Thomas, with whom he spent some time after the concert. "Friday last," he wrote to Gardner, "I passed a few happy hours with Mr. Thomas who really must care for my music to be so kind to me."[33] During the 1902–3 season Thomas conducted Loeffler's *La bonne chanson* in Chicago and in January 1904 the *Villanelle*.

The BSO repeated the same tone poems in January 1903. As with every other Loeffler composition, the orchestra also played the works out of town, this time in New York and Philadelphia. A number of reviewers began at this time comparing Loeffler to Richard Strauss, whose music was first performed by the BSO in Boston in 1893. One unique review in New York in fact called Loeffler "the Elgar of Blue Hill, the Richard Strauss of Back Bay."[34] The comparison to Strauss was a particular favorite of Lawrence Gilman's, who consistently preferred Loeffler's music. However, though both composers were modern tone poets, since the two were actually quite different, the comparisons disappeared after a short time.

The 1902–3 season was Loeffler's last as an orchestral musician. Few letters from the last few seasons survive, and no anecdotes about the orchestra occupy their pages. He did mention a few visits with friends—Raoul Pugno, Edward de Coppet (founder of the Flonzaley Quartet)—and a visit to the laboratory of the inventor Nikola Tesla. In Philadelphia he witnessed another accident when a derrick, used to build a fifteen-story building, dropped six tons of iron beams to the street opposite the place where Loeffler stood. "Although the street was full of people and vehicles none of the passers-by was hurt. That's life, isn't it? And it is odd to think that there were a million chances of losing existence at that moment and after all not one life lost. It is for that perhaps that one endures so much."[35]

One of the most significant out-of-town events was his meeting the

Schirmer music publishing family. He met Grace Schirmer first, then her husband, Gustave, who was "definitely going to publish my 4 Kahn romances this winter."[36] Schirmer also decided to publish four of the viola songs, *La mort de Tintagiles, La villanelle du Diable,* and *Deux rapsodies.* Thus encouraged, Loeffler committed himself more fully to a career as a composer.

At the conclusion of the 1902–3 season, Loeffler and Kneisel realized the resolutions they had made in 1890 and, along with the entire Kneisel Quartette, resigned from the orchestra. In May 1903 Loeffler wrote to Gericke about his resignation:

> As you may have learned through Mr. Higginson I have asked him to kindly release me from my position as second concertmaster of the Orchestra—which request he has granted me—
>
> I have taken this step for the following reasons, the first of which is that I find the work now, after playing twenty-one years in the orchestra, too wearing on my nerves. One of the other reasons is, that I need the time for my own work.
>
> I do not wish to leave the orchestra however without telling you that I appreciate very much your having put some of my works on the programs of your Symphony Concerts and that I feel very grateful for the beautiful manner in which they were there played.
>
> Please accept with my thanks, my best wishes and kind regards.[37]

Loeffler resigned but did not divorce himself from the orchestra. Higginson continued to turn to Loeffler for advice and help, and Loeffler continued to conduct business negotiations for him and Charles Ellis, the orchestra's manager, particularly regarding the appointments of conductors and performers. Every year Loeffler had season subscription tickets and attended as often as he could, preferring a seat in the right balcony. Not only did he wish to hear the music but also to see his friends, both members of the orchestra and visiting soloists. Harold Bauer, Fritz Kreisler, and Heinrich Gebhard, in particular, had long associations as soloists with the BSO in the early twentieth century. Busoni also returned to Boston, on which occasion Loeffler presented him with Whistler's book, *The Gentle Art of Making Enemies.*

In January 1904 Loeffler himself returned to the orchestra to play *Tintagiles* in Boston, Cambridge, Baltimore, and New York. The New York concert occasioned the remark by a New York critic who noted that hardly a season went by without a Loeffler composition on the BSO programs, that "there is even a mild Loeffler cult in Boston, the city of cults."[38]

If such a cult existed, one faithful member would have been Gardner. For her and other friends Loeffler continued, after retiring from the orchestra, to play in private. In the spring of 1904, for example, Loeffler played the viola d'amore for a small group at Fenway Court. Gardner suggested that he include *Plaisir d'amour*, a song Loeffler had grown to detest.

> I have just learned that on the 28th there is to be an audience outside of your-honorable-(in the most japanese and respectful sense)-self and Mrs. and Mr. Berensen. Mr. Kneisel cannot be amused by a viola d'amour solo and as a distinguished musician which he is I respect him enough not to spoil his joy of being with you and revelling in the wonders which your genius has chosen and arranged for artists delight. You can easily imagine that I loathe the silly old tune of Plaisir d'amore-more-more-more-than any musician in the world. Particularly since Mr. Sillibert has given it to us on all occasions—which is to say the truth a horse dose. En petite comité I would do it *once more* and then forever swear to never do it again! but before brother musicians: NO![39]

Loeffler did play for Gardner and her guests, probably another program.

Another cult member would have been Georges Longy. Longy was conductor of the Orchestral Club that performed Loeffler's *Divertissement espagnole* and leader of the Longy Club, at whose concert the *Deux rapsodies* had been performed. On 25 January Longy presented Loeffler's *Ballade carnavalesque* (followed by a performance of *Plaisir d'amour*) at a Longy Club concert. This work was scored for flute, oboe, saxophone, bassoon, and piano, the saxophone part again written for Elise Hall, to whom Loeffler dedicated the piece.

This performance of the *Ballade* was the only one that occurred during Loeffler's lifetime. The reviews were disappointing, reminiscent of those of the Octette, which also was never repeated. Beautiful moments were acknowledged, but critics—even Hale—claimed to be mystified by the piece as a whole. Loeffler then withheld the piece, rewriting part of it into his orchestration of *A Pagan Poem,* upon which he worked from 1904 to 1906.

The critical failure of *Ballade carnavalesque* must have been doubly disheartening in that it was the only new Loeffler composition to be given during a year's time following his retirement. Compounding this disappointment were other distressing incidents concerning his compositions. In 1904 he wrote to Gardner:

> I should like to call your attention to the fact that Bostonians on the whole do not care to hear me play or to acknowledge my musicianship. Several have been singularly rude and independent about telling me all

about it. My independence therefore shall be just the same for justice's sake and never on any occasion or under any consideration would I ever play in such individuals presence again. It is only within a month when at one of the musical affairs of Boston, I was cruelly waylaid, foot padded and pommelled by one of Boston's 4000 for having allowed the 2 Piano and 3 Tr. piece to be repeated at your house a year ago. A young lady! Well enough of this—but I also have feelings![40]

Loeffler did indeed have feelings, especially about his music. He hardly had any perception of a "Loeffler cult" in Boston. Despite the support of friends like Gardner, Longy, and Gebhard, he was feeling misplaced and decided to change his surroundings. For the summer he settled in Dover; the winter he meant to spend in Paris. Contemplating his return from Europe, he considered moving to New York, where he had friends, including Kneisel and the Schirmers, who were just beginning to publish Loeffler's music, and consequently wrote to Rudolf Schirmer:

> I am going abroad to spend probably a year in Paris. Though I am very poor I feel that I need this costly change of surroundings for my future work. Boston grates on my nerves and this leads me to ask you the following question: do you think that I could make a fair living in New York without playing in an orchestra? I am through, I hope, with this latter occupation. I should like to teach some, if I could get pupils on the violin and musical composition. I do not ever wish to teach as much as I have heretofore, and get along with a little less money and compose more. . . . I should like New York very much. Could you not by any chance make use of my musical experience or ability in your editorial department. . . ? I am rather practical in technical musical matters.[41]

That a major source of his discontent stemmed from his composing and its reception is revealed in letters to Fay from October 1904. "About my own self I seem to get more and more unsettled. Am I writing musical nonsense or is my stuff the expression of a new personality in music, no matter how small? Some dislike one personally and carry this unfavorable prejudice towards one's work—others again act the reverse."[42]

Two weeks later, Loeffler commented on the importance of his composing and its relation to his personal well-being: "As ever I seem to forget my unfortunate striving for happiness only in composing and writing. Therefore also is my music somewhat melancholy and dreamy. But great art ought not to be so, I believe. Undoubtedly my music has on many a fine soul after a short time a hypnotic influence and power which comes from the essence of my own sad soul, but is that art? Who knows? And I must not think too much about that, for if I lose that interest in my work on account of lack of faith in myself I might just as well cease living."[43]

That his discontent stemmed from old causes as well is also revealed in these letters.

That I am unhappy for more than one reason you can imagine—but have I ever been happy—real happy? No. *That* lies in my temperament and is my curse. It makes my life, but for the spasmodic interest in musical composition, a very aimless one. But neither you nor anybody could change that. *Now* I should like to be with you, dear, in Dover— were I *there* I should wish myself to London or somewhere else. Is this uneasy state of mind a disease of the brain or can it be otherwise psychologically explained. Whatever it is, it would not help much to know its reason. I have always lived somehow rather from day to day like a passing visitor wherever I happened to be. Unhappy childhood is of course one of the prime explanations of such a nature and a man that never loved his father nor his memory has a hole in his soul which nothing can mend later.[44]

The decision to spend a year in Paris postponed further his marriage with Fay. Their engagement had already stretched out to eighteen years. Fay was, understandably, unhappy with his leaving. She referred to this separation as "the most painful and sorrowful period of my life" and wrote: "If only a letter from you would come! I long for it—but do not claim it. I claim *nothing* from you nor of you. You are free, absolutely free and if accidently a word or speech slips from me, which makes you fear I am claiming old rights or counting on old conditions, forgive me dearest Martin. I do not mean it so. Your interests will ever be dear to me and my affection will never change though I may have to conceal it for very fear of making you un-happy."[45]

She often expressed her anxiety at being parted.

My heart is so full it is not safe to let it speak its own say and I don't know how to curb its longing to tell you of the joy and sorrow your two dear notes from New York have brought me. The tears will flow . . . I only meant I appreciate and am overcome by your expressions of affection with which you try to console. . . . You are never out of my thoughts, and I am ever hoping, wishing, praying that you will find peace—peace—which your poor dear soul has not known for many a day—dearest Martin, I grieve for you as well as myself, for I know better than anyone how tender and sensitive is your real nature, the one you keep hidden most of the time.[46]

Loeffler was not insensitive to her feelings: "I know you have been unhappy, but believe me my unhappiness has been great, deep and boundless for more than one reason, too."[47] Fay's fears were not easily stilled, especially the fear that Loeffler would never return. "These are hard days," she wrote, "the long cold silence which *must* last for weeks and *may* last forever. I try to prepare myself for all that is possibly in store for me."[48]

Loeffler, however, declared: "Though I am very, very sad for more than one reason I could not help smiling at your idea of my having gone forever! How do you imagine myself getting along without your devotion, your friendship, your love? Well may you count upon seeing me again with you, dearest. But I was born under an evil star I believe for why should I be the source of so much grief and sorrow to others and last but not least to myself?" It was not Loeffler's intention to break off their relationship. In every letter, as in nearly every letter he had written on any trip, he expressed his love for her. "I think of you always, and I clasp you in my arms with all love and affection of which you are more than worthy. Beloved, you will be happy again."[49]

Loeffler never intended staying in Europe longer than a year. Perhaps he did not expect living in Europe to change anything. But his spirit was troubled enough to drive him into what Walter Damrosch termed a "voluntary exile." In September he sailed for Germany.

11

Europe (1904–1905)

"My plans for the winter," Loeffler revealed to Grace Schirmer, "are to stay in Paris and work and listen, and observe others, many of whom take themselves probably altogether too seriously. My hopes are great to find a good dramatic text for an opera in Paris. For I should like so much to have a work under hand that will take perhaps a year or two (or more) to write—and complete."[1] Loeffler also made the trip to see European conductors about his works and to visit his family.

Loeffler never enjoyed the crossing to Europe. In 1898 he wrote to Gardner. "The sea has a good hater in me. I loathe the sight of it, the smell of it—the sticky feeling of it. No wonder Rubinstein could get up nothing better than this cod livery emulsion called 'Ocean Symphony.'"[2] He made this journey on the *Kaiser Wilhelm II*. Fellow passengers who became companions for the voyage included Nahan Franko (Sam Franko's brother and a conductor of the Metropolitan Opera House), his wife, and Count Orlowski, "a polish nobleman who married a rich N.Y. woman . . . (I suspect he is a spendthrift)."[3]

After his ship docked in Bremen in mid-September, Loeffler went directly to Homburg, where his mother and sister were living. He found Helene suffering from a poisoned thumb, her entire arm in pain. He sent her to a specialist in Frankfurt who operated on her thumb while Loeffler was in Berlin.

This visit to Berlin was the first in many years, probably the only one made since his student years. He went at his mother's request to meet her relatives, "as," he explained to Fay, revealing perhaps a further consequence of his father's imprisonment, "they are all friendly again with my mother." "My mother's own cousin [elsewhere called 'aunt'], 'Frau Geheime Commerzienräthin' Kahlbaum," Loeffler related, "invited me for a week to Berlin and so here I am. The day before my arrival this lady's own sister had three strokes of apoplexy so there was some little gloom cast into the house. However my hostess, though she is 78 years old and appears 55, is very kind to me. She is enormously rich and you ought to have seen the carriage with footmen she sent me to the station! Her house, a very old one—and right in the business part of the city—stands in the middle of a park of very old trees which lead down to the river Spree. It is all quite splendid."[4]

He met a number of cousins.

This aunt of mine has two sons—one who is professor of chemistry at the Univeristy of Basel (Suisse) and the other one is also Commerzienrath like his father. . . . I was of course presented to all relations possible and had a rather agreeable visit. Of course I had to keep quiet often for some of my cousins like General-lieutenant von Kummer and his sons, all of which are high officers in the army, are patriotic Germans to the core. One of them is leading the war against the Hereros in Africa—another one was attaché to the German embassy until recently in Washington. Samoa is governed by another cousin of mine for the German government. Other relations were the family Coqui—very charming people whose cuisine one cannot possibly ever forget. One son wants to become a conductor and studies music with that aim in view. As he is rich he will probably succeed.—These people all meet in perfect class regularity and to have 35–40 of them sit to dine is customary with them.[5]

In another letter he mentioned other relations.

I visited also my mother's sister [Mrs. Werne King] whom I found in deep mourning—she had lost her only son—a man of my age [a sculptor]. Since the early age of 8 years he had been ill with a disease of the bone of his leg which he inherited from his father. Now at last he has died of it. He was married to an English lady with whom he had two daughters—the eldest who is an angel of beauty—has been ill in bed for the last three years and a half with consumption of the spine—as you can imagine inherited from her father and grandfather. It is one of the saddest families you can imagine. Fortunately they are also quite rich and can take care of this poor girl. There is now still another sister of my mothers alive whom I shall look up later; I begin to fear that there also I shall hear nothing but tales of woe. However I am destined to that now for they are all old people and seem all to be in mourning.[6]

Frau Kahlbaum invited Loeffler to play. "One day I played all my French songs to a little coterie at my aunts. Fortunately she had a magnificent Steinway in her music room. The compagnie was small but very select and intelligent and extremely musical in the very best sense of the word. My music enthoused all present and I was delighted how well they all spoke French and understood at first sight G. Kahn's poetry. All this was a success."[7]

To Gardner he wrote: "I am that much wiser to know that there are even in Berlin some nice, cultivated people. Of interest to you about them would be perhaps to hear that my aunt owns eight of the finest paintings of Adolf Mensell, who is considered very highly everywhere. He is undoubtedly the great German painter. Otherwise I found all these—my mother's people—very musical and to my surprise absolutely versed in modern French poetry and symbolism which made my music to them very pleasurable. After my departure from Berlin, fire destroyed the enormous chemical factories in Adlerhorst near Berlin, which were owned by my cousin and which means millions of marks loss to—the fire insurances."[8]

While in Berlin Loeffler thought also to visit friends. He missed seeing Richard Strauss, Joachim, and Halir but did see Busoni, "who lives right opposite my mother's sister. . . . He was glad to see me and I must say that I was thunderstruck at the magnificent home he has. You never saw handsomer furniture, all old dutch and french pieces, in your life—very fine pictures and a most magnificent library of fine, rare books, mostly first editions."[9]

Busoni was conducting a series of three novelty concerts in Berlin and wished to give *Tintagiles*. But since Loeffler felt that Busoni was "a mediocre conductor," as he confided to Fay, "I have not so far committed myself and am waiting for a chance to get at Nikisch whom I shall see in Paris where he conducts the Colonne concert the 31 Oct. Otherwise I saw Emil Paur who will give some of my music later in Pittsburgh."[10] Mottl also asked for the score of *Tintagiles,* which Loeffler promised to him.

Before returning to Homburg Loeffler revisited one of the many places he had lived as a child—his mother's old country seat (described in chapter 1), where some of the older people remembered his family. "It was all very stirring and I wish you'd been here with me. The trip cost me a couple of dollars but it was worth 100 to me."[11]

Loeffler did not prolong his visit to Berlin. He did not like the city, as he explained to Fay:

Berlin, though it is an enormously big city and rather beautiful in particularily the newer parts, it is nevertheless not a metropolis like London or Paris. It is too new—and what is old is hideous. The great park is wonderfully fine but the German Emperor has spoiled it with poor statues and too many of them. Yes, the Germans are a people of utter lack of taste. Everything here is now this rotten 'Art-nouveau'— their architecture, their ornamentation of all things—house trimmings, jewelry, etc. Their books are vile—their poets very minor—and their music—being the art of sound—is noisy—bigmouthed—conceited—'gueularde.' To be forced to live here would be a sentence of death to me. Their very language is impure—at times incomprehensible on account of coinage of new words to extirpate those of foreign origin or derivation rather. The women are shortwaisted—dressed in frightful taste—the men thinlegged, big stomached cusses.[12]

Loeffler returned to Homburg. Finding Helene still suffering pain in her hand and arm, they both went to Frankfurt several times to visit the doctor.

While in Frankfurt, Loeffler had several interesting musical experiences. He wrote at longest length about his meeting with Ysaÿe, who was in Frankfurt to play with the Opera House orchestra. "The orchestra played," Loeffler reported, "though it is one of the best in Germany, very perfunctorily Beeth. and Weber. I should say the Pops orchestra would have played much, much better. The wind instruments are poor players, and the orchestra plays, like most german musicians, without taste and unrhythmically." The program also included violin concertos by Mozart and Bruch and an overture by Goldmark. "Goldmark, an old man 78 years old, was there—but nobody seemed to pay much attention to him. This overture is his last work and it is pretty bad. It is anemic and trivial not to say banale."[13]

Ysaÿe's playing saved the concert for Loeffler. "I was bored by the antediluvian music, but when Ysaÿe began, I knew it was the playing of the orchestra which made Mozart unpalatable. Ysaÿe played very beautifully—he is the *one* singer left on our instrument." The real fun was his reunion with Ysaÿe. "At the *public rehearsal* here, it is customary to play all the orchestra numbers first and *all* the solo numbers at the end. So after the Bruch Concerto the people began to leave the theatre, when I stept up towards the stage and called Ysaÿe. You never saw anybody so delighted as he was. He jumped off the stage and embraced me before this large audience which laughed loud at this demonstration and his loud, emphatic exclamation: 'Loeffler—Loeffler—!' We then stayed together for the day."[14]

Between rehearsal and concert Loeffler visited "Anton van Rooy the famous Wagner singer. . . . His music room is one of the finest you ever could imagine. He had a number of friends with him (all bachelors) and we all went to the concert together to hear Ysaÿe again."[15]

Ysaÿe persuaded Loeffler to visit him in Brussels for a week. There he was given "their finest guest room where Saint-Saëns, Vincent d'Indy, G. Fauré, Debussy, Ducas as well as myself had often enjoyed Y.'s hospitality."[16]

Loeffler sat in on a rehearsal and attended one program of the Ysaÿe Concerts, a series his host had been directing since 1895. He judged the orchestra to be "quite of the first rank and as always in Belgium are the wind instruments throughout remarkable."[17] Of Ysaÿe the conductor, he wrote, "This man has undoubtedly genius, for though I have always credited him with great gifts and accomplishments, he nevertheless amazed me by his conducting and rehearsing."[18]

The highlight of the program, which included Ysaÿe's own *Poème élégiaque* and music of Schumann and Wagner, was, in Loeffler's opinion, d'Indy's new second symphony. "A more unique, almost entirely original and architecturally interesting and imposing work one cannot easily imagine."[19] To Gardner he commented: "It is a most curious mixture of modernism and classicism. The expression, the harmonic progressions, the themes are tout de qu'il y a de plus moderne [all that which is most modern] and on the other hand is the plan of the work, the architecture, the facture so intellectually classic qu'on n'en revient plus de l'effet extraordinaire que produit en vous cette mixture d'extrèmes [that one is lost in astonishment at the extraordinary effect that this mixture of extremes produces in you]. The orchestration of it is quite marvellous. It was given with enormous verve and temperament by Ysaÿe who really is a genius."[20]

"The great disappointment," he related to Fay, "came through Van Rooy who telegraphed, that he would not be able to come for the concert as he was still in bed. And therewith came so much excitement and worry into my Brussels surroundings, that Ysaÿe became ill and had to go to bed, where he stayed always until rehearsal or concert time. Finally they found a substitute in Felix von Kraus (one of this years Bayreuth festspiel sängers). Though far from being a substitute for Van R. he nevertheless sang at least decently. The concert went well and after it Y. went to bed for another day."

"On that day," Loeffler continued, "I discovered that Mme. Ysaÿe sang and that quite well, and so we spent a whole afternoon rehearsing my 4 viola songs and in the evening (Y. had invited Van Hout, the famous Belgian Altoist) we performed them—I at the piano with Mme. Y. and Van Hout. We played each song twice to the delight of Y., Chaumont [a student of Ysaÿe], Van Hout, Dern (another pupil of Y.'s) and particularly Théophile Ysaÿe, a pianist of reputation and a composer. They all found my music exceedingly original = sans être tourmentée [without being tormented] = and yet very beautiful. In one word they were all delighted."[21] In return Loeffler was not accorded the pleasure of hearing Ysaÿe play his *Divertissement,* which Ysaÿe had wanted to perform in 1900. Ysaÿe returned the score at this time, claiming that it was too difficult.

Loeffler and Ysaÿe went to Verviers, where Ysaÿe assisted in a concert by Victor Vreuls, a student of d'Indy's, whom Loeffler judged to have "not much talent to my mind, but seems to have a pretty good opinion of himself."[22] At Verviers Loeffler met a number of musicians with whom he and Ysaÿe spent a delightful day sightseeing.

> Next day Y. invited [Albert] Dupuis [composer], Vreuls, [Alfred] Massau [cellist], Lovençon [cellist], [Louis] Kéfer (directeur du conservatoire de Verviers and also chef d'orchestre du Concert), [Jan] Hambourg [violinist] and me for a long drive. We started at 2 P.M. in two hacks and drove two hours distance from Verviers to La Gillette. . . . The weather was midsummer and heavenly—the mist hung over the mountains and the memory of it all is never to be forgotten. In my carriage was Dupuis (a man five foot 6 inches tall of which length most of it is neck and body—his legs are very short and bowed and the man at a distance is a very funny sight), Massau the eternal farceur, Hambourg, et moi. Without ever mentioning Vreuls name, his work was by all of us so destroyed by criticism without even mentioning even one of his works that it was, when I think of it now, a masterful conversation and very funny too. Before we left the inn M. Kéfer, being an elderly man, gave Eugène Y. in the name of Vreuls and Dupuis an étui with cigar and cigarette holder mounted in gold and a golden match box. Y. was much surprised and pleased. (He had given his assistance for nothing.)[23]

Loeffler and Ysaÿe traveled on to Cologne, where they parted, Ysaÿe to go to Berlin to play with Nikisch and Loeffler for Homburg, where he found his sister almost cured. At this time Loeffler managed to see two conductors in Frankfurt, Gustav Kogel and Siegmund von Hausseger. The latter invited Loeffler to a rehearsal, where Loeffler was not impressed. "He is nervous, angular, and does not care whether the brass drowns the melodies or themes by holding fundamental harmonies."[24]

In general, Loeffler was not impressed with the entire state of music in modern Germany. "In Germany everything is so absolutely against my own feeling in regard to *everything* that I see but France before me now. I mean musically. Of course France is really not a musical country—Germany is. In this latter there is music everywhere—but to my taste pretty bad. In France there is comparatively little but somehow it seems more interesting. There is probably no country in the world where there is so much bad music made and played as in Germany. It may of course be my own fault for I have created myself undoubtedly an atmosphere of my own and perhaps the air is a little too rarified to be healthy." Watching Hausseger led him to comment, "All these German musicians are a noisy lot—beginning with R. Strauss, as composer as conductor. Exceptions are Nikisch, Weingartner, Mottl, and Richter, all *not* Germans."[25]

The inclusion of Strauss's name here is surprising, since later (1910) Loeffler spoke of Strauss as "a man of exceptional gifts, though not necessarily the greatest living composer. He has assimilated everything. I think that in 'Salomé' he has even assimilated Debussy, although, of course, he has used Debussy's discoveries in a more direct and even brutal manner. But in 'Elektra' Strauss has become himself—shaken off, at last, all that had been hindering him. I mean the learning accumulated in his student days." In the same year, he also said, "Now some speak against Strauss. I believe this is chiefly because they do not understand the man or his music." At the end of his life, after a performance of *Salomé*, he said, "When I hear such music, I feel as if I knew nothing at all."[26]

While Loeffler was deprecating German music, he was still in his unhappy state. After about a month in Europe he wrote, "You ask me, dearest beloved Elise, if I have found contentment and happiness.—I wish I had but I seem to be incapable of happiness or merriness. As ever I seem to forget my unfortunate striving for happiness only in composing or writing."[27] He would be unlikely to forget his unhappiness in an unforgiven Germany.

Later during this European sojourn (in March) Loeffler visited Vienna and was no more impressed than with Berlin. "What a one horse town Vienna is! I am very much disappointed. Es ist die Stadt der Trottl. [It is the city of idiots.] The theatres are nice as far as the buildings are concerned, but what singing, what acting! The orchestra here seemed better than anything in Germany but it plays a gentle 2d fiddle to our Boston orchestra only."[28]

On the whole, when Loeffler commented on European orchestras and players, he concluded that America, in particular the BSO, had better men. "On this side of the water," he wrote to Gustave Schirmer, "there is only one orchestra of first quality and that is the Conservatoire Orchestra in Paris."[29] In another letter, however, he wrote, "On the whole, I think we play better in Boston on the violin than they do now here in Paris, for out of practice as I am, everybody seems to admire my playing."[30]

He did not comment on specific figures in Vienna. Mahler was then conductor of the court opera. Elsewhere Loeffler indicated that he did not like the music of Mahler. For example, Margaret Chanler (sister of the Boston author F. Marion Crawford), after attending a BSO performance, related: "I told [Loeffler] of my enthusiasm for the Mahler [second] symphony and how I had broken an engagement to hear it a second time. He was surprised, shocked: 'What,' he cried, 'you extraordinary woman, you listened to all that dreadful stuff and went back to hear it over again? It seems hard to believe.'"[31] Elsewhere Loeffler called Mahler's music "pitiable stuff," at the same time recalling "M. Mahler's exquisite outbreak at Mrs. Rudolph Schirmer,"[32] a comment suggesting that Loeffler cared as little for Mahler personally as for his music. (This incident probably occurred in February 1911 when the New York orchestra, then under Mahler's direction, played Loeffler's *Villanelle*.)

At the beginning of November Loeffler returned for another visit with the Ysaÿes at Brussels. He attended a further Ysaÿe Concert, composed entirely of music by Théophile Ysaÿe, with whom Loeffler was greatly charmed. "I found him to be an humble, somewhat timid but poetic soul. He is one of César Franck's pupils and was very intimately connected with Jules Laforgue, the ever lamented French poet who died at the age of 27."[33] Elsewhere he wrote, "Eugène is a genius, a heart as great as Liszt's was . . . a generous friend, camarade and all that, but Théo can be all that and now read at once in 'Les Grotesques' by Théophile Gauthier his essay on 'Théophile' and find out what Théophiles are on the whole!"[34]

Loeffler enjoyed Théophile Ysaÿe's music, especially the symphony, "his masterpiece," which he persuaded Gustave Schirmer to publish.[35] When the symphony did appear, in 1908, it bore a dedication to Loeffler, "which expression of regard," Loeffler wrote to Schirmer, "I value highly."[36] Loeffler's own high regard for Eugène Ysaÿe was manifested with dedications—to *Tintagiles* and *Le son du cor s'afflige vers les bois*, both then in press. A copy of *Une nuit de mai* is also inscribed to Ysaÿe.

One evening Loeffler played his viola d'amore for Ysaÿe, whom he reported as saying, "You have the sound that I myself have, my friend, that Wieniawski had, it is truly beautiful the sound that you draw from your instrument." Despite the mutual admiration and all the good times they had together, the Ysaÿes did not draw Loeffler out of his melancholy state. "Of course I am not an amusing guest to have at any time," he confessed. "I seem to live more and more an inner life which excludes necessarily exuberance of spirit and demonstration in general."[37]

After a ten-day visit, Loeffler and the Ysaÿes all went to Paris, where Loeffler settled for several months. The Théophile Ysaÿes returned to Brussels, and the Eugène Ysaÿes went to America. Loeffler wrote to Gardner to ask her to receive them at Fenway Court, declaring, "Y as a violinist is now simply perfection. Never since Wieniawski has there been so much temperament combined with tenderness, verve, elegance and style in one artist."[38] Gardner did invite the Ysaÿes to lunch; however, Ysaÿe cut short his Boston visit and did not see Fenway Court. Unfortunately his first concert in Boston was not well attended; Fay reported that he "postponed" (canceled) the second and returned early to New York.

Loeffler, at this time, was still in Paris. As in 1900 he was somewhat disappointed. "Paris has changed very much—even the old book stores on the Seine are not what they were. They don't seem to have anything decent."[39] Shortly, however, he reported to Grace Schirmer, "On the whole, Paris is quite the same place it always was, with a few changes perhaps. . . . At the theater one still finds a high standard reigning as far as acting is concerned as well as mis-en-scène." Loeffler attended concerts principally to hear new works, such as Charpentier's *Louise,* which he did not care for (nor for the "odor of gas from a chronically leaking gaspipe which one may justly call le parfum de loge de concierge mal éclairée! [perfume of a badly lit porter's lodge]"[40]), and works by d'Indy, Fauré, and Debussy, which he did like, and to hear fine artists. Most of Loeffler's reports from Paris, however, concern not concerts but the people he met and remet there.

Alone in Paris, Loeffler settled into a pension in the Rue de la Bienfaissance. "To my great dispair I find that I can hear a piano-teacher give lessons in the next house. His piano must be standing right against my wall—so you see that I shan't be happy again."[41] On the contrary, it so happened that Loeffler's next-door pianist was his friend Harold Bauer. Loeffler attended at least one Bauer concert in Paris, given jointly with Pablo Casals and Susan Metcalfe (who married Casals in 1914).

Loeffler fared well in Paris. "At Sylvestre the famous violin makers I am most admired for my playing," Loeffler wrote within two days of arriving in Paris, "which makes me feel as if there were no great violinists left in Paris. It seems all so curious to find people astonished at what I can do." In November Loeffler dined with Sylvestre and his wife. "We talked a lot and parted the best of friends."[42]

Loeffler met several Americans in Paris. "Just imagine that last night at the hotel stepped up to me Hadley, an American composer who won the Paderewski prize (500$). He came over here to study with Vincent d'Indy but very likely he will instead study with me, I shouldn't wonder!"[43] Hadley evidently did not study with Loeffler, but the two did spend some time together.

Among other Americans there was Jack Tilden, to whom Loeffler mentioned, near the end of November, that he was looking for an opera text. Tilden arranged for Loeffler to meet an Englishman named Strong "who knows all Parisian poets, writers and playwrights." Strong took Loeffler to a reception given by Mlle. de Pretz, "the intimate friend of Maeterlinck and Leblanc (his wife) [his mistress]. . . . At Mlle de P. meet all the literary swells of the town." Not all the "swells" were there when Loeffler went, but his hostess was diverting. "She is an enormous woman—speaks English like a native, composes songs (tommy rot of course) and is like all big fat people, amiable. There was not anybody there of importance that evening but I shall go again to her house."[44] Reports of other visits to Mlle. de Pretz are not preserved, though he mentioned elsewhere that she was recommending librettists to him.

That Loeffler did not get a text was not for lack of effort on Strong's part.

> Strong took me to a café where literary notabilities frequent a great deal. We sat down at a table with a certain George de Bruard, journalist and crack swordsman of Paris, founder of a club called "the Mousquetaires"—; with him sat three other men of whom one was the famous Erneste La Jeunesse. This latter chap wrote "L'amusement et l'ennuie de nos contemporaines" a book which created a great deal of comment and sensation a few years ago, but I must describe him to you. Imagine his hair very fussy—parted in the middle and standing off his head on both sides—he wears a brown *plush* hat—under all that a face which protrudes forward mostly at his mouth—he is clean shaved. His eyes are very small besides being kept pretty tightly closed. In his right eye he keeps the smallest monocle you ever saw. He wore an old used up brown jacket, under it a gorgeous Louis XIV westcoat. An enormous pin held his necktie together with the aid of something that looked like a scarf ring. In the button hole of this coat lappelle he wore a piece of jewellry. He had on his westcoat 2 watch chains and then imagine on his dirty hands with which he gesticulates from time to time a good deal rings on every finger way up to the joint. These rings are besides not at all beautiful but very cheap trash—Amethyst, carbuncle and that sort of thing. At first he seemed drunk to me for he seemed to snooze when all at once he broke out with the voice and timbre of voice of a little girl of seven with some extraordinary remark or witticism. This man is considered the wit of Paris and of course he seems very brilliant. The effect this being has on you is indescribable. His mouth pouts so

extraordinarily and then this small childs voice which always begins by saying to Bruard: "Tu parles trop, Bruard, tu m'ennuies" [you talk too much, Bruard, you bore me] in the most peevish manner is enough to make you roll under the table. Of course you do not laugh, because somehow rather you are somewhat awestruck by these people which are all that which they are most convincedly so. Finally we broke up, all of us, and I have been through a new sensation of a kind.[45]

Two years later Loeffler wrote, "During my sojourn in Paris I met frequently La Jeunesse, who was a great friend of Oscar Wilde's during the latter's stay in Paris. To be admired by La Jeunesse for wit, humour, esprit, and genius means indeed a great deal. . . . In a way he is the limit—namely in his bearing, his clothing which practically amounts to a maskerade and his private life, hélas funny though not moral." Loeffler thought his books "very amusing and witty to anybody that is somewhat au courant of French literary life. But often he pokes fun (though good fun) at men, much—very much his superiors."[46]

The search for an opera text continued. "Fantoms of all kinds in the shape of opera texts seem to hover round in the air about me. One I have read—by an American lady. Utter rubbish. Tilden holds before me Vielle-Griffin a French poet. Barrett Wendell [a Harvard professor of English] still another—an American I believe. Mlle de Pretz yet another one. This latter one I may meet next week. If I get a text, I am going to leave Paris at once, for life is dear here and I am too poor to enjoy the opera or theatres."[47] Loeffler did not get his libretto, nor did he leave Paris for another six months, but he did meet other writers. Théophile Ysaÿe had given Loeffler a letter of introduction to Gustave Kahn, though Loeffler's letters do not mention a meeting. He met Stefan Zweig, who, though he did not produce a libretto, made a translation of Rollinat's *La villanelle du Diable* for publication with Loeffler's tone poem.

There were many memorable musical meetings as well as literary ones. "Paris," he wrote to Fay, "is full of cliques like Boston. There are the Debussyists, the Fauréistes and then the Schola-Cantorum d'Indyists. I shall try to get at all of them the little while I am going to be here."[48] In November Loeffler and Hadley visited the Schola Cantorum and met "a man whose music is wonderful"—Vincent d'Indy.[49] He described the meeting to Fay: "The other day I met M V. d'Indy who was very cordial and who wishes me to play at the Schola cantorum some time later—perhaps on the viole d'amour. We talked about a lot of things most of which are not worthwhile putting on paper. . . . To come back to d'Indy. He is 52 years old, very amiable, rather common looking, yet he is bright and witty. You can see that like most teachers of fame he is used to blind admiration. He is apparently fond of teaching and has a talent for it."[50]

In a 1910 interview Loeffler commented further on d'Indy: "A paragraph in D'Indy's course at the Schola Cantorum says 'good counterpoint cannot be written without a pure heart' (and this may well be so). D'Indy is a figure from the fourteenth century. He believes that in art there is a principle higher than what is only beautiful, and he upholds his beliefs with what amounts to fanaticism. He has a prodigious intellect and a consuming passion for knowledge. He learned German that he might read Goethe, as he learned English to know Shakespeare. He looks into you, this Torquemada, with his calm and piercing eyes, and at the end of an hour or less, without your knowledge, knows exactly what you are."[51]

A warm friendship immediately formed between Loeffler and d'Indy, and on several occasions Loeffler was able to observe d'Indy and his followers. "He has grouped about himself a regular clique (tout comme chez nous—Lang) mostly young noblemen with a great deal of interest in music but rather little talent. For instance one of them wrote some mélodies and half a trio—all this is the result of 12 years of work. This is of course not d'Indy's fault. Though he is a great musician I think he is nevertheless of bad influence on the young men for they *all* do the same that he does which is not always good by any means."[52]

Loeffler met d'Indy again at the home of René de Castera, where d'Indy and his student Blanche Selva played. "d'Indy's playing is as I hear not good for his touch is dry and unsympathetic. But he certainly has made *a great musician* out of his pupil Miss Selva. She is now 21 years old, rather short, weighs 200 pounds or over, can walk 20 Engl. miles a day, give lessons on the piano all day, studies all night for herself. She is a giant of physical power. . . . last year she played in Paris in public over 200 new piano pieces, sonatas, trios, etc.! Besides that she played at Schola cantorum concerts all the original piano composition of J. S. Bach. . . . She has the genius and physic for hard work, yet she does not play like a plodder." That evening she played works by d'Indy's pupils "too 'tormenté.'" Loeffler and Selva played together violin sonatas by Franck and Bach, and "we admired each other most sincerely."[53] After returning to America, Loeffler tried to help Selva find playing engagements in the United States, not only because she was gifted but also "because it can only do good all round, to help things getting lifted out of the ruts.

E♭ Concerto	Liszt	Brrrrrr!
Concerto	Henselt	Brrrrrrrr!
Concerto	Grieg	Brrrrrrrrr!"[54]

In early December Loeffler called on Fauré. "I rang the bell and the door was opened by himself. . . . As it was late in the afternoon and rather dark he at first did not recognize me but when he did he was very cordial. We talked a long time together and finally he said he should like to introduce me at Mme la princesse de Polignac, his and Sargent's great friend. There he also expressed the wish of playing his Sonata with me. He gave me a rendezvous at the Madeleine Cathedral to go up to the organ loft last Sunday which invitation I followed and enjoyed. . . . At the organ were also that morning a young lady (now supposed to be F.'s mistress) and André Wormser, the composer of the pantomime 'L'enfant prodigue.'"[55] On several occasions Loeffler called on Fauré, at times taking his own music.

"I have seen G. Fauré a good deal lately," Loeffler wrote to Grace Schirmer, "and still find him charming as a man. He does not compose anything nowadays and I believe he is through with his say! He is an old beau and I fear he still has fair society woman too much on his mind to ever do anything again. Sargent writes me the other day that he hears Fauré is becoming 'gaga' (i.e. old, silly, peevish yet childish!) However I never liked him for what he was going to do but for what he *has* done. His music and personality has been a dear companion to me for many years." Though he feared that Fauré was "played out and written out," he still greatly admired the elder composer. "Fauré," he wrote in 1929, "was perhaps the greatest and most gifted musician since Rameau in France. . . . How gifted, how handsome, how lovable he was!"[56] In America Loeffler negotiated with Schirmers for the publication of Fauré's Quintette, op. 89, published in 1907.

Loeffler formed another friendship, this with Mme. Chausson, widow of the composer, at whose home "meet all the modern, fine musicians."[57] Ysaÿe had introduced them at a restaurant during Loeffler's first evening in Paris and had given Loeffler a letter of introduction to her, including the following paragraph: "You will judge for yourself the musician of taste, the poet, and harmonist that he is; I adore his music for the depth of sincerity and *personality* that are revealed in it; I think that there is in all that he does a *powerful interest* and I do not doubt a second that that will please you."[58]

Loeffler was charmed by Chausson, "the personificated French lady! She is so attractive and when I spoke to her about her unfortunate husband and my admiration for his beautiful works she was visibly touched by my words. She made the most delightful impression on me, though she was very reserved in her bearing."[59] In December, at her invitation, Loeffler called on Chausson. "Her house is quite a small palace for she is a very rich woman. The place is full of livried servants, and you may imagine my surprise and delight when I was introduced into a little den with a big piano in it . . . and in which the walls were covered with the finest paintings by Degas and others equally famous." After some conversation Chausson "made me play some of my songs to her which she liked very much."[60]

Chausson gave a dinner party in Loeffler's honor, to which also came Dukas, Silvio Lazzari, Pierre de Breville, René de Castera, and his artist brother. After dinner Loeffler and Lazzari played the latter's violin sonata.

Lazzari invited Loeffler to lunch with him and Weingartner and included Loeffler in other musical and social activities. After returning to America, Loeffler helped arrange the publication of Lazzari's *Six Mélodies* by Schirmer's.

Loeffler did not write, at this time, any impressions of Dukas. On another occasion (in 1907) he made a reference to an opera of Dukas's as "the chef d'oeuvre de genre ennuyeux [masterpiece of the tedious style]."[61] Loeffler never named Dukas among the composers he admired in Paris.

Loeffler did like de Breville. "In M. de Breville I learned to know a most rare and exquisite man and mind. He is very good looking, has a slight english reserve in his manner, yet a great personal charm. This man is not unknown to my soul from some preexistence I am sure."[62] De Breville, along with Chausson, offered his support to Loeffler to have one of his compositions performed by the Société Nationale. To that end, Loeffler wrote to Schirmer for an advance copy of his *Rapsodies*, then being published.

D'Indy had also been invited to Loeffler's dinner but was conducting his opera, *L'étranger*, in Lyons. For a less reputable reason, as Loeffler explained to Grace Schirmer, Debussy, also invited, did not attend.

He has gone away with some other man's wife, namely a Mme Bardac of great fame in Paris as an intelligent amateur singer. In fact she used to be Fauré's great interpreter and number of other things. Her husband is a kind of Parisian Wertheimer, immensely rich besides being a jew [from whom Loeffler had had an invitation to dine in 1900, declined in favor of staying with his family in Homburg]. During Debussy's escapade Mme Debussy shot herself, but did not succeed in killing herself, for the other day I saw her in the street. She merely perforated her stomach with a bullet—excusez du peu! Debussy who enjoys by the way a very bad reputation, has left her without a penny and she is actually begging for the most necessary things in life at his friends houses doors. She used to be a 'mannequin' at some famous ladies dress-maker when he married her.[63]

Loeffler also wrote to Fay about the affair:

Debussy wanted to get divorced from his wife who did not want to marry him at all in the beginning. She was a poor "ouvrière" and was willing to live with him but for his sake did not want him to marry her. He insisted however and so they married many years ago. They had no children. Debussy is considered here as absolutely devoid of any morals, in fact has the most awful reputation. His best friend, the finest, most celebrated architect in Paris, said to him once "Claude, tu n'as jamais tué?" [Claude, you have never killed?] Debussy had to come back from Nice where he had gone with Mme Bardac by order of police. He found at his house the last letter of his wife before she shot herself and two hundred francs in bills enclosed. He carefully put the bills in his pocket and tore the letter up. Then he had to go to the hospital with the commissionaire de police to see his wife. There he said to his wife: Pourquoi fais-tu tout ce tapage? Tu te passeras de moi—Tu es encore très bien—tu peux vivre avec un autre." [Why do you make all this row? You will do without me. You are still very well—you can live with another.] Though I have no right to throw a stone at this man it made me ill to hear all that.[64]

After visiting his wife, Debussy returned to Mme. Bardac in Nice, thus missing Loeffler's dinner with Mme. Chausson. Though Loeffler may never have met Debussy, the two did correspond. (The Debussy letters are now missing.)

Whatever he thought of Debussy the man, Loeffler loved his music. Walter Damrosch, also in Paris in 1905, recorded some of Loeffler's enthusiasm. "To my surprise and delight I found Loeffler there living in absolute seclusion in a little hotel on the rive gauche. Some mysterious soul trouble had sent him abroad into voluntary exile for the time being. We were together daily and he told me with great excitement of the new opera at the Opéra Comique 'Pelléas and Mélisande' by Debussy. He had already heard it three times, but insisted on accompanying me so that he could enjoy my pleasure in hearing it for the first time."[65] When back in America, Loeffler also went to New York for the American premiere of *Pelléas*.

In 1910 Loeffler spoke at great length (for Loeffler) on Debussy:

Debussy is, or was, a genuine innovator. He expresses himself, it is true, within a small circumference, but in that little kingdom he is supreme. I think that he hears more than any of us in nature. At least he is more conscious of his sensations and more successful in expressing them. I believe that if it were possible to hear the grass growing he would set it to music!

As for his seven-toned scale, he need not harp on that, as he has done to an annoying extent in such of the piano pieces, for instance, as the "Pagodes" and "Les Cloches à travers les Feuilles." Saint-Saëns, Fauré, and others knew all about whole-toned intervals some time before Debussy was famous. Fauré has written some exquisite music to "Pelléas et Mélisande." You would be surprised to see how much of Debussy's partition, extraordinary as it is, could be dispensed with without loss to the drama. Fauré wrote his music for Mrs. Patrick Campbell, and only where music was very essential. On the other hand, you could take bodily many of Debussy's compositions in the smaller forms and you would probably be surprised to find that they would fit in almost anywhere without loss to the coherency and the appropriateness of the beautiful score. "Pelléas"? The reason is that in the first place, Debussy's natural idiom is so well adapted to the text of Maeterlinck. But if for nothing else we should have to thank the composer for preserving intact the atmosphere of the play.

Debussy, from the first, steered for himself. We have in France the opposite wing, the followers of Franck. There is d'Indy. Debussy calls himself a pagan.[66]

Although many who have admired Debussy's music have also liked Ravel's, Loeffler was reported to have "bristled" at Ravel's name.[67] In 1912 he wrote to Grace Schirmer: "Somehow, this man's pretention is to me unbearable. He edits deliberately what is not his. On the very first page [of his ballet] he presents his principal theme, which is Debussy pure and simple. One of the dances later on is a copy of a 'Barentanz' by Bartok, one of the ultramodern, anarchistic, bloody-revolutionists of hungarian musicians. . . . The difference between Debussy and Ravel is that the former has true genius, the latter colossal nerve and pretention. Ravel presupposes, I believe, that nobody knows Debussy's music. As to Claude Debussy, there can be no longer any doubt, he has written himself down to immortality as we human beings understand it."[68] Loeffler's opinion of Ravel must have tempered with time, for in 1925 Loeffler mentioned Ravel as one of the few European composers to whose new music one could look forward with anticipation of pleasure.[69]

Loeffler's dislike of Ravel, as also of Dukas and Mahler and later his mixed feelings toward Koussevitzky, may have been due in part to an antisemitic prejudice, a part of his German culture that unfortunately remained with him after he left his homeland. As with his antipathy toward Germany, his antisemitism did not preclude his admiration and support of individual musicians; however, it was a feeling he never completely overcame.

Loeffler also met the composer Edouard Bron, who inscribed his *Berceuse* for violin and piano to his "excellent ami," "Monsieur Loeffler-Tornov"—the name under which Loeffler had published his own *Berceuse.*

Among performers Loeffler met Pablo Casals, Jacques Thibaud, and probably also Alfred Cortot and renewed his acquaintance with Raoul Pugno. Casals sent Loeffler concert tickets and professed admiration for Loeffler's own music. Years later, while in America, on learning that Loeffler had written a new piece for cello, Casals asked for the first performance rights. He received not only the rights but also the dedication.

Loeffler also admired the playing of Thibaud. Though he did not consider Thibaud a good teacher and noted that "[César] Thomson hated him," Loeffler himself called him "a 'charmeur' as a player."[70] In 1910 Loeffler was reported as regarding Thibaud as "the undoubted successor of Sarasate in elegance, beauty of tone, and possibilities of cantabile playing."[71]

Loeffler intended meeting Henri Casadesus, having heard of his skill at playing the viola d'amore. If not at this time, he did know Casadesus in later years. During this visit he did meet Louis van Waefelghem, cofounder of the Société des Instruments Anciens, who played, composed, and arranged pieces for the viola d'amore. Loeffler owned several of Waefelghem's arrangements (including the *Plaisir d'amour* so admired by Gardner) and at least one original composition, *Soir d'automne,* his copy inscribed by Waefelghem to "mon collègue et cher ami Loeffler."

A former student of Loeffler's, Arthur Hartmann, was also in Europe and also played the viola d'amore. Hartmann was signed to perform *Tintagiles* with Nikisch, who, like Ysaÿe and Mottl, conducted *Tintagiles* in 1906. Although on arriving in Europe Loeffler had said of his music, "I am not over-sanguine about its reception in the old country or rather the old world. It may possibly be a good symptom if it displeases the old foggies?" his efforts were meeting with some success.[72] *Tintagiles* and the *Divertissement* were both performed repeatedly in Europe because of this trip.

At the end of the year, Loeffler returned to his family and spent Christmas with them. The New Year found Loeffler, though still based in Paris, once again traveling about Europe.

Since Loeffler was meeting a number of conductors on his own behalf, it was an admirable opportunity for Higginson to entrust Loeffler with the assignment of interviewing conductors for the position with the BSO, again opening since Gericke was to leave Boston at the end of the 1905–6 season. In February 1905, therefore, Loeffler returned once again to Berlin to interview conductors. Not his official report to Higginson but rather confidential comments in his letters to Fay survive to record his activities and opinions. In Berlin he saw Scharrer of the Philharmonic and Sänger of the National Theatre, whom he thought "secondary" conductors, and Nikisch. About Nikisch he wrote: "I don't think it a good plan to take him back, were he willing to come for I think he is a cad. But there is no danger of his leaving Leipzig for [Nikisch had several conducting positions] and has an income from all this worth of 140,000 marks!" Loeffler also went to Dresden to see Schuch, "though to my mind he is out of the game"[73] and to Munich to see Mottl. He had already met Weingartner and declared, "I cannot like that man. He undoubtedly has great qualities as a conductor but is after all only a sort of travelling conductor virtuoso, like Paderewski."[74]

Loeffler's preference was for Karl Muck. In Berlin he heard Muck conduct *Tristan und Isolde* and a new opera by Leoncavallo. Between concerts, bearing a card of introduction from Busoni, he visited the conductor. To Fay he described both Muck's conducting and the interview.

> I was very much impressed with the Routine and Virtuosity with which he led orchestra and singers through all the difficulties of this marvellous score [*Tristan*]. I should like to caracterize him and his conducting in the following words: great Routine, great virtuosity, good memory, good ear, a lot of go, verve, nerfe, life, yet without fire or much warmth or enthusiasm. A man, I should say, that one might stand a great deal longer without getting tired of or nauseated with than for instance Weingartner. He is however not to be had before 1907. He is interested in all good music and by the way asked me: are you the man that wrote a Divertimento for Violin and orchestra which Halir played with me? When he found I was the man he told me a great many nice things about it. He thought the orchestration so wonderfully fine and "geistreich"! [spirited]. . . . To my mind he would be a very good man for Boston, for whatever he may seem to lack in fire and warmth (in spite of a great deal of nerve and life) may be due to the players of the orchestra in which the wind instruments are mediocre and the violins pupils of Joachim who play without warmth or vibrato, though technically good.[75]

Doubtless Loeffler's official recommendation to Higginson was, in essence, the same. Ellis negotiated with the Kaiser for Muck's engagement beginning in the fall of 1906.

In 1905 another piece of significant business was entrusted to Loeffler, the negotiation of d'Indy's engagement as guest conductor of the BSO. Loeffler arranged a contract that Ellis found "exceedingly clever" and handled all the arrangements.[76] He concluded these negotiations in Medfield, after returning to the United States in the spring.

Loeffler's announcement of his return was the news for which Fay had been fervently waiting. Throughout his European stay she inquired after his happiness and well-being, both hoping for but fearing his finding his happiness in Paris. "Now that you are in Paris," she wrote in November, "the city of your heart's desire, I can think of you as being nearer happiness, perhaps as happy and content as you will ever be, and I hardly believe you can care for or be interested in any news from Charles St."[77]

But Loeffler replied, "How happy I might be in working . . . in Dover next summer. Or don't you want me back there? Also, dearest, is it worth while to make me more unhappy by being cruel to me? Why do you write to me that now that I am in Paris I won't care to hear news from Charles Street! You don't believe that yourself. And how can you say on the last page of your letter 'I don't believe you will read as far as this, but if you do etc.' You make me shed tears when I needed your kindness—for everybody under the sun is worthy of consolation, even I. You know you are in my thoughts always—therefore, pray, go on being kind to me, dearest."[78]

Neither Paris nor the company of his friends had been the antidote to Loeffler's malaise. Though his letters are filled with anecdotes of delightful and amusing times, he wrote that he could never be as merry as his friends. Of an evening with Ysaÿe he wrote: "we passed a jolly evening together—though I enjoyed it I never seem to get into real gaiety—, which is, I fear, a constitutional shortcoming of mine—for the gayer people get the quieter I seem to get. All this is of course regrettable and I fear somewhat maladife. But after all, what is not to be regretted about me? I had no boyhood, no real youth with customary follies—nothing—nothing—. However this is not interesting."[79] Yet Loeffler had made friends in Europe. He had charmed people in Paris and Brussels as he had in Boston. After his return to New England, he was able to maintain many of these friendships, even renewing them when the Europeans visited America.

Loeffler had achieved his purpose of becoming au courant with musical events and people in Paris. In addition, he forged strong ties with French musical life. He continued his efforts to help French music and musicians whenever he could. Immediately upon his return to America, for example, he persuaded the BSO to purchase Chausson's Symphony, op. 10, which they performed the following January. He persuaded Schirmer to publish music of Lazzari, Théophile Ysaÿe, and Fauré, and perhaps others. He recommended Jean Marnold, a music critic and editor who was interested in the American writing market, to Richard Aldrich. Loeffler became something of an ambassador for French music in the United States. In return France accepted, admired, and honored Loeffler. In the year following his return to America, in March 1906, he received the first of his French distinctions—election as an officier of l'Académie des Beaux Arts.

Loeffler also achieved his purpose of interesting European conductors in his music. However, he was not able to produce new compositions. Before leaving for Europe, he had complained to Grace Schirmer that he could not finish his piano piece in Boston because "I never could find time in my lesson giving existence in Boston."[80] In Paris he could not finish it. "Paris is not a place to work in," he explained to Fay, "unless one were to live here always. If one has two, even only minor engagements, one is through with the best part of the day. Then, as I have said before, the houses are so uncomfortable and d...ly cold that one rather goes out than stay in."[81]

For several reasons Loeffler was looking forward to returning to Massachusetts. "In a month or so I shall be back and a great many memories will be shelved away to live upon as a stimulus where they were good and to compare, unfavorably, where they weren't nice. And so I shall enjoy being back with you, dearest Elise, and some few friends and also back again to regular work. I return with new interest to Amerika and with joy and I may write something decent before long for there aren't many more years to do it in. I am also happy at returning in early summer so as to enjoy our New England country with you again."[82] At the end of May, Loeffler sailed for home.

12

Pilgrimage to Peace

The summer of 1905 found Loeffler back in Massachusetts. Since Fay did not want to live in New York, he gave up the idea of moving there, but, though he retained a studio on Charles Street, he lived apart from Boston. He made his home in Medfield, approximately seventeen miles southwest of Boston, where Elise and Temple Fay had purchased a house (the Pfaff Mansion on North Street) in 1905.

Loeffler had not resolved his doubts and anxieties about his composing. "Sometimes I ask myself," he wrote to Grace Schirmer over a year after his return, "what I am writing music for. It certainly is not played much. I am unable to decide on my own behalf whether there is any fine quality in it or not. In questions of art of course the majority is always in the wrong—shall this for the present console me and my courageous publishers? I do not know. To please them and you and a few—very few—other friends has been keeping me marching on, unconscious of the rest."[1]

Some who observed Loeffler commented that he himself was one of the obstacles to the promotion of his own music. Though he did submit his scores to conductors, to some competitions, and to publishers, he did not push it publicly. Lawrence Gilman observed that "his indifference to celebrity, to the promotion of his reputation, was for years almost incredible."[2] Loeffler disliked publicity, so disliked intrusions into his personal life that he even eschewed talking about his music.

On a few occasions Loeffler provided programs for his music but usually did not reveal in-depth information about the creative process of his music. Upon supplying a short program to Oscar Sonneck for inclusion with the printed score of *Poem*, he wrote, "The shorter the notice the better. . . . I have the cook's aversion of having people inspect the kitchen."[3] Elsewhere he said, "If only some of these composers knew better than to talk. Too often when they talk, they talk nonsense and spoil the effect of what they compose."[4]

Yet, by not talking, he appeared indifferent to his own music. Critic Olin Downes declared, with reference to Loeffler, that "if a composer does not go down into the marts of trade, or propagandize shamelessly and persistently for himself, the musical organizations and the public in general remain content with one work or another which has happened to attract popular attention. The rest of the composer's output, unless he has an aggressive publisher to act for him, will in the course of human nature await the discoveries of future years."[5] Shameless and persistent self-propagandizing simply was not in Loeffler's nature. Thus, while Loeffler lamented that only a few evinced interest in his music, simultaneously many wondered at his own indifference.

Still Loeffler continued to compose. Since he had not found an opera libretto, he worked for the next few years mostly on short pieces. For the first time, he turned to English and American poets for texts. Regarding American poets, Loeffler said five years later, "Strange how I have stumbled on texts not American, although Edgar Allan Poe and Walt Whitman have appealed to me very strongly, especially Whitman. . . . It would be difficult to set Whitman to music, his verse is so rugged, and yet, as I said, I am very fond of his writings."[6] Eventually Loeffler did compose some music to Whitman's verses; however, he set Poe first.

During the summer of 1905 Loeffler composed *Four Poems* to texts by Poe, George Cabot Lodge (son of Senator Henry Cabot Lodge), and Dante Gabriel Rossetti. They were first performed by Susan Metcalfe and Heinrich Gebhard in Boston in 1906, and critics were quick to notice in this set the subtle change in temperament noted in the few years before his visit to Paris. Gilman commented, "He has turned from those moods of foreboding and terror that have so often enchained his imagination, to a region of inspiration which has often yielded at once a nobler impulse and a deeper beauty."[7] Though colored by poignancy, nostalgia, and some sadness, the songs were quite outside the realm of the morbid and macabre of the previous decade.

Having just immersed himself in the musical culture of France, Loeffler composed his English songs, unsurprisingly, in a style similar to his French songs. The poetry itself invited this treatment since it was in a vein with Symbolist poetry and Loeffler would ever be attracted to that which was rich in image and exquisite sentiment—the sort of poetry that prompted the phrase, "Ah, Bear in Mind this Garden was Enchanted," to be printed on the cover.

As the century advanced, while Loeffler's music became more

strongly allied with the French style, so did his reputation. An increasing familiarity with French music in America, particularly after the advent of Debussy's music, brought with it a wider recognition of Loeffler's aesthetic alliances—though ironically it may have been familiarity with Loeffler's music that helped prepare many Americans to receive Debussy's music.

In his own time it was recognized that Loeffler was not a follower or imitator (though admittedly an admirer) of Debussy or any other one composer. Engel, for example, wrote that Loeffler "staked his claim in the Klondike of tonal sheen and shimmer long before the great rush for the 'impressionistic' placer began," and Philip Hale wrote that Loeffler "had heard his own scale, shaped his harmonic system, found out his instrumental expression before the talent of Debussy was fully appreciated, even in Paris."[8] But since Loeffler and Debussy did develop along some parallel lines, comparisons between the two were inevitable. Loeffler's greatest admirers, however, staunchly and justifiably defended his individuality. Gilman strongly stated, "Their temperaments and their styles are irreconcilable. It is this elementary and indisputable fact which makes the suggestion of an obligation on Loeffler's part unworthy and inconsiderable."[9]

Loeffler's Frenchness was recognized in his own time as being, in D. G. Mason's terms, "inclusively French."[10] "From his early Parisian years," E. B. Hill elaborated, "one can trace records of the appreciation of Bizet, Lalo, and even Chabrier. The stylistic precision of Lalo, the piquancy of Bizet and the boldness of Chabrier were all productive of reaction. More obvious was the harmonic and melodic subtlety of Fauré, in which modal suggestions are so frequent."[11] Hale posited that if Loeffler were influenced by anyone, it was Chabrier and Fauré. Still, those who recognized influences upon Loeffler's music continued to write of his distinctive individuality.

In late 1905 the French composer with whom Loeffler was most occupied was d'Indy, who arrived in Boston in late November, by the terms of the contract Loeffler arranged, to appear exclusively with the Boston orchestra as its first foreign guest conductor. D'Indy spent three weeks in the United States. On the first and second of December, he conducted the orchestra in Boston and thereafter in New York, Philadelphia, Baltimore, Washington, and Brooklyn.

D'Indy had come to America to conduct French music only and, therefore, did not conduct any of Loeffler's own music, as Loeffler said in explanation, "I belong to the Americans and am perfectly happy and proud of it."[12] In New York, however, d'Indy did get involved with Loeffler's music at a private concert at Arthur Whiting's, documented by D. G. Mason: "One of the most memorable evenings at [Whiting's] studio in East Fortieth Street was that of December 10, 1905, during the first visit of Vincent d'Indy to America, when Loeffler's *Rhapsodies* were played by Whiting, piano, Georges Longy of the Boston Symphony Orchestra, oboe, and the composer, viola, and the French poems on which they were based were read aloud with exquisite expressiveness and distinction by d'Indy. Later Francis Rogers sang Loeffler's four songs with viola obbligato. Present were the Kneisel Quartet, the Flonzaley Quartet with Mr. de Coppet, Walter and Frank Damrosch, Richard Aldrich, Lawrence Gilman and W. J. Henderson, Gustave and Rudolph Schirmer, and a few others. Arthur Whiting played the piano parts magnificently, and was the animating spirit of the whole occasion."[13]

D'Indy played with the Kneisel Quartette his String Quartet in E Minor and Piano Quintet in A and with the Lovejoy Club his Clarinet Trio. In both Boston and New York he met, through Loeffler, many musical figures, such as the Schirmers (with whom, according to Fay, he was not very civil), Walter Damrosch, Heinrich Gebhard, and other interesting people including Isabella Gardner, who herself took d'Indy through Fenway Court. Loeffler later revealed d'Indy's favorite painting there to have been Crivelli's *St. George and the Dragon*. At Harvard University he lectured on César Franck.

Damrosch had wanted to schedule a performance of *La mort de Tintagiles* in December, but Loeffler, busy with d'Indy's visit (and other engagements), settled on dates in January. Therefore, after d'Indy's departure and after the holidays, Loeffler returned to New York "with my anti-diluvian friend viola d'amore" to perform the solo part himself, his only performance with an orchestra other than the BSO.[14] This performance of *Tintagiles* was the first of many performances of Loeffler's music by the New York orchestras, but the last in which Loeffler would ever participate.

In making trips to New York to perform or attend performances of his compositions, Loeffler did not usually go alone. "Entre nous," he wrote to Damrosch, "there is a comical side to my New York visits, for whenever I am going, it seems like Spring to stir up hibernating Boston to do likewise, at least in my immediate circle of friends. I do not take this homage too seriously, as it is mixed up with a large percent of achats [purchases] of latest corsets and frills of various sorts. As I have a sense of humor, I enjoy this once a year or so. . . . As I am writing this, chuckling to myself, you will please not think me sour or ungrateful, for I am really fond of these friends. . . . Having said so much, may I say that Mrs. G, Miss Fay and Mrs. Slater are coming for the concert."[15]

Loeffler's next trip to New York was apparently in February for a Kneisel Quartette concert at which Loeffler, Longy, and Gebhard performed Loeffler's *Rapsodies*. In March, Frank Damrosch included Loeffler's *Psalm* in a concert of the Musical Art Society. In April Loeffler, Longy, and Gebhard played the *Rapsodies* in Boston, both at a Kneisel Quartette concert and at a private recital of his songs, sung by Susan Metcalfe, in the music salon on Commonwealth Avenue of another of Loeffler's patrons and friends, Fanny Mason.

Around this time Halir revived Loeffler's *Divertissement* in Europe, performing it in Leipzig under Muck, in Berlin under Strauss (19 October 1905), and in Breslau and Cologne. In 1906 the European performances of *Tintagiles* took place, and in May of the same year it was also performed in Cincinnati. Of Loeffler's early orchestral works, *Tintagiles* was the most often performed. *Les veillées de l'Ukraine* and the *Divertissement* (except for the European performances) were not performed after 1899. *Morceau fantastique* was performed for the last time in America in Philadelphia in March 1905; Alwin Schroeder performed it one last time in Frankfurt in 1907 under Mengelberg.

The biggest orchestral news in Boston in 1906 was the arrival of the new conductor, Karl Muck. During the spring Boston bid its final farewell to Gericke, who ended his tenure by conducting a benefit concert for the sufferers of the San Francisco earthquake and fire. Muck arrived in the fall, after which Ellis wrote to Loeffler that everyone liked his conducting and, best of all, it suited Mr. Higginson.[16]

Together Muck and Loeffler would score a great triumph with Loeffler's piano and orchestra work; however, it was still not finished at Muck's arrival. During the summer of 1906 Loeffler worked diligently at it and at other works. He finished a choral piece, *For One Who Fell in Battle*, two German songs, *Vereinsamt* and *Der Kehraus*, and two or three songs by Yeats.[17] As Fay wrote to Gardner, "he has not been loafing."[18]

The Irish and German songs reveal that, despite the impression made by the four English songs, Loeffler was still fascinated by the fantastic. The poems by Yeats tell of the *sidhe*, the spirits of ancient Irish legend. "They are poetry of glamorous atmosphere," wrote the critic of the *Transcript* after the songs' 1909 premiere. "They are poetry of spectral voices. . . . They are poetry of dream figures and dream sensations vision made words. They are tinged beside with haunting melancholy, and each poem contains irresistible and long-lingering phrases. Each invites to the subtler speech of tones, and Mr. Loeffler's imagination must always find subtle expressions for the glamorous images it has seen and the phantom voices it has heard."[19] *Vereinsamt* is pure melancholy, and *Der Kehraus,* a story of an unknown, strange guest who appears at a dance and takes hold of the bride, is one of Loeffler's haunting *Dies irae* pieces.

The first new composition to be performed was the eight-part a capella choral setting, *For One Who Fell in Battle,* which Fay claimed was "different from everything before."[20] It was dedicated to Henry Higginson, a former major in the Civil War, "in memory of the comrades who never returned from the war." The poem was written by T. W. Parsons, a local writer, the model for "The Poet" in Longfellow's *Tales of a Wayside Inn.*

After a rehearsal Loeffler was disappointed in the work and wrote to Grace Schirmer: "I will humbly admit, that innovations in writing for concerted voices are practically impossible. I have experimented and—I have lost. The singers sing my intervals out of tune—in spite of good work on their part—and in parts where the voices are amassed, the effort is deplorable."[21] When Wallace Goodrich conducted the premiere in December at Jordan Hall with the Choral Art Society, it was well enough received, though recognized as a complex, involved piece. Loeffler held onto the work but then allowed it to be published in January 1911. Almost immediately he had Schirmer's withdraw the composition and issue a revision, *Ode for One Who Fell in Battle,* first performed in March 1912 by the Cecilia Society.

Though Loeffler felt he had failed with this chorus, he had an undisputed success with the premiere of *A Pagan Poem,* a fantasy scored with obbligato piano, English horn, and three trumpets. A musical impression of a maiden's love song and a sorceress' spell to draw her wandering lover home, the music is motivic, with behind-the-scenes trumpets repeating throughout the refrain of the sorceress until moving onstage for an exultant conclusion.

The BSO performed *A Pagan Poem* first, in October 1907, at Fenway Court, where the chamber version had been done, at Gardner's last elaborate concert before she divided her music room into two more museum rooms, the Spanish Cloister and the Tapestry Room. In November the BSO gave the piece its public premiere in Symphony Hall. Immediately *A Pagan Poem* was critically acclaimed as Loeffler's masterwork to date. It became his most popular orchestral work.

The *Boston Journal* proclaimed, "Of its brilliancy there can be no question. Its mere conception was a brilliant feat of imagination. So, too, was the development of the composer's fantastic ideas." Henry T. Parker of the *Boston Transcript* commented that "hitherto Mr. Loeffler's music has had the voice of a kind of poetic magic. There was a subtle spell in it. The music is poetic still, but now the voice is human and of clear passion. . . . That voice is more potent, that future seems more believable, because in him is a quality that is rare among the tone-poets of our time."[22] Also enthusiastic, Philip Hale of the *Boston Herald* declared, "In general conception, in breadth and stability of structure, in the inherent beauty and poignancy of the melodic thought, in harmonic and contrapuntal euphony, in sonorous symphonic treatment of the theme, in original and highly poetic orchestra expression, in an imaginative flight that rises far above fantasticality, in the fundamental and abiding qualities that turn what would otherwise be temporarily engrossing into that which survives the passing years, the 'Pagan Poem' is not only Mr. Loeffler's masterpiece, it is a work that is remarkable without the limiting thought of period or country." Lawrence Gilman, writing in *Harper's Weekly*, raved, "It contains page after page of extraordinary and overwhelming beauty; and throughout it holds captive the imagination. . . . this work must be ranked deliberately, I am convinced, not only as the most important and noblest of Mr. Loeffler's deliverances, but as the most original, imaginative, and significant piece of orchestral writing that has come out of America."[23]

Heinrich Gebhard was the pianist at the premiere. A more enthusiastic performer of Loeffler's works could not be found. He performed *A Pagan Poem* with various orchestras sixty-six times in twenty years and declared that "each performance was for me a glorious experience."[24] Elsewhere, Gebhard said: "It is to me one of the most wonderful pieces in musical literature. I adore Loeffler and all his writings. The 'Pagan Poem' is so absolutely unique; it is quite unlike anything else I know. The piano in this work is used in an entirely different way. It is almost as though the pianist were rhapsodizing with the orchestra and commenting on the themes given out by the orchestra. It is almost as though I were improvising. The musical form of the composition is utterly different from anything else. My admiration for Loeffler and his compositions is boundless."[25]

With the success of *A Pagan Poem* came also a choice opportunity for self-promotion. Yet Loeffler's reticence ruled over his desire to promote his music. Loeffler was frequently asked to comment on the writing of *A Pagan Poem*, yet said little more than, "There is no special story connected with my writing 'A Pagan Poem.' The text is a masterpiece. I could not possibly say how I got the inspiration. All I know is—it came to me" and continued to say, "I do not care to express myself as to my music, for I write for the joy of writing—there is absolutely no money in composing."[26]

This reticence did not change with time. "Loeffler's modesty as a man," wrote Linton Martin in 1935, "the fact that he never descended to tub-thumping on behalf of his own music, or any form of personal promotion, may account in some measure for the infrequent presentation of his music. This evidently genuine indifference to attention was eloquently exemplified in a chance chat the writer had with Loeffler when his best known and probably greatest work, 'A Pagan Poem,' was played for the first time here at the Philadelphia Orchestra concerts under the direction of Leopold Stokowski on December 5, 1919, a mere matter of eighteen [thirteen] years after it had been written. Asked whether he thought it odd that his work had been ignored or neglected until that time, and invited to discuss his musical philosophy, his achievements and personal predilections, Loeffler physically and figuratively shrugged his shoulders and displayed vastly greater interest in expressing his unbounded enthusiasm for the Philadelphia Orchestra."[27]

Loeffler did allow *A Pagan Poem* to be committed to print, and in 1909 it was published by the firm of G. Schirmer. Gustave Schirmer himself had died in July 1907, before the premiere of the work, but he had known the composition and persuaded Loeffler to publish it before its performance. Loeffler dedicated the score to his memory. The Kneisel Quartette also honored the memory of Gustave Schirmer with a concert in December 1907 at which they revived Loeffler's Quintet, which they had last performed in New York in 1902.

Soon after *A Pagan Poem* achieved such solid success, Loeffler received national honor as a composer. In 1908 Horatio Parker and Arthur Whiting proposed his name for membership in the National Institute of Arts and Letters, declaring on the nominating papers, "Mr. Loeffler is regarded by musicians as a composer having perfect mastery of his technique with large variety of musical substance and admirable refinement of method. He is an outstanding figure among American composers and would add distinction to the membership of the Academy."[28] Loeffler was elected and, in April, accepted membership.

Despite the success of *A Pagan Poem,* Loeffler did not attempt another orchestral composition for many years. Although there were performances of earlier works while Loeffler was composing in other genres, ten years passed before the BSO presented a new Loeffler work.

Not all of Loeffler's time was occupied with composition. In 1906 St. Edwards Church in Medfield gave Loeffler the opportunity to train his own choir in chant practice and performance. Loeffler devoted many afternoons to teaching chants from square notation to his choir of approximately a dozen boys. (Though two girls with deep voices were admitted to the choir, according to one of the singers herself, it was always termed a boys' choir.)

Loeffler had long loved Gregorian Chant. "It is perhaps the purest—certainly the only mystical music we know of," he wrote to Grace Schirmer. "St. Gregory himself (590–604) called it the 'melody of language.' Mozart adored it so that he is known to have said 'I would give all my glory as a composer to have been the composer of a single preface.'" Loeffler had studied treatises on chant practice. Although he believed that "Gregorian Chant ought to have neither organ accompaniment nor harmonies put under it" and did not like any of the existing harmonizations, since "the children are not artists," he wrote a very few, extremely simple organ accompaniments for them.[29]

Loeffler told a Medfield reporter that "with my little choir I can work patiently and accomplish much, and the little fellows do their best to help. They have wonderful voices, and once they get the meaning and the intention of the Gregorian modes, they find it simple and interesting work."[30] Loeffler rehearsed the Latin texts (and meanings) and the music with the boys and performed it at services. "It is of course out of the question for me to change the chants for every Sunday, but when we have learned something new, we give it."[31] The choir completely changed the quality of the music in the church, and Loeffler received the thanks of the archbishop of the diocese.

The choir gave several concerts, usually on programs with Loeffler's students and friends. Loeffler had given his first Grand Sacred Concert at St. Edward's in September 1905 when he, students Nina Fletcher and Gertrude Marshall, and Heinrich Gebhard presented the program, Loeffler performing an unnamed solo for viola d'amore. Apparently the first concert with his boys' choir occurred at Christmas time in 1907. Thereafter, Loeffler's students and his choir gave mixed concerts for several years, at least through 1911. Some of these concerts were supported by his patronesses in Boston who often attended, affording Medfield sudden, brief, but memorable glimpses of Boston's haute monde in their country town.

Loeffler composed a few pieces for the choir. His *Ave Maris Stella* was scored for the choir, solo soprano, strings, piano, and organ. He began but never finished another composition for the choir and baritone, four horns, two or four doublebasses, harp, and organ. The text was from Kahn's *Les palais nomades* and was to have been called *Poème mystique.* In December 1907 Loeffler wrote to Grace Schirmer, "I have written for the children a Christmas Carol on William Morris' 'Christmas Carol' which they sing well."[32] The carol does not survive.

Gardner, always interested in Loeffler's activities, helped as she could with his choir. Upon Loeffler's mentioning that the boys had a baseball team and wanted baseball suits, Gardner, an avid fan of the Boston Red Sox, bought the suits and delighted the boys. She also contributed to the fund for a new church organ and always supported Loeffler's concerts.

In Boston Gardner took up another of Loeffler's ideas, namely, that she invite Damrosch to Fenway Court to give the lecture on *Pelléas et Mélisande* that he had given before the January 1908 New York premiere of the opera. Gardner, who years earlier had been one of a group of Boston ladies to invite Damrosch to present lecture recitals on Wagner's Ring cycle, adopted the idea and relied on Loeffler for help with publicity and other arrangements.

Loeffler's work was again interrupted and his life saddened by a new series of personal trials and griefs, all within a year's time, beginning with the summer of 1908. In July Loeffler lost an old friend when Temple Fay died. He had been ill for some years, which had been a matter of great concern to Elise, for the two had lived together all their lives.

Born in 1845, Temple Fay had entered business early in life. A menu for a dinner in his honor in 1900 pictured a number of scenes from his career: working for John E. Thayer and Bro. 1860–65, wrecked at sea 1865, striking for the Wakefield Ralston Company in 1866, agent for Weld and Company in China. His business had been the East India trade. In the last years of his life he lived with Elise in Medfield. Shortly before his death, Loeffler wrote to Grace Schirmer that he often visited Temple during his illness, for "Mr. Fay likes to have me around him and sometimes at night it quiets him to have me in his room."[33] Temple Fay and Martin Loeffler had long been good friends. When Loeffler applied for citizenship, it was Fay who appeared as his character witness. To him Loeffler dedicated *The Wind among the Reeds* (two of his Yeats songs), which appeared in print five months following Fay's death.

Loeffler then suffered another personal affliction. His eyes gave out, only permitting work for three to four minutes before causing pain in his neck and head. "This falls on me like a curse," he wrote to Grace Schirmer.[34] By the fall, Loeffler's eyes had recovered their strength, and he was able to return to his work.

In another six months, however, his life was once more disrupted by family tragedy. In March 1909 his mother died in Germany. Then, in late March, Erich disappeared from his apartment on Columbus Avenue. A week passed and then another during which Martin and Erich's friends conducted a futile search. In April he was found by a Mrs. McLeod from whom he had taken a room in a lodging house on West Springfield Street under the name of Frederick Jacobs. During the night of April 7, after carefully opening the window in the hall to admit fresh air to the house around his room, he stopped up the cracks in his own room and ran a tube from an open gas jet to his mouth. On account of the smell of the gas, his room was opened, and he was found dead at 4:30 on the morning of April 8.

The newspapers reported that he was said to be despondent over the death of his mother. One reported that he had been fretting over the possibility of his not being able to retain his position in the orchestra, though another reported that "Erich was rated at Symphony Hall as a brilliant musician. He had recently renewed a two years contract with the orchestra."[35]

He left three notes, one for his brother and one for his former landlord, neither of which have survived; the third, addressed to the landlady of the lodging house where he died, was reproduced in the *Boston Globe*: "Dear Mrs. McLeod, I am sorry for the trouble I am about to cause you, but it is not my fault. Whisky is the cause of it all." The additional comment in the *New York Times* that he had vainly kept up a struggle against the liquor habit for a quarter of a century— his entire time in the States—suggests that Erich's unhappiness stemmed from the same source as Martin's, that Martin Loeffler had not been alone in supporting a deep, abiding personal grief.

Little is known of Erich Loeffler. He followed his brother to America in 1883 but did not live with him. He never became an American citizen like Martin; neither did he ever accompany Martin on his visits home to Europe. He played with the BSO until his death, and Philip Hale wrote at that time that he was "a violoncellist of unusual natural ability, of careful, thorough schooling and of long experience. A modest man, singularly distrustful of his own skill, he was content to remain in the background, when he could easily have had a prominent position in the musical life of this city."[36] Erich Loeffler's public playing was almost entirely confined to the orchestra, although he did for a time play with the Listemann Quartet. Unlike Martin, he did not make a career as a soloist or as a recitalist. He did not mingle with Boston society as Martin did. He never married; nothing is known of his personal life. Two curious fragments of simple compositions,

Darkies Patrol and *Coon Jig,* bearing his name, survive among Martin Loeffler's own papers. Loeffler kept none of Erich's other writings, though he saved letters from his other brother Raphael to Erich, as well as Erich's music and his cello. Undoubtedly Martin felt Erich's death keenly, which, coupled with his prevailing reticence about his family, led him to destroy any personal items left by his brother.

Following a service held at Loeffler's residence in Medfield, conducted by the Reverend Spence of the Medfield Unitarian Church and attended by several members of the BSO, Erich was buried in Medfield. In May Martin Loeffler left for Frankfurt to see his sister and stayed in Europe until the fall. Most of that time he spent with Helene; however, he also visited the Benedictine Monastery at Maria Laach for a week's stay at two different times. He first arrived there on 22 May. In the guest book he listed his profession as choir director and gave as the reason for his visit the study of choral practices.

Heinrich Gebhard visited Maria Laach with Loeffler. "When I spent six weeks in Europe with him . . . we lived for a week in a quaint little hotel in Maria Laach (Rhine Province) near the fine old Romanesque Benedictine Monastery, where the monks have preserved Gregorian Chant in its purest form. Through letters of introduction which Mr. Loeffler had, we were most warmly received by the Abbott, and were shown the inside of the monastery, a privilege granted to few outsiders. Every afternoon from 4:00 to 7:00, in the beautiful chapel, we heard wonderful singing of the chants by the monks—an unforgettable experience."[37]

Loeffler was profoundly impressed by the music at the abbey, but of immeasurable importance to him were the talks he had there with the Benedictines. "The talks I have had with two dear friends there have at last put my exasperated soul at peace. But I have yet so much to learn 'de humilitate'! My friends know what had befallen me in these last years and a ray of understanding came to me at the rest and peace after two days stay in the monastery, when I was told by one of my friends there that all in the monastery had prayed for me and those departed ones dear to me. . . . it affected me deeply as being very beautiful."

He shared these sentiments with Grace Schirmer, who had lost her husband two years earlier. "At first the cruel shocks of events seem to awaken one to the realities of life in their horror, until at last there comes a balm in the form of life becoming more spiritual, and we seem surrounded by gentle phantasms, and thoughts come to us that mellow what is still hard in us and our caracter. This ripening is undoubtedly due to the bitter experiences of life, but also to all that, which was noble, elevated and rare in those that have gone from us and the spirit of which now surrounds us and fortifies us as an elixir of a new, more spiritual life."[38] In a letter written years later to Gardner, acknowledging her gift of a book by Thomas à Kempis, Loeffler wrote, "He has initiated me into mysticism and I owe to it beautiful hours of meditation, the acceptance of the inevitable and true hope for a future. . . . An old Benedictine monk gave me—years ago—a little edition of the Original (in Latin)."[39]

Loeffler had finally found peace. His life became visibly more spiritual. He did not, however, formally ally himself with any church. Raised a Protestant, he was sympathetic to Catholicism, but wrote three years later to Grace Schirmer, "I also have found and find peace—but I have to go into retreat and seclusion. In the world I am driven out of churches by priest and minister. . . . Is the mystical side of the church dead?"[40]

Loeffler evidently had grown up with strong religious faith. In 1883 he wrote, "As a child I asked God many times, 'do you love me, dear heavenly father' and I felt his response so sure in my little heart." But at the time of that writing, still filled with hurt and cynicism about life and people following his father's trials, he continued, "and at present? I doubt many things. Like a diamond in its mine we live here below. In vain we pray, ask 'where are we going?' to find the return road, and 'why are we?'" In another letter that same month he wrote, "Often God has become incomprehensible when I look at eternity or the universe with frightened eye: all is chaos, incomprehensible."[41] These doubts troubled him. His visit to Maria Laach was immensely important as a long-sought resolution of his confusion, strengthening his faith and reestablishing peace in his life.

The spiritual change in Loeffler's life was registered both in his letters and his music. The penchant for the macabre and morbid, so frequent in his early writings, disappeared. Loeffler remained a Symbolist, a mystic, a visionary but with a new optimism. The motto of his earlier life, the *Dies irae,* was replaced by *Deo gratias,* which he quoted in compositions (e.g., *Hora mystica* and *Canticum fratris solis*) and copied into Gardner's guest book.

Loeffler was still unable to reunite his family. His attempts to persuade Helene to return to America with him were unsuccessful, as he confided to Gardner: "My sister, who is in delicate health as you may know, will not return to the United States with me. Unfortunately she has no desire to see America and prefers living alone, that is with friends of course, to living with me if it has to be in America."[42] In July Fay sailed to Europe and spent a month with Martin and Helene in Frankfurt. Loeffler followed her home in September. Helene never did come to America, though Loeffler renewed the invitation, and neither did Loeffler return to Europe.

Loeffler's trials were not over. Within the year he was again in physical distress, "in intense pain, suffering from a 'professional neurosis' for which I am under treatment at present. I am practically in a harness, from my hips up to my jawbone—all this to keep two tendons at rest in the back of my neck. If this will not cure my ailment, I shall write an essay on the bankruptcy of science!"[43]

Spiritually, however, Loeffler had indeed come to a turning point. Back in Boston, during the autumn of 1909, Loeffler first met Carl Engel, who (speaking with the editorial "we") described Loeffler as he appeared at this time. The contrast to 1885, when Loeffler's father died, could hardly be more striking.

> We were introduced to Loeffler at the end of a Boston Symphony concert, remembered mainly for the extraordinary gown worn by the soloist, Geraldine Farrar, that fairly shocked the staid Back Bay. Loeffler took us by the arm, and starting right in with a friendly sort of inquisition, walked us down Huntington Avenue to the St. Botolph Club. There we sat down at a table, for ale and cheese, with two other men who were to become staunch friends of ours: Philip Hale and Henry Eichheim (then still a member of the Boston orchestra). The talk, dominated by Hale's incomparable verve and cyclopaedic erudition, merrily swung all the way between the sublime and the ridiculous. It was great fun.
>
> The next time we saw Loeffler was, a few days later, in his studio on the second floor of a row-house on Charles Street. It was the late afternoon. A violin pupil, who eventually became the conductor of a symphony orchestra, had just finished his lesson and was leaving. Loeffler had previously looked over some manuscripts of ours, to French texts, and had asked us to play and sing them for him. We went at it with our heart in our mouth and our fingers in a knot. But Loeffler's evident interest and encouraging comment (likening the songs to Fauré's!) soon eased the tension. When we had done, instead of being dismissed, we were taken to dinner at the Tavern Club. The discovery of a kinship in literary tastes, especially as certain French authors were concerned, quickly established the ground for animated discussion. After dinner he invited us to accompany him to a vaudeville show at Keith's, where his joy over the jokes and antics of the comedians was undisguised. That evening sealed a friendship, the glow of which not even death can cool.[44]

As there were losses, so also were there gains in 1909 and the years to come—peace of spirit, new and great friends, as well as a new venue. By the end of 1910 he had a new home, household, family, and new visions for the future.

13

The Farmer of Medfield

By the end of his life Loeffler had acquired the reputation of a recluse, in large part due to his retreat to the countryside of Massachusetts. Most of his summers and most of his time since retirement from the orchestra had been passed in the country. Finally, about 1909, Loeffler made a permanent home for himself in Medfield, purchasing his own property on South Street. On one of his lots stood an old farmhouse, which he proposed to renovate into his home. The house and grounds, as reported in an article on the renovation in *American Homes and Gardens,* needed major repair.

> It had been unoccupied for many years and through neglect was fast falling into decay, the exterior battered and worn, and the interior uninhabitable; its very forlornness repelling any would-be purchaser, lacking projective imagination.
>
> The large estate on which the cottage stood was so neglected that the grass land was worn out, and intermingled with rank grass were thousands of weeds. The barn, joined to the house by a shed, seemed absolutely past redemption. . . . the once neat paling fence had been torn down so that only a remnant remained, dilapidated and sagging, with posts decayed.
>
> The apple trees still standing, through constant neglect, were the homes of armies of caterpillars and infested by hordes of gypsy moths, trees leafless and sadly in need of pruning they hardly promised to yield to attention.[1]

The architect whom Loeffler asked to do the job of restoration decided that it could not be done; therefore, Loeffler drew up his own plans and himself directed the workmen. The latter he found particularly trying, as he complained to Gardner: "No more building for me! Of all the disgusting disappointments, carpenters are the principle purveyors. They are nothing but wood butchers. If Nature were not so pretty around my house, I think I should sell out today. . . . When building, life passes by quickly as in a series of hideous nightmares."[2]

But the job got done. Gardner, as usual ready to help, offered a selection of wall paper. Loeffler chose an Oriental gold paper for his music room (later simply a living room).

Loeffler designed his home around the original features of the house, the open fireplace, the wide-board floor of the dining room, and the open-beamed ceiling of the living room. He filled the hall and living room with books and portraits of poets, composers, and musicians, and hung several original artworks by Sargent, Bunker, Zorn, Frank Benson, and Dodge McKnight. A copy of Sargent's portrait of Gardner stood on his desk. His favorite poet, Verlaine, was represented by four different etchings (one by Zorn, a gift from Gardner) and a framed autograph letter.

In short time Loeffler expanded his estate when he purchased additional property across South Street where stood another deserted house. This he converted into a music studio. The music room occupied the entire front of the building. Into this room he moved his two grand pianos, violins, violas, violas d'amore, Erich's cello, a guitar, koto, Aeolian harp, as well as many of his photographs and portraits of famous composers and musicians. At either end of the room, on the walls below the high vaulted ceiling, he hung Fay's large models of Oriental junks. Behind the studio he had a room for guests.

Loeffler restored the land as well. He cultivated his fields, planted a myriad of flowers, trained rambler roses over trellises at one end of the house, kept a garden where he produced his own vegetables and small fruit, and revived the orchard. He literally brought the place back to life.

The view from the main house overlooked a tributary of the Charles River and Mount Noon. The presence of the river prompted Gardner to send a further gift, a canoe, to which he responded, "I am very much delighted with this beautiful gift and thank you most sincerely for your great kindness in giving it to me. I dare say, I ought now to learn to swim first before using it? I will however take my chances."[3]

Once the building was finished, Loeffler was quite pleased with his home. He created the setting for the life that suited him best—that of a gentleman farmer. Although he returned frequently to urban settings, he much preferred country life and to be known as "Charles Martin Loeffler, the farmer of Medfield."

Loeffler moved into his new home in November 1910. In December he brought to it, finally, a new wife. On 10 December 1910, at three o'clock, Martin Loeffler and Elise Fay were married at the home of Mr. and Mrs. Frank Webster on Commonwealth Avenue in Boston. Elise was given in marriage by her sister Theresa; Martin was attended by Heinrich Gebhard. They were married by the Reverend Edward Cummings of the Exeter Street Church. Outside of the Webster family and the attendants, there were no guests.

The reasons for Loeffler's extraordinarily long engagement and for his final decision to marry are not known. During the early years, Loeffler was concerned about Fay's wealth and wanted to prove his ability to succeed without marrying for money. There are also indications that Fay had obligations to her brother. That Loeffler's brother never married, nor Helene until late in life, support the supposition that, for the rest, the answer may lie with Loeffler's deep-seated, family-related melancholy, which he was never able to lay to rest until the summer of 1909. In 1900, for example, while in London, he wrote: "To tell you to what degree I miss you and that I love you, I can not. My soul is with you, dear, for, little that you think: forever. And it is what I have best in me to give you. I have, if I may speak so, a reticent heart and a very tender soul—better bringing up or other conditions might have made me more acceptable in every way. Well as you know me, there is a little corner that is not yet to you as to me—it is the state of my soul—but no matter—I love you well, better and more than ever, and I know that knowing that will cause you pleasure."[4]

Very little is now known about Elise Loeffler. She remained offstage with regard to Loeffler's public life and in the background of his social life. Few references to her, beyond Loeffler's own rhapsodic comments from the 1880s, survive. In 1904 he compared her to Théophile Ysaÿe's wife. "She is kindness, goodness herself to Théo and everything that lives and breathes on this planet. To Théo she is what you are to me, an inspired devotion by love with the great difference of Théo's superiority to me as a caracter."[5] Loeffler reported Mrs. Severance as saying in 1924, "I have never known anybody with whom I fell in love at first sight so deeply as with Mrs. Loeffler. Although I only had the pleasure of talking with her for ten-fifteen minutes, her bearing, her lovely speaking voice and the lovely beautiful expression of her face I shall never forget."[6] Elise was apparently an astute business woman and was described as vigorous, self-reliant,[7] and, in late life, as rather strict and formidable.

Elise's devotion to Martin Loeffler was life-long and steadfast. His to her was also. His letters reiterate his love and devotion to her, and to the end he signed himself "your old faithful Martin." Loeffler dedicated three of his compositions to Elise: *Adieu pour jamais, Poem* for orchestra, and *The Passion of Hilarion,* the last worded "to my best friend, my wife."

After the marriage, the Loeffler household consisted of Mr. and

Mrs. Loeffler; Percy Read, described by Gebhard as "the faithful, efficient chauffeur, factotum, and general chore-man";[8] Mary Mc-Nary and Margaret Hastings, their cook and maid.

The Loefflers did not become complete recluses. Loeffler often traveled, especially to Boston to teach, visit, and attend concerts. He attended BSO concerts weekly, preferring the Friday afternoon performances to allow time for the return journey. At home, the Loefflers often received friends, as well as a steady stream of students. However, to a great extent, in Medfield the Loefflers did live a secluded life.

It was never an idle existence. In addition to his musical work, Loeffler had to manage his land. The combined Loeffler-Fay estate, named Meadowmere, extended over about 145 acres. The Loefflers maintained it as a working farm, growing their own fruit, vegetables, and fodder for the livestock, and keeping hens and cows for the household eggs and milk. Loeffler also kept horses, both to work the farm and to ride. His favorite was an English thoroughbred named Ferocious. Loeffler was accounted an excellent horseman and connoisseur of horses. The critic Richard Aldrich, for example, successfully treated a horse after seeking Loeffler's advice. Although Mrs. Loeffler purchased an automobile, Loeffler did not have the interest to learn to drive, preferring a horse-drawn carriage to the "benzene buggy."

Loeffler loved animal life. He always kept dogs about him and enjoyed the wildlife with which he was surrounded. In a later year he expressed his concern for the preservation of wildlife in a letter to a neighbor boy: "Now let me tell you this much, if all men loved animals as much as you and I do, this world would be a better world. Never point a gun at anything alive. In walking through the woods or the meadows I feel very lonely! Every game bird or wild duck has been shot. Deer one never sees nowadays. They have been butchered by human beings so much less beautiful than they were! In this country every wild animal will soon be exterminated. This begins now in Africa even! What hellyens men are! I shall always love you for your tender heart and regard for animal life. In this communion of spirit I remain forever your affectionate friend."[9]

Loeffler sketched a *Girl and Boy Guides Prayer Hymn* with a text beginning: "Hear our humble prayer, O God, for our friends the animals, In Thy Hand is the soul of every living thing, And we bless Thee that Thou carest for the dumb creatures of the Earth. We bless and praise Thee for Thy joy in their beauty and grace and the desire to share Thy love for them all."

He wrote contemptuously to Grace Schirmer of Teddy Roosevelt's reputation as a big game hunter, "shooting down mountain lions . . .

from treetops with bullets that would kill a full grown elephant (not to speak of perhaps fifteen hounds and another half dozen heroes, armed like the hero of San Juan, assistance)."[10]

Frank Benson, landscape and wildlife artist, remarked that Loeffler "had a most sensitive perception of worthwhile things around him, and of the wild things of the country where he lived."[11] Carl Engel discoursed on this aspect of Loeffler's nature at more length.

> We have elsewhere characterized Loeffler as a *seigneur campagnard*; he was that in the fullest meaning of the words. He loved his farm, loved it with a very real sense of proprietorship, and loved it with a mystic veneration of Nature in her eternal round of the seasons. However much he cherished good company, he liked seclusion, he resented intrusion.
>
> We shall never forget a broiling hot day in the summer of 1914 that Loeffler had chosen to make the tour of his extended fields and woodlands, to nail "No trespassing—no shooting" signs to appropriate trees; Loeffler, picturesquely clad in old linen trousers, a silk shirt, and covered with an oddly shaped straw hat that probably had cost a large sum when new, set out with a hammer and a box of nails under his arm. It was our privilege to lug the step-ladder and carry the signs. The journey was long and arduous, the heat unbearable. But Loeffler, undeterred, could think of nothing but the eminently useful occupation of warning away marauders and of protecting such bipeds and quadrupeds as had selected his domain for their abode.
>
> Loeffler was a great fancier of horses. He kept thoroughbreds for many years. He drove and rode them. He cut a handsome figure on his mount. But he could groom a horse as well as any stable-boy, and personally fed and watered the animals many a time. With dogs he had a special way. The two airedales would drop by the hearth with a deep sigh of content when he picked up his fiddle.
>
> Extremely generous and altruistic at heart, Loeffler nevertheless had acquired—by adoption, perhaps—that Puritan belief in the sanctity of possession. To him a trespasser was an outlaw. At one time a band of gypsies had been variously reported as camping and stealing in the vicinity of Medfield. The Loeffler ménage was thrown into violent commotion. Loeffler swore that the first gypsy he encountered on his grounds, would be shot at sight. The gypsophobia had reached its apex, when one still and moonless night Loeffler was awakened by the sound of prancing hoofs, on the tarvia road, that came to a sudden stop in front of his house. He jumped from his bed, gun in hand, leaned out of the open window and shouted into the night at the invisible riders. He bade them give instant response, turn their horses, or be prepared to receive his shot, when—out of the darkness—came a long-drawn, placid "moo-oo-oo": the neighbor's cows had broken loose!

Perhaps it was Loeffler's long communion with Nature that had so extraordinarily sharpened his senses. You might walk with him, and abruptly, in the midst of an intense debate, he would point ahead and whisper: "See that fox?" Before you had a chance to discover the beast it had vanished. Or, passing a pond, Loeffler would stop and hold you back with a quick clasp of your arm: "Watch the turtle raise its head!" You would be vainly searching long after the barely distinguishable dot had disappeared beneath the surface of the water.

One afternoon, gathered round the hospitable dinner table with Loeffler and Mrs. Loeffler, we were startled out of our conversation when Loeffler jumped from his chair and exclaimed: "Listen to the bird, she's in distress—it must be a snake!" Clamorous summons brought in a hurry Mr. Read, the magnificent factotum who still serves the Loeffler household as he has done for over thirty years. The bird in question was agitatedly fluttering before the entrance door, over which thick vines were twisting their shady branches, hiding a nest with young ones. Loeffler looked up—the next moment: "There, Read!"—and faithful Read had seen what his master had spied, but what not one in ten would have so promptly discovered. Mr. Read thrust his hand into the vines, pulled out a long black snake—indistinguishable from the vines except when in motion—and shattered its head on the flag-stones. It was the work of an instant. And when the snake lay dead in the roadway, the mother-bird hopped round it with excited chirps to make sure that the danger had passed; then *she* flew back to comfort her twittering brood. They owed their lives to Loeffler's incredibly sharp perception.

This quickness, this alertness of observation was at the bottom of Loeffler's critical faculty. He had trained himself to see, to hear, to feel just a little faster than anyone else. And having observed, he would compare; and having compared, he would discriminate. And there you have all that mortal man can expect to learn; for in discrimination lies the root of all wisdom.[12]

Country living offered difficulties, of course. For example, in 1920 he wrote to Damrosch: "I have been snowed in and under for over 25 days, cut-off from my village and of course from Boston. Horses cannot get through the snow and train service has stopped. The snow is at the height of the wooden fences in the road. Labor is scarce and so there we are—waiting for a general thaw which will probably carry us away, house and all, with the flood. In drifty places the snow is fifteen feet high. Fortunately we have our farm products and canned goods and on snow shoes I can go to the village for yeast-cakes! All this explains why I could not have score and parts straitened out."[13]

The Medfield community was well aware of Loeffler's presence among them. Since Loeffler enjoyed his privacy, he was not the most visible member of the community, but he could be met at the railroad station, at St. Edward's Church, passing on his hay wagon, riding, or taking a drive in the motorcar. Whether he was seen or not, however, the community was well aware that it had a famous musician in its midst who sometimes brought the cream of Boston society to their town. Reactions to Loeffler personally varied. To some he was aloof and forbidding. Others found him a charming and delightful person, an old-world gentleman. To still others he was a good friend.

For good reason, however, Loeffler acquired a reputation as a recluse. His heart's desire was to compose; for that he required solitude. Fay wrote to Gardner, "He has never had a place so much to his liking to work in—over in the cottage, in his little music room he can work the whole 24 hours undisturbed if he chooses, and no one goes in and out but Mab the puppy."[14] Loeffler alleged to a Medfield reporter that he could do twice as much work in half the time in the country as in the city. "Out here in the country one can play as much as one wants without danger of police interference. Have you ever heard musicians composing? Yes? Then perhaps you can understand why the police interfere."[15] In the country he only had to contend with "the sensation of having squirrels in the attick while trying to compose music."[16]

Composing was not Loeffler's only musical occupation in Medfield. He had his choir and his teaching. Loeffler was one of the most respected and popular teachers of his time. Though until 1920 he continued to see students at his studio on Charles Street, many came to his studio in Medfield. Each summer about a half dozen students would board in Medfield. Others commuted, either by motorcar or by train. For a first visit Loeffler would meet his students at the train station and take them to his studio in his horse-drawn carriage. Subsequently the students would take a cab or walk down South Street to the studio, and the sight of his students, walking from the railroad station to his house, became familiar to Medfield residents. Some students played without piano accompaniment; on other occasions Heinrich Gebhard, who spent every other summer in Medfield, would be there to play.

Loeffler was reputedly not an easy teacher. As reported in a music journal: "He limits his class to those pupils who are equipped for his work. . . . As a teacher he is not yielding. Often severe and sarcastic, especially if a student fails to do his bidding, he is the kindest of men and deeply appreciative of honest, hard work. Toward the gifted he has no leniency, especially if gifts are accompanied by slipshod and variable work. . . . If a principle is not understood, he never allows a student to slight a passage. Everything must be mastered."[17]

A few anecdotes have survived about Loeffler's teaching, one from the same journal: "A very talented pupil came to Mr. Loeffler recently and remarked, after the teacher had illustrated his lesson, 'You seem to be playing more beautifully than ever, Mr. Loeffler.' The teacher smiled and replied, 'I am not playing better than usual. It is you who have gained in discrimination. You are *listening* better every day. This is one of the first steps of culture."

Engel reported another incident: "A young violinist came to Loeffler one day to play for him. Before the visitor had sounded a note, Loeffler asked to see his instrument. He held it in his hands and examined it. Then with an almost contemptuous droop of his lips, he snapped out: 'You have a rotten right arm, or else there wouldn't be that rosin on the finger-board.' The poor fellow was ready to sink into the ground; but before Loeffler was done, he had not only restored the young man's courage, but he sent him away with priceless and infallible advice."[18]

Loeffler was a highly critical teacher. He was fussy about every point; every detail had to be right. He stressed intonation and left interpretation to the student. He could, at time, be caustic in his criticism. He once told a young lady, "You have a vibrato like a dying gander."[19] On the other hand, as Engel related, he could also be kind and generous. Two students may be quoted directly.

Herman Silberman reported that "in 1924 I began studies with Mr. Loeffler, each week taking the train to Medfield, and then a cab to his studio, where we spent the entire afternoon to-gether. He was most kind to me, and very liberal with his time during the three years I studied with him. It was a wonderful experience for me, for, in addition to being a consummate violinist and musician, he was a person of the highest refinement, ideals, and culture. In later years he invited my string quartet to Medfield for coaching, with no charge for his time."[20]

Samuel Gardner wrote: "I did know the great Charles Martin Loeffler. He was my violin teacher for one year, way back when I was nine and one half years old [1900]. I've never forgotten those extraordinary moments. I was living in Providence, R.I. I needed a more advanced teacher than was available in my town. My ambitious father got the name of Loeffler through some Boston Symphony musicians when they used to come to Providence for their concerts. We prevailed on him, or my father did, for an audition. I was immediately accepted. He was so sweet. His price for lessons was $8.00 per. Mother told him of our extreme poverty. He said, Mamma, can you pay $2.00 a lesson, plus the train fare from Providence if $2.00 for two. My folks undertook it. Loeffler gave us back the money for about 40 lessons after the season."[21]

Loeffler was popular among his students. One reported that he was almost a cult with his pupils; it was usually "Loeffler said this" and "Loeffler said that."[22] Walter Damrosch revealed that "several very talented and very pretty girl pupils simply adored him as some of them confessed to me in later years."[23]

Many of Loeffler's students became good orchestral violinists; several, including Silberman, Beale, Del Sordo, Gerardi, were admitted to the BSO. A few, including Nina Fletcher, Gertrude Marshall, and Carmela Ippolito, appeared as soloists with the BSO, and a few had concert careers. Nikolai Sokoloff became an orchestral conductor. Others became teachers themselves.

While still with the BSO, Loeffler had been the teacher of Arthur Hartmann. Hartmann began his career in 1887 as a child prodigy in Philadelphia. He had a successful concert career touring the US, Canada, and Europe and in Paris played in recitals with Debussy. According to Samuel Gardner, when Hartmann debuted in Paris, he angered Loeffler by never mentioning him as his teacher. Evidently the two were reconciled. In Berlin in 1905 Hartmann inscribed a copy of his *Ungarische rhapsodien* "For M. Loeffler with apologies Arthur Hartmann," and Hartmann played the solo part of Loeffler's *Tintagiles* in Europe. In a letter from 1911 Hartmann declared that Loeffler was his only true master.

Two favorite students from the early years of the century were Nina Fletcher and Irma Seydel. Nina Fletcher's name appeared frequently in the Loeffler-Fay correspondence during the time of Loeffler's stay in Paris. She played some recitals with Heinrich Gebhard and in 1909 performed with the BSO.

Irma Seydel was another prodigy, who made her debut at age eleven. Loeffler arranged several recitals for her in Medfield in 1908 and 1909 and in Boston in 1910 and 1911. She received complimentary reviews (in which reference to her training by Loeffler was not omitted). Loeffler was evidently quite proud of her; for her 1911 concert he lent her a Stradivarius. Between 1912 and 1920 she performed seven times with the BSO. She became concertmistress of a Boston women's orchestra conducted by Ethel Leginska and had success as a concert violinist in Europe.

The student to whom Loeffler referred as his "pride and joy" was Gertrude Marshall. It was she to whom he felt he had most fully passed on his art, and it was to her that he referred many prospective students. She became one of Loeffler's best friends during the last two decades of his life.

From among his many women students Loeffler formed, in 1908, the American String Quartette. Marshall was the first violinist and leader of the group. The other members changed over the years: second violin was played by Evelyn Street, Ruth Stickney; viola, by Ethel Bankart, Edith Jewell, Adeline Packard; cello, by Georgie Pray-Lasselle, Susan Lord Brandegee, and Hazel L'Africain Theodorowicz. The quartet rehearsed on Mondays when Marshall would drive the members down to Medfield. Loeffler coached the group and played viola, though he never played in their concerts.

The quartet first performed in Medfield on 18 November 1908, with the assistance of Heinrich Gebhard, who then played with them on other occasions. Their Boston debut occurred on 15 January 1909 in Cheney Hall, and a performance in Steinert Hall followed in March. The quartet was a success. They toured the country—the West in 1912, the South and Texas in 1917—and maintained a successful existence into the 1920s. In February 1917 with Renée Longy (piano) they gave the American premiere of Jean Huré's Piano Quintette.

Loeffler also coached other chamber groups including Silberman's quartet and, at the request of Carl Engel, the National String Quartet. This quartet stayed in Medfield during the summer of 1925 and received Loeffler's help without charge—Loeffler's custom for coaching.

At the same time that Loeffler was promoting the careers of his students, he himself was infrequently to be seen on stage in performance. In February 1909 he performed his *Rapsodies* again with Longy and Gebhard at a Longy Club concert, but after that he rarely played in public.

According to Gebhard, Loeffler did not give up playing in salons until after the World War. He wrote the following referring to 1903–18, but though the two did continue to play together through the war years, the large audiences Gebhard remembered were probably from before 1914.

> During those years there was also a lively interest in music among the wealthy and high society of Boston. . . . Mr. Loeffler and I had 'worked ourselves up' into quite a 'team,' practising sonatas for violin and piano. We had many beautiful engagements, giving sonata-recitals at some of the most fashionable homes in and around Boston. We played for Mr. and Mrs. Montgomery Sears at their grand mansion, corner of Commonwealth Avenue and Arlington Street (now an Officers' Club), for Miss Fanny P. Mason at her lovely residence 211 Commonwealth

Avenue, for Mr. and Mrs. Henry Lee Higginson at their large and charming apartment, for Mr. and Mrs. Charles Sumner Bird, in the exquisite blue and gold music room at 'Endean,' their beautiful estate in East Walpole, and for Mrs. Horatio M. Slater at her magnificent Manor House in Readville. We often played at these places with munificent fees. The audiences, between one hundred and one hundred and fifty people, were not only brilliant and highly cultured but for the most part truly musical. It was a joy for Mr. Loeffler and me to give those concerts.[24]

Loeffler also played in private for friends whom he invited to Medfield. A substitute member of the American String Quartette recalled that once a year Loeffler would have a concert in his studio, he playing viola, always with a distinguished guest invited. One year it was John Singer Sargent, another Elizabeth Sprague Coolidge.[25] Loeffler enjoyed entertaining his friends in Medfield. He never lost his taste or knack for fine conversation. Among those friends who have left impressions of Loeffler in Medfield are Frank Benson, Heinrich Gebhard, Amy Lowell, and Carl Engel.

Frank Benson was an Impressionistic painter educated at the Museum of Fine Arts School and in Paris. He had a studio in Boston and taught at the museum school until 1916. Loeffler may have met Benson as early as the 1880s, when Loeffler knew Benson's fellow artists Grundmann and Bunker. They may also have met through the Tavern Club, which Benson joined in 1892, but surviving correspondence dates only from 1916. The two shared, besides an interest in art, a love of wildlife. Benson was particularly well known for his etchings and paintings of natural subjects—"everybody had to have a Benson print of ducks," reported one Boston society lady.[26] Loeffler owned several of Benson's etchings and paintings. Benson designed Loeffler's bookplate and in 1919 did an etching of Loeffler himself.

Benson recorded part of a conversation he had with Loeffler. "One night in Medfield as we sat before the fire he asked me questions about design in painting. (He was always deeply interested in that art); 'Tell me,' said he, 'just how you go to work to give form to an idea.' This was something I had never thought of formulating in words, but I did the best I could, very clumsily it seemed, and when I had finished I asked if it conveyed anything to him; 'Why, my dear Frank,' he said, 'if you but change the names of things, merely alter the nouns, you have described the way I compose a piece of music.'"[27]

Heinrich Gebhard actually became a neighbor of Loeffler's (as did also Georges Longy).

I bought myself a smaller farm in nearby Norfolk, which I had "fixed up" into a comfortable summer home, where I spent a number of summers with my mother and two sisters, later with my wife [1920] and child. Every other afternoon I went over to the Loeffler's, and Loeffler and I always played two or three hours together. We began to study seriously the literature of sonatas for violin and piano. Gradually we learned the violin-sonatas of Bach, Mozart, Beethoven, Schubert, Schumann, Brahms, Strauss, Grieg, Franck, Fauré, Debussy, D'Indy, St. Saëns, Ropartz. We practiced hard and finally moulded ourselves into quite a "team.". . .

From 1903 until 1918 in the winter seasons I spent every other week-end with the Loefflers in Medfield. They were both wonderfully friendly and kind to me, and of course they had my admiration and deep affection. I often drove in the country with Mr. Loeffler or hiked through the woods with him, while we discussed music, art, literature, and the "riddles of the universe." Quite often there was some distinguished guest. A number of times it was John Singer Sargent. The great painter's personality was magnetic, big-hearted, and warm. Outside of his profession he had one hobby—music. He played the piano quite well, and loved to play four hand arrangements of orchestral music. So several times I played with him. He had a pleasing touch and was a remarkably good reader, but he used atrocious fingerings. It was amazing how his fingers could glide through intricate passages with his "impossible" fingerings! And he had such a good time doing it. I loved to listen to him discoursing on art with Loeffler. I remember once his saying how important fine workmanship was. He said, "No matter how God-inspired a work is, it has to be a finished art-work in order to last." How true that is.

Pablo Casals, the exquisite cellist, and his wife, the lovely singer (Susan Metcalfe) were at "Meadowmere" several times. Povla Frijsh visited there for four weeks once. . . .

When D'Indy was in America, besides my playing with him at Mrs. Slater's, I saw a good deal of him at "Meadowmere."[28]

It was almost inevitable that, when finally introduced, Amy Lowell and Loeffler would become friends, their tastes being so very similar. Lowell loved French poetry as Loeffler did and became an unconventional poet, as Loeffler was an unconventional composer, by her alliance with the French school. She also enjoyed French music. At her elegant family home in Brookline, she sponsored a series of recitals from 1913 to 1916 for a small group of friends nicknamed "the Devils," including Gebhard and Engel, at which Gebhard played programs of music featuring modern French music—Franck, Debussy, Fauré, Ravel, d'Indy. Loeffler was invited to the first of these concerts, but the late hour precluded his becoming a "Devil."

Lowell was a great fan of the BSO and had friendships with several musicians and composers, including Engel, Hill, Carpenter, Antheil, Rogers, and Eva Gauthier. Several of her poems were written with musical themes, and several were set to music. Lowell appreciated, as did the French poets, the kinship between the poet's and composer's arts. She delivered a lecture in 1919 at Harvard on the subject, "Some Musical Analogies in Modern Poetry" (the first lecture given by a woman under Harvard's patronage).

Lowell and Loeffler became great friends. As each of her volumes of poetry and prose appeared, she sent a copy to Loeffler, and each drew forth from Loeffler warm and sincere compliments. Commenting on one of her prose works, he wrote:

> Every new Book of yours is an event to me, but this last one I welcome quite particularly for all the illumination it brings. One closes the book finally with regret and gratitude—regret, that the pleasure has come to an end and gratitude for the hours of delight one has been allowed to spend in your company.
>
> This book again has all the marks of your rare personality and in meditating over all that you had to tell us, the mind wandered back to your own poetry, which so evidently places your genius amongst the great delights of one's life. Pray, receive again my humble words of homage.[29]

The sincerity of his expressions to Miss Lowell is borne out by a passage in a letter to Engel: "Your friend Amy Lowell's book on Keats apparently is out but, as far as Boston is concerned, there doesn't seem to be much comment on it so far. They are always so d....ly cautious in blowing trumpets for what seems to me ought and must be a great literary event."[30]

As Loeffler discussed art and music with Benson, so also he took the opportunity to discuss the kinship of inspiration in poetry and music with Lowell. For example, he wrote to her:

> When you insist on not knowing as much as you would wish to know about music, I can only accept this as referring to the metier part of our Art, for Poets are seers who understand intuitively what they behold without preliminary study or learning. The study of metier has been condensed, even with great musicians, particularly those who were autodidacts, into an amazingly short time for the reason, namely: that to have seen and heard meant to them the "fait accompli" of having grasped and understood the essence of phases and means of expression. I do not mean, of course, that the average musician need not arduously study his art and just trust in luck. It all depends on the slow or quick perception and comprehension of the individual. The game, is in two words: the chace after beauty. Lucky the artist who can 'capture the

Goddess'! [an allusion to Lowell's poem "The Captured Goddess."]
You are so eminently successful, that I marvel at, on reading my
particularly favorite poems amongst yours, how many new and delicate
shades in poetical fancy and unerring verbal choice I discover in them.
Again, there are in your lines felicitous and genially modulative turns
which retain their strength of affecting us after even a thousand readings and remain immortally fresh in their appeal. I have found this so
also in the best of music.[31]

Loeffler frequently invited Amy Lowell to Medfield to attend his
concerts and to visit. Lowell heard Loeffler play in his studio, declared
that "those rare afternoons in which you play to us are among the
happiest moments of my life,"[32] and wrote a poem about it, "Violin
Sonata by Vincent d'Indy," dedicated to Loeffler.

> A little brown room in a sea of fields,
> Fields pink as rose-mallows
> Under a fading rose-mallow sky.
> Four candles on a tall iron candlestick,
> Clustered like altar lights.
> Above, the models of four brown Chinese junks
> Sailing round the brown walls,
> Silent and motionless.
>
> The quick cut of a vibrating string,
> Another, and another,
> Biting into the silence.
> Notes pierce, sharper and sharper;
> They draw up in a freshness of sound,
> Higher—higher, to the whiteness of intolerable beauty.
> They are jagged and clear,
> Like snow peaks against the sky;
> They hurt like air too pure to breathe.
> Is it catgut and horsehair,
> Or flesh sawing against the cold blue gates of the sky?
>
> The brown Chinese junks sail silently round the brown walls.
> The windows are black, for the sun has set.
> Only the candles,
> Clustered like altar lamps upon their tall candlestick,
> Light the violinist as he plays.

Carl Engel, whose picture of Loeffler as the *seigneur campagnard* is
quoted above, saw Loeffler on many occasions and was one of those
privileged to hear him play. In spite of Loeffler's own professions of
being a has-been in 1914, Engel declared in 1925: "he does not stand
still. He keeps surmounting higher and higher violinistic problems,

goes on spinning his tone ever purer and warmer, for his own satisfaction and that of a few privileged beings. To hear him in his quiet music-room on his New England farm . . . to hear him interpret sonatas of Bach, Handel, Brahms, Fauré, and d'Indy is, indeed, one of Baudelaire's 'grandes jouissances.'"[33]

The image of Loeffler that Engel cherished was like that in Lowell's poem. "One prefers to picture the lonely man of noble and monastic mien in his spacious study, with the Chinese junks hanging motionless from the rafters, the two dogs stretched before the embers in the large fireplace, the soft light of wax tapers in slender iron candlesticks, an autumnal evening haze spread in fantastic patterns over the meadowland, the ethereal voice of a violin cutting into the silence and singing a passionate phrase—yes, in those moments one waits for the *fratres* to look in, for a little music, on their return from vespers, nay for Our Lady herself to steal through the deepening dusk and make her benign presence felt, as she was wont to do, in days of long ago, at Groenendal."[34]

Loeffler enjoyed his life in Medfield. It was a life of great activity and hard work but finally also of peace, contentment, and artistic refuge.

14

Opera

For years Loeffler had wanted to write an opera. By 1908 he still had not found a libretto, but he did then become involved in the world of opera when Boston acquired its own resident opera company.

Before the twentieth century, Boston, though frequently host to visiting opera companies, had no resident opera company. Then in 1907 the impressario Henry Russell came to Boston with the Naples San Carlo company. Because of a financial panic in New York which affected the company but not Boston, Russell turned for help to a local businessman and opera enthusiast, Eben D. Jordan. By the time the San Carlo company left Boston, Russell and Jordan had decided on a collaboration and in 1908 revealed their plans to form an opera company. Russell became director of the Opera House; Jordan, president of the opera company. Loeffler served on the board of directors, formed of a number of eminent men including Loeffler's fellow composers Frederick S. Converse and George W. Chadwick. Converse, also vice-president of the company, quickly raised subscriptions for the boxes.

A new building was built for the opera. Hitherto, visiting companies, including opera, musical comedy, ballet, and minstrel shows, had performed in theaters. Jordan purchased a site for a new house on Huntington Avenue, near Symphony Hall. At the end of the year, the foundation stone was laid. Within it was a bronze casket containing musical memorabilia of the time, including music by Beach, Chadwick, Converse, Damrosch, Hadley, MacDowell, Paine, Parker, and Loeffler.

The Boston Opera Company was formed of both European and American singers; the chorus members came largely from the New England Conservatory. The principal conductors were Arnaldo Conti and Wallace Goodrich. The productions were put together with great care. "From the moment I became director of the Boston Opera House," wrote Russell, "it was my ambition to give the finest performances in the world, and, thanks to the cooperation of those who worked with me, I think I may say that we maintained a high standard of excellence."[1]

When the proposal for a resident opera company was first made public, Loeffler had grave doubts about its success. He wrote to Grace Schirmer: "Boston is all aflame with the excitement of getting permanent (what an *absurd* word!) opera. M. Eben Jordan is going to build an Opera House. . . . if the San Carlo Opera Cie. is a specimen of what we are going to get, we shall become the laughing stock of the U.S. I am pessimistic about the matter."[2] However, Loeffler's fears were not borne out. From its premiere performance, on 8 November 1909 with *La Gioconda,* the Boston Opera Company was an artistic success.

Unfortunately, almost from the beginning, the opera was in financial jeopardy. The opera was only in its second season when Loeffler wrote to Gardner about the matter.

> We of the Opera House are in the midst of a crisis which will either turn to losing this excellent institution for good after this season, or having it vitalized by getting the public to support it more generously than heretofore, so that it may continue indefinitely. . . .
>
> Does the Boston Public not know, that it only has the finest concert organization, namely the Symphony Orchestra, through the unlimited generous public spirit of our great Mr. Higginson, and that it does not generously enough support even this now world famous orchestra so that it pays for itself? I know, there are many unthinking people, that believe the attendance sufficiently great at the Symphony concerts, to pay for the entire support of the orchestra. A short time ago, some well to do individuals in one of the offices of Symphony Hall gloated over their success of getting their Symphony Season tickets cheaper by one Dollar this year than ever before! This is really an inverted case of savages in Africa getting tawdry glass beads in return for their ivory. To expect the highest in any art for next to nothing is expecting the impossible.
>
> Mr. Jordan generously came to the fore last year in paying the enormous deficit of 90,000$ and this year, in spite of remarkable performances with an efficient orchestra and Chorus, excellent conductors, admirable vocalists and stage settings, comparable to the best in Europe, the outlook forebodes nothing good, unless the public shows more interest.[3]

Loeffler probably wrote similarly to other of his wealthy and influential friends in Boston, because his concern was not unfounded. The opera continued in financial trouble for the few years of its existence.

A temporary assignment in the world of opera came to Loeffler in 1910, two years after Mr. Gatti-Casazza of the Metropolitan Opera in New York offered a competition for an American opera. In December

1910 the jury was announced: Walter Damrosch, Alfred Hertz (of the Met), George W. Chadwick, and Loeffler. As Loeffler wrote to Gardner, "I accepted to be one of a jury of four, to judge for the Metropolitan Opera Co. the best Opera written by an American born Composer and now my troubles have begun! There are 24 operas to go through!"[4]

A curious event interrupted the judging process. The entries were divided into four groups, which rotated among the jury members. A package of two operas, which Damrosch was sending to Chadwick in Boston, was stolen from the express company's truck before it left New York. The thief undoubtedly had trusted to luck to steal something valuable. Luckily the scores were soon recovered when Policeman Donahue became suspicious of a man carrying a bulging bundle under his arm for which he was unable to give a satisfactory account. He brought his suspect to the police station, where Lt. Underhill, who had providentially just read of the opera theft while returning from his holiday, recognized the package for what it was. The anonymity of the manuscripts, all identified by pseudonyms, had been preserved by this quick action, and the judging resumed. In May 1911 the winner, *Mona* by Horatio Parker (not in the stolen package), was announced.

On May 2, after the jury reached its decision, Chadwick and Loeffler, en route back to Boston, stopped at New Haven to give Parker the news personally. Since Parker was out of town, each wrote him their congratulations. Loeffler's letter was the occasion for both personal compliments and patriotic sentiment.

> The rather gigantic job of reading through 24 opera scores is done! Ouff! And one breathes easier again. The work was all the more wearisome to me, as I was the one that had "Mona" *first* and then 23 more or less indifferently interesting ones (in grade down to very punk!) *after*. Therefore, my pleasure and fun was over after the first score perused, and the rest was one long, wearisome, tragi-comical *corvée*, with very few rays of sunshine in it. All this confidentially! Let me tell you, my dear Parker, how happy I am that you should have written this score, and how easy you have made it to me—to us—to strew palms and laurels at your feet. . . . Well, to have awarded you the moneyed prize was the least, the easiest thing to do; the greatest fun is to sincerely applaud your performance, long live America, long live the gifted of this land, you and admirable Brian Hooker, the great painters and architects and the *tutti quanti* that make this land one of the wonders of the world![5]

Damrosch was disappointed by the competition, finding the majority of entrants "pathetic in their clumsy ignorance of the most ordinary standards of technique and of ordinary requirements for operative purposes."[6] "I would have been happier," he wrote to Loeffler, "if the competition had been open to American musicians foreign born, and that I could have handed the Ten Thousand Dollars to the one man who should get it, if indeed he would ever stoop so low as to write an opera, and that is Charles Martin Loeffler."[7]

Loeffler's work for the Boston and New York opera companies undoubtedly stimulated his own desire to compose an opera. Having left Paris without a libretto, he continued his search in America, with ideas and suggestions coming from various friends, including George Cabot Lodge and Amy Lowell. Finally, about 1912 Loeffler settled on a play by William Sharp (pseudonym Fiona McLeod), *The Passion of Hilarion.* Sharp, having died in 1905, did not know of Loeffler's interest in his work but probably would have been pleased. He had written to Lawrence Gilman in 1904, "Some time ago a friend played to me one or two lovely airs by Mr. Loeffler, and I was so much impressed by their unique quality and their atmosphere of subtle beauty that I wrote to find out what I could about this composer."[8]

The story of Hilarion appealed to Loeffler. It was set principally within a Catholic church in Spain, allowing for the use of both chant and Spanish color. The dramatic conflict was between religious commitment and romantic love. Although the play was written in English, Loeffler composed the work with both English and Italian texts. "There must be opera in English," he wrote to Walter Damrosch, "but at present there cannot be, as nobody knows how to sing in it."[9]

Loeffler composed the opera during 1912 and 1913. He kept the project secret from all but three or four people, including Gardner, to whom he wrote in May: "My work slowly progresses. Qui va piano va sano? Let us hope so. I shall consult you soon after this work of mine which, of course, I intend to be my best. There are some questions of mise en scène which shall have to be solved. You probably will find some genial way."[10]

To Damrosch he also confided his progress. "I have been all summer on my farm finishing my dramatic one act, incidently making hay and repairing decayed apple trees. How seriously one works away at a thing like a musical composition! As if the world were waiting for it!"[11]

On 28 December he wrote to Gardner, "Today I expect to finish my Opus! At least the orchestral score." Loeffler's incurable penchant for revision kept him at work on the score in 1913, but he had taken *Hilarion* far enough to declare to Gardner in the same letter, "Now I am waiting to hear from our very Honorable Poet of the East—I have already in mind how to begin the thing!"[12] Loeffler was referring to Okakura Kakuzo and his play, written expressly for Loeffler to set to music, titled *The White Fox.*

Okakura was one of the exotic and highly talented people whom Loeffler met at Fenway Court. A native of Japan and graduate of Tokyo's Imperial University, Okakura was a merchant's son who took to artistic study and commerce after meeting Ernest Fenollosa. After Fenollosa returned to America in 1890, Okakura remained in Japan, where he was concerned with preserving Oriental art from growing Western influence. During a selling trip to America, he met John LaFarge, who gave him a letter of introduction to Gardner. With her help he became advisor and later curator of the Department of Chinese and Japanese Art (much of whose collection originated with Fenollosa's work in the Orient) at the Museum of Fine Arts, where he remained until 1913. In that year he returned to Japan, where he died.

Loeffler liked Okakura, whom he called a "marvel of wisdom and poetry and art."[13] He valued highly Okakura's *Book of Tea* (on the subject of Oriental aesthetics). Elise wrote, "We have sent several copies abroad and Martin bought a copy for himself, because 'he wanted it near at hand' which means on the table beside his bed."[14]

Loeffler never carried *The White Fox* project through. First Okakura could not make changes he asked for, and second a misunderstanding arose regarding his right to adapt the libretto himself. In 1920, when Loeffler became aware that two other composers, Terhune and Miramor, each wanted to set the play, he wrote to Gardner: "Of course if I had had your consent to *adapt* the play by changing the literary part and the dramatic arrangement, I should have continued writing the music to the play. I had already begun the first scene, but found some of the sentences too awkward for musical setting. . . . If you are willing to have the adapted and verbal changes made for operatic purposes [by Terhune], why shouldn't I be the one to have that privilege, for the play, offered you in hommage by the poet, was meant by the poet and you to be set to music by me, wasn't it?"[15] Gardner replied that Loeffler did indeed have all rights to the play (and so wrote to Terhune and Miramor) and that Loeffler could make changes. Still, Loeffler failed to complete the opera.

While Loeffler was working on *The White Fox,* he looked for an opportunity to have *Hilarion* staged. He wrote to Walter Damrosch in April 1913, asking him to recommend his work to the New York opera directors. If he had thought about the Boston Opera Company, he was disappointed by circumstances out of his control. The troubled company filed bankruptcy proceedings in May 1915. Though reconstituted as the Boston Grand Opera Company, it merely finished out its season. The house was sold to the Shuberts in 1918, and though it continued to host visiting opera companies, it never again housed a resident opera company.

But another problem existed regarding staging Loeffler's opera. He had not even considered until he had finished the score that the major love duet, which occurs in the confessional box of the church, was a scene which would not be allowed on an opera stage—not in proper society. Later Loeffler thought of persuading the BSO to produce a concert performance of *Hilarion,* but that project never materialized. Staged or not, the opera was never performed in any form.

Loeffler worked on two other uncompleted operas, *The Peony Lantern* and *Les amants jaloux* (libretto dated 1918), for both of which only sketches survive. The libretto to the former was written by Loeffler himself, based on an idea given to him by Okakura. He wrote two versions of the libretto, one set in Japan (*The Peony Lantern*) and one in China (*The Lantern Ghosts*). This may well be the libretto that he sent to the Metropolitan Opera Company, which the Met misplaced and had no knowledge of when Loeffler made enquiries in 1917. In response, Bodansky then wanted to see Loeffler's score. When Loeffler explained that he had discontinued work on it, they asked if it would be ready for the next season. Unfortunately, Loeffler did not finish it.

Since Loeffler worked primarily on his operas for several years after his return from Germany, few other new works came from him at this time. Two earlier works, however, were premiered in late 1909. One was *The Wind among the Reeds,* his settings of Yeats's poems "The Hosting of the Sidhe" and "The Host of the Air," composed during the summer of 1906. In October David Bispham and Woodruff Rogers performed the songs at Jordan Hall. In December the Kneisel Quartette gave the first performance of *Le passeur d'eau,* his 1900 revision of the second movement of the Sextuor of 1891, which Loeffler had dedicated to the memory of Denis Bunker.

Older compositions were also performed. These performances were facilitated by the appearance, beginning in 1903, of published editions of Loeffler's music. In that year Schirmer's had begun to publish Loeffler's music and through 1911 issued *Quatre mélodies* (1903), *Quatre poèmes* (1904), *Deux Rapsodies, La villanelle du Diable, La mort de Tintagiles,* (1905), *Psalm 137, A Pagan Poem, The Wind among the Reeds* (1909), *For One Who Fell in Battle,* and *Ode For One Who Fell in Battle* (1911). Then a hiatus in publishing occurred, probably a result, in part, of Loeffler's devotion to his operas. He had intended to give Schirmer's also the *Divertissement* and *L'archet* (after writing a fuller accompaniment), but neither was published.

The publications that did occur, however, allowed a wider performing field for his music. Between 1908 and 1912, while Max Fiedler conducted the BSO, only one Loeffler orchestral composition was heard in Boston, the *Villanelle* in 1910. However, orchestras of other cities—Pittsburgh, Chicago, New York, Cincinnati, and Philadelphia—were performing his works. In a stunning article written by Lawrence Gilman for the *North American Review* in 1911, Gilman stated, "After a quarter-century of curiously deliberate activity, of quiet devotion to what would have seemed to many an impossible ideal of perfection, he is at last coming into his own."[16]

The widening performance field also included parts of Europe. *A Pagan Poem* was performed in Zurich in May 1910 as part of the National German Music Festival, which included three orchestral and choir concerts. On the final day *A Pagan Poem* was directed by Volmar Andreä, conductor of the Philharmonic "Tonhalle" concerts, with Rudolf Ganz at the piano. It was reviewed in papers of Zurich, Lausanne, Mannheim, Berlin, and Amsterdam. In Lausanne *A Pagan Poem* was judged "an enchantment" and "one of the high points of the festival."[17] From all quarters Loeffler received praise for those elements of his music by then so familiar to Boston audiences: colorful modern harmonies, beautiful melodies, and, especially, ingenious instrumentation. The next European performance of *A Pagan Poem* was, apparently, a Proms Concert conducted by Henry Wook in 1917.

For One Who Fell in Battle was also performed in England, at a Promenade Concert and at a Halifax Madrigal Society concert. Probably at the former Percy Grainger heard the piece and in 1914 wrote to Loeffler: "I can't refrain from telling you how it touches and thrills me . . . what delicious clean partwriting, and how inspired and felt every line, and all so personal and unusual all the time, yet so splendidly *singable* every bit. It has been a real event in my life coming in touch with this wondrously spiritual soulful and uplifted creation of yours and I cannot say how I long to hear a really glowing performance of it."[18]

In 1911 Loeffler celebrated his fiftieth birthday. Unaccountably it was an occasion unmarked by the BSO, although in New York Damrosch conducted the *Villanelle* in February. In June of that year Loeffler himself included his new song *Hommage (Je te vis)*, sung by Mrs. J. S. Fay, in a Grand Sacred Concert at St. Edwards.

With the return of Muck in 1912, seasonal performances of Loeffler's works by the BSO resumed, beginning with *A Pagan Poem* in 1913 and *La mort de Tintagiles* (with Emile Ferir as soloist) in 1914 and 1915.

During 1913 both the New York and Philadelphia orchestras performed the *Villanelle*. Also in New York in 1913 the Kneisel Quartette once again played Loeffler's Quintet, reviewed as "a fresh, spontaneous and delightful piece of music of old fashioned frankness. It vibrates with melody and it glows with opulent harmony. Graceful, fluent and melodious in thematic matter, clear, well balanced and solid in part writing, it works itself out in a lucid, symmetrical shape and leaves the hearer with a refreshed mind and a warmed fancy."[19] Never before had the adjective "old fashioned" been attached to anything Loefflerian.

Also in 1913, Maggie Teyte, who earned a reputation as an interpreter of Debussy's music, came to Boston on a concert tour and met Loeffler, who introduced her to his songs. "She liked them tremendously and studied them," declared Gebhard, who was engaged by Fanny Mason to accompany Teyte at a concert at her home, on 11 February 1913.[20] Teyte sang a program of selections from three of Loeffler's published song sets.

With the exception of *Hommage* and the *Ode for One Who Fell in Battle,* however, between 1910 and 1916, no new works by Loeffler were premiered. Much of this time was simply consumed by opera composition. From the middle of the decade, however, new works issued forth from Loeffler's farm in Medfield, where the "recluse" once again became involved in world events.

15

War Years

The tranquility of Loeffler's life in Medfield was disturbed by the outbreak of war in Europe in August 1914. While there was still hope that the conflict would be over quickly, it did not deeply affect American life. But from the beginning it affected Loeffler. For one thing his sister was still in Germany. The only surviving war-time correspondence from Helene is a postcard sent in August 1916, at which time she was in Scheveningen, Holland, with her husband, violinist Friedrich Gaffkÿ. The postcard told Martin that they intended to settle in Homburg, from where her postwar correspondence was indeed addressed.

But, despite his concern for his family and friends in Germany, Loeffler's sympathies were not with what he called "criminal Germany."[1] The war rekindled Loeffler's old antipathy towards the German government, and his hopes and anxieties were allied with his beloved France. Increasingly Loeffler became solicitous over the plight of France, and gradually it affected his activities and his work.

A curious result of the outbreak of the war was that the Cincinnati Orchestra, whose conductor, Ernst Kunwald, was in Europe and whose return was in doubt, approached Loeffler to consider "breaking away from your moorings and delightful surroundings for the difficult and exacting work entailed by an orchestral season," presumably an invitation to take over as conductor.[2] However, Kunwald did return to his position, which Loeffler, happily retired from the concert stage, would not have accepted.

The war caused Loeffler to value even more, if possible, his moorings and surroundings, not only his home but also the world of music and poetry in which he lived. Upon receiving a copy of *Sword Blades and Poppy Seeds* from Amy Lowell, Loeffler wrote, "At this time, so full of horror and intense hatred, your book comes as a consoling, reassuring message, with new revelations. After all, my dear Miss

Lowell, nothing matters much but art—and the power of expressing a new phase of it."[3]

Music had always been Loeffler's great consolation, and it continued so to be, especially his own composition. Both Damrosch and Muck made attempts to get him to return to the concert stage as a soloist when they conducted *Tintagiles,* but Loeffler refused. "The fact is," he insisted to Damrosch, "I have given up fiddling in public."[4] He later declined an invitation to play at Elizabeth Sprague Coolidge's Pittsfield chamber music concerts and also resisted Gardner's invitation to play for her guests (though not for her), writing: "There is a time for everything, but the time to hear me play whatsoever is now by gone. I have not touched a violin for so long, that it would be an imposition on anybody to listen to my playing. It also places me in an unfair light. I am too 'journalier' nowadays, and you know, that I have given up playing to people, except now and then at home, if 'le coeur m'en parle.' Please realize with me, that I am nothing now but an old has-been. . . . Please understand, dear Mrs. Gardner, my repugnance at playing before people at this late date. It is dictated by a quite proper sense of dignity, wisdom, and appreciation. I have also given up skating lately."[5]

During 1915 and 1916 Loeffler produced several new compositions apparently unaffected by world events. He revised, in 1915, his *Poem* for Orchestra, a work of tranquil lyricism. During the summer he composed a new orchestral work even more deeply in a spirit of peace. *Hora mystica,* which he called a one-movement symphony, was a musical impression of Loeffler's visit to Maria Laach. It grew out of his spiritual experiences there as well as the experience of hearing the Benedictine choir, with which, twenty years later, Loeffler was still enchanted: "Pianissimos so soft that no strings could equal them, and yet perfectly resonant through the whole cathedral."[6]

Loeffler himself provided some commentary on the symphony for the BSO program.

> The mood is one of religious meditation and adoration of nature. A lonely pilgrim winds his way through a land of ever-changing enchantments, where clouds moved like a procession of nuns over the hills, or descended upon a lake, changing it into a mysterious gray sea. From far away came a curious tolling of village church bells. On the slope above, a shepherd piped to his flocks. At last the pilgrim stood before the cathedral of a Benedictine Monastery, contemplating its beauty—even the grotesque beauty of the gargoyles, placed on the house of worship to ward off evil spirits. In the church, with its rose-window still aglow

with the last evening light, the office of compline—known to the Benedictine monks as *Hora Mystica*—was tendered to God, and peace descended into the soul of the pilgrim.

"Here then," commented Lawrence Gilman, "was to be a translation into music of the meditations and the moods of one who, having (as the Upanishads say) crossed over all the sorrows of the heart: having wandered and dreamed upon the hills and in the fields and valleys, had now turned his heart inward toward the silence of that holy of holies where, 'with half-parted lips, the Infinite murmurs its ancient story,' and where there is a light that shines, as Shankara tells us, like a light within a vase."[7]

The music of the symphony was based on three pieces of Gregorian chant: *Tu autem in nobis es, Domine,* particularly its response *Deo gratias; In manus tuas, Domine, commendo spiritum meum;* and *Salve Regina.* It also employed a succession of notes from the monastery bells—B♭, D♭, E♭, F, A♭, B♭. The conclusion of the symphony incorporates a unison male chorus, inspired by the monks' singing of the office. In 1915 *Hora mystica* was Loeffler's own "reassuring message."

Hora mystica was chosen for production at the 1916 Norfolk Festival of the Litchfield County Choral Union. This festival was held annually in June in the hills of Connecticut on the estate of Mr. and Mrs. Carl Stoeckel, who had built, in composer Henry Gilbert's words, "an unpretentious but wonderfully perfect auditorium." Under the direction of Stoeckel, the festival had achieved national importance, particularly with his institution of cash prizes for two new works, generally by Americans, to be produced at each festival. Gilbert praised the festival. "The American composer has here the opportunity of bringing his work to performance amid almost ideal conditions. Beside conducting all rehearsals and the performance he is given every practicable assistance and is treated with deference and respect."[8]

Hora mystica went into rehearsal in May with the Philharmonic Orchestra of New York and set Loeffler back to work, as he explained to Lowell: "I am in the depth of mire—for wrong notes in orchestra parts are nothing but mire—wallowing in it and shoveling the infernal stuff out of my music. In simple English: I am correcting the orchestra parts of my symphony."[9]

The performance was on 6 June. Loeffler himself, in an unwonted appearance, conducted. Lawrence Gilman, who attended the performance, was enchanted: "The music was evocative, transforming. As we listened, the long June twilight failing slowly through the lilac-scented stillness outside became, for us, one with the enchantment that entered the soul of the pilgrim who spoke to us from the music. Through the open doors and windows of the encircling hills, a deepening purple against the luminous amber of the sunset sky; the hushed valley with its distant shining stream; the tremulous stillness of the fields: these things were touched with magic, caught up and merged, by the witchery of the tone-poet, into the pictures unfolded in his music—became one with the communicated vision of the rhapsodist."[10]

The symphony had a number of supporters, including Fritz Kreisler, who, to use Loeffler's expression, "boomed" it to Walter Damrosch. Loeffler had given the score to Muck but also promised Damrosch a copy. The BSO presented *Hora mystica* in March 1917, followed by a performance by the Chicago orchestra. The copyist, however, failed to produce the music in time for a New York performance, by which time Loeffler decided to withdraw the work, which he felt was too long, for revision. He never did finish the revision despite conductorial interest, including Stokowski's 1923 threat: "I warn you that sometime in August a noisy, dirty Ford will draw up at your door, and I shall bother you again until the symphony is finished."[11]

In Boston the symphony received compliments from the critics. Downes, in the *Boston Post,* observed, "This writing impresses one as having, in its best estate, a subtlety and a fineness not hitherto approached, not even by Loeffler." Parker at the *Boston Transcript* commented, "Not a few know the spiritual passion and the spiritual splendor that may suddenly flame white and high in great cathedrals from the celebration of High Mass. This passion and this splendor, the music of 'Hora Mystica' bears into the world of nature and then lifts high heavenward."[12]

In 1915, while Loeffler was writing his symphony, he heard from Busoni, who was then himself composing a new work. Busoni described the work as a piece on an American Indian theme for string instruments and six wind instruments. He intended to dedicate it to Loeffler if he could finish it to his satisfaction. Evidently he did not.

About this time Loeffler's expertise on French composers was called upon for the Boston Music Company publication of Saint-Saëns's *Havanaise.* Loeffler edited the piece, published in 1916.

That same year Loeffler wrote a new composition for cello, *Poème (Scène dramatique)* pour violoncelle solo et piano (ou orchestre). (The orchestral score, if written, is now missing.) Pablo Casals, who was in the United States in 1916 and heard that Loeffler had written a new work for cello, made inquiries through the singer Povla Frijsh. Loeffler not only sent Casals the work for its premiere but also dedicated it to him.

Casals liked the work, writing to Loeffler, "The writing of this piece is indubitably of a perfection and logic . . . equaling the most subtle writing of Mozart."[13] The music for *Poème* was "drawn from an unpublished opera," as Loeffler wrote on the title page, with a snatch taken from his *Ballade carnavalesque*. A one-movement piece, it begins with the somber marking "monotone et sinistre," continues "assez lent" throughout, and is embellished with Spanish color, producing the title used at Casals' concerts of *Poème espagnole*. Casals performed the work in New York, Boston, and Spain. In New York's Aeolian Hall and Boston's Jordan Hall, accompanied by Ruth Deyo, he performed on 28 January and 24 March 1917. On the same program Susan Metcalfe-Casals performed two of Loeffler's songs. John Sargent wrote Loeffler from New York that he intended to stay over to hear that performance.

The *Poème* was well received, drawing, for example, the comment, "Mr. Loeffler weaves suggestion of romance and of poetry out of subtle harmonies that curiously color the music and intrigue the ear, while by no slight feat of invention, imagination and resource they blend as curiously into background of Spanish rhythm, color, suggestion." Downes wrote, "This music, charged with melancholy and with an eloquence sometimes fiery and sometime languorous, is a revelation of a certain side, perhaps surprising to some, of the temperament of Charles Martin Loeffler."[14]

Also in March a Charles Martin Loeffler Programme, organized by Longy, was presented in Jordan Hall. Longy, Adeline Packard (a Loeffler student), and Renée Longy performed the *Rapsodies*. *L'archet* was performed by the Cecilia Society, Povla Frijsh, Gertrude Marshall, and Heinrich Gebhard. Frijsh, who was to Loeffler's mind "the greatest artist among singers,"[15] also gave the Boston premiere of four of Loeffler's songs, *Ton souvenir est comme un livre bien-aimé, Hommage, A une femme,* and *Boléro triste*. These four songs had all been written years earlier, the first two at least by 1911 and the latter two in 1904 and 1900. The first three are lyrical love songs, the last a pungent, exotically colored setting of a macabre Kahn poem. *A une femme* and *Boléro triste* were written in two versions—with and without a part for scordatura violin. Frijsh sang the songs without violin.

Loeffler's work in 1917 and 1918 was hindered by new medical problems. In January 1917 he told Walter Damrosch that he had refrigoric paralysis of the right side of his face. Elise wrote to Gardner, "though he suffers no pain, he is very uncomfortable. . . . The doctors want him to keep on with his work and do everything as usual and promise everything will come out all right soon."[16] During the summer Loeffler was hospitalized for an undetermined time and unknown treatment. He was home in Medfield during the fall and winter, but in July 1918 had to go back to the hospital. Despite all these problems, Loeffler did as the doctors advised and, as much as possible, kept on with his work, which then included war work.

By the close of 1916 it had become clear that the war in Europe was not to be settled quickly. Many efforts were organized in America to help the Allies to several of which, such as ambulance funds and liberty bonds, Loeffler contributed. He also sent money to d'Indy to be contributed to the Association Nationale des Veuves et Orphelines. He joined the Musicians Unit of the Red Cross Special Fund, of which Paderewski was honorary president and John McCormack treasurer. He was a benefactor of L'aide affectueuse aux musiciens. And he also organized his own benefit concerts.

Loeffler produced two concerts at St. Edward's in Medfield for the benefit of the Red Cross, in June of 1917 and 1918. His patrons included Amy Lowell, John Sargent, Isabella Stewart Gardner, and several other loyal Boston patronesses, such as Fanny Mason, Sarah Sears, and Mabel Slater. The music chosen was that of Handel, Purcell, Tchaikovsky, Franck, d'Indy, and Albeniz. A highlight of these concerts was Loeffler's arrangement of the Franck piano quintet for double string quartet and piano. According to Engel, "Nobody knows the Franck Quintet who has not heard it with a small orchestra replacing the string quartet, under Loeffler's direction."[17] Loeffler claimed that it was so popular that he had to repeat it five years running.

Gebhard recalled other benefit concerts. "During those four [war] years Mr. Loeffler and I played ten sonata-recitals for the benefit of the Red Cross, giving our services free, of course. We performed these ten programs at "Meadowmere," in the lovely spacious music-room (the house on the other side of the road). We charged $5.00 a ticket, and were able to get about eighty people (mostly society) to come to each concert. It was a grand pleasure to send about $4000 to the Red Cross."[18] In March 1918 E. B. Hill at Harvard University organized a concert for the American Friends of Musicians in France. Loeffler's *Rapsodies* were performed by Georges and Renée Longy and Louis Bailly, with Amy Lowell reading the Rollinat poems. Hill relied on Loeffler's advice for the control of the money.

The war came closer to Loeffler when young Americans volunteered for service in France. Several of his choir boys enlisted in the American Expeditionary Forces. Loeffler wrote to each and sent gifts of money.

The son of Loeffler's old friend John J. Chapman had joined the Foreign Legion in 1914 and in February 1916 became a pilot of the Franco-American Aviation Corps. While stationed at Verdun, in June 1916 he was shot down by German aircraft and was the first American aviator to be killed in the war. During the year following, Chapman collected his son's letters to his family and with his own "Memoir" of Victor and Victor's mother published *Victor Chapman's Letters from France*. In June 1917 Chapman sent a copy to Loeffler, who read the book during his summer hospital convalescence. He described his response to Chapman.

> During the weary hours of recovery, when the body was so weak, the mind so sensitif, the heart so tenderly sympathetic, I meditated many hours over what you and your heroic boy had revealed to me. . . .
> After reading your book—while still at the hospital—I evolved in my thoughts, on all that I had learned of father and son, music, of which I should like to tell you in a few words the meaning. My work is in three parts and for stringed instruments. The first part called "Musique" is expressive of the mystical, the unconventional, the predestined, the heroic, the bizarre and the dramatic. The second part is called "Le Saint Jour de Pâques" with a wonderful chant of the Roman Liturgy "Resurrexi, et adhuc tecum sum, Alleluia: etc, etc" for the theme. The 3d part I have entitled "Paysages" (en France). It is a poetic conception of the field of action of the hero.[19]

The composition was *Music for Four Stringed Instruments*. The original version was completed in October 1917. He rewrote the conclusion in 1918 after which the first performance was given by the Flonzaley Quartet in New York on 15 February 1919, sponsored by the Society of Friends of Music. The Loefflers and Gardner attended the first performance in Aeolian Hall. Charles T. Griffes was also in the audience. Four days later the quartet was performed privately at Fanny Mason's in Boston.

Loeffler rewrote the quartet during the winter of 1919 and 1920. During this time he wrote to Gardner that "for the past six weeks, I have worked steadily on my quartet which I have rewritten entirely and which stands now on better legs. During those hours of critical contemplation of what I had done last year, the Siamese national hymn often came to my mind: O-wa ta-na Siam" [written to the opening measures of *America*].[20]

Music for Four Stringed Instruments was a deeply personal state-ment. The first two movements use as thematic material two Gregor-ian chants from the Easter Mass: *Resurrexi* and *Victimae Paschali.* The third movement is a tone poem picturing the landscape of France, the funeral and apotheosis of the hero; the apotheosis uses the chant melody *In paradisium.* The theme of the quartet is *Resurrexi;* the music is an expression of spiritual victory, a statement of faith.[21]

The Flonzaley Quartet played the quartet on several occasions, including a performance in London. Quartet member Adolpho Betti recognized the religious nature of the quartet in his comments to Loeffler. "It seems to me like a vast poem (an actual tryptich, is it not?) on the contemplation of death—such as one finds in the frescos of certain of our great Primitives. . . . There are pages that one would say were conceived in one of our churchyards, in the shade of cypress trees and in the midst of flowers that garland old graves. . . . Its true place would be, it seems to me, in a church; not in a large city church, where there is always something fossilized in the air, but in a small country church as there are in our homeland in Italy, where by an open door enter the great breath of the country in flower and the always powerful hymn of nature."[22]

Loeffler also undertook, in 1917, to write a song for the soldiers. He chose verses from Walt Whitman's "Drum Taps" and set them to very energetic music for unison male chorus and piano or small ensemble. He sent it to a publisher who neither published nor returned the score. Perhaps because the Whitman piece was lost, Loeffler wrote to Lowell, "Have you written anything lately that could be set to music by such a presumptuous fellow as myself? I mean something for the young soldiers to sing—in march form or song? If you have would you like me to try it?" Lowell replied, "I grieve to say that that patriotic song does not come, and I fear it never will. That is not my method of expression, I regret to say."[23] Loeffler was not able to give the soldiers a song.

Toward the end of the war Loeffler had another opportunity to help France directly. The Paris Conservatory orchestra was planning an American tour. Otto Kahn, of the Metropolitan Opera and chairman of the Franco-American Association for Musical Art, took charge of the tour. Loeffler became involved through Henri Casadesus.

Loeffler saw Casadesus several times from 1917 to 1919. Founder of the Société Nouvelle des Instruments Anciens, Casadesus had come to America in 1917 to give concerts with his ancient instruments. His tour brought him to Boston in January of 1918 and 1919. But, before that, he made a special trip to Boston to see Loeffler. The Ministrie de l'Instruction Publique et des Beaux Arts had conferred the honor of Officier de l'Instruction Publique on Loeffler. Casadesus delivered the diploma in November 1917.

Throughout his stay in America, Casadesus remained in close touch with Loeffler, through whom he was able to approach Higginson, Ellis, and other Bostonians about the proposed tour of the Conservatoire orchestra. Loeffler became chairman of the Boston arrangements. A major task he assumed was the raising of a sum of money to guarantee the tour. On this business he wrote to Lowell:

> I come a-begging this time! It cannot fail to interest you, that the Orchestra of the "Société des Concerts du Conservatoire" of Paris, the finest orchestra in the world, numbering 82 or 5 players with their distinguished conductor M. Messager, will come over next fall for a concert tour of 50 concerts, if we in Boston can raise a guarantee fond of 9000$ for three performances in our town. I am happy to say, that yesterday we succeeded in raising 6000$.
>
> I feel at rest in knowing that you cannot think me presumptious in appealing to you, our great and beloved poet, you so identified with French culture to help us in our endeavor to bring this fine enterprise to a victorious end. To have your name on our list would be a great moral help and a great honor.
>
> The French orchestra is not coming over to make money for money's sake, but "France" wishes to be heard, and who is the American that would deny her the opportunity?[24]

Lowell, like many others, did subscribe, ensuring the orchestra's visit. Before they arrived, however, Boston's own orchestra experienced its own trials that threatened its survival.

German supremacy in American concert life, where the majority of musicians, conductors, and repertoire were German, had long been established. During the war, however, violent anti-German sentiments held by many Americans, suspicious of all things German, affected the musical world, changing concert programs and the personnel of musical organizations. Many musicians in American orchestras lost or left their jobs because of the war. In Cincinnati, for example, in December 1917 Kunwald was arrested and interned as an enemy alien. The incident, unfortunately, was neither unique nor rare. (Loeffler himself, though German, escaped discrimination and suspicion by virtue of being thought French or Alsatian.)

Boston had its own war against Germany, which nearly destroyed the BSO itself. Many of the musicians of the orchestra were German, as was Muck (though a naturalized Swiss citizen). Popular as he had been before 1917, suspicion arose that he was an enemy alien, a spy.

A false story spread that he refused to play the national anthem, creating great antipathy towards Muck in Boston and other cities where the orchestra played. Higginson would not dismiss Muck, yet popular agitation became so intense that in March 1918 Muck was arrested by the federal government and interned in Georgia (with Kunwald) as an enemy alien.

When the Muck affair exploded, Higginson was eighty-four. He was very much distressed by the whole affair. In addition, after Muck's arrest, the fate of about one-third of the orchestra players was in doubt. Loeffler wrote to Casadesus: "Our government has not yet decided on the subject of about 30 musicians of the orchestra (aliens or enemy aliens). Mr. Higginson can hardly, for the moment, think about the continuation of his enterprise. He finds the task of replacing thirty musicians too overwhelming."[25] In February Higginson decided to give up his private ownership of the BSO. In April the orchestra was incorporated, the management entrusted to a board of trustees. At the same time Charles Ellis, who had been the orchestra's manager from its beginning, resigned. It was then the trustees who bore the burden of the survival of the orchestra.

The Muck affair must have been difficult for Loeffler also, though how he felt about Muck at this time is unknown. The most he is known to have written on the Muck arrest is a comment in a letter to Grace Schirmer: "What do you say to all the amazing things that have happened lately in Boston? I am sincerely sorry that these troubles could not have been spared Mr. Higginson. However our government knows what it is doing I am confident."[26]

Muck had originally come to Boston on Loeffler's recommendation. During Muck's first season Loeffler wrote to Grace Schirmer: "I trust you liked M. Muck 'though I fear he does not take his position very seriously! This is of course *very confidential!* From what I hear through musicians of the orchestra there is a great deal of joking going on during the rehearsals—sometimes even during concerts. The learned Dr. amuses himself at time by beating 3/4 time while the orchestra plays 4/4 as in 'Die Meistersinger' vorspiel. That kind of joke is very German and 'widerlich' [repulsive] to me. But the children of the BSO enjoy it and him!"[27]

Muck had been, however, very much admired as a conductor and had returned for a second term (his two terms were 1906–8 and 1912–18). He had respected Loeffler as a composer, had conducted Loeffler's new works, *A Pagan Poem* (during three seasons) and *Hora mystica,* as well as *La mort de Tintagiles* (two seasons). Loeffler had shared his opera with Muck, in fact wrote to Damrosch, "If *you* and

Dr. Muck consider my score and libretto of value, I should consider it a great honor if you were to propose this work of mine to Mr. Cravath, Mr. Gatti, and possibly to Mr. Toscanini."[28] There is no reason to suppose that the relationship between Muck and Loeffler continued to be other than cordial; however, at the end of his life he gave a student the impression that he liked Muck not at all.[29]

Following Muck's removal, the orchestra was without a conductor. Ernst Schmidt, the assistant conductor (also an "alien") finished the season, but a new conductor had to be found. For the first time, Germany was completely overlooked in the search for a conductor. The trustees considered many possibilities, including the conductors of France.

France was also looking at Boston. Casadesus, who assumed leadership in looking for positions for French musicians in America, wrote to Loeffler to recommend French conductors. Loeffler's first choice was the Belgian Ysaÿe, who had telegraphed to Loeffler in November 1917 that if Muck resigned he would replace him but who took the position in Cincinnati vacated by Kunwald. Loeffler also spoke to Higginson and the trustees about Casadesus's recommendations, specifically Rhené-Baton and Camille Chenillard. He also recommended Guy Ropartz and perhaps others as well. For a brief moment the choice seemed to be Chenillard; however, the definitive announcement, not made until September, declared that Pierre Monteux would come up from New York to conduct the first month after which the season would be given to Henri Rabaud.

The BSO was no longer a German orchestra. For five years it would be directed by French conductors, followed by the long directorship of Serge Koussevitzky. The membership of the orchestra also changed. Muck himself had engaged French woodwind players when he returned in 1912. In 1918, after a number of German players left or were dismissed, Loeffler campaigned for French musicians, and several French musicians were employed.

A new era had, in a sense, begun for the BSO. The war changed not only the personnel of orchestras but also the repertoire. Although music of countries other than Germany had been performed before the war, the war gave these countries, particularly France and Russia, a real chance to be heard.

The music of France had its chance, not only with the appointment of a French conductor in Boston but also with the visit of the Conservatoire orchestra in the fall of 1918. Their first concert in America was at the Metropolitan Opera House in October. In Boston they performed music of Bizet, Beethoven, Debussy, Saint-Saëns, Franck, and

Berlioz. When the orchestra came to Boston, Loeffler had the opportunity to hear the orchestra he had judged in 1904 to be the best in Europe. He also enjoyed a reunion with friends, such as Alfred Cortot, the soloist with the orchestra, and with Casadesus, who, just the next month, performed *Tintagiles* with the St. Louis Symphony.

Rabaud stayed with the BSO only one season. He joined the orchestra just one week after Monteux had conducted Loeffler's *Poem* (the revision of *La bonne chanson*) in Boston, Washington, Baltimore, and New York. He and Loeffler became good friends. Rabaud looked to Loeffler for advice and help in a variety of matters—English texts, introductions to musical figures, the choice of a doctor, and other personal and professional concerns.

Loeffler considered Rabaud "a warm hearted man, an exquisite musician!"[30] To Gardner, he wrote: "Personally I bear M. Rabaud a sincere affection and really believe him to be one of the most high minded of men I have known." Recommending Rabaud "for innate nobility of mind and heart," Loeffler arranged for Rabaud to meet Gardner, as he had done for Casals, Cortot, d'Indy, the Flonzaley Quartet, and others.[31] It must have been a particularly pleasant occasion for Loeffler, since about this time he renewed his own friendship with Gardner, a friendship he feared he had lost, as he declared to her: "Many little incidents within the last year or so—incidents connected directly or indirectly with the war and personal enemies of mine— made me feel and fear, that I had lost your once so friendly regard."[32] (Curiously, Loeffler had also written to Engel in 1917 to thank him for expressions of friendship "in these days of intense aversions."[33])

Whatever the "incidents" so vaguely alluded to here, Loeffler had not lost Gardner's friendship. Indeed, what prompted Loeffler's letter was Gardner's gift to him of her Stradivarius violin, so often loaned to Loeffler for his performances. Loeffler wrote: "One of the pleasures in playing the beautiful Stradivarius was, that it belonged to you and that you entrusted it to me. . . . I hardly know now, how to express to you how deeply I am moved in rereading your kind letter. Your presenting me with the beautiful Stradivarius is so generous a gift and so much proof of your kindly sentiment for me, that I feel as if I had fallen out of a dark cloud. I am deeply grateful, dear Mrs. Gardner, for all your kindness, but I am above all most happy to know of your affectionate regard for me. In thanking you with all my heart I assure you of my gratitude and affection at the same time."[34]

Loeffler rather quickly lost Rabaud's association in Boston. After returning to Europe, however, Rabaud continued to correspond with Loeffler, keeping Loeffler up to date on events in Paris. He continued to consult Loeffler about English texts, particularly for his composition *Riders to the Sea*. He did not, however, take Loeffler's advice to decline the directorship of the Conservatoire. "I advised M. Rabaud," Loeffler wrote to Gardner, "not to accept such an offer as it would hold him down to work which would prevent him from composing. However his conscience is terrifically New Englandish, in spite of my sound advice, that to write some fine scores was his first duty to the story of fame."[35]

Rabaud's first choice for a successor was Gabriel Pierné; his second, Pierre Monteux. When Pierné did not accept, Rabaud with Loeffler's second recommended Monteux. Judge Cabot proposed Monteux's name to the trustees and wired Monteux. Monteux accepted and remained with the BSO until 1924.

During Monteux's first season, all Boston lost a great benefactor with the death of Henry Higginson in November 1919. Loeffler lost a good and loyal friend who had supported him throughout his entire career, both as a violinist and as a composer. From Loeffler's first years in Boston Higginson had relied on him to help with the selection of new orchestral personnel; his final correspondence with Loeffler included consultation over the replacement of Muck. This high regard for Loeffler's talent and judgment was also respected by the trustees.

While Loeffler continued to work for the BSO, he also had a hand in the workings of a new Boston orchestra, the Boston Musical Association, founded by Georges Longy in 1919. It was short-lived but in that time performed several new works in Boston, for which purpose it had been founded. The string section of the orchestra owed a heavy debt to Loeffler's tutelage. Loeffler's student Gertrude Marshall was concertmistress; she, Nina Fletcher, and Carmela Ippolito (all Loeffler's students) appeared as soloists, and other Loeffler students were members of the orchestra. Occasionally the American String Quartette appeared on Association programs. Loeffler held a sustaining and supporting membership in the association. For the association's program cover Loeffler lent a drawing done for him years earlier by Denis Bunker.

Loeffler's postwar work included more than helping Boston's orchestras and promoting French music and musicians. He continued to help people in Europe after the war as he had during it. Loeffler assumed much of the burden of support for his sister and her husband, sending them packages of food and gifts of money. Helene never recovered financial independence. In March 1921 her husband died; it took years to receive the money he left in trust for her, which, in any case, was severely devalued through inflation. Loeffler continued to send Helene food, clothing, money, and other gifts. Despite her hardships, she never consented to join her brother in America.

Loeffler continued to raise relief funds. On 4 June 1919 he held a concert for the Benefit of Devastated France at the Unitarian church in Medfield. (After the Armistice, since the Roman Catholic church disallowed concerts being held in their churches, Loeffler no longer used St. Edward's.) As part of this concert, the first performance of Loeffler's *Hymne* for soprano, five-part strings, organ, and piano was given. Povla Frijsh, Heinrich Gebhard, and Albert Snow (from the New England Conservatory) were the featured performers. The *Hymne* is characteristic of Loeffler's sacred music with its rich and sweet mood of devotion. That this piece sprang from feelings engendered by the war is evidenced in the prayer itself: "O thou who will come to judge the world at the last day, we beseech thee protect us with the arms of thy grace against our enemies."

Among those who attended the performance was John Singer Sargent, whom Loeffler saw often during and after the war. In 1917 Sargent did a charcoal portrait of Loeffler standing in Sargent's studio beside the model for the rotunda of the Boston museum which Sargent was redesigning for mural decorations. Sargent, Loeffler, and Gardner together heard the organist Joseph Bonnet in 1918. Another evening these three planned to spend together, with Sargent's sister Emily, to see *Pelléas et Mélisande* had to be cancelled when illness prevented both Loeffler and Gardner from going. Loeffler sincerely enjoyed Sargent's company, as he wrote to Gardner in January 1920: "I had some pleasant hours with John Sargent. He was lovable, indulgent, and amazing as ever. How keen his appreciations are in literature and music for instance! To have known him and you, dear Mrs. Gardner, has been one of the great privileges of my life."[36]

Together Loeffler and Sargent helped Fauré, whom they had heard was in straitened conditions, by sending a gift of money. Loeffler wrote to Sargent: "The two thousand francs are now on the water for our friend Fauré. . . . I believe Fauré will be pleased, not only with your letter but even with mine, and no doubt will swallow the friendly and affectionate 'administration.' At all events, I have this off my mind and heart. It was very good of you to step in so generously into the helping scheme."[37] Loeffler also continued to help Fauré get his music published. In 1919 the Boston Music Company published Fauré's Sonata for Violin, op. 13, edited by Loeffler. Fauré gave Loeffler permission to orchestrate his compositions, and Loeffler did an orchestration of Fauré's *Elégie* for cello and made arrangements of several other pieces (all unpublished). Fauré, appreciative of all of Loeffler's efforts on his behalf and frankly fond of Loeffler, in November 1921 offered Loeffler the dedication of his second cello sonata, op. 117, "in remembrance of the affectionate interest that you have always witnessed towards my music and myself."[38]

There were other friends whom Loeffler helped. During 1921 he contributed to a Golden Jubilee for César Thomson in Brussels, and he also contributed to the support of Strasbourg University, again part of France.

In 1921 Loeffler's attention was again directed to d'Indy, who (with his new wife) in December returned to America and was guest conductor of the BSO. "What joy to see you again," d'Indy wrote a month before coming. "I have often thought of you, believe me, and about our talks on Art and Aesthetics, and it seems to me that that will begin again naturally as if there had not been an interruption of 17 years!"[39] Loeffler hosted d'Indy in Boston, took him to Fenway Court and to the Tavern Club for an honorary lunch. He attended a concert given by d'Indy at Copley Plaza Hotel. He had hoped to arrange, for this visit, a performance of d'Indy's *St. Christopher* by the New York Met. Although Ziegler and Gatti-Casazza discussed the idea, Loeffler was unsuccessful.

Loeffler's efforts on behalf of French musicians during and after the war did not go unrecognized. Casadesus and Rabaud were determined to ask the French government for recognition of all that Loeffler had done. In April 1918 Loeffler received a letter of appreciation from the Haut Commissariat. On 12 July 1919 Loeffler received word from the director general of the French Services in the United States that he had been elected a *chevalier* of the Légion d'Honneur. In 1920 the Académie des Beaux Arts, of which Loeffler had been a member since 1906, unanimously elected him as a *correspondant* replacing Max Bruch.

In 1920 also, Loeffler began serving as a member of the Honorary and Advisory Board of the new Franco-American Musical Society, founded by Germaine and Robert Schmitz. The society began issuing a journal in 1923; however, in 1926, having broader international interests, the publication was renamed, after the new name of the society, the *Pro-Musica Quarterly*.

Loeffler being one of the Americans most expert on French music, the new attention to the music of France placed him in his element. As ever he kept current with French music, and in 1923 he was able to advise a student then in Paris to remain under the influence of "the valiant Mm. D'Indy, Gédalge, and Mr. Koechlin with all of whom I hope you are having the time of your life. Or perhaps not? Do you like the other gang better? I mean the '5' or less, or still another latter 'chapelle' whose members will have yet to prove their quality and 'raison d'être.' . . . M. Gédalge is the man to guide and to lead you through all the intricacies of double counterpoint and fugue to free composition. . . . Maître d'Indy will stand by you with his good judgement of esthetics in art, composition and orchestration. Of Mr. Koechlin I know less, but had the pleasure of hearing 4 Chorales for Orchestra which I found very interesting." Loeffler noted that audience reaction to Koechlin's music had been cool, as he recalled it had been to Debussy's *L'après-midi d'une faune,* when no one applauded. "I often think of that gruesome silence, after that so delightfully Mozartean piece of music as 'le grand silence des Mufles' [the great silence of muzzles]. All tadpoles have not evoluted as yet into humanly feeling beings!"[40]

Occasionally the people of France had the opportunity to hear Loeffler's music. On 9 March 1920, for example, his *Rapsodies* were performed at the Salle Erard by the Société Française de Concerts. Another occasion arose when the French Minister of Fine Arts invited Walter Damrosch to bring the New York Symphonic Society to visit France in 1920. While the bulk of the three programs Damrosch devised consisted of European music, two Americans were represented—Loeffler and John Powell, the latter of whom accompanied the orchestra to play the solo part of his own *Rapsodie nègre* for piano and orchestra.

When Damrosch approached Loeffler about the concert, Loeffler suggested his own favorite among his orchestral works, *A Pagan Poem.* As alternatives he suggested Griffes's *Kubla Khan,* "an excellent, though ultramodern work,"[41] Hill's *Stevensonian Suite,* or Carpenter's *Perambulator,* which he felt suited the current taste of Parisians.

When *A Pagan Poem* was felt to be impractical (probably because of the juxtaposition to Powell's piano piece), *Poem* for Orchestra was scheduled, although Loeffler felt it was "old fogeishness" and feared for its reception,[42] as he confided to Damrosch: "to tell an old and beloved friend the truth: I would rather not have any of my stuff played in Paris. It will not be received, from the point of view alone of having been written by someone with a name of Germanic resonance, but with sincere antagonism. I have ever been, and during the war all the more so, most loyal and devoted to France: this has been more than duly recognized by the French government and all Frenchmen that know me. But I believe that my instinct and delicacy of feeling in this matter is correct in expressing to you most sincerely my request of cutting me out of your plans."[43]

Again Loeffler recommended substituting *Kubla Khan*. However, Damrosch replied: "I think you are wrong in your fear of any antagonism whatsoever. In the first place, I found the French curiously free from such war psychosis as demonstrated itself here during the war from some of our hectic women music fans. And secondly, your name is held in high esteem by musicians and critics in Paris."[44] Loeffler then consented and attended rehearsals in New York. "The rehearsal," he wrote to Gardner, "took place in a small hall, just large enough to hold the orchestra *only*! You may imagine what it sounded like! All pianos sounded forte and the latter almost raised the roof of the building! Such, in a word, are the tribulations of a composer! Poor Walter D. of course could not help it."[45]

Loeffler's *Poem* was performed on Damrosch's third and final program in Paris. The series was attended by several of Loeffler's friends including d'Indy, Fauré, Messager, and Rabaud. The orchestra then toured France, Italy, Belgium, Holland, and England.

Other European performances of Loeffler's music took place during the years after the war, including *Tintagiles* in Stockholm (1919), Berlin (1923), and Christiana (1923); *Villanelle* in London (1920); *A Pagan Poem* in Barcelona (1922) and Amsterdam (1926); *Poem* in Stockholm (1926); and *Deux rapsodies* in Strasbourg (1923). He started to acquire an international reputation, though he gave little credence to it, commenting to Engel, "What the devil is all the hububb about in London, putting me in a Cyclopedia? Nobody knows me there nor ever will."[46]

Despite his own feelings about it, Loeffler was, for an American composer of his time, exceptionally successful having his music performed. His position as a composer, both internationally and nationally, was increasingly respected and acknowledged during the last decades of his life.

16

Dean of American Composers

Settled into his country home, the Farmer of Medfield was acquiring a reputation as a recluse. Yet Loeffler was still an active, influential, and visible figure in the musical life of the country.

In Boston itself, Loeffler's eminence and respected position as a composer was reaffirmed during the war years by his unanimous election by his colleagues as president of the Composers Club of Boston. Founded in 1916, the club essayed to meet once a month from October to April "to promote social and artistic fellowship among composers; to perform, or facilitate the performance of, compositions of its members; and to further acquaintance with works of American composers who are not members of the Club."[1] Charter members were Percy Atherton, George W. Chadwick, Philip Greeley Clapp, Chalmers Clifton, Frederick S. Converse, Carl Engel, Arthur Foote, Henry F. Gilbert, Wallace Goodrich, William C. Heilman, E. B. Hill, Clayton Johns, Loeffler, Arthur Shepherd, and Walter Spalding.

Percy Atherton, club secretary, described the club's short life. "Briefly, the Club enjoyed a rather tenuous existence: partly owing to our imminent involvement in World War I, but quite as much because the members, listening to the works of colleagues, tended to accept them far too politely. One altogether missed the fiery art-discussions and disagreements traditionally associated with similar situations in and out of Parisian cafés and studios. Of course, with us Bostonians the volatile Latin temperament was all too conspicuously lacking. The Club breathed its decorous last after its second year, leaving but a regrettably slight ripple on the musical waters of Boston's 'Back Bay.'"[2]

Historians have designated the composers in Boston of Loeffler's time as the "Boston School" or the "Second New England School" (the first New England school having been William Billings and his contemporaries). There was no school in the sense of a deliberate banding together to espouse the same ideals and create in a vein. But as a consequence of education (most Boston composers were students of J. K. Paine or G. W. Chadwick, both educated in Germany), convention, or preference there was a decided classical and Germanic bent to musical aesthetics and composition among Boston's composers.

Conservative classicism being the prevailing aesthetic, many were reserved about Loeffler's music, associated as it was with Decadence and the avant-garde. Arthur Foote, for example, whose tastes continued in a direct line from Dwight and Dresel, cared little for Loeffler's music. D. G. Mason also, although he recognized Loeffler as an accomplished French composer and admired some individual compositions, was out of sympathy with Loeffler's general aesthetic. He differed from Arthur Whiting (a former Boston composer who had moved to New York), whose view Mason recorded: "Whiting's best beloved composers, I suppose, were Bach and Brahms. . . . His taste was broad enough, however, to include a good deal of impressionism also, especially Debussy, Ravel, and his friend Loeffler—though he was by no means unaware of its decadent qualities. Someone once called Loeffler's pieces 'a mass of decay.' 'Yes,' agreed Arthur, 'but such swell decay!'"[3]

Loeffler's music was admired by a number of composers besides Whiting. Expressions of this admiration may be gleaned from correspondence to Loeffler.

Percy Atherton: "I want to express to you my admiration of your latest Opus [*Hora mystica*]. . . . While I must confess that to my non-ultra ears many passages were 'difficult' of comprehension (especially at a single hearing) I had at all times the consciousness that the man behind the music knew exactly what he wanted and expressed that conviction with power and masterly technique."[4]

Chalmers Clifton: "After a second hearing of your symphony, I cannot forbear writing you of my renewed impression of its beauty of conception and rare technical achievement. But more important and fundamental is its compelling mysticism which emanates from a sensitive soul." And "Every time I listen to this masterpiece [*A Pagan Poem*], I am greatly moved by its beauty of sound, subtle evocation of mood, and superb craftsmanship."[5]

Frederick Converse: "I think them [*Poem* and *Villanelle*], without exception, the best modern works that we have had for some years, both in point of inspiration and workmanship. I call them masterworks." And "[*A Pagan Poem*] is one of the things that I like best in all music."[6]

Walter Damrosch: "Your 'Pagan Poem' we produce because it is a great work, but if your compositions were only half as good as they are, I should perform them every year."[7]

Henry Eichheim: "[*Malay Mosaic*] is dedicated to you in warmest and deepest homage . . . it is not an adequate expression of all the gratitude I feel toward you for the rich and wondrous experience I had in hearing your noble and beautiful music during so many years of our companionship."[8] (Eichheim dedicated three other compositions to Loeffler.)

Wallace Goodrich: "[*Poem*] is a noble and beautiful work—as full of imagination as it is clear in expression—and a rarely beautiful combination of loveliness in both the musical content and the orchestral color. It was more than a pleasure to hear it—it did one good."[9]

E. B. Hill: "I find it [*Hora mystica*] a noble and elevated work full of beauty, poetic thought and a remarkable atmosphere of spiritual contemplation and reverence. In this latter respect it is quite unique among modern works, which reflect so much of the temporal and so relatively little of the eternal! It is exasperating to hear a piece of so much depth and concentration of substance only once, and I hope that it will be repeated very soon."[10]

B. J. Lang: "Your playing and the composition itself were a joy to my heart—the perfection of one and the delightful originality of the other were absolutely satisfying. We at this house are proud of you to the fingertips."[11]

D. G. Mason: "However divergent our aesthetics may be I have always admired your thoroughness of workmanship, and I consider it high praise that you should wish to hear anything of mine a second time." And "I want to tell you how delighted I was with your Irish Fantasies last night. They held one's interest every moment, their rhythmic life carried one along, many places were appealingly expressive, and the orchestration splendid. I wish I could hear it again."[12]

Arthur Shepherd: "I have just this moment finished playing the last measures of "La cornemuse" and have experienced that rare feeling—indescribable but permeated with a joyful gratitude—that overtakes one, when suddenly confronted with *true beauty*!"[13]

Arthur Whiting: "I have just been looking over your two rhapsodies (oboe, viola, pianoforte) not having seen them for several years, and I am bound to say they are masterpieces that give me absolute satisfaction and joy. However you feel about them, there isn't a grey hair or a rheumatic joint in one page, and years are the real test of vitality."[14]

Other testimonials were written for publication. Carl Engel wrote several articles praising Loeffler. Walter Spalding, in one of his books, wrote that "the composer of greatest genius and scope in America is undoubtedly Charles Martin Loeffler."[15] In a posthumous tribute, E. B. Hill, an enthusiastic admirer of Loeffler and one of the few possibly influenced by his style, called him "an unparalleled figure in our recent musical life."[16]

In some cases, support of Loeffler's work from fellow composers was manifested by more than written tribute. Damrosch, for example, enjoyed conducting Loeffler's works. For another example, Arthur Shepherd, who had conducted the Musical Art Society in Boston for three years, resigned in 1917 in protest against certain of the society's officers' refusing to permit a performance of Loeffler's *Psalm*.

Organizations also honored Loeffler. In January 1920 the National Institute of Arts and Letters awarded Loeffler their Gold Medal, "given yearly to the person judged to have distinguished himself in his particular profession."[17] In 1928 he received (at the same time as Eugene O'Neill) an honorary degree from Yale, "as an eminent representative of a noble art, a creator and interpreter of beauty in melodic forms."[18] In 1931 he was elected to the American Academy of Arts and Letters (the inner body of the National Institute of Arts and Letters, limited to fifty people).

Loeffler also received prizes, commissions, and continued critical acclaim. He was sought after to serve on musical competition juries, including the North Shore Music Festival Association, Elizabeth Sprague Coolidge's chamber music competitions, and the Paderewski Competition. In addition, he served as an honorary member of music committees, including those for the Salzburg Festival Playhouse in 1922 and the Sesquicentennial Exposition in Philadelphia in 1926.

Though he never joined a school faculty, Loeffler helped during the formation of the New York Institute of Musical Art and the Juilliard School, was consulted by the Fontainebleau School of Music for Americans, and was invited to address the student body at the Curtis Institute. In a journal article proposing a National Conservatory, Charles Henry Meltzer stated his first choice for director would be Loeffler, "admired by all who know how long and well he has worked for art."[19]

There was hardly a more respected musical figure in America. Loeffler the "exotic" had become a recognized "dean of American composers" (as he was called in more than one obituary).

In turn, Loeffler had a very good opinion of American music and American composers. "There is a great deal of talent rampant in our glorious land," he wrote to Elizabeth Sprague Coolidge, specifically in reference to composers.[20] He admired and encouraged American composers and enjoyed attending performances of their works, as evidenced in the following selection of his remarks on individual composers.

On J. A. Carpenter: "I have always had a predilection for Carpenters gift as a musician and I am delighted at his great success."[21]

On Frederick Converse: "This week, at the Symphony, we are having Fred. Converse's New Symphony which to me is a very noble work, expressive of his own noble soul. I cannot tell you all the good I find in this man, all the good I think of the man and the musician"; and "I enjoyed Converse's 'Job' as a fine sustained effort of a man of great talent."[22]

To Walter Damrosch: "Having plowed away and wallowed in storm for some time on my own One Act play, I know of the difficulties, the doubts and hazards that one encounters in the business of writing an opera. It is therefore with genuine admiration, that I take off my hat and bow low to him, who could write the Score of Cyrano. . . . While the musician listened during the hours of the performance, the friend in him was carefully kept apart. When, however, the musician's heart began beating more and more warmly the friend and the musician became again at one in their joy."[23] (Loeffler had traveled to New York expressly to see *Cyrano,* returning by train the same night.)

To Carl Engel after an examination of Engel's manuscripts: "I don't know what your religion is . . , but when you go to bed tonight thank God He made you what you are."[24]

To Wallace Goodrich: "Your score promises great delight from my point of view, and I am happy to think that a friend wrote it whom I must admire the more for it."[25]

On Horatio Parker: "I was in hopes that he would write some more, for here is a man who has something to say."[26]

To Rabaud Loeffler recommended Parker's compositions and also Hill's, as a consequence of which Hill's *Stevensoniana* was performed by the BSO in March 1919. To Koussevitzky he recommended Eichheim's music, and *A Chinese Legend* was performed. Loeffler also recommended Shepherd and Engel as composers to Coolidge, and Griffes and Carpenter to Damrosch.

Publicly Loeffler voiced his support of American music on more than one occasion.

As to American music, so-called, I am very hopeful as to its outcome, for you have some composers who have done excellent things—although I personally may not agree with all these same writers may say. . . .

I think that Americans are very talented: I cannot imagine any one saying to the contrary, for any country should be extremely proud of the composers and opera singers whom America has already produced. Yes, America is all right. See what Theodore Thomas did for music! People who do things here have a chance given them. There is the symphony orchestra—it has graciously treated American compositions on a perfect parity with those of other nations, giving an equal chance to all.[27]

"This country," he said elsewhere, "is quick to reward genuine musical merit, and to reward it far more generously than Europe. Our best orchestras are surpassed nowhere, and they are as ready to perform native works as those of the recognized European masters. A land that produced Theodore Thomas, and that supports so many great musical organizations of the sort he established, need not be ashamed of its musical status."[28]

"As a man," Loeffler declared, "I am very fond of America and Americans."[29] Loeffler liked much in American literature, as well as music, not only poetry but also the humor of such writers as Mark Twain and Will Rogers. As he read and praised Lowell's books on French poets, so also he read and praised John Macy's book, *American Literature*. Arthur Shepherd wrote: "I remember his expression of regret that he had not been born in America! I have in my possession a set of wild-west stories by Clarence Mulford ('Hopalong Cassidy,' etc.) presented to me by Loeffler. What a paradox from a musician who was once almost like a family member in the home of G. Fauré."[30]

For all that Loeffler loved America and had found a place of distinction and influence among American composers, he was, however, never fully accepted as an American composer. "Americans," wrote Deems Taylor, "who know his music are inclined to classify him, almost subconsciously, as a French composer; and the French call him an American. . . . His music . . . spoke a language that we weren't used to; it sounded foreign. Nothing that we were accustomed to associate with American. And so, while we admitted that, technically he was an American composer, we didn't quite believe it."[31]

Loeffler had the same doubt. Though he once wrote, "I belong to the Americans," he did not quite consider himself an American composer.[32] Before entering one of Coolidge's chamber music competitions, he wrote to inquire if he qualified as an American composer (he did). He did not consciously seek to be American as a composer by adopting some sort of ethnic American style. He dabbled with some American musical materials but was not involved in any attempts to create nationalistic American music. But he did support others so involved.

Loeffler helped the Wa-Wan Society, founded by Arthur Farwell to be "a national organization for the advancement of the work of American composers, and the interests of the musical life of the American people."[33] Its executive board consisted of Chadwick, Loeffler, Gilman, Ernest Kroeger, Frank Damrosch, and Spencer Traske. Farwell shouldered the bulk of the work, especially the Press. Allegedly, "Loeffler was the only figure to show extraordinary interest, and his comments about accepting manuscripts were thankfully received by Farwell and [Henry] Gilbert."[34]

Arthur Shepherd remarked:

> I recall the somewhat snobbish attitude of various musicians and "big-wigs" of the established order, and there were, of course, many lively discussions on the side concerning the artistic merit of the Wa-Wan output. One composer, however, of unquestioned eminence was openminded and very cordial to the new spirit manifested in this venture. I refer to Charles Martin Loeffler, whose genius and culture was always an incentive, and many of us owe to him more than can actually be put down in words. . . . he was an influence by reason of a most impressive culture; critical acumen taste and artistic integrity unmatched by his immediate Boston Contemporaries. He too saw the urgent need for us fellows to emancipate ourselves from the incubus of German romanticism.[35]

Loeffler's *Les soirs d'automne* was performed on the first concert of the Wa-Wan Society in New York (28 February 1908), but Loeffler's compositions were not published by the Wa-Wan Press. A few were published by C. C. Birchard and Company in Boston. This company, which first published music for school chorus and orchestra, turned during the 1920s to publishing orchestral works with the aim of helping American composers, beginning with the works of E. S. Kelley, Henry Hadley, and Arthur Shepherd. Birchard published four of Loeffler's last works: *Evocation, Beat! Beat! Drums!,* and posthumously *Prière* and *The Passion of Hilarion.* After the death of Rudolph Schirmer in 1919, Loeffler lost his last tie of sympathy with that firm, but Schirmer's did publish a few more of Loeffler's scores. The Society for the Publication of American Music, of which Loeffler was an honorary member, chose *Music for Four Stringed Instruments* for publication in 1923. *Canticum fratris solis* was published by the Library of Congress six years later.

In contradiction to the esteem granted Loeffler as a composer was the fact that he did not gather a school or disciples around him. He is known to have taken at least four composition students, but he did not have the reputation as a composition teacher that he had as a violin teacher. Those who did receive compositional instruction were John Beach, Alexander Steinert, Kay Swift, and Francis Judd Cooke. Shepherd may not have been a student but he did relate that "the best lesson I ever had" occurred when he took a violin sonata to Loeffler and together they read through and discussed it.[36]

Alexander Steinert, who had been referred to Loeffler by Gardner, claimed that Loeffler was the finest teacher in composition he ever worked with, that he knew the orchestra from A to Z, and that his view of composition was based on classical structure and order in music.[37]

Kay Swift was even more enthusiastic about Loeffler as a teacher. She had been a great fan of Loeffler's music long before meeting him. When she went to live in Cambridge and took piano lessons from Heinrich Gebhard, she asked about Loeffler. After a while Gebhard talked to Loeffler, who said he would see Swift if she could come out to Medfield. She did, and Loeffler arranged to give her lessons on alternate Saturdays. Later she remarked, "In looking back I thank heaven for having known Loeffler whose music I had known for some years and admired tremendously, listened to with avid interest—and then finally to meet him and then have him willing to teach me and listen to my music, I cannot imagine anything more inspiring and more helpful to someone trying to do some work along these lines."[38]

According to Swift, Loeffler always showed interest and was very attentive and very constructive. When she brought him music, he would never say, "That's wrong" or "terrible" or "That isn't the way you should develop this theme," but rather he would say, "Do you think it would be more interesting if you did this or that sort of thing?" He was not ex cathedra, and he had such widespread interests that Swift was never ashamed of any kind of music that she might take to him. In particular she found him to be a "master of the orchestra."

The "master of the orchestra" had a number of admirers among the nation's orchestral conductors, as well as its composers. In Boston his compositions had been performed by every conductor since 1891 (except Rabaud, although Monteux conducted *Poem* at the beginning of Rabaud's one season), and the tradition was continued by Serge Koussevitzky, who joined the BSO in 1924, following Monteux. In New York Loeffler's music was conducted by Mahler, Damrosch, Walter, and Stransky; in Philadelphia, by Molinari, Scheel, and Stokowski; in Baltimore by Siemann, Schelling, and former BSO member Strube; in Cincinnati by van der Stucken, Kunwald, and Reiner; in

Cleveland by Sokoloff; and in Chicago by Stock. The most keen to conduct his music, apparently, were Damrosch, Stransky, Stokowski, Stock, and his former student Sokoloff.

In postwar America Loeffler was still considered by many as a modern composer. In 1919, for example, when Varèse organized the New Symphony Orchestra of the New York Federation of Musicians "to be devoted to the most advanced contemporary music," Loeffler's *Pagan Poem* was chosen for the first season (along with music by Varèse, Bartok, Debussy, Griffes, Satie, Ravel, Roussel, and others).[39] The work was actually performed during the second season under Artur Bodansky.

To other minds, by the 1920s Loeffler was no longer modern. In the face of the new wave of the avant-garde—Varèse, Antheil, Schoenberg, Stravinsky—Loeffler had become an ivory tower composer, removed from the present. As at the beginning of his career, Loeffler's critics were split. Some criticized Loeffler for not being timely, for not belonging to the age of skyscrapers and industrial modernism (what they perceived as reality). For example, Copland described Loeffler and Griffes as escapists: "As composers, they seemed quite content to avoid contact with the world they lived in. Unlike the poetry of Sandburg or the novels of Dreiser or Frank Norris, conscious of the crude realities of industrial America, you will find no picture of the times in the music of Loeffler or Griffes."[40]

However, some continued to perceive the relevance of Loeffler's visions. "Often in Loeffler's music," wrote Gilman for Loeffler's seventieth birthday, "we are brought close to immemorial things—to sorrow and loveliness and transport and faith and the haunted destiny of man, his terrors and fantasies and dreams; so that we may find ourselves wondering if this is not, perhaps, art of the sort that can afford to be indifferent to the hues of time."[41]

Loeffler himself was quite aware that to many he was, to use a term he favored himself, an old fogey. Responding to Engel's request in 1926 to perform *L'archet,* Loeffler declined, saying, "The music is, since the reign of the Internationalists, apparently (or possibly in fact) demodé." Elsewhere, in a discussion on the subject of the depiction in art of the realities of the war, he concluded: "Our imagination of artists will see nothing but ugly nightmares, and what is engendered by these will be music similar to rachitic children, born too late, with black whiskers, bald heads and horseteeth. It would not be beautiful. For all of us it is much better to live in a world of unrealities. . . . Idealism and loftiness of spirit, that alone counts."[42]

However Loeffler was rated during the 1920s and 1930s, his music continued to be played. The BSO continued to regard Loeffler's music as a staple of its repertoire, and all the major orchestras vied for the privilege of introducing Loeffler's new music.

Through the 1920s Loeffler's composing continued unabated. He returned in 1920 to work on *The White Fox* but again abandoned it. During the winter of 1919 and 1920 he worked on two projects mentioned in a letter to Gardner in which news of his work seems hardly as important as that of his beloved wildlife.

> This last snowstorm has again tied up railroad and "electrics" and the snowdrifts at the end of my street toward Medfield are simply formidable. I have kept up feeding my poor friends the birds. The family consists of pheasants, crows, 10,000,000 blue jays, tree sparrows, juncos, starlings, chicadees (5,000,000) and two partridges. I have four feeding stations on the place. I have found a new way of feeding the larger birds by tying ears of corn on the tree branches. Obviously I am feeding a lot of marauders and thieves like crows and blue jays, but lately I discovered a roosting place of two partridges whom I see now daily under the same tree where I feed them. The quail—I fear—have perished from hunger this winter. There are now a great many foxes, at all events their tracks are crossing our meadows about every 50 feet. The snow is a great revealer of wild animal neighborhood existence.
>
> I am pegging away in these days, composing or concocting Machiavellian finger exercises for violinists without imagination. Nature has created a great many vacuums besides hollow nuts!—
>
> At present I am writing an a capella chorus for mixed voices to the words of the Angelus. This is of course nothing for Boston (with its asinine, medieval hatred for anything connected with the Mother Church) but when it is finished I shall play it to you.[43]

Loeffler wrote the violin exercises for his students, rather than for publication, although a set of thirty-five were posthumously published. He used at least one of his own exercises in his composing, a passage of continuous sixteenth notes for the first violins near the end of *Evocation*. His *Angelus* for eight-part a capella choir appears to have been intended as part of a larger work, *Drei Marienlieder*, never completed. It was never performed.

In 1920 Kreisler consulted Loeffler about performing the *Divertissement*. "He has always," wrote Loeffler to Gardner, "been fond of me and by appointment we both spent Saturday together (in Boston, in the Copley-Plaza ball-room where there is a Piano) playing through your 'Divertimento,' which it was 'convenu' he should play next winter with orchestra everywhere. He was very enthusiastic over the composition, though I assured him, that the best thing about it was, that your name ornamented my title page."[44] But the *Divertissement* was not revived. In April 1923 Kreisler did perform Loeffler's arrangement of Chabrier's *Scherzo-Valse* at Carnegie Hall, which Ysaÿe had performed in Boston earlier.

Loeffler began a new orchestral work in 1920. In this year the Irish Free State was established, and during the summer Loeffler revised and orchestrated his Irish songs, *The Wind among the Reeds*. He then composed three other orchestral songs, two on texts by Yeats and one by William Heffernan (the Blind). Loeffler's comments on the composition to Gardner again set his composing in its rural setting. "During Gebby's [Gebhard's] wedding trip I have been busy getting our hay crop in the barn which has taken a little over two weeks and so much of anxiety about rain and so forth spoiling the crop is over. In my spare hours I have been orchestrating some songs for tenor (McCormac) and orchestra on words by Yeats.... The first two I had written some time ago but have changed for the better. The last [the third] is very recent. It is somewhat 'reely and jiggy.'"[45]

The five fantasies are each brilliantly orchestrated and evocative of the Irish spirit, each in its own way. In the first two, tales of the sidhe who ride in the wind and who steal brides, Loeffler evokes moods both of powerful glamor and of subtle menace. *The Fiddler of Dooney*, however, is light-hearted and fun, while the song of the dying fox hunter is tinged with nostalgia. The fifth fantasy, *Caitilin Ni Uallachain*, sets parts of a Jacobite poem originally written in Gaelic. Loeffler used an English translation of this poem but also labored, with the help of an Irish priest, to set the original. But when McCormack saw it, he declared he could not sing a word of it, and the Gaelic was forthwith abandoned. Whatever the language, the music, in its fervent nationalism, is one of the most intense pieces Loeffler, a life-long opponent of political oppression, ever composed.

In March 1922 McCormack appeared with Monteux and the BSO to sing three of the *Fantasies*—*The Hosting of the Sidhe*, *The Fiddler of Dooney*, and *Caitilin Ni Uallachain*. Critical and audience response was enthusiastic. Parker of the *Transcript* declared, "For once new pieces by Mr. Loeffler had carried all before them." In the *Post* Downes enthused, "It was an extraordinary experience for any hearer. It provoked a demonstration of unqualified enthusiasm, not from an audience of partisans, but from musicians and everybody else capable of response to music of extraordinary color and evocative power."[46]

McCormack's performance, despite a cold, was reported to be remarkable, especially in the fervent *Caitilin*. Downes declared, after quoting the quatrain beginning "We will not bear the chains we wear,"

"When he sings this, you may be a crustacean, a crocodile, or a member of the Loyal Coalition, but you will think the hair is rising on your head, and the gooseflesh will course up and down your spine!"[47] Loeffler dedicated the song to McCormack.

The orchestra and McCormack repeated the performance in New York that same month, just before St. Patrick's Day, and were enthusiastically received. From the beginning Loeffler had thought of the fantasies in terms of McCormack's voice. His judgement had not been mistaken.

Despite the overwhelmingly positive reception of the *Fantasies,* the reviews afforded Loeffler another opportunity to express his disdain for critical interpretation. After the premiere, he wrote to Grace Shirmer: "The critic of 'The World' thought I was trying to be too clever in depicting 'smoke' after Yeats' line 'were gone like drifting smoke,' when I merely modulated back to B major! How pretentious it ever is and will be to try to read what is in another man's mind. However, all that sort of expressing an opinion on a new piece of music on the spur of the moment is purely haphazard anyhow. It cannot be otherwise. Jim Huneker said once that most music criticisms had the value of everyday conversations."[48]

In 1922 Loeffler became interested in a musicological work. Coelestin Vivell of the Abbey of Sechau had prepared a *Glossarium musicum,* a lexicon of Latin musical tracts from antiquity and the middle ages.[49] Loeffler strove to have it accepted for publication. He, Frank Benson, and Gardner contributed a tenth of the sum Vivell thought he needed for publication, and Loeffler pressed Engel to help. Engel submitted the proposal to Oscar Sonneck, vice-president of Schirmer's. When Vivell died in 1923, publication plans were evidently abandoned.

Loeffler composed a new chamber work for string quartet and harp in 1921 and 1922, *Historiettes,* a set of four musical portraits or "Preludes to Imaginary Tragicomedies." In 1921 he wrote to Gardner, "The motto might be said to be 'crime as a fine art.'" By the summer of 1922 the order of movements, titles, and the character of one prelude had changed, but not the intent. The Preludes were "little observations on the criminal 'insouciances' of the modern, developed Gorilla called man! One motive goes through these compositions, namely the one of 'evil and the devil.'"[50]

After Franz Kneisel became interested in this new work, Loeffler sent him the parts for his students to play. His accompanying letter provides some explanation of the music, given here following the final titles (in their final order) and the dedications.

1. Historiette du mariage de Pierrot Fumiste (dedicated to Mrs. John L. Gardner) "belongs to a little comedy by Laforgue, entitled 'Pierrot Fumiste,' whose characters, whom the whole world knows, his wife Colombine and himself, make fools of themselves. The music is a little in the style of the 18th century."

2. Historiette des tribulations de M. Punch (dedicated to Pablo Casals) "deals with the medical man Mr. Punch, who in all disagreeable and perplexing situations helps himself with the one simple medicine, namely the cudgel! Quarrels with his wife (Judy), bawlings of the kids, meddling of the police, even at the end that of the devil who would fetch him are successfully fought out by the universal character Punch with his cudgel."

3. Historiette de Batyoushka Raspoutine (dedication intended for Fanny Mason but withheld at her request) "deals with the peasant monk, drunkard, impostor, and fakir Grishka Raspoutine, who was murdered by a mob in St. Petersburg. His corpse was thrown into the Neva at night."

4. Historiette de la Senorita Conchita Piquer (dedicated to John S. Sargent) "characterizes a great artist, a Spanish gypsy, whom I heard two years ago sing in New York in a small comic opera, 'The Wildcat.' The music must naturally speak for itself."

"A small motive runs throughout the four movements, representing that something of the devil that there is in all human beings."[51]

In July Loeffler visited the Kneisels in Blue Hill, Maine. "It was most delightful to be once more with my old pal," Loeffler wrote to Sonneck. "He is a perfect host and his kin form the most lovable, harmonious family I have seen for years."[52] Kneisel's students played Loeffler's new piece, and then seventeen of them (evidently four players per part plus a pianist), Loeffler, the Kneisel family, Felix Kahn, Richard Aldrich, and Henry Krehbiel—in two cars and a truck—motored to Seal Harbor to play the piece with Carlos Salzedo, whom Loeffler had consulted while writing the harp part. Though Loeffler seemed pleased with the performance by Kneisel's students, the composition did not have a public performance.

During 1923 publication of Loeffler's compositions recommenced, after a hiatus of twelve years, when both *Music for Four Stringed Instruments* and *Poem* were published.

In 1924 Loeffler was approached by the Concord Players to compose music for their production of Yeats's *Countess Cathleen*. Loeffler wrote one or two songs (now lost) for voice, viola, harp, and piano. Due to a transportation mix-up, Loeffler missed his opportunity to hear the music. That mischance was, however, a relief to the musicians, who had believed Loeffler to have been in the audience on the one night (when the singer, flirting backstage, missed his cue) that their performance fell apart.[53]

Loeffler also composed music for areas other than Boston and its neighbors. His *Irish Fantasies* were the last of his works to be premiered by the BSO. When Monteux left Boston in 1924, Loeffler's ties with orchestra personnel may have simply diminished.

Loeffler liked Monteux very much. When Monteux returned to Europe during the summer of 1922, Loeffler wrote to Engel: "Monteux has sailed to Paris and is going to rake in the Legion of Honor from what I hear. Please, do not mention this to anybody. I should be sorry if there were to be a hitch, for M. deserves this recompense. He has given us excellent performances and programs. I am sorry, that somehow he does not hit it off with the big audiences as other and not better men sometimes do. . . . I for one am glad that he is to be in Boston for another two years."[54]

Monteux left the BSO in the spring of 1924. During his years with the orchestra he had introduced a number of important new works to Boston. He had favored music of Americans—Carpenter, Converse, Foote, Griffes, Hill, MacDowell, Mason, Powell, D. S. Smith, and, of course, Loeffler, whose *Poem, Five Irish Fantasies, Tintagiles,* and *Pagan Poem* he conducted. In addition Monteux presented new works by French, English, Italian, and Russian composers. Among his most notable premieres in Boston was his presentation of Stravinsky's *Rite of Spring* in January 1924. Shortly afterwards, he directed the work in Europe and wrote to Loeffler: "Where then is my beautiful Boston orchestra? And, is it permitted to call 'orchestra' what I am now directing? Where are my beautiful quartet sonorities?? It seems to me that I am conducting a gramophone!! It is frightful—and the world finds that superb!! What a real pity that I was never able to take the Boston orchestra to Paris when I had the joy of being its conductor! One would have seen that it is a beautiful orchestra."[55]

Loeffler himself admired the orchestra under Monteux's hand. "Our band," he wrote to Gardner in 1920, after commenting on Damrosch, Stransky, Stokowski, and Bodansky, "still sounds very beautiful to me and superior," and commented similarly to Richard Aldrich, "I hope that you feel as I do, that our orchestra plays better and better from month to month."[56] After leaving Boston, Monteux, like Rabaud, continued to correspond with Loeffler. Also like Rabaud he took Loeffler scores with him to Europe. In 1924 he conducted *Poem* in Stockholm.

In May 1924, Rabaud wrote to Loeffler about Monteux's successor, Koussevitzky, who, he reported, had success in Paris "playing by preference the most ugly music one could imagine hearing."[57] There are no indications that Loeffler had any hand in the appointment of Koussevitzky as the new music director of the BSO. He had helped Georg Schneevoigt (who had conducted Loeffler's works in Europe) receive an appointment as guest conductor in 1923; yet when Monteux did not return (as Loeffler no doubt wished), Loeffler's unofficial position as advisor to the BSO management appears to have ended.

It has been said that Loeffler did not much care for Koussevitzky as a conductor. A letter from Helene to Martin in 1926 makes reference to "some little personal antipathy that he instills in you."[58] Yet Loeffler did admire Koussevitzky as a contrabass player, and letters do exist from Loeffler complimenting Koussevitzky on his conducting of Stravinsky's *Symphonie de Psaumes* and his own *Canticum fratris solis*.

Loeffler granted Koussevitzky performance rights for each of his new orchestral compositions (after premieres elsewhere), as well as for *Poem, Tintagiles,* and *A Pagan Poem.* Koussevitzky also performed Loeffler's compositions out of town. However, other cities were no longer dependent on the BSO for performances of Loeffler's music. Orchestras, chamber ensembles, choral groups, and singers other than those in Boston were performing Loeffler's compositions, even on occasion bringing them back to Boston.

Loeffler's new orchestral composition of 1924 was his tone poem *Memories of My Childhood: Life in a Russian Village.* It depicts scenes from Loeffler's years in Russia, each of which is identified by annotations in the score (in Russian in the manuscript). It employs Russian themes, and the orchestration, emphasizing deep registers, using supplemental instruments such as four mouth-harmonicas (as well as the combination of celesta, piano, and two harps that he favored in his late orchestral works), and accented by a large percussion section including bells, xylophone, and several types of drums, evokes the sound of Russia.

Loeffler submitted the score to the North Shore Festival Association competition. Out of eighty-three submissions, it was awarded first prize ($1,000) and was consequently premiered in Evanston, Illinois, by the Chicago Symphony Orchestra.

The behind-the-scenes story of the selection of *Memories* as the prize winner has been amusingly told by Deems Taylor, one of the judges (the others being Adolf Weidig and Ernest Schelling).

> One work in particular struck us as being head and shoulders above the
> rest. It was a symphonic poem, called *Memories of My Childhood,* with

the subtitle, *Life in a Russian Village.* [The scores were submitted anonymously.]

... It seemed inevitable that this work would win on the first ballot, and that our meeting wouldn't take over fifteen minutes. That is not exactly what happened.

You may remember that in the early twenties we enjoyed a witch-hunt in this country that hadn't been equalled in excitement and gusto since the Salem affair, a couple of centuries ago. Only this time it wasn't witches we were hunting, but Communists.... And as he looked again at the title-page of the work that we all thought was so good, one of our judges suddenly smelled tainted gold.

"Life in a Russian Village," indeed! was the general purport of his remarks. Did we actually mean that we were going to sit there and award this prize to some Russian immigrant, presumably unwashed, probably with whiskers, and indubitably in the pay of Lenin and Trotsky, some insidious alien who was adopting this dastardly means of taking the bread out of the mouths of honest American composers? A thousand ... oh, fifteen hundred times ... no!

That, of course, was exactly what the rest of us did mean that we were going to sit there and do. [It was pointed out that if the composer were an alien, the prize would not be awarded to him.] ...

But our friend was hard to convince. It was obviously his conviction that if we awarded the prize to the composer of *Life in a Russian Village,* a large Russian army was going to arrive and put Evanston to the torch before midnight.... it was a very long day ... we finally won. About six o'clock, only two hours and a half before the concert, our all-American judge reluctantly yielded to superior numbers and stronger lungs, and consented to cast his vote for *Memories of My Childhood.* To do him justice, I must say that when the envelope containing the composer's real name was unsealed, and he discovered that the prize had gone to Charles Martin Loeffler, a man who had sat at the first desk of the Boston Symphony Orchestra for twenty-one years, who had not a drop of Russian blood in his veins [and without, it may be added, any sympathy for the Bolsheviks], and who had been an American citizen for more than half his life ... when he discovered that, I must say that his face took a mean revenge, and turned the color that is usually associated with Communism.[59]

The end of the story as told to Loeffler by L. W. Spofford, president of the association, was that immediately after the announcement of Loeffler's name as winner, all the judges began questioning him to make sure he had not become confused, for they said it was unlike his style and he was Alsatian, not Russian. When finally convinced, they all expressed admiration for Loeffler's versatility in producing a composition so unlike his previous works.[60]

On 30 May 1924 Frederick Stock conducted the Chicago Symphony Orchestra in the first performance of *Memories*. It was quickly taken up by the orchestras of Cleveland, Boston, Philadelphia, and New York.

Loeffler turned to the genre of orchestral song once more when commissioned by Elizabeth Sprague Coolidge for a new work for the opening of Coolidge Hall at the Library of Congress. The new auditorium was built at the library following Coolidge's donation of the funds for its construction. To it, in 1925, she moved the chamber music festivals that she had held in Pittsfield, Massachusetts, since 1918. Loeffler, who had been able to attend at least a few of the Pittsfield festivals (once, in 1920, as a judge), had great—reciprocated—respect for Coolidge.

Upon hearing the news of the project, Loeffler wrote to Coolidge: "I cannot describe to you my deep emotion, while listening to Carl Engel's telling me of your last truly inspired Act of giving a Temple of Music to the Library of Congress in Washington. Such thoughtful generosity seems indeed to descend on music, on musicians and the American People like a blessing from Heaven. Please, permit me to lay my most respectful homages at your feet, in appreciation of this donation, so important and far reaching in effect. . . . Your kind request that I should write a Chamber-orchestra-piece of Music for the great occasion of dedicating the Hall, inspires me with awe, and in deep humility I now stand before you, wondering whether I am worthy of the honor, and whether I ought to dare and acquiesce to your request. I should, in truth, love to write something for you, dear Mrs. Coolidge, which should above all be a 'pièce d'occasion.'"[61]

The music that Loeffler wrote was something, he said, "which I always had the intention of putting on paper," a setting of St. Francis of Assisi's "Hymn to the Sun."[62] "It might have been expected," wrote Gilman, "that Mr. Loeffler would at some time be attracted by the thought of a musical setting of St. Francis's poem. A spiritual mystic, a profound and pentrating student of medieval thought and art, an authority upon Gregorian plain song and the recondite subject of the ecclesiastical modes, he is ideally fitted for such an adventure."[63] The "mystic" scored his *Canticum fratris solis* for soprano accompanied by an ethereal chamber orchestra composed of flutes, English horn, horns, celesta, piano, two harps, and strings. The vocal part is through-composed, though most of the sections are related by use of the *Laudato sia, mio signore* motive that recurs, with some variation, at the head of most of the verses.

After finishing the score, Loeffler sent it to Engel for his opinion. "You will find interwoven a few Gregorian melodies [*Deo gratias,*

Kyrie eleison, Resurrexi] and alas, to the young Iconoclasts horror there is even a 'Canon à l'octave' in my music!"[64] He gave Engel the freedom to remove the piece from the program "if the thing is not suited for your opening Concert, or if it seems long or too-o-o long." Engel made no such decision. Loeffler's *Canticum,* along with Stock's *Rhapsodic Fantasy* and F. Jacobi's *Two Assyrian Prayers,* was performed on the first program of the first festival of chamber music held at the Library of Congress on 28 October 1925. The solo part was sung, upon Loeffler's insistence, by Povla Frijsh. Loeffler attended the performance but declined to conduct, allowing Stock to direct his piece.

Coolidge was delighted with the *Canticum,* dedicated to her. It was also well received critically. *New York Times* critic Richard Aldrich commented: "The work shows a sustained strength, an unflagging potency and depth of expression, and with all its freedom of treatment has a remarkable concentration and intensity. It has what all modern works have not, originality of idea and the quality of beauty."[65]

In November the Chicago orchestra included the composition on a program in Coolidge's honor, which Loeffler himself attended. Coolidge also proposed European performances to which Loeffler was at first opposed, as he was five years earlier when Damrosch took his *Poem* to Europe. "My experience," he explained, "has taught me, that composers of this country are not treated fairly in the old countries of Europe." Indeed, Loeffler indulged in quite a tirade against contemporary European practices.

The various Mutual Admiration Societies of England, Germany, and the other countries of the Continent—mostly Internationalistic in appearance, but chauvinistic in reality, are to a man, against *everything* coming from this country, except our—dollars! Carpenter had no luck in Paris, nor did Eichheim, if I may judge from the French Press notices. For the most part, American Music is presented—if at all—insufficiently rehearsed and in the end insufficiently played. Those of us who ever sent any compositions to the committees of the various Salzburg, Zurich, Prague International festivals, invariably found, that their packages had never been opened even. Too much has been done and is being done now in our country for young foreign composers as yet without fame, but much notoriety, whose compositions on the whole have but very little intrinsic musical value. Nobody asked for a new Quartet by poor old Fauré, who was to the very end in dire need of money! Instead, a certain Internationalistic Press clamored for "le dernier cri" of Mr. Milhaud. A new Quartet by H. Rabaud, a master-musician, might be of interest—no! Mr. Honegger comes first. d'Indy is still alive, a great musician—probably Mr. Tansmann will, for to us unknown reasons, be crowding the old masters out of limelight. And so it goes on. Interest in Strauss is dead, yet even in his Alpine Symphony he again proved himself a great master-architect in creating a "sustained effort." Outside of him, who is there now in Europe but Schoenberg, Ravel, Stravinsky and possibly Malipiero, to whose new works we can look forward with anticipation of pleasure? Of course there still is Vincent d'Indy who has just written a Piano Quintet and Henri Rabaud a very fine musician, who ought to be encouraged to write chamber music, for he knows and loves the great masters more than anybody I know. The old world is exhausted and half insane since the war. We suffered hardly at all from it, and we have hardly anything in common with Europe musically. Most of *their* new stuff means very little to us, with the exception of the men aforenamed: Strauss, Schoenberg, Ravel, Malipiero, Rabaud, d'Indy, Stravinsky. Europe *does not want* our music. I understand it and hence have no desire to impose my music on them.[66]

Loeffler did concede that "to have Hans Kindler for my interpreter would be my heart's desire!" and Coolidge eventually won Loeffler over. She arranged successful performances in the spring of 1926 in Paris, Brussels, Milan, and Oxford, and in September 1927 in Vienna and Prague.

Loeffler composed further music based on the "Hymn to the Sun" when Daniel Sargent—a fellow member of the Tavern Club and, in Loeffler's opinion, a "delightful poet"—asked Loeffler to provide music for his Franciscan play *The Reveller*. Several other club composers had written works for various club entertainments—for example, Chadwick's *A Quiet Lodging* for "Narrenabend" (Fool's Evening) and Owen Wister's *Il Commendatore* and his prohibition opera, "Watch Your Thirst." Loeffler had earlier written an overture for two violins and piano for a minstrel show; he set *The Reveller* for Christmas 1925.

Sargent's one-act play was about a young troubadour who tried to out-match St. Francis in singing. Loeffler composed seven songs, each using a medieval or Renaissance melody which he found in an *Antologia antiqua* of Italian poetry and music edited by Eugenia Levi. The music was scored for voice, viola, and piano, with a closing chorus to the seventh verse. With the exception of the *Reveller's Song* the verses were Sargent's translations from the "Hymn to the Sun."

Loeffler agreed to the project because he liked the play but had some regrets about the decision. Originally told the singer playing St. Francis would be a tenor, he had to transpose the music when he discovered the singer actually to be a baritone. The rehearsals necessitated repeated trips in and out of Boston. Finally, the performance was marred, as Loeffler described to Engel: "Such out of tune singing . . . you never heard. The Chorus-master, a charming fellow, singer and musician, must have had about 3 cocktails too many! The funny thing was that neither the Pianist nor I were conscious of what was going on on the stage, as we were placed in a small room behind the stage. *They* could hear us but we could not hear *them.* Philip Hale said: 'the Chorus was pretty badly out of tune' so we knew. . . . The Chorus master fast asleep in our little backroom during the first scenes! I did not know how he led his flock when he was called to do *his* job! I am laughing still!"[67]

In 1925 and 1926 Loeffler wrote the last two songs that he is known to have composed: *Vieille chanson d'amour,* an exquisite strophic setting of a fifteenth-century French text, with plaintive verses leading to uncharacteristic florid melismas, and *Prière,* to words by Roger Dévigne, a brief, touching prayer set as both a song and a four-part chorus. Also in 1926 Loeffler composed a new work for violin and piano entitled *Cynthia,* an ethereal essay in musical moonlight. Like the *Vieille chanson, Cynthia* remained unperformed, in manuscript; later he reworked small sections into his orchestral work, *Evocation.* With such works as *Vieille chanson, Cynthia,* and *Evocation*—particularly with the increasingly frequent passages of gliding parallel chords—Loeffler's alliance with French Symbolism became even more pronounced.

Simultaneously, however, Loeffler continued his eclectic manner of composing. *Norske Land,* for example, composed during the late 1920s, is based on two Norwegian tunes and a "ranz des vaches" (Alpine herdsman's melody) and was originally scored for viola d'amore and piano. He revised the work for either viola d'amore or violin under the title *Eery Moonlight.* Yet again he revised the work, newly titled *Norske Saga,* for contrabass or contrabass and viola d'amore and piano. In 1929 Loeffler presented the contrabass version to Koussevitzky as a "humble mark of profound admiration." On that occasion he wrote to Koussevitzky, "There remains in my ear still the memory of the sonorities all together unexpected as well as beautiful that you have known how to create and draw from your beautiful instrument" and referred to "the mysterious and tonal alchemy of which you are the unique musician."[68]

Loeffler's work frequently took him out of his country retreat to travel to New York, Philadelphia, Washington, Chicago, Cleveland—cities where his music was performed or his expertise needed. Loeffler planned a trip to Europe for 1923 but cancelled it, evidently owing to his wife's ill health. Loeffler's own ill health also prevented trips to Europe. In 1927 Helene wrote: "I think that it is because of the . . . hernia, that you are prevented from making an ocean voyage. You never told me the reason why you have never come to see me again, and I had persuaded myself that it was because of antipathy for our country that you obstinately stayed away."[69]

Fortunately, a number of letters written by Loeffler to his wife survive from the 1920s, documenting some of his American trips. The year 1924 may be taken as an example of Loeffler's out-of-town traveling. In February Loeffler visited Washington to help Engel with some work at the Library of Congress. In June he was in New York meeting with his publishers and with Stock. An operation then kept Loeffler in Medfield during the summer, but in October he returned to New York to work as an examiner for the Juilliard Foundation, then auditioning students for its new conservatory of music. Also in October Loeffler went to Chicago for the Chicago Symphony Orchestra's performance of *Memories*. In November he journeyed to both Philadelphia and Cleveland for performances of his *Poem*. During December he returned to New York as a consultant for the Juilliard Foundation.

The Juilliard work was somewhat out of Loeffler's ordinary routine. Juilliard had approached Loeffler to assume a post as professor of violin, but Loeffler refused for Elise's sake, explaining to Richard Aldrich, "The fact is, were I to accept your offer would mean a very lonely life for Elise, my wife, who depends very much on me and who is, although not actually ill, far from being well. In a word it would probably break up our living in the country altogether."[70]

The school also wanted César Thomson, who had just come to America to teach at the Ithaca School of Music. Loeffler recommended his old friend as the greatest teacher he knew, declaring, "All these Thibauds and Enesco's are delightful players, . . . but as teachers I do not see these men with the same eye [as Thomson]."[71] Loeffler declined to fill in the time Thomson could not teach and also declined to teach for only three months. Allegedly Juilliard sent students to Medfield to study with him during the summers.[72] And for two years Loeffler auditioned students in the fall.

Throughout all his trips Loeffler was entertained by numerous old friends and new acquaintances. In Cleveland, for example, Loeffler was invited to the spectacular estate of Mr. and Mrs. John L. Severance, who later donated a million dollars towards the construction of Severance Hall. He also attended a concert by the Cleveland Quartet, which included his own *Rapsodies,* at the home of Severance's sister, Adella Prentiss, who had "the most magnificent house you ever saw: filled with Rembrandts, J. Reynolds, Corots etc. It is just like a Museum."[73] He was entertained on more intimate levels as well. In Cleveland Loeffler had a wonderful visit with the Sokoloff family, to whom he was "Uncle Martin." (Sokoloff's second child, named Martin, was in fact Loeffler's godchild.)

Loeffler had the opportunity to attend several concerts (not just those of his own music), for example, the New York premiere of Honegger's *Le Roi David,* and to go to shows. He also took time to indulge other interests, like seeing "Mr. Delano's Norwegian and Arabian horses which was a great pleasure" and visiting with Aldrich in Scarborough, New York, Dr. Decan, "the famous chemist who found the world famous Decan's fluid which saved so many hundred thousand wounded soldiers lives."[74]

The concerts of his own music were the source of both delight and dismay. They were also the occasion for some of the more interesting comments in his letters, those dealing with the conductors, orchestras, and composers Loeffler encountered on his trips.

Loeffler's greatest complaint in Chicago was the hall: "The echo in that empty hall was terrific! One could hardly distinguish the various harmonious changes. Therefore I had very little pleasure in listening to my piece [a rehearsal of *Memories*] . . . Now by the way, the hall, which was built for Theo. Thomas. When he heard how awful it was he became ill and died 3 weeks after! He just conducted 3 concerts in it. I understand when the hall is full there is no echo but the sound is dead!" In addition: "One flaw I found at once namely that the piano part was badly played—in parts left out by a perfect duffer of an organist who did the murderous job! We hope to have a better man today—at all events they will try to get one. The trouble is of course the Union! The good Pianists are mostly non-Union men." Nevertheless, "I am glad I came for I must make a few changes in the indications for tempi etc."[75]

Elsewhere Loeffler expressed distaste for the union. After Damrosch asked him to perform the solo part of *Tintagiles,* Loeffler replied that he would—if the M.P.U. were willing. To Damrosch he also commented, after Damrosch's trip to Paris to engage French players, "Your frenchmen arrived safely, but what a reception those poor devils did get from the Union! Vive la liberté! (Quelle blague!) Ours is a beautiful but *not* a free country."[76] Loeffler commented on the union again in 1925. "The *Union* watches over the orchestra to squeeze more money out of the Association so, to my amazement 2 numbers were omitted last night, for had they not been omitted, the concert would have lasted 5 minutes overtime, which would have cost the festival Association 500$. The only way to do, therefore, was to biff the 2 Schubert numbers."[77]

This occasion was a performance by the Chicago orchestra at Evanston, where his *Poem* was played. The lack of rehearsal time there concerned him, though Stock "has a great deal of experience for cramming in much work in few minutes!" and he concluded after the second rehearsal, "Stock's orchestra has a very fine tone quality—quite unusually so and that helps and consoles."[78] The pleasantest part of that Evanston visit, he claimed, was meeting Percy Grainger again. Loeffler sacrificed one night's concert to help Grainger alter orchestral parts for a performance the next evening and was glad to do it. "He is such a nice, lovable and talented fellow. I am really happy of having met him again." Loeffler enjoyed hearing Grainger's music as well as his own *Poem*—more so evidently than the competition works—"5 Muttpieces," neither good nor bad.[79]

On another trip to Chicago itself (1925) Loeffler again worried about lack of rehearsal time: "26 hours travel is *somewhat long* to hear an improperly rehearsed composition played—*if* they don't play it well. But I am not going to worry about it. If they all get out and loose their places let them. Fortunately Stock knows his orchestra. So, there you are: people say and think 'What fun it must be to hear your music played!' Rats! If it's bad enough, one can at least laugh about it. Fine it can hardly be, unless I am sorely mistaken."[80] Unfortunately Loeffler's post-performance reaction is not recorded.

In Cleveland Loeffler was quite happy. "They are treating me grandly here! The orchestra plays magnificently, con amore, and my piece [*Poem*] was *never* played like this before! So I am really delighted to the utmost," and Loeffler declared, "Sokoloff is my best and most loving interpreter."[81]

Loeffler also sent wonderful reports from Philadelphia, which, he wrote to Engel, "used to be called: the home of funeral marches," but added, "this latter good old town is now taking a wonderfully high place in the musical world. You will nowhere hear better concerts than these given by Stokowski." Stokowski, he wrote, "is a great conductor and has the finest orchestra in the world, no doubt about that." He was particularly impressed by the orchestra's "precision not to be found elsewhere."[82]

Loeffler admired Stokowski very much: "But what a worker the man is. 3 hours rehearsal in the morning, 3 hours Record-making. In the evening orchestral rehearsal in the Curtis Institute with the Students. Today, Concert-day, this morning rehearsal of 2 hours; in the afternoon concert. After the concert I am going to St. for dinner. . . . After each rehearsal he takes a hot bath, after the concert a bath and massage. He conducts everything with the left arm, his right one being used up."[83]

Loeffler heard not only his own music but also the quite different music of Varèse. "Varèse's composition will bring about a public protest!!! Watch the papers! The orchestra itself is enraged at his music! I believe St. does it for advertising sake. This side I do not understand in him, who gives Bach so divinely!"[84]

Loeffler even had occasion, while out of town, to comment on his own Boston orchestra. In New York for a performance of *Canticum fratris solis,* Loeffler wrote: "Koussevitzky, the orchestra and Povla covered not only themselves but me and the Canticle of the Sun with not only Glory but with tonal beauty not often found anywhere. All three of us were applauded to the Sky and called on the Stage at least 5 times. At last I have heard the work under most wonderful conditions."[85]

But the traveling itself did not appeal to Loeffler, no more than when he was an orchestral musician. From New York he wrote to his wife: "[Grace Schirmer] was glad to see me and of course won't go to Ch[icago] if you don't. In a way she seemed also slightly relieved and I am the only goat in the case! Why did I write this piece! Serve me right." In Philadelphia he wrote: "I am getting enough of this travelling. To Cleveland unfortunately I must go and then for a 5 years rest! New York is not so bad for I feel at home but Philadelphia makes me homesick more than even Chicago with all its pickpockets."[86]

Loeffler also left his beautiful farm to take innumerable short trips into Boston. The Boston orchestra still commanded his loyalty and respect; however, Boston itself was not so much to Loeffler's tastes as it had been in the nineteenth century. In 1923, for example, he wrote: "Boston is getting stuffier and stuffier and will soon graduate to the astounding grade of 'the largest village on earth.' As my friend [Ned] Tarbell might say, 'Dark, dark brown Boston.' The enthusiasms of this little town are perhaps the most perplexing and disheartening symptoms of dry rot."[87]

During the next year, after visiting Washington, he wrote to Engel (with allusion to Rollinat's *L'étang*), "How refreshing it all was to get away from that stagnant old pool full of old, blind fish and frogs—that old pool called: Boston."[88] Upon regretfully declining the Juilliard post, he confessed to Aldrich, "When I left the B Symphony Orchestra I always lived in the hope, that I might someday change my domicile to New York but alas, it never came. I always disliked Boston."[89] He stayed near Boston because Elise did not wish to leave.

Until 1920 Loeffler kept his Charles Street studio, but in that year the city took over that section of property. Still Loeffler frequented the homes of his friends, the concert halls, and his clubs, the Tavern Club and St. Botolph Club.

The St. Botolph Club had been formed in December 1879 "for the promotion of social intercourse among authors, artists, and other gentlemen connected with or interested in literature and art."[90] Francis Parkman, who once took the thirty-year-old Loeffler fishing, was its first president, and early members included J. Q. Adams, W. D. Howells, Phillips Brooks, and Henry Cabot Lodge. The pianist Harold Bauer, a guest in Boston, wrote enthusiastically about the club: "Henry Mason, then artistic director of the Mason and Hamlin firm founded by his father, introduced me at the St. Botolph Club, and I thought that I had never met such an aggregation of artistic and interesting people as in this delightful place, although I was familiar with the Savage Club in London, the only institution of the kind to which it had some resemblance."[91] Loeffler joined the St. Botolph Club about the turn of the century. From 1921 to 1928 he served as vice-president of the club while Frederick Converse was president.

The only place in Boston where Loeffler continued to play, apparently, was Fenway Court, and there he played only for Gardner herself, who during the last years of her life was a house-bound invalid. Sometimes Loeffler sent the American String Quartette to her but also himself frequently visited her to play with Gebhard—when the pianist was available. "Gebhard," he wrote to Gardner in 1920, "an altogether too much married gentleman now, has been away for over two weeks—then returned for a few days to play a little Sonata concert in Steinert Hall with a Mr. Keller—gave some 1500 piano lessons to support his wife and the many, many children he will never, never have—then departed again for another two weeks to Canada doing there all the young ladies schools in the form of Piano recitals and bringing home loads of riches."[92]

In 1924 Loeffler lost his old friend. Isabella Stewart Gardner died in July of that year. Her death severely diminished Loeffler's ties to Boston; as he told Aldrich, "since I lost my great friend Mrs. Gardner, this town means next to nothing to me."[93] As a final service to her memory, when the Gardner Museum opened in 1925, Loeffler arranged the program for the Harvard Glee Club, conducted by Archibald T. Davison.

Gardner was only one of several dear friends who died in the mid-1920s. In November 1924 Fauré died. Just months later, Loeffler received a letter from Povla Frijsh in which she quoted Fauré as having said, smiling, "Loeffler, I like him *very much*."[94] In April of the next year, John Sargent died. Loeffler had been looking forward to Sargent's projected return to American in 1925 and involving him with Mrs. Coolidge's music hall; however, Sargent died in London before he could return.

A memorial for Sargent occurred at the Museum of Fine Arts in November and December 1925. Loeffler arranged the music for the opening of the Sargent exhibit and loaned his Sargent watercolor, *Interior of a Church (Cathedral of Toledo)*. At Symphony Hall the BSO performed *Siegfried's Funeral Music* from *Gotterdammerung* in his memory in April; Loeffler's *Poem* was coincidentally on the program. Loeffler also wrote a tribute to Sargent for a biography written by Evan Charteris, including: "It is unusual to meet so marvellously endowed a man possessing such simplicity of manner, such goodness of heart, such genuine human kindness in his nature. He had the innate bearing and dignity of a noble man. His life was to my mind the fullest imaginable, for he was ever alert, in his joy over the petal of a flower, over a feather of a small bird, the mystery of the propelling power of a little snake in the grass. . . . He just was a glorious exception as genius always is, and just could not help being almost omniscient with so exceptional a memory as was his. . . . To have appreciated the honor of enjoying also his friendship may explain to you the profound affection in which I hold today his memory."[95]

Amy Lowell died the month following Sargent. Just the month before Loeffler had been a sponsor of a "Complimentary Dinner" in her honor. Then in March 1926 Loeffler wrote, "Another chapter closed in my life."[96] Franz Kneisel had died. Since his retirement from the BSO, Kneisel had devoted his time to his quartet (dissolved in 1917), to teaching and miscellaneous musical activities and had not continued as a Boston resident. He lived in New York (where Loeffler attended his funeral) and had a summer house at Blue Hill, Maine, where Loeffler visited when possible, renewing their friendship.

Although the loss of each of these friends saddened Loeffler, neither he nor his music reverted to the morbidity of his early life. Much of his musical attention during the 1920s was given over to new sounds, new idioms, new ideas. The 1920s were the Jazz Age; they were also Loeffler's jazz era.

17

The Jazz Age

"I am frightfully addicted to 'Jazz,'" Loeffler wrote in 1925.[1] Loeffler's sister wrote that she did not understand this interest; and in polite Boston society, where jazz was not considered quite respectable, there must have been similar bewilderment. But Loeffler loved it and did not conceal his passion. He listened to it, played it, recommended recordings to his friends, attended recording sessions, and even tried his hand at composing it.

Loeffler's interest in every kind of music amazed his student Kay Swift, particularly on one occasion when he discovered she was taking tap dancing lessons and said, "I'd like to do that. I think if you could arrange it, I'd like to take some tap dancing lessons."[2] (Lessons were not arranged since Swift was, at that early time, so much in awe of Loeffler).

Engel wrote, "Often eccentric in his likes and dislikes, Loeffler was never blind to merit. . . . Late in life, he remained young enough to pay his respect to jazz." Engel (using the editorial "we") continued: "We owe to him—resident of sober Medfield, Mass.—our first introduction to the gaieties of the Cotton Club in Harlem, N.Y.! Mr. Duke Ellington's trumpeters could throw Loeffler into pardonable ecstasies. We well remember the night in New York when we took Loeffler to hear the first 'Little Show' . . . in the first row of the orchestra, and his keen delight with the clever instrumentation."[3] It was Loeffler's custom to visit Harlem during his New York visits. On one trip to New York he "looked up old 'Handy' in his lair at the D'Eauville."[4] He enjoyed Handy's *St. Louis Blues* immensely—in fact, was once overheard in Medfield playing it when the eavesdropper was expecting to hear Mozart or Beethoven.

Elise described one of her husband's jazz excursions to Gardner. Following their attendance at the opera in New York in December 1920, while Elise returned to the hotel, Loeffler went with some friends to a small ball, as he said "just to look in for 5 minutes," but

Elise did not see him again for hours. "I had to stay awake to let him into the room and had made up my mind that at 4 o'clock I would telephone to the police to look him up, as I felt sure something awful had happened to him! but it seems there were 2 jazz bands playing at the ball, the best in New York, & when they learned Martin was there, they laid themselves out to play everything they knew and in their best manner. He was immensely interested in the music, which he had never heard well done before and really had a wonderful time—Sorry he had to come away when he did 'for fear I might be anxious'!!"[5]

That same month, Loeffler himself wrote to Gardner about a "spree" he and Elise had in Boston at the Westminster. "We took dinner in the winter garden, with which dinner was thrown in a whole concert and a most wonderful jazz band. While the singing was boresome, the band was too wonderful for words. Most people of course danced. But the players! Violin, Piano, Saxophone, Bass, Drums, Cymbals, and Xylophone! Every one of these six players a creation of Hofmann's Phantasie tales, in other words, a crazy genius. I enjoyed it hugely. At ten Elise retired to rest her weary bones and I remained until midnight listening to these gifted fellows. God be thanked, that it should matter, that things, all things, should be done to perfection."[6]

Loeffler had his preferences in jazz as in all music. Always abhorrent of pretense in music, which he felt to be the essence of the "crooner," Loeffler drafted a short (unfinished) paper to decry this "blight." In part it reads: "Our popular music has genuine charm, both melodic and artistic. In its orchestral arrangements, sometimes for not more than 6–7 players, it offers a color palette of sonorities of incredible wealth and variety. It delights us with surprises of rhythmic and harmonic ingenuity and beauty. All this is offered in the shortest dance and song forms imaginable, played so marvelously that one can remember it only as of an evanescent, fleeting impression. It is in a way an art of chamber music playing which in its expressiveness vies with what music really ought to be: namely the purveyor of delight and amusement."[7] "*Good jazz*," he wrote a young friend, "is lovely, and often humorous and witty." Yet its composition should be seriously undertaken like any chamber music. He advised his friend to "write something for Whiteman's wonderful Orchestra as one writes Quartets for the Kneisels or Flonzaleys."[8]

Among Loeffler's friends in the jazz world was the Boston band leader Leo Reisman. While Reisman was playing in a Boston hotel, desiring to improve his general musicianship, he took various music lessons, including violin lessons with Loeffler. Swift recalled that

Loeffler always made a point of going to Reisman's recording sessions. She accompanied him once; he stayed there all day, and it did not bore him a bit.[9] Mr. and Mrs. Reisman (who named their son Charles Martin) were Loeffler's guests at Medfield, where the quiet of the country made their sleeping difficult. Loeffler eventually composed a piece for Reisman's orchestra, *Intermezzo (Clowns)*, premiered in February 1928 at Symphony Hall.

Another jazz figure whom Loeffler adored was George Gershwin. Loeffler met Gershwin while in New York in April 1927 for a performance of his *Music for Four Stringed Instruments* by the Musical Art Quartet. Following the performance Swift gave a party for him, during which she surprised him with a performance of his *Quatre poèmes,* sung by Greta Torpadie, and also introduced him to many of her friends. It was a big party, Swift having invited many musicians and people she thought he would like, including Heifitz, his sister Pauline, and her husband, the critic Samuel Chotzinoff. Among them also was George Gershwin, who, as usual, played. Gershwin's music gave Loeffler such keen pleasure that the two immediately struck up a firm friendship. According to Swift, everyone at that party, including Gershwin, was thrilled to meet Loeffler and know him as an entertaining, light, and lively wonderful person—not just the noble, austere wonderful person of his reputation. Like Gershwin, he was filled with vitality and enthusiasm, of which his feeling for Gershwin's music was one example.[10]

After returning to Boston, Loeffler wrote to Swift, "I am grateful to you for so many things that you have brought about for me so delightfully, that I know not where to begin. The music in your house was very beautiful in which you, Miss Rosanoff [cellist with the Musical Art Quartet] and George Gershwin stand out 'en première Ligne.' It was a revelation to hear the latter play his Concerto, hear him sing his songs and—to know him."[11] Loeffler set Gershwin apart from his confrères both "for his unusual gifts which often touch on genius, and for that rare something indefinably lovable in the man."

Loeffler and Gershwin kept up their friendship. Loeffler attended what Gershwin shows he could in New York, attended rehearsals and shows in Boston, and, of course, Gershwin's appearances in Symphony Hall. They also corresponded. Loeffler was quite frank in his admiration of Gershwin, as he wrote to Gershwin himself.

> As to yourself, it is needless to say that I have pinned my faith on your delightful genius and on your future. You alone seem to express charm, grace, and invention amongst the composers of our time. When the Anthlands and Coptheils ed tutti quanti will be forgotten, and Janitors,

Chorewomen, Dead-heads and Press-reporters no longer will have to sit up (on their la-beinols) at the formers musical antics, you, my dear friend, will be recorded in the Anthologies of coming ages.

I am looking forward with keenest expectations of consoling delight to your latest work. If you can't have me now, I'll see you in New York to hear your music. Here is to the Store of Wisdom! To Sanity! To 'La gaya scienza'! And how much you possess particularly the latter! Ye Gods![12]

It was not simply that Loeffler liked Gershwin's music but that he thought him a great American composer. According to Gebhard, Loeffler considered Gershwin "the spokesman for our music, for the American people."[13]

Gershwin sent Loeffler complimentary, inscribed copies of his music (inscribed, for example to "my dear friend, Charles Martin Loeffler, in greatest admiration and affection") and issued several invitations to Loeffler to visit him—as did Loeffler to Gershwin when the latter came to Boston. One of the invitations from Gershwin, for example, was to join him in Ossining in June 1927. Apparently, Loeffler had previously communicated to Gershwin that he could not accept for he wrote to him: "It can however now be arranged and I may follow my hearts desire and spend 24 hours or so in your delightful company . . . . If you are deep in the throes of writing the music for your new show and can't spare a few hours for interruptions, treat me ever as a friend: à la bonne franquette. At all events we can share three meals together for 'Causeries intimes.'"[14] It chanced, however, that Loeffler suffered an eye complaint in July and could not go out of reach of his specialist. The Gershwins returned to New York that same month for rehearsals of *Strike Up the Band,* and Loeffler's consolation was that his doctor promised that he could go to the show.

When in March 1928 Gershwin intended going to Europe, he told Loeffler of his plans. Loeffler responded with some advice about visiting d'Indy: "Have a good time while away in France and do a lot of writing. If you could get near M. Vincent d'Indy to study for a while, principally orchestration, and take in some of his ideas on tonality and free form you would fare well and some day thank me for having spoken to you of him. He is a grand old gentleman. His orchestration is marvelous in sound and uncannily thoughtful and clever. He has the genius for teaching. If you do not find what you are looking for over there, go on writing just the same and come out to me in Medfield, make me happy with your presence, your new works and your magnificent pianism." He continued with comments on Gershwin himself: "There is something Mozartean about your stuff, something beautifully personal and frightfully simple. Am I kidding or fooling you? Would I try to discountenance a violet or the Ave Deum by Mozart? No more than you, dear George. Your brother Ira has some of the similar quality in him. Dieu Merci, for the two of you."[15]

In September 1928 Gershwin wrote to Loeffler that he had finished writing *An American in Paris* and part of the orchestration and wanted to show it to him. If Loeffler could not come down to New York, he would go to Medfield. The visit did not come off, but Loeffler did attend the premiere—with a seat in Gershwin's box—in December. He had also been invited to the postperformance party for Gershwin, but "Mr. Glaenzer, who had kindly invited me to go to his house after the Concert, had however forgotten to tell me where his house was or is. At the last moment I found myself a lost waif on the Streets of N.Y."[16]

But Loeffler wrote not primarily of regret but of his excitement at hearing the music. "It was a great delight to hear your last work a week ago. The spirit of it was enchanting and contagious. I am sorry I had not the advantage of seeing your score before the performance to render myself account whether the Trombone had followed your intentions in its solo (further along in the piece) or just played nobly in a somewhat "bonasse" or "domesticated" sort of style when perhaps a pinch or "Soupçon" of red pepper in the form of the Wa-wa mute or a chapeau haut de forma might have lightened the Gershwinian twinkle of the eye. However that might have been, Walter Damrosch gave your work a fine performance, even to the Trombonist who played *too* beautifully, everybody seems to be on his metal."[17]

Thinking that perhaps the violins might be overworking their "enticing" opening motif, he did suggest that the nasal English horn timbre or something of that sort might step in there (which it now does). But that one criticism was far outweighed by expressions of admiration. "Your work to me seemed delightful and a seven-mile-boot-step-forward, so to say a promise kept and to us realized. I was happy to be there, see and speak to your beautiful Mother, and applaud you. . . . One more word, my Dear George, I believe more than ever in a bright future for you!"

In 1932, after Gershwin sent Loeffler a copy of his biography written by Goldberg, Loeffler wrote to compliment him on *Girl Crazy*, which he had seen twice in New York the winter before and to thank him for the book. The biography he judged to be a "fine book on a beloved and supremely gifted musician: namely you! If I had written it (the book) I dare say the account of you personally, and of your great musical charm and gifts would have been more glowing. . . . I cannot help thinking of you but with great warmth and delight, for all that your art has brought into my life, for the friendship you seem to feel for your old friend."[18]

When Gershwin played with the BSO in 1932, Loeffler was, of course, there. "I enjoyed thoroughly George Gershwin's 2d Rapsody his last work," he wrote to Grace Schirmer. "It is delightful and stimulating, full of rhythmic life, finely orchestrated and played by beloved George and our fine orchestra and the inimitable Koussevitzky à merveille."[19] Loeffler was also in the audience and visited backstage in January 1934 when Gershwin appeared with the Leo Reisman orchestra (conducted by Charles Previn) at the beginning of Gershwin's twenty-eight-city tour.

Loeffler enjoyed musical shows by other composers as well. In June 1929 he wrote to Engel describing a show by Werner Janssen: "I must say I enjoyed Boom-Boom immensely! The music is delightful, the Jazz excellent, full of spirit and good tunes. . . . The Dancing all through was amazing! And one felt that the music made it so! But ye gods, if I can't, through you or Werner, know Nell Kelly, I shall *die* a sorry man! . . . I was—I am spell bound: those unforgettable Aesops eyes—vide Velasquez' painting! This lady is half demon half godess!!!!!!!!!!"[20]

Loeffler did more than enjoy and play jazz music. He tried his own hand at composing using jazz elements. John Erskine recorded that Loeffler remarked that "if he had his work to do again he would explore the marvelous possibilities of the jazz orchestra."[21] During the 1920s Loeffler dabbled with the possibilities. He worked on some pieces for voice and dance band (perhaps intended as a suite)—one of which, *Creole Blues (De 'tit zozos),* he finished—and he composed *Clowns* and possibly also a tango for Reisman's orchestra.

Clowns was his major work for jazz band. Reisman's orchestra performed it on 19 February 1928 at Symphony Hall in a concert entitled "A Programme of Rhythms." The program included several short pieces by a host of composers including Handy, Gershwin, Grofé, and Kern. Loeffler's *Intermezzo (Clowns)* began the second half of the program. For the program booklet accompanying the performance, Loeffler supplied a poem on clowns by Verlaine and a prose piece on the same subject by Théodore de Banville. Both are completely unrelated to the text of the piece, but, evidently, not to the inspiration, which so often for Loeffler lay not only in musical ideas but also literary ones.

In two other compositions Loeffler incorporated elements from popular music into otherwise classical compositions. In *Historiettes,* following three different movements (outlined in chapter 16), Loeffler composed a fourth movement inspired by a musical show. In the original outline this movement was entitled *Slavin in "Silence and fun" (un nègre).*[22] The movement as finally composed was *Historiette de Senorita Conchita Piquer,* a portrait of a Spanish gypsy he had seen in the show *The Wildcat.*

Loeffler's partita also has four differing movements, one of which was influenced by popular music. Loeffler began this new chamber work in 1930 at the request of Elizabeth Sprague Coolidge for her Chamber Music Festival in Chicago that October. Since Wanda Landowska was among the musicians engaged to play, Coolidge suggested that Loeffler might write a composition for harpsichord and viola d'amore. Loeffler decided on "the delights of a 'Partita' for viole d'amour and clavecin in four movements. Not strictly of course in the ancient manner, somewhat free and particularly of our time."[23]

While working on it, he revealed to Coolidge the same meticulous attitude Denis Bunker had observed with Loeffler's first chamber work. "I'll let the first movement rest for a week or ten days, then read it through and criticize it as if it had been written by some fellow whom I thoroughly despise, to find the weak spots." Loeffler had additional rewriting to do after Landowska had to cancel. He revised the already completed parts and reworked the remaining music for violin and piano. He did not wish to give up the work. "I wish to the saving of my soul that I might succeed writing not only a work that would really please you but also should be worthy of you, my beloved and most honored friend. In the meantime I am having the most beautiful time working at my Partita, a form which I choose for the delightful freedom it gives to my imagination. The great 'Snorters,' it seems to me, have been written and tho' that may be true of Partitas 'également,' yet, see the great beauty of moods expressed by titles as well as by charm and delight in the great Cantor of Leipzigs 6 Partitas!"[24]

The "ancient manner" is recalled in the first two movements of the work. The first, *Intrada,* is an introduction and fugue that incorporates a motto formed of Coolidge's initials (perhaps homage to JSB as well as ESC). The second, *Sarabande,* is a set of variations on a theme by Johannes Mattheson. The final movements are more "particularly of our time." The fourth, *Finale des tendres adieux,* is an arpeggiated essay in lyrical French beauty.

The third movement, however, is another matter. Entitled *Divertissement* and originally subtitled *La princesse nègre,* the movement is a hodgepodge of minstrel, ragtime, tango, and other jazzy elements and ideas. From the moment the work was premiered by Jacques

Gordon and Lee Pattison, reaction to this movement was mixed. It was not to everyone's liking. Allegedly Coolidge was offended by it. In a performance of the Partita at the Gardner Museum in 1934, it was omitted. In other performances, such as that at the Library of Congress in 1937, it was retained.

Loeffler, who had had the opportunity while traveling with the BSO to cross the country and hear the variety of its music, turned to indigenous American music for composition on only a few other occasions during his career. He arranged some southern tunes, including *Carry Me Back to Old Virginny*, in his *Rêverie-Barcarolle* for violin, *Were You There* for the viola d'amore, and *Dixie* for a Tavern Club minstrel show. He also made an arrangement of two cowboy tunes (one being *The Lone Prairie*) for the eminently Loefflerian, though not indigenous American, combination of viola d'amore, saxophone, and piano.

In these pieces, Loeffler was not making any attempt to be American by quotation, any more than he sought to be an American composer by innovation (of a peculiarly American sound). His use of American material, combined with his use of all national materials, may be considered American if by "American" one means "cosmopolitan," which, according to one European, "is comparable to nationalism in Europe."[25] Yet Loeffler was American primarily by being a resident of America who composed freely, as he wanted, which for Loeffler meant using a wide variety of material. Like America, Loeffler was a great assimilator.

He did not, however, assimilate everything. Apart from jazz, Loeffler was not always receptive to modern music and never incorporated many new developments into his style. His opinion of contemporary music was divided. He admired several composers of the then modern school. In an interview in 1931 for *Musical America* he said, "'Stravinsky is still the first among living composers, and Prokofieff is second.' Then after a pause he said, 'And there is no third.'"[26]

Percy Grainger recorded an incident that might indicate that Loeffler did not rate Stravinsky so highly. In 1922 both were judges at the Evanston Music Festival and heard a program of Stravinsky's music. Grainger was thrilled with *Firebird,* but Loeffler remarked, "It's such awful old stuff to anyone brought up in Russia, as I was. There isn't a passage, an effect in the Firebird that he hasn't lifted bodily out of Borodin or Balakirev or some other source well known to musicians in Russia, but not always known to musicians outside of Russia."[27]

But Loeffler really did admire Stravinsky's music, with some exceptions (e.g., the piano concerto). What he was actually protesting to Grainger was the equation of nationalism with originality. On another occasion, when asked about the symphonies of Sibelius, he replied: "That is not originality. That is nationalism, and, myself, I do not particularly care for cod liver oil. I had once a volume of more than seven hundred Norwegian tunes. They were very interesting in melody, as well as harmonically and rhythmically. Since I first looked them through I have never been able to find a piece by Grieg which I could not duplicate on some page of my book. It is the same with Russian composers, who often display such wealth of color and who are simply falling back upon the national storehouse."[28]

As with Stravinsky, Loeffler expressed conflicting opinions about the music of Varèse. To Elise in 1927 he wrote from Philadelphia, "Varèse's composition will bring about a public protest!!!"[29] In 1931, however, he said: "I was fortunate enough to hear the Philadelphia Orchestra when they played 'Hyperprism.' It would be a negation of all the centuries of musical progress if I were to call this music. Nevertheless I seemed to be dreaming of rites in Egyptian temples, of mystic and terrible ceremonies which history does not record. This piece roused in me a sort of subconscious racial memory, something elemental that happened before the beginning of recorded time. It affected me as only music of the past has affected me."[30]

Loeffler did not care for many modern compositions. He disliked the music of Copland (a "second-hand Schönberg"[31]), Antheil, Honegger, and, as illustrated in the following comment, Milhaud: "I really believe this world is growing insane politically [referring to the Bolsheviks], socially, musically and artistically! People stay away, particularly the young, when a quartet by Beethoven is being played, but run to New York to hear a new quartet by Milhaud!"[32] Loeffler was not opposed to modernity on principle but simply did not care to experiment with atonality, serialism, and certain other new ideas. He was ever hopeful for the future of music, as he declared to Coolidge, "Music is eternally delightful as regards the masterpieces prior to the war; so interesting now in petto, awakening ever new expectations of some beautiful page of music yet to come."[33]

More beautiful pages of music were yet to come from Loeffler, though his output in the 1930s diminished. Loeffler's health was slowing his pace and turning him into more of a recluse than ever. But in his final years he continued on as well as he could. New experiences and new work still lay ahead.

Charles Martin Loeffler at age 16, courtesy of the Medfield Historical Society

Charles Martin Loeffler and Elise Fay, April 1886, from the author's collection

Martin and Helene Loeffler, 1887, from the author's collection

Denis Bunker's pen-and-ink drawing for the cover of Loeffler's Quatuor, 1889, courtesy of the Spenser

The Boston Symphony Orchestra conducted by Artur Nikisch, 1891, courtesy of the BSO Archives

The Kneisel Quartette (left to right: Franz Kneisel, Alwin Schroeder, Louis Svecenski, and Otto Roth), courtesy of the Medfield Historical Society

Sketch of Loeffler by Anders Zorn, February 1894, courtesy of the Isabella Stewart Gardner Museum, Boston

Loeffler in 1894, courtesy of the Medfield Historical Society

Loeffler's apartment, showing his portrait by Léon Pourtau, courtesy of the Medfield Historical Society

Loeffler, Heinrich Gebhard, and two students—Miss Squires and Miss Furlong—courtesy of the Medfield Historical Society

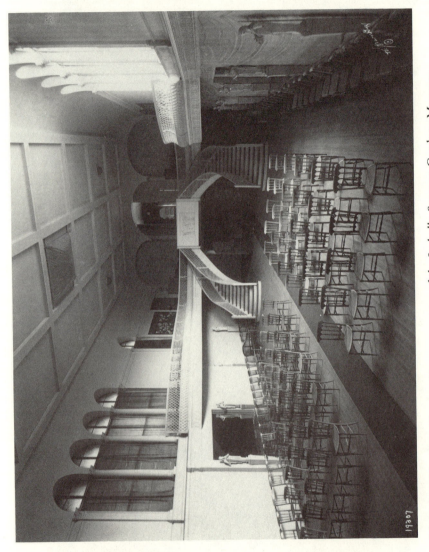

The Music Room at Fenway Court, courtesy of the Isabella Stewart Gardner Museum

Vincent d'Indy in New York in 1905, seated front center to the right of Loeffler and Kneisel (front left), Arthur Whiting and Frank Damrosch (front right), members of the Kneisel Quartette, and others, courtesy of the Library of Congress

Erich Loeffler, courtesy of the
Library of Congress

Helene Loeffler, courtesy of the Library of Congress

The Farmer of Medfield, with his dog and his horse, courtesy of the Medfield
Historical Society

The Loeffler house, after restoration, and the Loeffler living room, both courtesy of the Medfield Historical Society

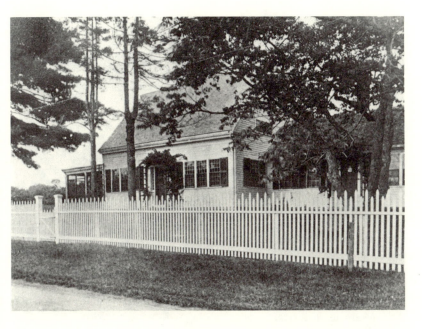

The music studio exterior and interior, courtesy of the Medfield Historical
Society

Loeffler with Irma Seydel, courtesy
of the Medfield Historical Society

The American String Quartette, courtesy of the Library of Congress

Loeffler at the window of his music studio, c. 1919, from the author's
collection

The Yellow Room in the Isabella Stewart Gardner Museum contains Loeffler's portrait by John Singer Sargent and a case of Loeffler memorabilia, including a cast of his hand, courtesy of the Isabella Stewart Gardner Museum

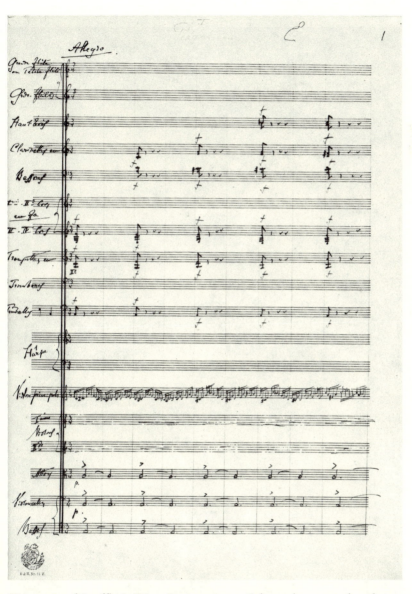

First page of Loeffler's *Divertissement* pour violon solo et grand orchestre, 1894, courtesy of the Isabella Stewart Gardner Museum

Loeffler in his music studio, c. 1930, courtesy of the Medfield Historical Society

18

Adieu pour jamais

In 1929 Loeffler fell dangerously ill. He had angina pectoris. During his hospitalization (in October and November) he translated eighty-one of Lao-Tse's Proverbs from German. "Since my illness," he remarked to Grace Schirmer, "I need the meditative and contemplative thoughts of Lao-Tse to calm and steady my mental balance and make the short time, possibly still allotted to me, worthwhile to live through with human interest and warmth."[1] Loeffler had been ill many times before; he had had so many operations that in 1927 he wrote Engel that he had been advised by surgeons "not to go through the ordeal of another surgical operation as the tissues were so extraordinarily delicate that nothing could hold stitches."[2] Angina was the last illness Loeffler had to endure.

Outwardly Loeffler accepted this illness as stoically as all the others he had endured. After angina was diagnosed, he would not travel alone and, in fact, canceled a trip to Chicago to hear his partita because he had a cold, but he tried not to let it intrude into his life. Once, soon after an attack, when a neighbor met him out walking in the woods and protested, in concern for his health, he replied, "Oh, it's just like mal du mer—when you have it, it's pretty bad, but when it's over, it's over."[3] To Gertrude Marshall he wrote, "There is one thing that provokes me, namely medical experts say that physically I am in perfect condition but my heart is what one might call an Ingersoll 1$ watch! That is supposed to be a consolation!"[4]

Although Loeffler's pace and his output diminished, during the 1930s he remained as active as he could. He continued to enjoy the simple but rich pleasures of his life. In 1930, for example, he was a guest at a garden party given by Marshall. Afterwards he wrote: "What is happiness? Well, *this is it!* This afternoon *was* it and the everliving Memory of it, *is it!* I cannot remember since the days of Mrs. Gardner's honoring me similarly of having lived through so delightful, truly happy hours as those on that wonderful June afternoon! The

Garden, the flowers, the trees—that cherry tree!, the tent, the thieving birds and you, my admired and beloved friend at my left and your Mother . . . and the genial, hospitable spirit of Mr. Wit hovering over it all. Not a flaw in all of it!"[5]

Several performances of Loeffler's music took place each year in the country. By the end of his life the BSO had given one hundred and seventeen performances of his music, and in October 1930 their performance of *A Pagan Poem* was broadcast, becoming the first live radio performance of a Loeffler work. Earlier in 1930 a dance version of *A Pagan Poem,* choreographed and directed by Irene Lewisohn, performed by the Neighborhood Playhouse Company with the Cleveland Orchestra and Harold Bauer (piano), took place in February in New York (simultaneously with Molinari's performance of the same piece in Carnegie Hall). Among the featured dancers was Martha Graham. Lewisohn designed the dance according to her own interpretation of Loeffler's music, about which Loeffler commented to Engel, "I liked her interpretation of Pagan Poem. It is very refined, but the end is *not in accord with my music*!"[6]

Early in that same year (1930) Casadesus and Koussevitzky were to have done *Tintagiles* but were not able to agree on a date before Casadesus returned to France. In 1930 the piece was performed by the Manhattan Symphony Orchestra, conducted by Henry Hadley, and in 1932 Koussevitzky conducted the work (with Jean Lefranc). Bruno Walter conducted it in New York the next year.

The year 1931 was a celebration year for Loeffler—his seventieth birthday. The occasion was honored by special performances by the orchestras of Boston, New York, and Cleveland, by newspaper tributes, essays by Philip Hale and Lawrence Gilman published by the Boston Music Company, as well as personal communications.

In February 1931 Loeffler's last orchestral composition, *Evocation,* was premiered. It had been commissioned for the opening of the Cleveland Orchestra's new home, Severance Hall, and the inspiration for the work was the actual building of the hall, as Loeffler explained in a preface to the score:

> The imagined form of this music is to tell the building of a beautiful temple of the Muses; of the god Pan's rhapsodic lay and the nymphs' love for him; of their vain endeavors to fetter him to their beloved sunny fields whence Echo is listening, listening for the pure fun of answering; of Syrinx, Pan's most beloved naiad, whom Artemis metamorphosed into a reed to save her from Pan's amorous pursuit; of the strange account given by the Singing Stone of itself; awed by solemn wonder at it we now seek the little stream running down the hills to meet us, the

reeds bowing to us in the breeze. The nymphs are still calling, "Pan, abide here on these sunny greens."

Loeffler further commented in a letter to Sokoloff: "The very beginning of the music, namely the fugue out of which grows the one most important theme a few pages later on, suggested itself to me on account of its harmonically chaotic theme, alike, as I imagined, to the matter which in confusion marked the beginning of the fine temple of music which the architects had in mind. By designed order these men used their material i.e. stone and marble to erect what will soon be known as 'Severance Hall.'"[7]

Evocation was scored, as the title page reads, "for women's voices and modern orchestra." The modern orchestra includes three saxophones and a vibraphone (or vibraharp). Realizing that saxophones were unheard of in a symphony orchestra, Loeffler wrote to Sokoloff, "How now about the 3 Sax's? Ye gods! Take, if you can, Jazz-players. There are some good ones in every large city."[8] Loeffler had investigated the possibility of having panpipes built, to a special scale, to suit the verses about Pan. Eventually the idea was dropped, but a vibraharp was specially constructed to accompany the Singing Stone (recited in a hushed tone offstage).[9] Loeffler's research into panpipes was not, however, without effect on the score, for they are suggested in the melodies of the flutes, especially one melody Loeffler had heard performed by goatherds in the Quartier Montmartre. Novel orchestration extends also to the timpani part, which, in the first bars of the score, contains an amazing eleven-tone chromatic passage within a span of a minor tenth—written with the assurance of Cleveland's timpanist that he could play it.

As at the beginning, so also throughout the score both orchestration and harmony produce a myriad of lush and exotic effects in the score. The Singing Stone passage, for example, scored primarily for vibraharp, harp, and piano, has an enchanting theme, constructed on a pentatonic motive, delicately supported by fluctuating chords built on roots a diminished fifth apart. The transition back to the chorus includes beautiful gliding parallel chords, and the chorus itself concludes on a chord with an unresolved second. For all its special effects, however, there is a subdued beauty and restraint to *Evocation* appropriate to the pastoral Greek verses Loeffler chose for his women's chorus.

The opening of Severance Hall was a gala occasion. In the Severances' box were Mr. and Mrs. Loeffler, Mr. and Mrs. Sergei Rachmaninoff, and Mrs. William Curtis Bok, founder of the Curtis Institute of Music. Carl Engel and Irene Lewisohn were also in attendance. After the event Tristam Livingston composed a poem about *Evocation.*

> In olden days the alchemist essayed
> To find a wealth distilled from tin and lead;
> Culled ancient learning all his life to aid
> A search that brought him poverty instead.
> So one who treads, in music or in art,
> A shorter path to riches and to fame,
> (Himself the necromancer's counterpart)
> Leaves to posterity a scarce remembered name.
> But Loeffler, in his laboratory found
> The singing stone which other men had sought,
> That yielded music from the very ground;
> And, reverent of the mystery he wrought
> Exquisite tapestries, where fold on fold,
> Ecstatic song is thread of molten gold.

After returning to Medfield Loeffler wrote a letter of appreciation to Adella Prentiss Hughes including the remark: "Elise said to me the other day, 'Would you like to live in Cleveland?' and I said simply, 'Yes.' As long as there are people there with such pluck as you, dear Adella, and people to whom you look up and believe in, Cleveland seems to me like Weimar during its great days—a truly ideal place."[10]

In the next few years, several other Loeffler works were given at Severance Hall, including a repeat performance of Lewisohn's dance version of *A Pagan Poem* (with pianist Beryl Rubinstein) on a program with Stravinsky's *Firebird* and staged versions of Debussy's *Nocturnes* and Griffes's *The White Peacock*. Sokoloff and his orchestra premiered another Loeffler composition, *Beat! Beat! Drums!* (also called *Drum Taps*), in November 1932. After this work had been lost by a publisher for more than ten years, Loeffler retrieved it through a copyist and orchestrated it. As sensitive to the nature of the poetry here as in his lush and sensuous choruses for women's voices, Loeffler evoked in this chorus the strength and ruggedness of Whitman's verses. In Cleveland, it was performed by a chorus of 200 voices in unison, accompanied by winds, brass, and percussion. The performance in Cleveland was followed in December by one in Boston by the Apollo Club.

Boston also followed Cleveland in presenting *Evocation.* In April 1933 the BSO with the Cecilia Society conducted by Arthur Feidler performed it on one of its broadcast concerts. After the performance Loeffler consented to speak over the air, an interview unfortunately not preserved.

Several concerts of Loeffler's music took place in 1934, including performances of *Psalm 137,* both by the MacDowell Club and by the New England Conservatory; the partita by the University Glee Club of Providence; *Memories* by the Baltimore Symphony Orchestra; and *Evocation* by the BSO, a performance which took the piece to New York.

What was to be, during his lifetime, the final concert composed entirely of Loeffler's compositions was given at the Gardner Museum on 24 April 1934. The Tapestry Room (used for concerts after Gardner redesigned the music hall into two museum rooms) was crowded; people were standing in the rear. Loeffler's portrait by Sargent was hung at the front. Wallace Goodrich opened the concert with the following remarks:

> We are met together to honor one who for a long time has honored us by his presence and activity in our midst.
>
> We are mindful of Mr. Loeffler's long service as one of the leading members of the Boston Symphony Orchestra; of his preeminence as an artist; of his activity as a teacher, and of the high ideals and example which he imparted to his pupils and caused them to make their own; and by no means least, of the very great and distinctly outstanding contribution he has made to creative music in all forms, in our country.
>
> Mr. Loeffler: we all feel this in our hearts more deeply than I can say. We, your friends, gathered here, ask you to accept this, our tribute in your honor, as the expression of our appreciation, of our admiration, and of our gratitude.[11]

The program included the partita (without the third movement) performed by Richard Burgin, BSO concertmaster; six songs sung by Olga Averino, and the *Canticum fratris solis* performed by Averino and a group of about twenty-five musicians from the BSO conducted by Burgin. After each performance Loeffler rose from his seat to lead the applause and escort the performers to the anteroom. He presented each soloist with a gift. He gave Averino a copy of *The White Fox* and expressed a hope that she might be able to sing in a concert performance of *Hilarion,* a performance that never occurred.

A tribute of another sort also occurred in 1934 from the Tavern Club. Part of the club's fiftieth anniversary celebration included the execution of a commemorative triptych, planned by Ives Gammell. It bore the names of Holmes, Chapman, Lowell, Cushing, Paderewski, Adamowski, and Loeffler,

Along with the celebrations and the honors, there were new occasions of personal grief for Loeffler during his last years. Georges Longy died in 1930. In November a memorial concert, given at Jordan Hall, featured *La cornemuse,* so often performed by Loeffler, Longy, and Gebhard. In 1931 Loeffler lost two other old friends, Eugène Ysaÿe and César Thomson. Loeffler had sent a former student of his own, Herman Silberman, to study with Thomson. Just an hour before the third scheduled lesson, Thomson suddenly died. "I have lost in him," Loeffler wrote to Silberman, "a Great friend! The world a great genius in whom the Spirit of Paganini was revived! There is unfortunately today nobody that is comparable to him as a phenomenal Virtuoso and teacher." Thomson was to Loeffler, as he wrote to Rabaud, "le grand et cher Maître."[12]

During the 1930s also, Loeffler had cause once again to be distressed by unhappy world events precipitated by his repudiated native country. In January 1933 Hitler had become chancellor; after two months he was voted the powers of a dictator. By that same time he had already aroused the concern and ire of Americans who deplored his policies and actions. In March 1933 Artur Bodansky conceived the idea of sending a cable to Hitler, a protest against his persecution of musicians, to be signed by outstanding musical artists in the country. Loeffler and ten others responded immediately. The following cable was sent:

> The undersigned who live and execute their art in the United States of America feel the moral obligation to appeal to your excellency to put a stop to the persecutions of their colleagues in Germany, for political or religious reasons. We beg you to consider that the artist all over the world is estimated for his talent alone and not for his national or religious convictions.
>
> We are convinced that such persecutions as take place in Germany at present are not based on your instructions, and that it cannot possibly be your desire to damage the high cultural esteem Germany, until now, has been enjoying in the eyes of the whole civilized world.
>
> Hoping that our appeal in behalf of our colleagues will not be allowed to pass unheard, we are Respectfully yours, [signed by Toscanini, Walter and Frank Damrosch, Koussevitzky, Bodansky, Bauer, Gabrilowitsch, Alfred Hertz, Loeffler, Fritz Reiner, and Rubin Goldmark; Stock added his name the next day].[13]

Three days later the National Socialist commissarial head of the Radio Department issued an order that the music and recordings of the signers of the cable would no longer find a place on the programs of German broadcasters or in the concert halls.

Loeffler also received news of Germany from his sister, who wrote frequently and commented on conditions in Hitler's Germany. Loeffler continued to support his sister, but he had no further opportunity to help France or his own country as in World War I, since he did not live to see them at war again.

Loeffler's life became increasingly restricted. He had ceased teaching violin and his one composition student, Francis Judd Cooke, was as much a companion as a student. Loeffler had, of course, also given up riding. Read would take the Loefflers for rides around the countryside in the automobile, but the Loefflers rarely traveled more than that.

Because of his own or his wife's ill health Loeffler had to decline nearly every invitation issued by the American Academy of Arts and Letters for their meetings and concerts in New York, including his own ratification as well as a request to serve (in 1932) on their music committee. His final trip to New York was probably that made in April 1934 when the BSO performed *Evocation* at Carnegie Hall.

The Loefflers discontinued their weekly trips to the symphony concerts about 1934 but listened to Saturday night broadcasts. Cooke often played phonograph records for Loeffler. Marshall continued to visit, bringing chamber music (and necessary performers) to play, but finally, during a rehearsal of a Brahms quintet, when Loeffler, playing viola, got lost, he stopped playing. It was the last time he was heard to play.

Although denied many activities, Loeffler still had his books. He respected reading so much that he autographed a portrait to Cooke with the quotation from Voltaire:

> Quel est le plaisir le plus durable?
> Sans doute c'est l'étude.
> Plaisir toujours nouveau
> Qu'augmente l'habitude.
>
> What is the most lasting pleasure?
> Without doubt, it is study.
> An ever new pleasure
> Augmented by habit.

During the last two to three years of his life, Loeffler finished no new compositions. The last work he saw published was the *Five Irish Fantasies*. He was not really composing, although he did want to revise *Hora mystica*. Cooke made a piano reduction of the score, which he played for Loeffler night after night, but nothing more came of it. Cooke tried to interest Koussevitzky in the piece, but Koussevitzky at the time was preoccupied with Stravinsky. When, in 1933, the American Academy of Arts and Letters put together a collection of members' autograph pages for a volume of *Le Manuscrit autographe,* Loeffler chose a page of the *Salve Regina* ending of *Hora mystica.*

Loeffler had already written his musical farewell—the fourth movement of his partita, composed in 1930. This movement, called *Finale des tendres adieux,* was, so Loeffler wrote in a letter, "a little sad, a little gay."[14] Loeffler allegedly said to Marshall, "This is for all of you—you are all in it."[15] The main theme of the movement is a variation of the melody of his *Prière.* The work closes poignantly with a quotation of the title motive of his song *Adieu pour jamais*—Farewell Forever.

In July 1934 Loeffler suffered a heart attack that nearly killed him, but, although his heart stopped, he was revived. Helene also had heart trouble—as had their mother—and simultaneously, as Loeffler feared to hear of his sister's death, Helene feared to hear of Martin's.

Loeffler lived another year, for the most part staying in Medfield. In September 1934 he motored to Boston to lunch with Carl Engel. Engel described the meeting.

> He paid us a touching compliment with the words: "it isn't for everyone I'd make the trip." He bore the marks of his physical suffering. But his razor-blade mind still showed occasionally its flashing edge. His mood was genial, reminiscent. The good things of the table still appealed to him. His wonderful eyes would still twinkle as he unraveled some favorite story, not less amusing for being not altogether new. His precarious cardiac condition did not prevent him from asking the waiter to bring some particularly rich cigars. He acknowledged eagerly how charmed he had been with the person of Arnold Schoenberg. His thoughts roamed the length of contemporary music. On hearing the hotel musicians play a certain composition, he made a face and confessed that for him the appeal of Carl Maria von Weber had long ago ceased. From one thing to another, the talk swayed along its circuitous course, not as fast perhaps as formerly, but just as absorbing. . . . After that meeting, we had no other."[16]

Another broadcast of Loeffler's music occurred in New York when the New York Philharmonic performed Loeffler's *Poem* on 14 April 1935. At that time Lawrence Gilman delivered a special tribute—the last that Loeffler was to receive during his lifetime.

At 6:15 on the morning of 19 May 1935 Charles Martin Loeffler died. He was buried in the Fay family plot in Southborough. While it had been Elise's wish to outlive her husband, after his death she frequently told her attorney that she hoped God would take her so that she could join her husband.[17] Ten months later she, whose life it had been to wait on him and help him, was laid at his side. Helene, the last of the family, died in 1937.

All the major newspapers ran special obituaries. "The death of Charles Martin Loeffler," claimed one, "has removed from the American scene one of the most significant musical creators to have emerged during the past fifty years." He was acknowledged by others to have been "almost universally esteemed as the foremost composer of serious music in America" or, as Olin Downes wrote in the *New York Times:* "one of the most striking and distinctive figures that American music has known."[18] Further, Downes declared, "It was not Loeffler's fault if he became something of a cult of the sort for which Boston was famous. He was a most careful and fastidious workman, a passionate seeker after beauty, of a curious and somewhat cerebral temperament, a many-faceted man and a most distinguished artist."

"The death of Charles Martin Loeffler last Monday removed from the roster of American composers its leading name," wrote W. J. Henderson in the *New York Sun.* "Mr. Loeffler was not only the leading American writer of music, but one of the most distinguished in the world. . . . Mr. Loeffler was a supreme artist and the musical world will sorrow over his departure. Those who knew him will lament the loss of a man of fine culture, and of a most lovable nature."[19]

Frank Benson wrote a memorial address for the Tavern Club:

The musical world ranks him as a great artist, and that is what we have all known him to be, but, with all his splendid accomplishment, if you knew him well, you prized him as a man, an upstanding, steadfast friend, who . . . never yielded a point in the principles he believed in, or stood for anything but the highest and best. Indeed, I think he invested those he loved with the same qualities; and what greater tribute can one receive from another? . . .

I thought of him as one who lived always on the heights, touched by a light that only reached the upper regions, yet he loved all that was interesting in life, whether high or low.

And when the end came, and the world praised the work of the great poet composer I thought that to those who had been fortunate to know the man, he was even greater than his work.[20]

During the 1935–36 season several memorial concerts were given by the BSO and other orchestras. Special chamber concerts were given in New York at Schirmer's in January 1936 and at the Library of Congress in 1937. Between 1936 and 1938 four scores—*Prière, Hilarion,* Partita, and Quintet—and his violin studies were published.

Loeffler's friends, critics, and admirers took their leave of him in various manners. Carl Engel allowed the musical world to share his farewell to Loeffler, which he recounted in the *Musical Quarterly.*

It was a bright, fresh morning in May, the kind of Spring-day found only in New England. Large, billowy clouds pushed one another quietly through the blue, with smaller patches sailing past them at a little faster pace. Out of the young green, speckled with tender russet, the sun picked the thousands of dogwood blooms—creamy or pink—, gave luster to the daisies in the meadows, and drained the myriad lilac bushes of their fragrance. . . .

Through Jamaica Plain, by the flowery pond, through Dedham, across its quaint village common, through Dover woods, a tip of Walpole, into Medfield township sped the car. Familiar sites began to stir up a host of memories. There was the stationery shop, hard by the post-office, where, in August and September 1914, we used to stop on our bicycle to get the papers and anxiously scan the news from the front. There was the Catholic church—once the place of memorable concerts—, its clap-boards and jig-saw ornaments too shiny in recent paint. Just beyond the railway crossing the road turns to the left; at the next fork you take to the right. There was the farmhouse where we had spent a torrid but kindling summer. The car slowed down. A few hundred yards further on, from out thick masses of lilac and through the sheltering poplars loomed the roofs of the two buildings: the living quarters on the right, the "work-house" on the left. And there in the latter, which is practically nothing but one huge room—that had so often resounded with the polished strains of his music and the luminous tone of his violin—stood the coffin of Charles Martin Loeffler. . . .

A truly great life has come to an end, a grand personage has stepped from the scene. . . .

Is it possible that we have seen, resting upon a silenced heart, those bloodless, waxen fingers that we knew strong in life and capable of giving utterance to four cat-gut strings in a chant so moving that it hurt?

The sound has floated into space. If the echo lingers, it is in the lilacs that envelop the music house of Charles Martin Loeffler in Medfield. Let no one trespass—here is hallowed ground.[21]

The Loeffler Estate, Loeffler Prize, and Loeffler Collections

Loeffler bequeathed to the music section of the Academie des Beaux Arts $15,000 to create a prize, under the name Prix Ch. M. Tornov Loeffler to be given every two or four years to a Frenchman of at least four generations of French ancestry, "the author of the finest musical composition written within the course of the last 2 (or 4) years." The prize was established and continues to be given. Loeffler also bequeathed $20,000 to Les Amis du Conservatoire (Conservatoire National de Musique et de la Déclamation), of which he was a *membre donateur*, to create a fund, the Ch. M. Tornov Loeffler Fund, to be used for general purposes.

The bulk of Loeffler's estate was put in trust for the benefit of his wife and sister. Following their deaths, legacies passed to Philip Hale, Carl Engel, Nikolai Sokoloff, Charles Martin Reisman (son of Leo Reisman, probably a god-child, as were children of Engel and Sokoloff), and to four charities.

Mrs. Loeffler's will was noteworthy enough to receive press coverage. Her estate was valued at a half million dollars (the bulk of which, after liquidation, was divided among charities). Various Oriental curios and art objects were given to the Peabody Museum in Salem and her Sargent artworks to the Boston Museum of Fine Arts. She donated her husband's music manuscripts and copyright to them to the Library of Congress, which also holds the major collection of the Loeffler correspondence and iconography then possessed by Mrs. Loeffler. Other Loeffler manuscripts have since been donated to the Library of Congress and other libraries (see Appendix 2).

Various other items from the Loeffler estate (a baton, glasses, photographs, clippings, printed music, bookplates, calling cards, etc.) have been donated to the Medfield Historical Society, which also has a bust of Loeffler. A collection of Loeffler items is on permanent display in the Yellow Room of the Isabella Stewart Gardner Museum, Boston. Sargent's portrait is hung there above a display case containing photos of Loeffler, a program hand-written by Gardner of a concert including Loeffler's music performed at Green Hill, and a cast of Loeffler's hand done by Mabel Hunt Slater. In another case in the same room rests the viola d'amore that Loeffler presented to Gardner in 1903. Other items, including correspondence and musical manuscripts, are located in the Gardner Museum archives.

In May 1940 the first of the two houses owned by the Loefflers in Medfield was accidently destroyed by fire. The house that was formerly Loeffler's music studio is now privately owned.

19

A Proud and Wholly Personal Place

On the occasion of Loeffler's seventieth birthday, Olin Downes wrote a rather lengthy article for the *New York Times* in which he stated, "This article is neither tribute nor homage, because neither of these two things are needed. These words are in the nature of a protest. Why instead of kind words for a composer whose place will be established by his music and not by any words of contemporaries, do we not hear more of Mr. Loeffler's compositions?"[1]

For an American composer, Loeffler was not unsuccessful. But although his music was performed nationally and internationally to generally good reviews and enthusiastic audiences, several critics besides Downes, particularly those outside Boston, expressed the opinion that his music was not heard frequently at all and certainly less than it deserved. For a half century following his death, it was heard even less, with a consequent loss of familiarity to a wide audience even of his name.

One reason stemmed from the composer himself. Loeffler was one of the most meticulous, perfectionist, self-critical composers that ever lived. His compositions underwent frequent revision, and often he could never quite finish rewriting. Some compositions were not heard after the first performances, and others reappeared only years later after revision. Lawrence Gilman wrote, "it has often seemed as if his chief concern, after finishing a new work, were to conceal it from public knowledge."[2] In his later years Loeffler generally lost interest in his early works. He sometimes refused requests for permission to perform his music. He also withheld certain scores from publication, never quite getting them ready. "One felt," Gilman continued, "that he would far rather keep a manuscript in his portfolio or on his desk, with pencil and eraser handy, than yield it to the engraver, or even to a performer for experimental hearing."

Loeffler enjoyed success and liked to have his music performed for those who appreciated it. He spent some time trying to interest conductors in his work, but he simply did not push it publicly. There were even several occasions when he suggested that music other than his own be performed, for example, when he insisted that the Composers Club present Engel's violin sonata rather than his own songs at a dinner honoring Rabaud. Often he withheld his music because he preferred it to be unperformed than unappreciated.

Many times his music was unappreciated, and though he professed stoicism to outside opinion, he was very sensitive to it. To Harold Bauer he wrote, "There are so many celebrated . . . compositions in our orb that I do not admire and would not ever willingly listen to again except under administration of chloroform, that it would be utter arrogance on my part to mind meeting with indifference or antagonism in regard to my own works."[3] Yet in other letters he complained of people's disregard of his music, and a comparison of reviews of Loeffler's early compositions to subsequent revisions and to performance records reveals his sensitivity to criticism. Never was Loeffler quite sure of his own worth as a composer. He once observed, "The works of even great men, sooner or later, drop into the Ocean of forgotten things, so I fully realize and live under no delusions—being only one of the minim of minor composers—about my wet, moist, dank, and humid future!"[4]

Critical opinion, like audience opinion and the regard of his professional colleagues, was, understandably, divided. Some professional critics, like Hale, Gilman, Huneker, and Downes, quite frankly adored his music. Some had mixed feelings, for example, Louis Elson, who liked much about Loeffler's music but deplored his morbidity. Others were lukewarm or disinterested. Some openly disliked his music. Paul Rosenfeld, for example, who adhered to a quite different aesthetic, condemned Loeffler's music with nearly every pejorative possible— "derivative," "bloodless," "unsubstantial," "cold," "colorless," "uncreative," "sterile."[5]

Loeffler's music was unusual. "Not of his time was Charles Martin Tornov Loeffler," wrote Moses Smith in his obituary of Loeffler, "yet he was not comprehensible in another age."[6] He introduced a music— modern, exotic, Decadent, Symbolist—that many could not comprehend. It was not like anything they were used to. Even in later years, when Loeffler's music was more familiar and less avant-garde, he never belonged to the mainstream of compositional activity. During the 1920s and 1930s, his detractors called him an "ivory tower" composer, out of touch with modern times, which opinion has often been thoughtlessly passed on as a generalization on Loeffler's style.[7] Though the mystic and poetic nature of his music is one of its timeless charms, in his own day Loeffler was criticized for being modern and for not being modern, when, as Hale said, what should have been important was simply whether his music was good or bad.

Perhaps more than by impressions of its timeliness, however, Loeffler's reputation has been affected by considerations of nationality. As stated at the outset of this biography, Loeffler lived in an era highly conscious of nationality, one prone to view artists in terms of national expression and identity. At the beginning of his career, Loeffler's dual nationality—European and American—put him in a position to be favored by both traditionalists and nationalists, but as his career advanced, he never fell squarely into either camp. He did not belong to familiar Germany, and Americans were never quite sure if he were American. There was no French camp, nor did he form his own camp. Albeit his music was often admired for originality and individuality, these very qualities were stumbling blocks to minds prone to generalization, which had to fit Loeffler's music neatly into a school, style, or nationality to comprehend it, champion it, and later to see it in a historical setting. To these minds, Loeffler never quite fit anywhere.

There is no need now to exclude Loeffler as an American composer. America was the country for Loeffler. Composing as he wished, Loeffler was an American free spirit, subject, as was the country, to a world of influences but at liberty, as was the country, to make of them what he would. Yet during his lifetime, though at first his music aroused the interest of those looking for change in American music, many doubted whether Loeffler could be considered an American composer (despite the American propensity to claim anything that was original). Although charges of being un-American could apply to any number of American-born composers who themselves composed within a European tradition, they at least composed within a familiar tradition. Loeffler was not like most Americans. Walter Spalding, for example, wrote: "Although he has become a loyal American, and although his best works have been composed in this country, we can hardly claim him as an American composer, for his music vividly reflects French taste and ideals."[8]

The most frequently created image of Loeffler was that of a transplanted European, particularly a Frenchman. But Loeffler was not French. From a world view his American citizenship might suggest he was outside the mainstream of the European movement he was most closely allied with, which movement in America was outside the mainstream of American musical practice. In addition, the emergence of a French figure as leader of the Impressionist style relegated others, especially Americans, to inferior positions. Comparisons to Debussy gave many who did not know or comprehend Loeffler's music a way to peg him at last—yet here also he did not quite fit, nor should he. To assess Loeffler the eclectic by comparison to Debussy must inevitably either find Loeffler wanting as a Debussean or lead to the more just acknowledgement that, though allied to a movement, Loeffler had his own, independently developed, and different voice within it (which recognition may lead to a broader understanding of Symbolism).[9]

Loeffler has been called a cosmopolitan but also an exile or depaysé—belonging not to all countries but to none, which is probably more true with regard to his posthumous reputation. Yet had Loeffler been accepted wholeheartedly as an American composer, his posthumous reputation might have fared no better. To Europeans Loeffler was an American, and that, in his own opinion and in fact, was a handicap. Loeffler's fate has been shared by nearly every American composer of his generation, for American composers were simply considered second rate after Europeans by both Europeans and Americans. One review alone need be quoted: "Had [Loeffler] remained in Paris, among the wellsprings of his inspiration, who knows what heights he might have reached? For some unknown reason, he chose to live in what was then a land of musical primitives and unwittingly committed himself to limbo. Perhaps we Americans are to blame; if so, we may have lost a sorely needed genius."[10]

Ultimately, critical classification according to nation or school is irrelevant. James Huneker wrote, "I don't lean much on the map theory in music,"[11] and Loeffler himself agreed. "There is positively no type in music," he said. "Music is music. I . . . believe in music for its own sake, and not nationality in art. Of course, as a man, I believe in nationality, but in music—no! If there be such a thing it can have no interest for me. No there is no such thing as French or German music. I love all good music, and that is sufficient for me."[12] Huneker further wrote: "Let us judge a man by the sheer merits of his work, and if Loeffler doesn't lead all other composers here, then I'll wager Philip Hale the omphalic scale against the chromatic. Mr. Gilman thinks the same."

For this biography nationality was the starting point because of its profound influence on the man and his aesthetic. Influences of various nationalities on Loeffler's style have been remarked throughout. In closing, nationality has again been examined in relation to Loeffler's art because of the effect that definition by nationality has had on Loeffler's reputation. However, Loeffler's place in music history should not be defined, bound, or dependent on nationality. Loeffler belonged to America; he belonged to the world; and he belonged only to himself.

When Loeffler was seventy, Oscar Thompson wrote that "placing Loeffler has been one of the most perplexing tasks of those who have had to write about him."[13] More than difficult, trying to place Loeffler's music somewhere (e.g., according to boundaries he never recognized or by comparison to a composer he was not imitating) has been a disservice.

One of Loeffler's first fans, Philip Hale, called Loeffler "a singular apparition in music." Loeffler's first biographer, Carl Engel, wrote that Loeffler was *sui generis;* "he is that rare and comforting thing in life and art—a perfect anomaly." And E. B. Hill, though able to analyze Loeffler's debt to France, concluded: "He attained his own style and delivered his personal message."[14] Similar sentiments may be found in the writings of others of Loeffler's contemporaries. Though Loeffler may indeed be viewed as a Symbolist, as an American, as a European/American, or some other classification, he does not quite fit. In his life as in his art he stands apart. It is as an individual, composing to suit himself, that he should hence ultimately be recognized and his music examined.

Certain words from the past rather encourage a new examination of Loeffler's music. Many have already been quoted; to quote but one more, W. J. Henderson wrote, after a performance of *Evocation*: "We do not know of any other musician who could have written this work. It is essentially individual. It is one more disclosure of the fully stored mind and generous heart of a composer who is profoundly a scholar, instinctively aristocratic, a poet and a philosopher, born to dwell all his life in the sacred shades spread from the Erechtheum without ever making concessions to the urge toward popularity, without ever defacing his musical speech with shopworn devices of the market place or shibboleths of party, without parade of pomp or circumstance, he has made for himself a proud and wholly personal place as one of the definitely distinguished writers of his time."[15]

Our own study leads us to the same conclusion held by Loeffler's contemporary admirers—both in respect to the man himself and his music. Flaws there were and are, yet Loeffler and his music were unique and extraordinary. Loeffler lived through important times in musical history, for which, if only as a witness, he draws one's interest. Yet Loeffler was far more than a witness; he played a significant part in the development of his country's music—as violinist, teacher, composer, and man of judgment. His life was rich in activity, acquaintance, trial, and triumph. In his oeuvre are gems of musical composition of enduring beauty. Some of his music is so exquisitely wrought as to be breath-taking. His fate should not be to be lost in the ocean of forgotten things. The "proud and wholly personal place" Loeffler once made for himself should be among the distinguished artists of all time.

Solos Played by Loeffler
with the Boston Symphony Orchestra
Chronologically Arranged

Godard, *Concerto romantique,*
op. 35
 Boston 16–17 November 1883
 Fitchburg 29 November 1883
 Cambridge 6 December 1883
 Worcester 13 December 1883
 Cambridge 8 January 1891

Bruch, *Concerto, D Minor, no. 2,*
op. 44 (I)
Lalo, *Fantasie norvégienne*
 Boston 19–20 December 1884
 Salem 28 January 1885
 Cambridge 12 March 1885

Bach, *Chaconne*
 Boston 20–21 March 1885

Bruch, *Concerto, D Minor, no. 1,*
op. 26
 Boston 27–28 November 1885
 Cambridge 7 January 1886
 Washington 14 April 1886
 Cincinnati 17 April 1886
 Chicago 21 April 1886

Mendelssohn, *Concerto, E Minor,*
op. 64
 Boston 10–11 December 1886
 Cambridge 10 January 1887
 Pittsburgh 22 April 1887
 St. Louis 30 April 1887
 Chicago 7 May 1887
 Troy 18 May 1887

Lalo, *Symphonie espagnole (I-II-*
IV-V)
 Boston 11–12 November 1887
 Cambridge 2 February 1888
 Cambridge 12 December 1889
 New Haven 13 January 1890
 Boston 7–8 February 1890
 Philadelphia 12 February 1890
 Columbus 5 May 1890
 Minneapolis 12 May 1890
 Albany 23 May 1890

Bruch, *Scottish Fantasy, op. 46*
 Boston 23–24 November 1888
 Boston 30 January 1889
 Cambridge 7 March 1889
 Buffalo 2 May 1889
 Chicago 10 May 1889
 Cincinnati 14 May 1889
 Pittsburgh 16 May 1889
 Washington 18 May 1889

Bach, *Double Concerto, D Minor*
(with Kneisel)
 Boston 10–11 October 1890

Loeffler, *Les veillées de l'Ukraine*
 Boston 20–21 November 1891
 Cambridge 31 December 1891

Mozart, *Sinfonia concertante for Vi-*
olin and Viola (I) (with Kneisel)
 Boston 1–2 January 1892

Saint-Saëns, *Concerto, A Major,*
no. 1, op. 20
   Boston 24–25 February 1893
   Buffalo 4 May 1893
   Cincinnati 11 May 1893
   Chicago 15 May 1893

Bruch, *Romanza, A Minor, op. 42*
Saint-Saëns, *Concert-Piece, E*
Minor, op. 62
   Boston 16–17 February 1894

Loeffler, *Divertissement, A Minor*
   Boston 4–5 January 1895
   Boston 8–9 January 1897
   Cambridge 10 February 1898

   Philadelphia 14 February 1898
   Washington 15 February 1898
   New York 17 February 1898

Loeffler, *La mort de Tintagiles*
   Boston 7–8 January 1898
   Boston 18–19 March 1898
   Cambridge 7 April 1898
   Revision:
   Boston 15–16 February 1901
   Philadelphia 20 February 1901
   New York 21 February 1901
   Boston 1–2 January 1904
   Baltimore 12 January 1904
   New York 14 January 1904
   Cambridge 28 January 1904

Annotated Catalog of Works

LC Numbers: Since the majority of manuscripts held by the Library of Congress have been catalogued under one call number but those microfilmed have been assigned individual item numbers on the films, this catalog identifies most Library of Congress holdings by these microfilm numbers—e.g., LC26. The use of LC+ indicates that a catalogued item in the library was not microfilmed, and LC* that an item was neither catalogued nor microfilmed by the Library at the time that this catalog was compiled.

VOCAL WORKS
Songs
Voice and Piano

A une femme (A vous ces vers de par la grace)
Text:	Paul Verlaine, *Poèmes saturniens*
Composition:	1904
Premiere:	21 March 1917, Povla Frijsh and Heinrich Gebhard, Jordan Hall, Boston
Dedication:	à Mme. Richard Aldrich
Manuscript:	Score: holograph (4 pp.), LC1
Variant:	*A une femme* for Voice, Violin, and Piano

Adieu pour jamais (Chère apparence viens aux couchants illuminés)
Text:	Gustave Kahn, "Intermède XIV," *Les palais nomades*
Composition:	about 1899
Premiere:	10 May 1900, Julia Heinrich and George Proctor, Green Hill, Brookline, Mass.; Philip Hale, however, dates it 1899.
Dedication:	à Mlle. Elise Fay
Score:	*see Quatre mélodies*
Recording:	D'Anna Fortunato and Virginia Eskin, Northeastern Records 207
Transcription:	*Adieu pour jamais* for Violin and Piano

Ballad of the Foxhunter (Now lay me down in a cushioned chair)
Text:	William Butler Yeats, *Crossway*
Composition:	1920, Medfield, Mass.
Dedication:	To Dr. Henry Lee Morse
Score:	*see Five Irish Fantasies*

Boléro triste (Tant que l'enfant me préféra tel joueur de flûte)
Text: Gustave Kahn, *Chansons d'amant*
Composition: summer 1900, Medfield, Mass.
Premiere: 21 March 1917, Povla Frijsh and Heinrich Gebhard, Jordan Hall, Boston
Dedication: à Mme. Povla Frijsh
Manuscript: Score: holograph (4 pp.), LC*; Draft: torn page laid in LC41
Variant: *Boléro triste* for Voice, Violin, and Piano

Busslied, aus dem 16ten Jahrhundert (Gott wie sind meine Sünden so schwer)
Text: unidentified
Composition: n.d. The style points to a very early composition date.
Manuscript: Score: (10 pp.), LC10; bears no ascription for text or music, is uncharacteristic of Loeffler in style, hand, and use of German script

Caitilin ni Uallachain (How tossed, how lost, with all hopes crossed, we have been!)
Text: William Heffernan (the Blind), translated from the Gaelic by James Clarence Mangan and others, published in Mangan's *The Poets and Poetry of Munster.* The complete Gaelic setting may be found among sketches for the orchestral *Fantasies.*
Composition: 1920, Medfield, Mass.
Dedications: To Mr. John McCormack
Score: *see Five Irish Fantasies*

Domaine de fée. See Les soirs d'automne

A Dream within a Dream (Take this kiss upon the brow!)
Text: Edgar Allan Poe
Composition: 1905, Medfield, Mass.
Premiere: 10 April 1906, Susan Metcalfe and Heinrich Gebhard, Boston
Dedication: To Mrs. Gustave Schirmer
Score: *see Four Poems*
Recording: John Kennedy Hanks and Ruth Friedberg, Duke University Press, DWRM–6417–18

The Fiddler of Dooney (When I play on my fiddle in Dooney)
Text: William Butler Yeats, *The Wind among the Reeds*
Composition: 1920, Medfield, Mass.
Dedication: To Edward Johnson
Score: *see Five Irish Fantasies*
Recording: D'Anna Fortunato and Virginia Eskin, Northeastern Records 207

Five Irish Fantasies, for Voice and Orchestra or Piano
See also individual titles and *The Wind among the Reeds*
1. *The Hosting of the Sidhe*
2. *The Host of the Air*
3. *The Fiddler of Dooney*
4. *Ballad of the Foxhunter*
5. *Caitilin ni Uallachain*

Manuscripts:	Scores: holograph (7, 16 [9 & 7], 9, 11 pp.), LC44; 1–3: copy with corrections (11 pp.), Yale; Sketches: 3: sketch on last page of *Vassar College Song,* LC108
Publication:	New York: G. Schirmer, 1934 (9, 11, 11, 11, 13 pp.)
Recording:	1–3: D'Anna Fortunato and Virginia Eskin, Northeastern Records 207
Arrangement:	*Five Irish Fantasies* for Voice and Orchestra

Le flambeau vivant (Ils marchent devant moi, ces yeux pleins de lumières)

Text:	Charles Baudelaire, *Les fleurs du mal*
Premiere:	5 April 1902, Lena Little
Manuscript:	missing

Four Poems, Set to Music for Voice and Piano, op. 15
See also individual titles:
1. *Sudden Light*
2. *A Dream within a Dream*
3. *To Helen*
4. *Sonnet*

Manuscripts:	Scores: holograph (4, 6, 4, 5 pp.), LC83; 3: holograph presentation copy to Evelyn Benedict (4 pp.), Boston Public Library
Publication:	New York: G. Schirmer, 1906 (7, 7, 5, 7 pp.); reprint ed., Hunstville, Texas: Recital Publications, Ltd.

[*Four Songs* (LC title)].
See also individual titles:
1. *Marie*
2. *Madrigal*
3. *Les hirondelles*
4. *Rêverie*

Title:	These are probably the romances on Loeffler's list given in note 28 to chapter 9.
Manuscripts:	Scores: holograph (3, 3, 3, 3 pp.), LC104; 4: holograph (3 pp.), with corrections, LC91

Girl and Boy Guides Prayer Hymn–Sketch

Composition:	probably contemporary with *Prière* since sketches to both compositions may be found together
Manuscripts:	Sketches, LC25, LC84, LC*

Les hirondelles (Voltigez hirondelles, voltigez près de moi)
    Text: A. d'Hotelier
    Composition: probably mid-1880s
    Premiere: perhaps 1888, Philadelphia
    Score: *see [Four Songs]*

Hommage (Je te vis, je t'aimais)
    Title: The title *Hommage,* not on the manuscript, appears on the
                    program of the premiere and in Loeffler's writings.
    Text: Gustave Kahn
    Composition: 1908, Medfield, Mass.
    Premiere: 7 June 1911, Mme. J. S. Fay and Heinrich Gebhard, St.
                    Edward's Church, Medfield, Mass.
    Dedication: Povla Frijsh (on 21 March 1917 concert program)
    Manuscript: Score: holograph (6pp.), LC45

The Host of the Air (O'Driscoll drove with a song)
    Text: William Butler Yeats, *The Wind among the Reeds*
    Composition: summer 1906–7, Medfield, Mass., revised 1920, Medfield
    Dedication: To my friend Temple R. Fay
    Score: *see The Wind among the Reeds, Five Irish Fantasies*
    Recording: D'Anna Fortunato and Virginia Eskin, Northeastern Re-
                    cords 207

The Hosting of the Sidhe (The Host is riding from Knocknarae)
    Text: William Butler Yeats, *The Wind among the Reeds*
    Composition: summer 1906–7, Medfield, Mass., revised 1920, Medfield
    Dedication: To my friend Temple R. Fay
    Score: *see The Wind among the Reeds, Five Irish Fantasies*
    Recording: D'Anna Fortunato and Virginia Eskin, Northeastern Re-
                    cords 207

Der Kehraus (Es fideln die Geigen)
    Text: Joseph von Eichendorff
    Date: 1906, Medfield, Mass.
    Manuscripts: Scores (all bound with *Vereinsamt*): 3 holographs, each
                    with corrections (6 pp. incomplete, 7 pp., 8 pp.), Yale

Madrigal (Si les roses pouvaient vous rendre le baiser)
    Text: Paul Bourget
    Composition: probably mid-1880s
    Premiere: perhaps 1888, Philadelphia
    Score: *see [Four Songs]*

Marie (Ainsi quand la fleur printanière)
    Text: Alfred de Musset, *Poésies nouvelles*
    Composition: probably mid-1880s
    Premiere: perhaps 1888, Philadelphia
    Score: *see [Four Songs]*

Les paons (Se penchant vers les dahlias)
Text:	Gustave Kahn, "Intermède IX," *Les palais nomades*
Composition:	about 1899
Premiere:	10 May 1900, Julia Heinrich and George Proctor, Green Hill, Brookline, Mass.; Philip Hale, however, dates it 1899.
Dedication:	à John S. Sargent
Score:	*see Quatre mélodies*
Transcription:	*Les paons* for Piano; *Les paons* for Violin and Piano

Prière (Prayer) (Dieu des petits enfants) [also: *Prière brève*; subtitle *A short prayer for a charming grandmother to teach her grand-children* (on copyist manuscript)]
Text:	Roger Dévigne, translation by David Stevens
Composition:	Christmas, 1926, Medfield, Mass.
Premiere:	25 April 1934, Olga Averino, B. Zighera, Gardner Museum, Boston
Dedication:	To Mrs. M. Graeme Haughton (on copyist manuscript)
Manuscripts:	Scores: holograph (1p.), with sketches, LC84; copy with title page by Loeffler (1p.), LC85; Sketches: LC84, LC*
Publication:	Boston: C. C. Birchard, 1936 (3pp.); in *Solos for the Church Year*, New York: G. Schirmer, Inc., 1957.
Arrangement:	*Prière* for Chorus—Mixed Voices

Quatre mélodies, pour chant et piano, poésies de Gustave Kahn, op. 10.
See also individual titles
1. *Timbres oubliés*
2. *Adieu pour jamais*
3. *Les soirs d'automne*
4. *Les paons*
Manuscripts:	Score: missing; Sketches: 3: LC*
Publication:	New York: G. Schirmer, 1903 (7, 7, 7, 7 pp.); reprint eds., *Four Melodies*, Huntsville, Texas: Recital Publications, Ltd., *Four Songs*, Boca Raton, Florida: Masters Music Publications, Inc.; 2&4: in *50 Art Songs from the Modern Repertoire*, New York: G. Schirmer, Inc., 1939.

Rêverie (Laissez moi, mes amis, laissez moi solitaire)
Text:	unidentified
Composition:	probably mid-1880s
Premiere:	perhaps 1888, Philadelphia
Score:	*see [Four Songs]*

Les soirs d'automne (Les soirs d'automne au bois des peurs)
Text:	Gustave Kahn, "Lied IV," *Les palais nomades*
Composition:	about 1899
Premiere:	10 May 1900, Julia Heinrich and George Proctor, Green

Hill, Brookline, Mass., if the title on the program, *Domaine de fée,* is an alternate title, not the title of a lost song.

Dedication:	à Franz Kneisel
Score:	*see Quatre mélodies*
Recording:	D'Anna Fortunato and Virginia Eskin, Northeastern Records 207

Sonnet (Tell me again, and then lift up to me)

Text:	George Cabot Lodge, "Sonnet XXXIV," *The Song of the Wave*
Composition:	1905, Medfield, Mass.
Premiere:	10 April 1906, Susan Metcalfe and Heinrich Gebhard, Boston
Dedication:	To Mrs. H. N. Slater
Score:	*see Four Poems*

St. Agnes Eve–Sketch

Text:	John Keats, "The Eve of St. Agnes"
Manuscript:	Sketch, LC33

Sudden Light (I have been here before)

Text:	Dante Gabriel Rossetti
Composition:	1905, Medfield, Mass.
Premiere:	10 April 1906, Susan Metcalfe and Heinrich Gebhard, Boston
Dedication:	To Miss Susan Metcalfe; on manuscript: Mrs. B. C. Child
Score:	*see Four Poems*

Timbres oubliés (Timbres oubliés, timbres morts perdus)

Text:	Gustave Kahn, "Intermède IV," *Les palais nomades*
Composition:	about 1899
Premiere:	10 May 1900, Julia Heinrich and George Proctor, Green Hill, Brookline, Mass.; Philip Hale, however, dates it 1899.
Dedication:	à Mme. Henry P. McKean
Score:	*see Quatre mélodies*

To Helen (Helen, thy beauty is to me)

Text:	Edgar Allan Poe
Composition:	1905, Medfield, Mass.
Premiere:	10 April 1906, Susan Metcalfe and Heinrich Gebhard, Boston
Dedication:	To Miss Evelyn Benedict
Score:	*see Four Poems*
Recording:	D'Anna Fortunato and Virginia Eskin, Northeastern Records 207

Ton souvenir est comme un livre bien-aimé (first line)

Text:	Albert Samain, *Au jardin de l'infante*

Composition: by 1911
Premiere: 21 March 1917, Povla Frijsh and Heinrich Gebhard, Jordan Hall, Boston
Dedication: à Mme. J. S. Fay
Manuscript: Score: copy with text and annotations by Loeffler (6 pp.), LC107
Recording: D'Anna Fortunato and Virginia Eskin, Northeastern Records 207

The Travail of Passion
Text: William Butler Yeats, *The Wind among the Reeds*
Composition: 1906; a unique reference occurs in CML to GrS, 1 October 1906.
Manuscript: lost

Vassar College Song (As at dawn thy colors flame)
Text: unidentified
Composition: 20th century
Manuscript: Score: holograph (4 pp., complete though Loeffler has written on the title page "Only a sketch"), LC108

Vereinsamt (Die Krähen schrein und ziehen schwirren Flugs zur Stadt)
Text: Friedrich Nietzsche
Composition: 1906, Medfield, Mass.
Manuscripts: Scores (all bound with *Der Kehraus*): 3 holographs, all with corrections (4 pp., 4 pp., 5 pp.), Yale

Vieille chanson d'amour (xv siècle) (Hellas mon cueur n'est pas à moy)
Text: unidentified
Composition: 3 January 1925, Medfield, Mass.
Manuscripts: Score: copy with English text added in another hand (5 pp.), with typescript of translation, LC114; Sketches: sketchbook, LC*
Recording: D'Anna Fortunato and Virginia Eskin, Northeastern Records 207

The Wind among the Reeds, Two Poems by W. B. Yeats, Set to Music for Voice and Piano.
See also individual titles:
1. *The Hosting of the Sidhe*
2. *The Host of the Air*
Publication: New York: G. Schirmer, 1908 (10 and 9 pp.)
Revision: *see Five Irish Fantasies*

Voice, Violin, and Piano

A une femme (A vous ces vers de par la grace)
Text: Paul Verlaine, *Poèmes saturniens*
Part: The violin part requires scordatura tuning: f, d, a, e.

Composition: 1904, perhaps revised 1915
Dedication: à Mme. Richard Aldrich
Manuscripts: Scores: holograph (6 pp.), with corrections, LC9; copy (7 pp.), LC+
Publication: *Selected Songs with Chamber Accompaniment*, vol. 16, in Recent Researches in American Music. Madison, Wis.: A-R Editions, Inc., 1988 (6 pp.)
Variant: *A une femme* for Voice and Piano

Boléro triste (Tant que l'enfant me préféra tel joueur de flûte)
Text: Gustave Kahn, *Chansons d'amant*
Part: The violin part requires scordatura tuning: f#, d, a, e.
Composition: 1908, perhaps revised 1915
Dedication: à Mme. Povla Frijsh
Manuscript: Score: holograph (6 pp.), with corrections, LC9
Publication: *Selected Songs with Chamber Accompaniment*, vol. 16 in Recent Researches in American Music. Madison, Wis.: A-R Editions, Inc., 1988 (6 pp.)
Variant: *Boléro triste* for Voice and Piano

Voice, Viola (or Viola d'amore), and Piano

La chanson des Ingénues (Canon à l'octave) (Nous sommes les Ingénues)
Part: Catalogued by LC for viola d'amore for unknown reason
Text: Paul Verlaine, *Poèmes saturniens*
Composition: about 1893
Manuscripts: Score: holograph (5 pp.), with corrections, LC13; Part: holograph viola part, allegretto comodo, LC126
Publication: *Selected Songs with Chamber Accompaniment*, vol. 16 in Recent Researches in American Music. Madison, Wis.: A-R Editions, Inc., 1988 (7 pp.)

La cloche fêlée (Il est amer et doux pendant les nuits d'hiver)
Text: Charles Baudelaire, *Les fleurs du mal*
Composition: about 1894
Premiere: 30 November 1897, Lena Little, Loeffler, Mrs. Emil Paur, Steinert Hall, Boston
Dedications: à Mme. J. Montgomery Sears
Manuscripts: Score: copy (8 pp.), Gardner Museum; Parts: copy of voice part with English text, LC103; holograph viola part, LC126; Sketches: LC*
Publication: *see Quatre Poèmes*
Recording: D'Anna Fortunato, Patricia McCarty, and Virginia Eskin, Northeastern Records 207
Arrangement: *La cloche fêlée* for Orchestra with Solo Voice

Dansons la gigue! (first line)
Text: Paul Verlaine, "Streets I," *Romance sans paroles*

Composition: about 1893
Premiere: 30 November 1897, Lena Little, Loeffler, Mrs. Emil Paur, Steinert Hall, Boston
Dedication: à Howard G. Cushing; on manuscripts: à Mlle Camille Landhi (LC31), à M. J-K. Huysmans (LC32)
Manuscripts: Scores: holograph fragment bound with *Le rossignol*, LC95 (3pp.); holograph fragments bound with *Harmonie du soir*, LC31 (2pp.) and LC32 (1p.); Parts: copy of voice part with English text, LC126; fragments of viola part, LC126, LC31; Sketches: LC41
Publication: *see Quatre poèmes*
Recording: D'Anna Fortunato, Patricia McCarty, and Virginia Eskin, Northeastern Records 207

Harmonie du soir (Voici venir les temps où vibrant sur sa tige)
Part: The string part of the original holograph manuscript (LC30) is labeled for "viole d'amour ou alto."
Text: Charles Baudelaire, *Les fleurs du mal*
Composition: about 1894
Premiere: 30 November 1897, Lena Little, Loeffler, Mrs. Emil Paur, Steinert Hall, Boston
Manuscripts: Scores: holograph (10pp.), with corrections, LC30; holograph (10pp.) with corrections, LC32; incomplete copy with corrections by Loeffler (pp. 2–14), LC31; Parts: copy of voice part with English text, LC103; copy of viola part, LC31
Publication: in *Selected Songs with Chamber Accompaniment*, vol. 16, in Recent Researches in American Music. Madison, Wis.: A-R Editions, Inc., 1988 (12pp.)

La lune blanche (first line)
Text: Paul Verlaine, *La bonne chanson*
Composition: about 1893
Manuscripts: Score: copy with text and viola part notated by Loeffler (4pp.), each page of the manuscript scored through once diagonally, text incomplete, Gardner Museum; Part: holograph voice part, scored through once diagonally, text complete, Gardner Museum
Publication: *Selected Songs with Chamber Accompaniment*, vol. 16, in Recent Researches in American Music. Madison, Wis.: A-R Editions, Inc., 1988 (4pp.)

Quatre Poèmes, pour voix, alto et piano, op. 5.
See also individual songs:
1. *La cloche fêlée*
2. *Dansons la gigue!*
3. *Le son de cor s'afflige vers les bois*
4. *Sérénade*

Order: The published set was neither the original nor sole group-
ing of the viola songs. At one point six were bound
together in the order: *Harmonie, Dansons, Cloche fêlée,
Sérénade, Paysage,* and *Ingénues;* the premiere performance included the first four of these. The Gardner Museum manuscripts group *Rêverie, Lune blanche, Sérénade,
Paysage,* and *Rossignol.* English voice parts group *Dansons, Sérénade, Paysage, Cloche fêlée,* and *Harmonie,* and
a German voice part pairs *Le son du cor* and *Sérénade.*

Publication: New York: G. Schirmer, 1904 (14, 7, 7, 10pp.); reprint
eds., *Four Melodies,* Huntsville, Texas: Recital Publications, Ltd., *Four Poems,* Boca Raton, Florida: Masters
Music Publications, Inc., *Quatre Poèmes,* New York:
McGinnis & Marx

Rêverie en sourdine (Calmes dans le demi-jour)
    Text: Paul Verlaine, "En sourdine," *Fêtes galantes*
    Composition: about 1893
    Manuscripts: Score: copy with text and viola part notated by Loeffler
(8pp.), Gardner Museum; Parts: holograph voice part,
Gardner Museum; incomplete holograph viola part,
Gardner Museum
    Publication: *Selected Songs with Chamber Accompaniment,* vol. 16, in
Recent Researches in American Music. Madison, Wis.:
A-R Editions, Inc., 1988 (6pp.)

Le rossignol (Comme un vol criard d'oiseaux en émoi)
    Text: Paul Verlaine, *Poèmes saturniens*
    Composition: 1893
    Dedication: à Mme. Georg Henschel (on copyist score, LC95)
    Manuscripts: Scores: holograph (8pp.), with corrections, LC95; copy
with text and viola part notated by Loeffler (8pp.), Gardner Museum; copy (8pp.), LC95; Parts: holograph voice
part, Gardner Museum; incomplete holograph voice part,
LC*; holograph viola part, Gardner Museum
    Publication: *Selected Songs with Chamber Accompaniment,* vol. 16, in
Recent Researches in American Music. Madison, Wis.:
A-R Editions, Inc., 1988 (9pp.)

Sérénade (Comme la voix d'un mort qui chanterait)
    Text: Paul Verlaine, *Poèmes saturniens*
    Composition: about 1893
    Premiere: 30 November 1897, Lena Little, Loeffler, Mrs. Emil Paur,
Steinert Hall, Boston
    Dedication: à Raoul Pugno
    Manuscripts: Score: copy with text and viola part notated by Loeffler
(8pp.), Gardner Museum; Parts: holograph voice part

with French text, Gardner Museum; holograph voice part with German text, LC82; copy of voice part with English text, LC103; holograph viola part, LC126

Publication: *see Quatre poèmes*
Recording: D'Anna Fortunato, Patricia McCarty, and Virginia Eskin, Northeastern Records 207
Arrangement: *Sérénade* for Orchestra with Solo Voice

Le son du cor s'afflige vers les bois (First line) [also: *Paysage triste, Sonnet*]

Text: Paul Verlaine, *Sagesse*
Composition: 1893
Dedication: à Eugène Ysaÿe
Manuscripts: Scores: holograph fragment bound with *La chanson des ingénues,* LC13; holograph fragment (pp. 3–5) bound with *Le rossignol,* with corrections, LC95; copy entitled *Paysage triste* with text and viola part notated by Loeffler (5pp.), Gardner Museum; Parts: holograph voice part with French text, entitled *Paysage triste,* Gardner Museum; holograph voice part with German text, entitled *Sonnet,* LC82; copyist voice part with English text, entitled *Paysage triste,* LC82; holograph viola part, entitled *Paysage triste,* Gardner Museum; holograph viola part, LC 126; Sketches: in sketchbooks, vol. 2, LC126
Publication: *see Quatre poèmes*
Recording: D'Anna Fortunato, Patricia McCarty, and Virginia Eskin, Northeastern Records 207

Voice, Clarinet, Viola, and Piano

Rapsodies pour voix, clarinette, alto, et piano
L'étang
La cornemuse
La villanelle du Diable [Subtitle: Rondeau (on holograph score)]

Text: Maurice Rollinat, *Les névroses*
Composition: summer 1898, Medfield, Mass.
Dedication: à la mémoire de Léon Pourtau
Manuscripts: Scores: holograph (10, 10, 28pp.), with corrections, LC24; copy with text, annotations, and corrections by Loeffler (10, 10, 28pp.), LC*
Publication: *Selected Songs with Chamber Accompaniment,* vol. 16, in *Recent Researches in American Music.* Madison, Wis.: A-R Editions, Inc., 1988 (50pp.)
Revisions: *Deux Rapsodies* for Chamber Ensemble; *La villanelle du Diable* for Orchestra

Chorus
Women's Voices

L'archet, fantazia—légende pour soprano solo, choeur de femmes avec viola d'amour, op. 26 [for SSAA, soprano, d'amore, and piano]

Text: Charles Cros, *Le coffret de santal*
Composition: about 1897–99
Premiere: 5 March 1901, Julia Wyman (soprano), Loeffler (viola d'amore), Heinrich Gebhard (piano), Cecilia Society conducted by B. J. Lang, J. M. Sears home, Boston; public premiere: 4 February 1902, Wyman, Loeffler, Miss Hawkins, Cecilia Society, Symphony Hall, Boston.
Manuscripts: Score: copy (34pp.) with added English text, LC3; Parts: 2 copies of viola part, LC3, LC*; copy of choral part, photocopy, LC*; Sketches: LC*; Misc.: manuscript translation in unknown hand, typed translation, and notes in Loeffler's hand, LC3

Canticum Fratris Solis [SSA]

Original: *Canticum fratris solis* for Orchestra with Solo Voice
Manuscripts: Scores: holograph (32pp.) and copy with piano part (29pp.), LC Coolidge Collection

Psalm 137 (by the Rivers of Babylon), For Four-Part Chorus of Women's Voices with Accompaniment of Organ, Harp, Two Flutes, and Violoncello Obbligato, op. 3

Composition: about 1901
Premiere: 28 Feburary 1902, Choral Art Society; Albert W. Snow, organ; Heinrich Schüecker, harp; André Maquarre and Arthur Brooke, flutes; Alwin Schroeder, cello; directed by Wallace Goodrich, Church of the Messiah, Boston
Dedication: To my friend William P. Blake
Manuscript: missing
Publications: New York: G. Schirmer, 1907 (22pp.); piano-vocal score: New York: G. Schirmer, 1907 (19pp.)
Recordings: John Oliver Chorale, Northeastern Records, NR 226-CD; the Emma Willard Choir, Spectrum, SR-326

The Sermon on the Mount [SSAA, 2 viole d'amore, viola da gamba, harp, organ]

Text: St. Matthew 5:3–12
Composition: n.d.; probably about the time of *Psalm 137*
Manuscript: Score: unfinished holograph (14pp.), LC96

Men's Voices

Beat! Beat! Drums! For Men's Voices in Unison, Words from Drum Taps, by Walt Whitman [also: *Drum Taps (A Soldier's March Song), Soldier's Life*]

Parts: (a) piano; (b) 2 pianos; (c) piano and obbligato 4 trumpets, glockenspiel, bass drum, cymbals, fifes, drum; (d) band (6 piccolos, alto saxophone, 2 tenor saxophones, 4 trumpets, 3 trombones, tuba, 6 snare drums, bass drum, cymbals, 2 pianos)

Composition: 1917; d: about 1927–32, Medfield, Mass.

Premiere: 17 December 1932, Cleveland Symphony Orchestra, conducted by Sokoloff, with Cleveland Orchestra Chorus and Glee Club of Adelbert College

Manuscripts: Scores: (b) copy, Cleveland Orchestra; (b) copy (10pp.), titled *Soldier's Life (Drum Taps)*, LC*; (c) holograph titled *Drum Taps* (5pp.), LC7; (d) holograph condensed score, titled *Drum Taps* (8pp.), with corrections, LC7; ?(d) copy, Cleveland Orchestra; Parts: holograph 2-piano part, titled *Soldier's Life (A Soldier's March Song)* with corrections, LC7; unfinished 2-piano part, LC7; unfinished second piano part, LC7; parts for cello, violin 1 & 2, LC*; parts, Cleveland Orchestra; Sketches: orchestral version, LC7

Publication: (a) Boston: C. C. Birchard, 1932 (13pp.); (d) Boston, C. C. Birchard, 1932 (46pp.), facsimile of copyist score

Boys' Voices

Ave maris stella, For Boys' Voices, Solo Soprano, Strings, Piano, and Organ, After an Old Chant by Orazio Vecchi (1595) (Convito Musicale, Venetia, 1595)

Composition: about 1906–12, Medfield, Mass., for use by Loeffler's boys' choir, St. Edward's Church, Medfield, Mass.

Manuscripts: Score: holograph (5pp.), with corrections, LC4; holograph piano-vocal score (2pp.), LC4; Parts: holograph parts, LC4

[*Christmas Carol*]

Text: William Morris, "Christmas Carol"

Manuscript: lost, a unique reference occurs in CML to GrS, 21 December 1907

Mixed Voices

3 [Drei] Marienlieder, für gemischten Chor [SSAATTBB]
1. *Angelus Domini nuntiavit Mariae*
2. *Remember, O most pious Virgin Mary*
3. *The Litany of the Blessed Virgin* (latin words)

Composition: winter 1919–20, Medfield, Mass.
Manuscripts: Scores: holograph of *Angelus* (6pp.) LC48; draft of refrain
                 (2pp.), LC*

For One Who Fell in Battle, Eight-Part Chorus for Mixed Voices A Cappella,
Words by T. W. Parsons [SSAATTBB]
Text: Thomas William Parsons, "Dirge: For One Who Fell in
                Battle"
Composition: summer 1906, Medfield, Mass.
Premiere: 13 December 1906, Choral Art Society of Boston con-
                 ducted by Wallace Goodrich, Jordan Hall, Boston
Dedication: To Major Henry Lee Higginson in memory of the com-
                 rades who never returned from the war
Manuscript: missing
Publication: New York: G. Schirmer, 1911 (23pp.)
Recording: Westminster Choir School, NBC broadcast, 7 May 1937
                 (on tape at LC)
Revision: *Ode for One Who Fell in Battle*

Ode for One Who Fell in Battle, Eight-Part Chorus for Mixed Voices A
Cappella, Words by T. W. Parsons [SSAATTBB]
Composition: 1911, Medfield, Mass.
Premiere: 21 March 1912, Cecilia Society, Symphony Hall, Boston
Manuscript: missing
Publication: New York: G. Schirmer, 1911 (19pp.)
Original: *For One Who Fell in Battle*

Poème mystique [for boys' choir, chorus, 4 horns, 2 contrabass, harp, organ;
or baritone, choir, 4 horn, 2 contrabasses]–Sketch
Text: Gustave Kahn, *Les palais nomades*
First line: "Bon chevalier, la route est sombre"
Composition: begun 1907, Medfield, Mass.
Manuscripts: Sketches: LC126, LC*

Prière [SATB and piano or string quartet]
Text: Roger Dévigne, English translation by David Stevens
Composition: 1926, Medfield, Mass.
Manuscript: Score: holograph with piano accompaniment in another
                 hand (3pp.), LC+
Arrangement: *Prière* for Voice and Piano

Choral Accompaniment

[*Mass*] Kyrie, Benedictus, Gloria Patri, Credo, responses [also: *Charles Mar-
tin Tornov Loeffler's Organ Accompaniment to a Mass* (LC title)]
Date: about 1907, Medfield, Mass.
Performance: about 1906–12, Loeffler's boys' choir, Medfield, Mass.

Manuscripts: Scores: holograph (5pp.), LC14; draft of Credo with re-
                 sponses (4pp.), with corrections, LC14

Unidentified Voices

[*Matthew* 14:23–33]–Sketch
Manuscript: Sketch: LC*

DRAMATIC WORKS
Incidental Music

The Countess Cathleen [for voice, viola, harp, piano]
  Text: William Butler Yeats
  Composition: 1924, Medfield, Mass.
  Premiere: 8 May 1924, the Concord Players, Concord, Mass.
  Manuscript: lost

The Reveller by Daniel Sargent [for male voice, men's chorus, viola, piano]
  Language: English
  Composition: December 1925, Medfield, Mass.
  Premiere: 22 December 1925, the Tavern Club, Boston
  Manuscripts: Scores: Version 1 (for tenor): copy with variant sections 4
                  and 5 (10pp.), LC90; Version 2 (for baritone): holograph
                  (7pp.), LC90; Parts: Version 2: holograph viola part,
                  LC90; Sketches: Version 2: sketch of verse 4, LC90; Li-
                  bretto: typescript, LC90
  Publication: New York: Calvert Publishing Corporation, 1926 (10pp.)

Ouverture pour le T. C. "Minstrel entertainment" after southern and variety
show themes, pour 2 violons et piano
  Composition: n.d.
  Premiere: possibly used in the Hallowe'en and Minstrel Show, 29
                  October 1906, Tavern Club, Boston
  Manuscripts: Score: holograph (10pp.), LC66; Parts: holograph parts,
                  LC66

Opera

Les amants jaloux, Drame en deux actes et cinq tableaux d'après un Poème
de M.–Sketch
  Cast: Don Paez (baryton), Don Etur de Guadasse (tenor), Un
                  vieil officier (baryton), Un moine (basse), Le crieur de nuit
                  (basse) 4 Officiers (voix moyennes), Un vieux soldat (bar-
                  yton), Marquesa Juana d'Amiequi (soprano), Inès (mezzo-
                  soprano), La Belisa (mezzo-soprano), Doler (gitana
                  danseuse), chorus
  Scene: Seville, Spain

Language: French
Composition: 1918, Medfield, Mass.
Manuscripts: Sketches: laid in sketchbook vol. 3, LC101; Libretto:
                 bound holograph, LC Loeffler Collection of Literary
                 Works

The Passion of Hilarion, Opera in One Act and Two Tableaux, After William
Sharp's Play

Cast: Hilarion, a priest (tenor), Anais (soprano), young priest
                 (baritone), acolyte, beggar woman (mezzo), old man,
                 young gitana, chorus: church choir, peasants, gitanos
Scene: Spain
Language: English and Italian
Composition: 1912–13, Medfield, Mass.
Dedication: To my best friend, my wife
Manuscripts: Scores: unfinished holograph piano-vocal draft score
                 (158pp.), LC76; holograph piano-vocal score (161pp.),
                 LC76; incomplete draft condensed score (96pp.), LC74;
                 holograph (280pp.), LC75; Sketches: sketchbook,
                 sketches, and drafts (with deleted scenes) LC72, LC73,
                 LC74, LC126, LC*; Libretti: holograph with rough
                 sketches of set, with corrections, LC Loeffler Collection of
                 Literary Works; typescript text, LC75
Publication: Boston: C. C. Birchard, 1936 (278pp.), facsimile of holo-
                 graph full score

The Peony Lantern–Sketch

Cast: Hagiwara Shinzaburo, Yamamoto Shijo, Tomozo, Yusai,
                 Ryoseki, a vendor of singing insects, a blind flute player,
                 Tsuju-ko, O-Yone, O-Mine
Scene: Japan at cherry blossom time
Language: English
Composition: about 1919
Manuscripts: Sketches: sketchbooks, LC101; Libretti: bound and un-
                 bound holographs, LC Loeffler Collection of Literary
                 Works
Variant: *The Lantern Ghosts*

Unset Libretti

Duniascha, Romantisches opus in 3 Augzugen

Cast: Prinz Wassili Basarof, Graf Massalsky, Sitnikof, Pro-
                 kowitsch, Arkad, Matrvei Ylitsch, Duniascha, Arina, cho-
                 rus
Scene: 1720, Moskow
Language: German
Composition: possibly written by Loeffler's father

Manuscript:	bound, German script, LC Loeffler Collection of Literary Works

The Failure; or, There Is Somewhere Some Good in Most of Us [or: *Life, A little, true picture of life in two acts* (on reverse of title page)]

Cast:	Rev. Peter Horne, his invalid wife, Dippy Gallagher, Jimmy Hellburn, a woman singer, some musicians, 6 ushers, Milly, city people, villagers, morticians, florist
Scene:	a village in New York
Language:	English
Manuscript:	unbound holograph, LC Loeffler Collection of Literary Works

The Lantern Ghosts; or, Life Is But a Dream, An Oriental Play in 4 Acts (After a Narrative by O [Okakura] by Ch. M. Loeffler)

Cast:	Kiang-Tui, Dr. Hua, Tong, Liu, Pien Chiao, Sie-Thao, Feng-Hsien, Su-Su, chorus
Scene:	China
Language:	English
Date:	about 1919
Manuscript:	bound holograph (bound with *Les amants jaloux*), LC Loeffler Collection of Literary Works
Variant:	*The Peony Lantern*

The Tribulations of Mr. Pillgarlic, An Operatic Farce for Small and Full Grown People. Opera Buffa in One Act and Several Tableaux after Count P's and C's plays

Cast:	Punch (Mr. Pillgarlic), Judy, Policeman, Ghost, Mrs. Moosepecker, Mrs. Talkfast, Mrs. Tuneup, Buttons, Chimneysweep, chorus
Language:	English
Manuscript:	bound holograph, LC Loeffler Collection of Literary Works

The White Fox

Text:	Okakura-Kakuzo, *The White Fox: A Fairy Drama in Three Acts, Written for Music*
Cast:	Kohla, Yasuna, Kuzunoha, Ackeimon, damsels, fox maidens, huntsmen, soldiers, pilgrims
Language:	English
Scene:	Central Japan in pre-Ashikaga times, toward the end of the 14th century
Dedication:	The libretto is dedicated to "The Presence," i.e., Isabella Stewart Gardner.
Composition:	about 1913–14 and later, Medfield, Mass.
Manuscript:	missing; Sketches: LC mistakenly identified sketches for *The Peony Lantern* as being for *The White Fox*; Libretto: typescript, Gardner Museum

INSTRUMENTAL WORKS
Piano
Piano Transcriptions of Vocal Works

Les paons
    Arranger: probably Heinrich Gebhard
    Manuscript: Score: by Gebhard with additions by Loeffler (6pp.), LC*

Piano Reductions of Orchestral Works

See Orchestral Works:
Hora Mystica   *A Pagan Poem*
La mort de Tintagiles   *La villanelle du Diable*

Solo Violin

Danse bizarre, pour violon seul
    Composition: August 1881, New York
    Manuscript: Score: holograph (2pp.), with corrections, LC19

Requiem/Variations diaboliques sur le thème "Dies Irae, Dies Illa," pour violon seul [also: *Requiem d'el Signor Paganini/Variations diaboliques sur le thème "dies irae, dies illa"* pour violon seul]
    Composition: before 1894
    Manuscripts: Scores: holograph draft, 16 variations, with corrections, LC*; incomplete holograph (5pp.), 21 variations, LC*; incomplete holograph, 22 variations, (variations 10–22 torn in half—top half only survives), LC*

Violin and Piano

Airs tziganes, pour violon avec piano
1. Andante
2. Lento
3. Andante melancolico
    Composition: n.d., probably 19th century
    Manuscripts: Scores: variant movement 1, labelled Grave: holograph (6pp.), LC2; movement 1: incomplete holograph draft (2pp.), with corrections, LC2; movement 1: incomplete holograph, first two pages of Yale score below, LC2; movements 1–3: incomplete and unfinished holograph (pp. 3–11), Yale; movement 3: holograph draft (7pp.), LC*; Parts: movements 1 and 3: holograph, LC2; movement 2: holograph, LC*

Allegretto [also: Piece for violin and piano, apparently based on gipsy airs (LC title)]

Composition: 20th century; may be related to the *Divigations*
Manuscripts: Scores: holograph (11pp.), LC77

Barcarolle (d'après des mélodies arabes)
Composition: 19th century
Manuscripts: Scores: holograph (9pp.), LC6; incomplete holograph variant setting (5pp.), LC6

Berceuse, pour violon avec accompagnement de piano
Composition: about 1884
Dedication: à Monsieur H. Léonard
Manuscript: Score: holograph (4pp.), LC8
Publication: Paris: J. Hamelle, [1884] (5pp.)

Capriccio russe, pour violon et piano
Composition: about 1881–86
Dedication: dedié à mon ami Leop. Lichtenberg
Manuscript: Score: holograph (10pp.), LC12

Cynthia
Composition: 1926, Medfield, Mass.
Manuscripts: Scores: incomplete holograph (2pp.), LC126; copy, title crossed off (12pp.), with corrections by Loeffler, Yale; incomplete holograph draft, untitled, (3–9pp.), Yale; copy, untitled (8pp., introduction unnotated), with sketches for *Evocation*, Yale; Parts: unfinished holograph & 2 unfinished copies, all Yale

Divigations sur des airs tziganes, Fly to Her, My Swallow [also: *Repülj fecske'm*]
Composition: 20th century; may be related to *Allegretto*
Manuscripts: Scores: two unfinished copies of draft (2pp., 3pp.), LC20; three unfinished copies of draft, (2pp., 2pp., 1p.), LC*

Eery Moonlight (a little poem on two Norwegian airs and a "cattle call") set for violin or viole d'amour
Composition: about 1929
Manuscripts: Scores: holograph, untitled (pp. 1–4), Yale; holograph, untitled (12pp.), LC*; Part: holograph, for violin or viola d'amore, LC*; Sketches: LC*, Yale
Revisions: *Norske Land* for Viola d'Amore and Piano; *Norske Saga* for Contrabass and Piano and for Viola d'Amore, Contrabass, and Piano

Fantasie scandinave
Composition: 19th century
Manuscript: Part: holograph, LC*; accompaniment unspecified but unlikely to have been orchestral

Grave
  Composition: 19th century
  Manuscript: Score: holograph (5pp.), with corrections, LC28

Joe Bibb [also: *The Clown; Joe Bibb sinister clown*]–Sketch
  Composition: 20th century; possibly related to *Intermezzo (Clowns)* for
                    Jazz Orchestra
  Manuscript: Sketches, LC46

Partita, for violin and piano
1. *Intrada*
2. *Sarabande,* Variations on a theme by Johann Mattheson (1681–1764)
3. *Divertissement* [draft subtitle: *La petite Princesse nègre* or *créole*]
4. *Finale des tendres adieux*
  Composition: 15 May–June 1930, Medfield, Mass.
  Premiere: 16 October 1930, Jacques Gordon and Lee Pattison, Chi-
                    cago
  Dedication: To my great friend Mrs. Elizabeth Sprague Coolidge
  Manuscripts: Scores: holograph draft (variously paged), with correc-
                    tions, LC70; movements 1 and 3: holograph (9pp. &
                    9pp.); movements 3 (end) and 4: copy with corrections by
                    Loeffler (numbered 29–55), LC71; copy (43pp.), LC*;
                    Part: copy LC*; Sketches: LC70, LC*
  Publication: New York: G. Schirmer, 1937 (40pp.)
  Recordings: Jacques Gordon and Lee Pattison, Columbia 68820–23D
                    (in set 275); Louis Kaufman and Erich Itor Kahn, VOA
                    16" acetate (on tape at LC)
  Arrangement: Mattheson, *Sarabande,* Arrangements for Violin or Viola
                    d'Amore

Rêverie-Barcarolle, paraphrase sur des airs nègres, pour violon avec piano
  Composition: n.d.; perhaps contemporary with *Airs tziganes*
  Manuscript: Score: holograph (5pp.), with sketches, LC92

Romance russe
  Composition: 19th century
  Dedication: à mon ami W. P. Blake
  Manuscript: Score: incomplete holograph (6pp.), LC93

Sonata
  Composition: summer 1886. References to a sonata occur in letters and
                    BSO programs; the composition is either lost or unidenti-
                    fied.

Spring Dance (Danse norvégienne)
  Composition: 19th century
  Dedication: Dedié à mon ami César Thomson
  Manuscript: Score: holograph (8pp.), LC105

Tarantella
Composition: 19th century
Manuscript: Score: holograph (13pp.), LC106

Violin and Piano Transcriptions of Vocal Works

Adieu pour jamais
Arranger: Jacques Gordon.
Publication: New York: G. Schirmer, 1943 (7pp.)
Recording: Jacques Gordon and Carl Deis, Schirmer 2553 (in set No. 10)

Les paons
Arranger: Jacques Gordon
Publication: New York: G. Schirmer, 1943 (7pp.)
Recording: Jacques Gordon and Lee Pattison, Columbia 68820–23D (in set 275)

Violin and Piano Reductions of Orchestral Works

Divertimento tre pezzi di virtuosita, per il violino col orchestre [also: *Divertimento* für Violine mit Begleitung grossen Orchesters von Ch. M. Loeffler/Ubertragung des Orchesters für Klavier von Heinrich Gebhard (on Gebhard score)]
Arranger: Heinrich Gebhard, revisions by Loeffler
Composition: 1899
Manuscripts: Scores: by Gebhard (35pp.), Yale; copy with title page, revisions, and corrections by Loeffler (40pp.), LC23

Rapsodie russe, pour violon avec orchestre
Original: *Les veillées de l'Ukraine,* movement 1
Composition: about 1891
Manuscripts: Score: holograph (14pp.), LC88; Part: unfinished holograph, LC88; Sketch: titled *Introduction et capriccio russe,* LC*

Une nuit de mai, rapsodie d'après Gogol
Original: *Les veillées de l'Ukraine,* movement 2, version I
Composition: about 1891
Manuscripts: Scores: unfinished holograph with corrections (16pp.), LC63; holograph, Brussels Bibliotheque royale

III [also: Set of Variations, comprising the 3d movement of a larger work, apparently based on a Russian folk-song (LC title)]
Original: *Les veillées de l'Ukraine,* movement 4
Composition: about 1891
Manuscript: Score: incomplete holograph (10pp.), with corrections, LC97

Les veillées de l'Ukraine (d'après Nicolai Gogol), grande suite pour violon
solo et grand orchestre
>Original: *Les veillées de l'Ukraine* for Orchestra with Solo Violin,
>   1891 version
>Composition: about 1891
>Manuscript: Score: holograph (54pp.) without movement 2 (move-
>   ment 3 labelled as 2), with corrections, LC113

Viola d'Amore and Piano

Eery Moonlight (a little poem on two Norwegian airs and a "cattle call") set
for violin or viole d'amour
>Composition: by 1929
>Manuscripts: Scores: holograph, untitled (pp. 1–4), Yale; holograph,
>   untitled (12pp.), LC*; Part: holograph for violin or viola
>   d'amore (3pp.), LC*; Sketches: LC*, Yale
>Revisions: *Norske Land* for Viola d'Amore and Piano; *Norske Saga*
>   for Contrabass and Piano and for Viola d'Amore, Contra-
>   bass, and Piano

Entrada–Sketch
>Manuscript: sketch, LC*

Mescolanza "Olla Podrida"
>Composition: 20th century
>Manuscripts: Scores: holograph draft (9pp.), with corrections, Yale;
>   incomplete, unfinished holograph (pp. 5–11), Yale; holo-
>   graph (13pp.), with corrections, Yale; incomplete holo-
>   graph (6pp.), Yale; Sketches and Drafts: LC*

Norske Land, Rhapsody on two Norwegian tunes for viole d'amour with
piano accompaniment
>Composition: by 1929
>Manuscripts: Scores: incomplete holograph (2pp.), with corrections,
>   LC*; holograph (pp. 3–9), with corrections, Yale; copy
>   (11pp.), with corrections by Loeffler, Yale; Sketches: Yale,
>   LC*; Misc.: title page, LC126
>Revisions: *Eery Moonlight* for Violin or Viola d'Amore and Piano
>   and *Norske Saga* for Contrabass and Piano or for Viola
>   d'Amore, Contrabass, and Piano

Cello and Piano

Poème (Scène dramatique), pour violoncelle solo et piano (ou orchestre) [also:
Scène dramatique tiré d'un opéra inédit de Ch. M. Loeffler pour violoncelle
et orchestre, *Poème espagnole,* and *Conte espagnole*]
>Composition: March 1916, Medfield, Mass.

Premiere: 27 January 1917, Pablo Casals and Ruth Deyo, Aeolian Hall, New York

Dedication: To my friend Pablo Casals

Manuscripts: Scores: holograph (28pp.), with corrections, LC80; copy, title page by Loeffler (38pp.), LC80; Part: incomplete holograph, LC80

Recording: Luis Leguia and Alan Mandel, 7 January 1983 (on tape at LC)

Arrangement: orchestral version, missing

Contrabass and Piano

Norske Saga, divertissement (d'après deux motifs norvégiens et d'un ranz des vaches, tirés de la Collection Nationale de Musique Norvégienne publiée par Warmuth à Christiana)

Part: The solo part requires scordatura tuning: F#, B, e, a

Composition: April 1929, Medfield, Mass.

Dedication: à M. Serge Koussevitsky, humble marque de profonde admiration

Manuscripts: Scores: holograph (12pp., pp. 7–10 cut out), with corrections by Loeffler, Yale; copy (15pp.), Boston Public Library, Koussevitzky Collection; Parts: holograph fragment, LC*; holograph, Yale; 2 copies, Boston Public Library, Koussevitzky Collection; Sketches: Yale, LC*

Variants: *Norske Land* for Viola d'Amore and Piano; *Eery Moonlight* for Violin or Viola d'Amore and Piano; *Norske Saga for Viola d'Amore, Contrabass, and Piano*

Viola d'Amore, Contrabass, and Piano

Norske Saga

Composition: about 1929

Manuscripts: Scores: holograph, (11pp.), Yale; holograph, (pp. 7–10), Yale; holograph last page, Yale; Parts: holograph contrabass part, Yale; holograph contrabass part, Boston Public Library, Koussevitzky Collection; Sketches: LC*

Variants: *Norske Land* for Viola d'Amore and Piano; *Eery Moonlight* for Violin or Viola d'Amore and Piano; *Norske Saga* for Contrabass with Piano

Sketches For Unidentified Solo Parts

Rondo

Part: Unidentified though catalogued by LC for viola d'amore

Composition: n.d.

Manuscript: unfinished holograph draft (2pp.), LC94

Zapateado–Sketch
Manuscript: sketch, Yale

Violin Technique

Violin Studies for the Development of the Left Hand
Composition: 1920, Medfield, Mass.
Publication: New York: G. Schirmer, 1936 (20pp.)

Untitled Violin Exercises
Manuscript: holograph (14pp.), Yale

Chamber Ensembles
Strings

Music for Four Stringed Instruments [also: *Musique pour 2 violons, alto et violoncelle*]
1. Poco adagio [subtitle (on manuscript): *Musique*]
2. *Le Saint Jour de Pâques* (Easter Sunday)—Adagio ma non troppo
3. Moderato [subtitle (on manuscript): *A vol d'oiseau*
   Composition: 1917, revised 1918, 1919, 1920, Medfield, Mass.
   Premiere: 15 February 1919, Flonzaley Quartet, Aeolian Hall, New
                      York
   Dedication: To the Memory of Victor Chapman
   Manuscripts: Scores: 1917 holograph (44pp.), LC57; 1919 holograph
                      (22pp.), LC56; 1919 holograph with 1918 revision pasted
                      over (45pp., pp. 5–16 missing), LC56; final version holo-
                      graph (38pp.), with corrections, Yale; final version holo-
                      graph used by engravers, (32pp.), LC58; Parts: all
                      versions: copyist parts, LC*; 1917 violin 2 part, LC59;
                      Sketches: LC56, LC*
   Publication: New York: G. Schirmer, 1923, for the Society for the
                      Publication of American Music (37pp.)
   Recordings: The Kohon Quartet, Vox SVBX 5301; Coolidge Quartet,
                      Victor 15349–51 (in set M or DM-543)

Le passeur d'eau, poème (d'après Verhaeren), pour 2 violons, 2 altos et 2
violoncelles
   Original: Sextuor, movement 2
   Composition: summer 1900, Homburg von der Hohe
   Premiere: 10 December 1909, Kneisel Quartette, Fenway Court,
                      Boston
   Dedication: à la mémoire de Denis Bunker (artiste-peintre)
   Manuscripts: Scores: holograph (15pp.), LC98; copy (19pp.), LC99;
                      incomplete copy (18pp.), with a few corrections, LC99

Quatuor, pour deux violons, alto, et violoncelle [also: String quartet in A
minor (LC title)]

1. Allegro moderato
2. Tempo di Menuette (canon à l'octave)
3. Assai andante (con quasi Variationi)
4. Rondo pastorale
 Composition: 1889, Medfield, Mass.
 Premiere: Movement 2: 1889–90 season, Adamowski Quartette, Philadelphia; Movements 2 and 3: 12 April 1892, Adamowski Quartette, Union Hall, Boston
 Dedication: dediée à H. L. Higginson (on Bunker title page) or J. M. Sears (in a letter from Loeffler to Carl Engel, 26 March 1925)
 Manuscripts: Score: holograph, movements 2 & 3 missing (23pp., pp. 7–12 missing), with corrections, LC86; Parts: LC86; Misc.: title page designed by Denis Bunker, University of Kansas Museum of Art

Quintet, in One Movement, for Three Violins, Viola, and Violoncello [also: *Lyrisches Kammermüsikstuck; Eine Frühlingsmusik* (crossed off manuscripts)]
 Composition: about 1894
 Premiere: 18 February 1895, Kneisel Quartette with William Kraft, Union Hall, Boston
 Manuscripts: Score: holograph (27pp.), with corrections, LC87; Parts: copyist parts, LC87
 Publication: New York: G. Schirmer, 1938 (39pp.), edited by Adolfo Betti
 Recordings: The Phelps Family, ZRA Inc., QSD 301; Gordon String Quartet, Schirmer 2534–35 (in set No. 13)

Sextour, pour 2 violons, 2 altos, 2 v'celles
1. Allegro vivo e appassionato
2. Andante
3. Allegro conspirito
 Composition: begun about 1885, finished about 1892
 Premiere: 27 February 1893, Kneisel Quartette with Max Zach and Leo Schulz, Chickering Hall, Boston
 Dedication: Franz Kneisel in Freundschaft und Verehrung zugeeignet; Movement 2 subdedication: à la mémoire d'un ami D. B., Denis Bunker
 Manuscript: Score: holograph (13, 9, 12pp.), with corrections, LC98
 Revision: Movement 2: *Le passeur d'eau*

Mixed Instruments

Ballade carnavalesque [for flute, oboe, saxophone in Eb, bassoon, piano]
 Composition: 1902, Dover, Mass.
 Premiere: 25 January 1904, Longy Club (André Maquarre, Georges

Longy, Elise Hall, A. Debuchy, Heinrich Gebhard), Potter Hall, Boston

Dedication: à Mme. Hall (located on sax part)

Manuscripts: Scores: holograph (47pp.), with corrections, New England Conservatory; copy with a few corrections by Loeffler (81pp.), LC5; Parts: copyist parts, New England Conservatory

Deux Rapsodies, pour hautbois, alto et piano

1. *L'étang*
2. *La cornemuse*

Original: *Rapsodies* pour voix, clarinette, alto, et piano

Part option: Substitution of violin for oboe is mentioned in Loeffler's correspondence.

Composition: 27 September 1901, Dover, Mass.

Premiere: 16 December 1901, Georges Longy, Loeffler, Heinrich Gebhard, Chickering Hall, Boston

Dedications: 1: à la mémoire de Léon Pourtau; 2: à Georges Longy

Manuscripts: Score: holograph (14, 13pp.), with corrections, LC89; Parts: holograph parts, LC89; *L'étang:* unfinished holograph oboe part, ink, LC*; Sketches: *La cornemuse* sketch, LC89

Publications: New York: Schirmer, 1905 (42pp.); New York: McGinnis and Marx, 1979 (42pp.)

Recordings: John Mack, Abraham Skernick, and Eunice Podis, Advent 5017; Robert Sprenkle, Francis Tursi, and Armand Basile, ERA 1011; Bruno Labate, Jacques Gordon, and Emma Boynet, Schirmer 2531–33 (in set No. 10); Harold Gomberg, Milton Katims, Dimitri Mitropoulos, Columbia ML-5603; Ralph Gomberg, Albert Falvoce, Miquelle, Historical Concert, Casimir Hall, 4 April 1941, Curtis Institute disc 2370 (on tape at LC)

Historiettes, pour quatuor et hârpe

1. *Historiette du mariage de Pierrot Fumiste* (d'après J. Laforgue)
2. *Historiette des tribulations conjugales de M. Punch*
3. *Historiette de Batyoushka Raspoutine*
4. *Historiette de la Senorita Conchita Piquer "Du sang, de la volupté et de la mort"*

Composition: 1922, Medfield, Mass.

Premiere: July 1923, private performance by students of Franz Kneisel with Carlos Salzedo, Seal Harbor, Maine

Dedications: 1: to my friend Mrs. John L. Gardner; 2: à Pablo Casals; 3: [intended for Fanny Mason, withheld at her request]; 4: to my friend John S. Sargent

Manuscripts: Scores: drafts of *Pierrot* and *Punch* (2 each) (23, 15, 12,

23pp.), of *Raspoutine* (14pp.), and of *Conchita,* incomplete, (18pp.), LC33; holograph (22, 25, 23, 29pp.), with corrections, LC 35; Parts: holograph harp part, movements 1–3, with corrections, with annotations by Salzedo, LC34; copyist parts, LC35; Sketches: LC33, LC*

Octette [for 2 clarinets, 2 violins, viola, cello, bass, harp]
1. Allegro moderato
2. Adagio molto
3. Andante—Allegro alla Zingara
   Composition: about 1896
   Premiere: 15 February 1897, Kneisel Quartette with Léon Pourtau, P. Metzger, H. Schüeker, and E. Golde, Association Hall, Boston
   Manuscripts: Score: holograph (73pp.), with corrections, LC64; Parts: copyists parts, with corrections by Loeffler, LC65

Paraphrase on Two Western Cowboy Songs [for saxophone, viola d'amore, piano] [also: *The Lone Prairie,* western cowboy song]
   Composition: 20th century
   Manuscripts: Scores: unfinished holograph (5pp.), LC*; unfinished holograph (3pp.), with corrections, LC47; Part: sax part, LC47

Poème paien (d'après Virgil) [also: *Poème antique d'après Virgil*]
   Parts: a: 2 flutes, oboe, clarinet, English horn, 2 horns, viola, bass, piano, 3 trumpets; b: 2 pianos and 3 trumpets
   Program: Virgil, "Pharmaceutria," #8 in *Eclogues*; quotation from Virgil prefixed to score
   Composition: a. 1901-2, Dover, Mass.; b. 1902–3
   Premiere: b: 13 April 1903, Heinrich Gebhard and George Proctor, pianos; L. Kloepfel, H. E. Brenton, and J. Mann, trumpets; Fenway Court, Boston
   Manuscripts: Score: a: holograph (59pp.), with a few corrections, LC68; Sketches: sketch of motive and theme, LC*
   Revision: *A Pagan Poem for Orchestra*

Jazz Band

By-an'-By–Draft
   Instruments: voice, flute, English horn, clarinet, saxophone, trumpet, horns, violins, celeste, tenor banjo, piano, and others not identified
   Composition: 1920s; possibly meant for *Intermezzo (Clowns)*
   Manuscripts: Score: holograph draft, incompletely scored (4pp.), LC11; Sketches: LC11

Creole Blues ("De 'tit zozoz") (Creole Words); Tango-Drag for Jazz Orchestra [also: *Louisiana tango*]

Instruments:	trumpet, saxophones, trombone, traps, violin, banjo, bass, piano, voice
Composition:	finished December 1926 (at end), March 1927 (on title page), Medfield, Mass.
Manuscripts:	Score: unfinished draft, titled *Louisiana tango* (32pp.), LC102, catalogued by LC as Sketches for a suite for voice and dance orchestra; holograph (19pp.), LC18; Sketches: LC102

Intermezzo (Clowns)

Instruments:	flute (piccolo), violins, horns, saxophones, trumpets, trombones, tuba, doublebass, traps, tympani, tenor banjo, viola, pianos (celesta), xylophone, harp, and alternate instruments (cello, vibraphone, English horn, bass clarinet)
Program:	Text unidentified; the *Habanera* sketches and LC15 use text not included in the final score.
Composition:	1928, Medfield, Mass.
Premiere:	19 February 1928, Leo Reisman Orchestra, Symphony Hall, Boston
Dedication:	dedicated to Leo Reisman (on concert program)
Manuscripts:	Scores: holograph, with corrections (50pp.), LC15; holograph (67pp.), with corrections, LC16; holograph discarded pages (6pp.), LC17; Discarded drafts: incomplete holograph draft (8pp.) and sketches, headed with "Habanera Rhythm," LC29; Sketches: LC*

Mardi gras in New Orleans–Sketch

Composition:	1926, Medfield, Mass.; possibly intended as companion piece for *Creole Blues*
Manuscript:	Sketches, LC102

Old Creole Days–Sketch

Composition:	1926, Medfield, Mass.; possibly intended as companion piece for *Creole Blues*
Manuscript:	Sketch, LC102

[*Suite* for voice and dance orchestra]

LC has catalogued the sketches of *Creole Blues* (or *Louisiana Tango*), *Mardi Gras in New Orleans,* and *Old Creole Days* as Sketches for a suite for voice and dance orchestra. The finished copy of *Creole Blues* is headed "No. 2"; Loeffler may have intended a set of dance orchestra pieces, but the manuscripts are not so identified.

Todavia estas a tiempo (Tango)

Instruments:	clarinet, trumpet, trombone, guitar, drums, piano, bass, violins

Composition: The manuscript neither bears Loeffler's name nor is in his hand; "orchestration for Leo Reiman by his orchestrator" is written atop page 1 in Loeffler's hand.
Premiere: 1 August 1932, Ponds Program (on manuscript)
Manuscript: score by "J. Smith for Leo Reisman" (9pp.), LC*

ORCHESTRA

Cynthia's Dream–Sketch, LC*

Memories of My Childhood (Life in a Russian Village), Poem for Modern Orchestra
Composition: 1924, Medfield, Mass.
Premiere: 30 May 1924, Chicago Symphony Orchestra, conducted by Stock, Evanston, Illinois
Dedication: To my friends, Mr. and Mrs. John L. Severance
Manuscript: Score: holograph (48pp.), LC49
Publication: New York: G. Schirmer, 1925 (51pp.)
Recordings: Eastman-Rochester Symphony Orchestra, conducted by Howard Hanson, Mercury MG-40012, MG-50085, SRI 75090; NBC Symphony Orchestra, conducted by Arturo Toscanini, 7 January 1939 broadcast, Curtis Institute discs 1219, 1220 (on tape at LC)

A Pagan Poem (After Virgil), Composed for Orchestra with Piano, English Horn and Three Trumpets Obbligato, op. 14
Original: *Poème païen* for Chamber Ensemble—Mixed Instruments
Composition: 1904–6, Paris and Medfield, Mass.
Premiere: 29 October 1907, private performance at Fenway Court, Heinrich Gebhard with the Boston Symphony Orchestra, conducted by Muck, Boston; 22 November 1907, publicly, same personnel, Symphony Hall, Boston
Dedication: To the memory of Gustave Schirmer
Manuscripts: Score: holograph (108pp.), with corrections, LC69; Sketches: LC67
Publication: New York: G. Schirmer, 1909 (107pp.)
Recordings: Leopold Stokowski and his Symphony Orchestra, Capitol PAO-8433, P-8433/SP-8433, Seraphim S-60080; Eastman-Rochester Symphony Orchestra, conducted by Howard Hanson, Victor 18479–81 (in set M-876); Paris Philharmonic, conducted by Rosenthal, Capitol P8188
Reduction: 2 pianos, by Heinrich Gebhard. New York: G. Schirmer, 1909 (63pp.)

Poem, Composed for Orchestra [also: *Avant que tu ne t'en ailles, La bonne chanson,* originally paired with *La villanelle du Diable* as *Deux poèmes pour grand orchestre*]

Composition:	summer 1901, Dover, Mass.; revised 1915, Medfield, Mass.
Premiere:	11 April 1902, Boston Symphony Orchestra, conducted by Gericke, Symphony Hall, Boston; revision: 1–2 November 1918, Boston Symphony Orchestra, conducted by Monteux, Symphony Hall, Boston
Dedication:	To Elise, my wife
Manuscripts:	Scores: original: holograph (44pp.), with corrections, LC79; revision: holograph (53pp.), with corrections, LC78; Parts: percussion, LC*
Publication:	revision: New York: G. Schirmer, 1923 (60pp.)
Recording:	Eastman–Rochester Symphony Orchestra, conducted by Howard Hanson, Mercury MG-40012, MG-50085, SRI 75090

La villanelle du Diable, d'après un poème de M. Rollinat, Fantasie symphonique pour grand orchestre et orgue, op. 9 [Originally paired with *Poem* as *Deux poèmes pour grand orchestre*]

Original:	*Rapsodies* pour voix, clarinette, alto, et piano
Composition:	summer 1901, Dover, Mass.
Premiere:	11 April 1902, Boston Symphony Orchestra, conducted by Gericke, Symphony Hall, Boston
Dedication:	A Franz Kneisel
Manuscript:	missing
Publication:	New York: G. Schirmer, 1905 (84pp.)
Reduction:	4-hand piano, by Marcel Labey. New York: G. Schirmer, 1908 (33pp.)

Untitled [LC title: Sketch for a piece for string orchestra and organ]

Manuscripts:	unfinished holograph score (4pp.), with corrections, and parts, LC100

Orchestra with Solo Voice

Canticum Fratris Solis, Set for Voice and Chamber Orchestra to the hymn by St. Francis of Assisi in a modern Italian version by Gino Perera

Composition:	1925, Medfield, Mass.
Premiere:	28 October 1925, Povla Frijsh, directed by Stock, Washington, D.C.
Dedication:	Elizabeth Sprague Coolidge in profound admiration
Manuscripts:	Scores: unfinished holograph (46pp. draft), dated March 1925, Medfield; holograph (64pp.); copy (64pp.), with corrections; holograph piano-vocal rehearsal score (20pp.), with corrections; copyist piano-vocal rehearsal score (24pp.), with corrections; copyist organ-vocal re-

hearsal score (24pp.), with note on title page "this can be omitted"; Parts: copyist parts; Sketches. All in LC Coolidge Collection.

Publications: Elizabeth Sprague Coolidge Foundation, Library of Congress, Washington, DC, 1929 (95pp.); Piano-vocal score: Elizabeth Sprague Coolidge Foundation, Library of Congress, 1929 (23pp.)

Arrangement: *Canticum fratris solis* for Women's Chorus

La cloche fêlée and *Sérénade*

Original: *La cloche fêlée* and *Sérénade* for Voice, Viola, and Piano
Texts: Charles Baudelaire and Paul Verlaine
Composition: about 1895
Manuscript: Score: holograph (36pp.), with some corrections, LC81

Five Irish Fantasies, for Voice and Orchestra
1. *The Hosting of the Sidhe*
2. *The Host of the Air*
3. *The Fiddler of Dooney*
4. *Ballad of the Foxhunter*
5. *The Song of Caitilin ni Uallachain*

Texts: 1–4: William Butler Yeats; 5: William Heffernan (The Blind), translated by Clarence Mangan and others; the Gaelic is underlaid on some manuscripts.

Composition: July-October 1920, Medfield, Mass.

Premiere: 2, 3, 5: 10 March 1922, John McCormack with the Boston Symphony Orchestra, conducted by Monteux, Boston; 1, 4: (performed with 3): 7 November 1929, Edward Johnson with the Cleveland Orchestra, conducted by Sokoloff, Severance Hall, Cleveland

Dedications: 1 and 2: Temple R. Fay; 3: Edward Johnson; 5: To my friend John McCormack

Manuscripts: Scores: incomplete drafts of 4 & 5 (various pagings), LC41; holograph (5 is draft) (12, 16, 12, 18, 24pp.), with corrections, LC42; holograph (15, 20, 17, 24, 27pp.), LC43; Parts: draft vocal part of 5, with complete Gaelic, LC41; holograph score of vocal part with piano accompaniment, with Gaelic text partially covered over, LC44; Sketches: LC41, LC126, LC*

Publication: New York: G. Schirmer, 1935 (104pp.)

Recordings: Neil Rosenshein with the Indianapolis Symphony Orchestra, conducted by John Nelson, New World Records, NW 332; Eileen Farrell and CBS Symphony Orchestra, conducted by Bernard Herrmann, Rockhill; ncp 1444/1445: US Composers no. 29, (on tape at LC); 3 & 5: Eastman–Rochester Symphony Orchestra, acetate (on tape at LC)

Arrangement: *Five Irish Fantasies* for Voice and Piano; the voice parts of
                the piano and orchestral versions differ at some points.

Hymne, pour voix, quintette à cordes, orgue et piano [also: *Hymne d'église;
Hymne à Dieu; Prière* for mezzo-soprano, string orchestra, organ, and piano]
  Composition: about 1919
  Premiere: 4 June 1919, Povla Frijsh, Heinrich Gebhard (piano),
                 Albert Snow (organ), and strings conducted by Loeffler,
                 Unitarian Church, Medfield
  Manuscripts: Scores: 2 incomplete drafts, entitled *Hymne d'église* (4pp.
                 each), LC39; holograph (12pp.), with a few corrections,
                 LC40; holograph piano-vocal rehearsal score "for the
                 singer" (10pp.), with a few corrections, LC40; Parts:
                 copyist parts, LC40; holograph organ part, LC40

Orchestra with Chorus

Beat! Beat! Drums! See Men's Chorus

Evocation, On Lines from the Select Epigrams of the Greek Anthology, by J.
W. Mackail, For Women's Voices and Modern Orchestra
  Composition: August-September 1930, Medfield, Mass.
  Premiere: 5 February 1931, Cleveland Orchestra, conducted by
                 Sokoloff
  Dedication: To John L. Severance
  Manuscripts: Scores: incomplete holograph with corrections (32pp.),
                 LC26; holograph (47pp.), with corrections, LC27; holo-
                 graph piano-vocal rehearsal score (13pp.), LC27; Parts:
                 copyist parts for SSAA and speaker, alto flute, bass drum,
                 xylophone, tam-tam, LC27; parts for violin 1, violin 2,
                 viola, LC*; Sketches: LC25, LC33, LC36, LC*
  Publication: Boston: C. C. Birchard and Company for the Juilliard
                 Musical Foundation, 1932 (47pp.)
  Recording: ncp 1182/83 US Composers #6 (on tape at LC)

Hora mystica (The Mystic Hour), Symphony in One Movement, for Grand
Orchestra and Men's Voices
  Composition: summer 1915, Medfield, Mass.
  Premiere: 6 June 1916, Philharmonic Orchestra of New York, con-
                 ducted by Loeffler, Litchfield County Choral Union, Nor-
                 folk, Conn.
  Dedication: To Mr. and Mrs. Carl Stoeckel in admiration, affection
                 and gratitude
  Manuscripts: Scores: holograph (138pp., pp. 122–25 are blank but the
                 score is complete), LC37; copy, title page by Loeffler
                 (133pp.), with typescript of notes outlining differences
                 between score and parts, LC38; copy in the Fleischer

Collection; piano-vocal rehearsal score, privately printed
for Loeffler (8pp.), LC38; Sketches: LC36, LC76, LC101,
LC126

Reduction: for piano by Francis Judd Cooke, 1934 (49pp.), Cooke
Collection

Orchestra with Solo Violin

Divertissement, en trois parties, pour violon solo et grand orchestre, op. 1, a
minor
1. *Préambule*
2. *Eclogue*
3. *Carnaval des morts* (Variations sur le thème: dies irae—dies illa, à la
mémoire de Franz Liszt)
    Composition: 1894, Paris and Boston
    Premiere: 4 January 1895, Loeffler with the Boston Symphony Or-
chestra, conducted by Paur, Music Hall, Boston
    Dedication: dediée à Mme J. L. Gardner
    Manuscripts: Scores: holograph (79pp. as misnumbered, 86 actual
pages), with corrections, Gardner Museum; copy with
title page (in English) by Loeffler (30, 25, 48pp.), LC21;
copy with title page (in French) by Loeffler (36, 24, 64pp.)
LC22; copy in the Fleischer Collection; Parts: copyist solo
part, Cooke Collection; copyist parts, LC21; misc. pages,
LC*
    Reduction: *Divertimento* for Violin and Piano

Une nuit de mai, Rapsodie d'après Nicolai Gogol, pour violon et grand
orchestre et hârpe
    Original: *Les veillées de l'Ukraine,* movement 2
    Composition: 1890s
    Dedication: Hommage à Pablo de Sarasate (removed from LC62)
    Manuscripts: Scores: Version 1: holograph (47pp.), LC61; Version II:
holograph (43pp.), LC62; Version 2: copy with correc-
tions by Loeffler (49pp.), LC62; Parts: Version 2: holograph violin part, with corrections, LC62
    Reduction: *Une nuit de mai* for Violin and Piano

Les veillées de l'Ukraine, (d'après Nicolai Gogol), suite pour orchestre, violon
et hârpe
1. Introduction et pastorale
2. *Une nuit de mai (La noyée–Runa)*
3. *Chansons russes* [or *Doumka*]
4. *Les parobki s'amusent* [or *Carnaval russe*]
    Composition: begun about 1888, finished 1891, Wayland, Mass.; re-
vised summer 1899, Medfield, Mass.
    Premiere: 20 November 1891, Loeffler with the Boston Symphony

Orchestra, conducted by Nikisch, Music Hall, Boston; revision (without third movement): 24 November 1899, Franz Kneisel with the Boston Symphony Orchestra, conducted by Gericke, Music Hall, Boston

Dedication: à M. Henri L. Higginson

Manuscripts: Scores: original: holograph, without second movement (99pp., movements 3–4 renumbered 58–116), with corrections, LC109; revision: holograph, without second movement (105pp.), LC110; copy with second movement in the Fleischer Collection; revision: variant pages 32–36, LC110; Parts: revision: holograph violin part, (25pp.), LC112; copyist orchestral parts, without third movement (4th movement labelled as third), LC111

Arrangement: Movement 2 separated as independent composition, *Une nuit de Mai*

Reductions: *Les veillées de l'Ukraine, Rapsodie russe, Une nuit de Mai,* and III for Violin and Piano

Orchestra with Solo Viola d'Amore

La mort de Tintagiles, poème dramatique, d'après le drame de M. Maeterlinck, pour grand orchestre et viola d'amore, op. 6 [originally for 2 violas d'amore] [also: *Der Tod des Tintagiles*]

Composition: summer 1897, Medfield, Mass.; revised September 1900, Homburg von der Hohe

Premiere: 7 January 1898, Loeffler and Franz Kneisel with the Boston Symphony Orchestra, conducted by Paur, Music Hall, Boston; revision: 15 February 1901, Loeffler with the Boston Symphony Orchestra, conducted by Gericke, Symphony Hall, Boston

Dedication: A Eugène Ysaÿe (LC53 adds: en sincère amitié et profonde admiration)

Manuscripts: Scores: original: holograph (89pp.), German title, LC51; original: holograph condensed score (12pp.), LC51; revision: holograph (84pp.), with corrections, LC52; revision: holograph (93pp.), German title page, with corrections, LC53; publisher's proof with corrections by Loeffler (97pp.), LC54; Parts: copyist part for viola d'amore, labelled by Loeffler "old—not complete," LC*; copyist part for viola d'amore, LC*; holograph part for second viola d'amore, LC51; Sketches: LC*; Misc.: cover page for holograph score, Medfield Historical Society (bearing opus number 24)

Publication: New York: G. Schirmer, 1905 (97pp.)

Recording: Jennie Hansen with the Indianapolis Symphony Orchestra, conducted by John Nelson, New World Records NW 332

Reduction: 4-hand piano, by Marcel Labey. New York: G. Schirmer, 1908 (39pp.); unfinished 4-hand piano reduction (7pp.), LC54

Orchestra with Solo Cello

Morceau fantastique, pour violoncelle avec grand orchestre et hârpe [also: *Fantastic Concerto,* for violoncello and orchestra]
1. Allegro
2. Adagio
3. Allegro
4. Thème russe: Poco allegretto
5. Presto

    Composition: 1893, Medfield, Mass.
    Premiere: 2 Feburary 1894, Alwin Schroeder with the Boston Symphony Orchestra, conducted by Paur, Music Hall, Boston
    Dedication: Alwin Schroeder zugeeignet
    Manuscripts: Score: missing; Parts: holograph solo part, with corrections, LC50

Poème (scène dramatique), pour violoncelle et piano ou orchestre
    Original: *Poème (scène dramatique)* for Cello and Piano
    Manuscript: Despite the wording of the title page of the piano score and a letter from Casals referring to his being delighted with the orchestral score, no manuscript is known to exist.

Orchestra with Solo Saxophone

Divertissement espagnole, pour orchestre et saxophone
    Composition: summer 1900, Homburg von der Hohe
    Premiere: 29 January 1901, Mrs. R. J. Hall with the Orchestral Club of Boston, conducted by Longy, Chickering Hall, Boston
    Dedication: à Mme R. J. Hall
    Manuscripts: Scores: holograph (41pp.), with corrections; copy with additions (50pp.) (copy in the Fleischer Collection); Parts: copyist parts. All at New England Conservatory

Cadenzas for Violin and Orchestra Works by Other Composers

Johannes Brahms, Concerto, violin, op. 77, D major
    Premiere: 12 February 1897, Franz Kneisel with the Boston Symphony Orchestra, conducted by Paur, Music Hall, Boston
    Manuscript: holograph, LC118

W. A. Mozart, Sinfonia concertante, K. 364, E♭ Major
  Manuscripts: movement 1: 3 holographs; movement 2: 3 holographs; movement 3: holograph, Middlebury College

Nicolo Paganini, Concerto, violin, no. 1, op. 6, E♭ major
  Composition: early, possibly late 1870s
  Manuscript: holograph, with corrections, LC122

Camille Saint-Saëns, Concerto, violin, no. 1
  Premiere: 24 February 1893, Loeffler with the Boston Symphony Orchestra, conducted by Nikisch, Music Hall, Boston
  Manuscript: holograph, with corrections, LC124

Camille Saint-Saëns, *Morceau de Concert,* op. 62
  Premiere: 16 February 1894, Loeffler with the Boston Symphony Orchestra, conducted by Paur, Music Hall, Boston
  Manuscripts: two holographs, LC*

EDITIONS OF COMPOSITIONS BY OTHER COMPOSERS

Gabriel Fauré, Sonata for Violin and Piano, opus 13, edited by C. M. Loeffler
  Publication: Boston: Boston Music Company, 1919 (55pp.)

Camille Saint-Saëns, *Havanaise,* for the violin with piano accompaniment, op. 83, Fingerings and bowings by C. M. Loeffler
  Publication: Boston: Boston Music Company, 1916 (15pp.)

ARRANGEMENTS OF COMPOSITIONS BY OTHER COMPOSERS

Of the arrangements in Loeffler's collection some bear his name (as noted in the entries below), while others bear no attribution. It is possible that some of these others are copies he made, or some may be arrangements by Gertrude Marshall Wit, in whose hand many of the manuscripts are.

Violin and Piano

Solos for the Violin with Piano Accompaniment arranged by Charles Martin Loeffler
  ———Emmanuel Chabrier, Scherzo-Valse from *Scène Pittoresque*
  ———Henry Ketten, *Caprice Espagnole*
  ———Nicolo Paganini, *La clochette*
  ———Emmanuel Chabrier, *Habanera*
  Dedications: Chabrier, Scherzo-Valse: Eugène Ysaÿe
                  Ketten: Mrs. H. N. Slater
  Manuscripts: *La clochette:* holograph score (18pp.), incomplete part,

LC123; *Habanera:* incomplete holograph score (last 4pp.), LC*

Arrangement: *see also* violin and orchestra arrangement
Publication: Boston: Boston Music Company, 1909
Recording: Chabrier, Scherzo-Valse: J. Szigeti and N. de Mageloff, Columbia 68162D

Bach, Adagio, Largo, Gavotte I, 2 Passepieds
Manuscripts: Score: copy (8, 3, 4, 6pp.); Parts: holograph for Passepieds; copy for Passepieds. All LC*
Variant: *see also* viola d'amore arrangement

Bach, Rondeau de la Suite
Manuscripts: Scores: holograph (6pp.); copy (6pp); Part: holograph. All LC*

Fryderyk Chopin, Andante [Etude, op. 10, no. 6]
Manuscript: Score: holograph (4pp.), LC120

Chopin, Etude, op. 10, no. 7
Manuscript: Score: holograph (3pp.), LC120

Chopin, Mazurka op. 17, no. 4
Manuscript: Score: holograph (2pp.), LC120

Charles Gounod, *Berceuse* pour violon avec piano (d'après un manuscript par Charles Gounod)
Manuscript: Score: holograph (7pp.); Part, holograph, both LC*

Nicolo Paganini, Capriccio 24 (Thème et Variations), l'accompagnement par Ch. M. Loeffler
Composition: probably 1883, Boston
Manuscript: Score: holograph (6pp.), LC*

Guiseppe Tartini, *Il trillo del diavolo*
Manuscript: Score: copy, LC125. Not in Loeffler's hand and probably not his arrangement, but LC has suggested that Loeffler possibly realized the figured bass.

Viola d'Amore and Piano

Johann Sebastian Bach, Courante, transcrite pour viole d'amour et piano par Ch. M. Loeffler
Manuscripts: Scores: holograph (2pp.), LC*; copy (2pp.), LC*; Part, LC*; Sketch: Yale

Bach, Preludio 8, pour viole d'amore et piano arrangé par Ch. M. Loeffler Prelude en mi mineur [Das wohltempierte Clavier, Th. 1, no. 8]
Manuscripts: Scores: incomplete holograph (1p.), LC*; unfinished holograph (3pp.), LC116; copy (3pp.), LC*; Part: holograph, LC*

Bach, Praeludium (in A)
　　Manuscripts:　　Scores: holograph (2pp.); 2 copies (2pp. each); Sketch:
　　　　　　　　　　sketch. All LC*

Bach, Sonata en re, for viole d'amour and piano arranged by Ch. M. Loeffler
　　Manuscripts:　　Scores: 2 copies (7pp., 6pp.); Part: holograph. All LC*

Bach, Adagio, Largo, Gavotte, 2 Passepieds
　　Manuscripts:　　Score: *see* violin arrangements; Part: holograph for Ada-
　　　　　　　　　　gio, Largo, Gavotte, LC*
　　Variant:　　　　*see also* violin arrangement

H. T. Burleigh, arr., Negro spiritual, *Were You There,* for viola d'amore
　　Manuscript:　　Score: copy (4pp.), Loeffler corrections pasted over, LC*

Arcangelo Corelli, Gavotte by Corelli, Variations by Tartini
　　Manuscripts:　　Scores: holograph (6pp.); copy (7pp.), both LC*

Corelli, 2 Gavottes, transcrite pour viole d'amour et piano par Ch. M. Loeffler
[arrangement of Gavotte above, without variations, and in a different key]
　　Manuscript:　　Score: holograph (2pp.), LC*

Gabriel Fauré, *Berceuse,* op. 16
　　Manuscript:　　Part: copy, laid inside a print score on which Loeffler has
　　　　　　　　　　crossed out *violin* and penciled in *viole d'amore,* LC*

Fauré, Mélodie, transcrite pour viole d'amour et piano par Ch. M. Loeffler
　　Manuscripts:　　Scores: holograph subtitled "(En sourdine)" in E♭ (4pp.);
　　　　　　　　　　holograph in F (4pp.), both LC*

C. G. [sic] Gluck, Gavotte, arranged for viole d'amour and piano by Ch. M.
Loeffler
　　Manuscripts:　　Scores: holograph (2pp.); copy (2pp.); unfinished holo-
　　　　　　　　　　graph draft (2p). All LC*

Edward Grieg, A Song, arranged for viole d'amore
　　Manuscript:　　Score: holograph (2pp.), LC*

Joseph Joachim, Paraphrase on a Romanza, for viola d'amore and piano
　　Manuscripts:　　Score: holograph (5pp.); copy (5pp.), both LC*

d'après J-M. Leclair, *Tambourin* (vieille danse française), l'accompaniment
pour piano écrit et l'arrangement pour viole d'amour fait par Ch. M. Loeffler
　　Manuscript:　　Score: holograph (8pp.), LC*

Padre Martini, Canzone (en sol), viole d'amore et piano, acct. by Fritz Kreisler
　　Manuscript:　　Score: holograph (2pp.), LC*

Jules Massenet, Paraphrase sur une Mélodie, arrangé pour viole d'amour par
Ch. M. Loeffler, *Le crépuscule*
　　Manuscript:　　Score: holograph (2pp.), LC*

Milandre, Suite en re, Largo, harmonisé par Alexandre Béon
Manuscript: Score: copy (9pp.), missing, probably not an original arrangement

Myers, *Oriental Ditty* on a tune by Myers
Manuscripts: Scores: unfinished holograph (2pp.); unfinished holograph (pp. 5–6); Sketches. All at Yale

Nardini?, Canzona pour viole d'amour et piano d'un autheur inconnu (xviii siècle)
Manuscript: Scores: holograph (4pp.); copy (4pp.); copy with a different accompaniment than above scores (4pp.); Parts, holograph and copy. All LC*

Nicolai Rimsky-Korsakov, Hymn from *Le Coq d'or*, arranged for viole d'amore with piano accompaniment by Ch M. Loeffler
Manuscripts: Scores: holograph (5pp.); copy (7pp.), both LC*

Anton Rubinstein, Romance (d'après H. Wieniawski), arrangée pour viole d'amour par Ch. M. Loeffler
Manuscript: Score: holograph (5pp.), LC*

Domenico Scarlatti, Sonata in A Major, for viole d'amore and piano by Ch. M. Loeffler
Manuscripts: Scores: holograph (7pp.), with corrections, LC*; holograph (7pp.), LC*; holograph (5pp.), with corrections, Yale; copy (6pp.), LC*; Part: holograph, LC*

C. Scott, arr., *Irish Air*, arranged for viole d'amore and piano by Ch. M. Loeffler
Manuscripts: Scores: 2 holographs (3pp. each), LC*

P. Tchaikovsky, Serenade, op. 26
Manuscripts: Scores: 2 copies (10pp., 8pp.) Part: 2 copies; printed principal violin part of another editon with Loeffler changes for viola d'amore pasted over. All LC*

Eugène Ysaÿe, *Rêve* (en la) pour viole d'amour et piano
Manuscript: Score: holograph (6pp.), LC*; may be either a copy or an arrangement made by Loeffler

Composer Unidentified, Minuetto
Manuscript: Score: copy (4pp.) with corrections by Loeffler, LC*

Composer Unidentified, *Rêverie,* pour viole d'amore arrangée par Ch. M. Loeffler
Manuscripts: Scores: holograph (4pp.); copy (4pp.), both LC*

Two Violas d'Amore and Piano

Antonin Dvořák, *Idylle pastorale*
Manuscripts: Scores: holograph (3pp.); copy, bound with the following (9pp.), both LC*

Dvořák, *Sur l'eau*
Manuscripts: Scores: holograph (3pp.); copy, bound with preceding (9pp.), both LC*

Violin or Viola d'Amore (part not identified) and Piano

Johann Sebastian Bach, Allegro vivo
Manuscript: Score: holograph (6pp.), LC*

Bach, Preludio si mineur [*Das wohltempierte Clavier,* Th. 1, no. 24]
Manuscripts: Scores: holograph (3pp), LC117; holograph (3pp.), LC*; copy (3pp.), LC*

Bach, Praeludium [D Major]
Manuscript: Score: holograph (3pp.), LC*

Ole Bull, Mélodie
Manuscript: Score: unfinished holograph (1p.), Yale

Gabriel Fauré, 2 Mélodies
Manuscript: Score: holograph draft (3pp.), missing

Fauré, Mélodie [Andantino]
Manuscripts: Scores: holograph (3pp.), with corrections; copy (3pp.); Part: copy, bound with Gluck-Kreisler and Schubert. All LC*
Arrangement: There is also a part marked "E♭ alto," titled *Tuscany Song;* on the reverse side is a part for Fauré's Nocturne for E♭ Sax, LC*

Fauré, Mélodie ["Allegro molto"]
Manuscript: Score: holograph (4pp.), LC*

Fauré, Nocturne [from *Shylock*]
Manuscript: Score: holograph (2pp.), privately owned—Cooke Collection
Arrangement: There is also a part for E♭ Sax, LC*

Gluck-Kreisler, Melodie
Manuscript: Part: copy, bound with Fauré [Andantino], Schubert, and Air by Jean Huré [transposition of Air pour violoncelle et piano ou orgue], LC*

Louis de Caix d'Hervelois, *Musette* (1680)
Manuscript: Score: copy (3pp.), missing

Johannes Mattheson, Allemande [title page reads Allemande, Courante, Sarabande con tre variationi] [Suite xii]
Manuscript: Score: holograph (2pp.), LC*

Mattheson, Sarabande con tre variatione
Manuscript: Score: holograph (3pp.), LC*
Variant: Partita for violin and piano, second movement

Milandre, Contredanse
Manuscript: Score: holograph (4pp.), LC*, laid inside the part of
                      published transcription for viola d'amore by Waefelghem
                      of Milandre's Andante et Menuet; this manuscript is an
                      arrangement of the Menuet of the published music

Paganini, Capriccio
Manuscript: Part: holograph sketch, LC*

Franz Schubert, *Adagio Preghiera*
Manuscripts: Score: copy (3pp.); Part: copy, bound with Gluck-Kreisler
                      and Fauré [Andantino], both LC*

G. Tartini, *Air Adagio Soavemente*
Manuscripts: Scores: holograph (4pp.); copy (4pp.); copy (3pp.); holo-
                      graph of last page, with sketches; holograph arrangement
                      pasted in published score. All LC*

Composer Unidentified, *Mandoline*
Manuscript: Score: unfinished holograph (4pp.), LC*

Composer Unidentified, Mélodie (*Au bord de l'eau*)
Manuscript: Score: unfinished holograph (4pp.), LC*

Chamber Group or Orchestra

Gabriel Fauré, *Elégie* pour violoncelle et orchestre (orchestrée par C. M. Loeffler)
Manuscript: Score: holograph (15pp.), LC121

Fauré, Nocturne from *Shylock*
Manuscripts: Score: copy for viola d'amore, cello, and piano, laid in
                      piano score, Yale; Parts: for viola d'amore, cello, and
                      piano, laid in piano score, Yale; holograph parts (5-part
                      strings), laid in piano score, Yale; holograph part for E♭
                      sax, LC*
Revisions: There are also manuscripts for solo string and piano.

Pierre-Alexandre Monsigny, *Rigaudon*
Manuscript: Parts: holograph (for 4-part strings), located inside a pub-
                      lished arrangement of *Rigaudon* by Sam Franko, LC*

Violin and Orchestra

Isaac Manuel Francisco Albeniz, *Rapsodie espagnole*
  Manuscript: Scores: holograph draft 2-violin and piano score with
                   orchestration notations (12pp.), with a published score of
                   a 2-piano arrangement with notations by Loeffler, LC115

Johannes Brahms, [Ungarische Tänze, no. 5–6] [for solo violin and chamber
orchestra]
  Manuscript: Score: holograph (9pp.), LC119

Nicolo Paganini, *Rondeau à la clochette (Campanella)* pour violon et orchestre d'après Paganini par Ch. M. Loeffler
  Manuscript: Score: holograph, unfinished (12pp.), LC123

Viola d'Amore and Orchestra

Marais, Adagio/Chaconne, pour viole d'amour (et orchestré par Ch. M.
Loeffler)
  Manuscript: title page only, located inside a published copy of Marais's
                   Chaconne transcribed for viola d'amore by Waefelghem,
                   which has a few passages in Loeffler's hand pasted in, LC*

MISCELLANEOUS SKETCHES

A number of sketches at the Library of Congress remain uncatalogued.
Among these sketches, the following titles or headings appear on manuscripts
that cannot be classified according to genre: *Flamenca, Gothique, Lincoln,
Hommage à la très Sainte Vièrge, Federal March, Mexican Creoles, Maria ad
la cum, Hungarian Dance, Maria Am See.* There are, in addition, a number
of other sketches, fragments, and parts in the Library of Congress collection
that remain unidentified.

The sketch of *Las moyares corraleras; cancion espanola*, though catalogued
by LC as a Loeffler composition (LC55), is simply an unfinished copy of a
song in *Receuil de Romances, Bailes, etc. de Portugais et Espagnoles* (1862),
located at the Boston Public Library.

NOTES

Loeffler's letters are documented by the initials of sender and recipient, according to the table of abbreviations below, by date of letter or postmark [bracketed], and, in cases of Loeffler's correspondence when written away from home, by place of writing (at the first reference). Letters are located at the Library of Congress unless otherwise noted and with the following exceptions: correspondence to Isabella Stewart Gardner is used courtesy of the Isabella Stewart Gardner Museum, Boston; to Richard Aldrich, courtesy of the Edna Kuhn Loeb Library at Harvard; to Gericke, Lowell, and Chapman, courtesy of the Houghton Library at Harvard; to Sargent, courtesy of Richard Ormond; to Gertrude Marshall Wit, Herman Silberman, and Sam Gardner, courtesy of the families. Letters to Damrosch, Steinert, and Franko are located at the New York Public Library; to Goodrich, at the New England Conservatory.

RA	Richard Aldrich		ISG	Isabella Stewart Gardner
PA	Percy Atherton		SG	Sam Gardner
HB	Harold Bauer		GG	George Gershwin
AB	Adolpho Betti		HG	Heinrich Gebhard
DB	Denis Bunker		WiG	Wilhelm Gericke
HC	Henri Casadesus		PG	Percy Grainger
PC	Pablo Casals		WG	Wallace Goodrich
JJC	John Jay Chapman		DH	Dan Hamant
EC	Evan Charteris		EBH	E. B. Hill
AC	Albert Chatfield		APH	Adella Prentiss Hughes
CC	Chalmers Clifton		VI	Vincent d'Indy
FC	Frederick Converse		FK	Franz Kneisel
ESC	Elizabeth Sprague Coolidge		HK	Hugo Kortschak
WD	Walter Damrosch		SK	Serge Koussevitzky
ChE	Charles Ellis		BJL	B. J. Lang
CE	Carl Engel		HuL	Hubert Léonard
HE	Henry Eichheim		CML	Charles Martin Loeffler
GF	Gabriel Fauré		HL	Helene Loeffler
EF	Elise Fay		AL	Amy Lowell
SF	Sam Franko		DGM	D. G. Mason
PF	Povla Frijsh		PM	Pierre Monteux

HR	Henri Rabaud	LWS	L. W. Spofford
JSS	John Singer Sargent	AS	Alexander Steinert
GrS	Grace Schirmer	LS	Leopold Stokowski
GS	Gustave Schirmer	KSW	Kay Swift Warburg
ArS	Arthur Shepherd	EW	Edward Waters
HS	Herman Silberman	AW	Arthur Whiting
NS	Nikolai Sokoloff	GMW	Gertrude Marshall Wit
OS	Oscar Sonneck	EY	Eugène Ysaÿe
HaS	Harold Spivacke		

Newspaper articles were consulted not only from microfilm copies of the papers themselves but also from clippings in the press books and files of the Boston Symphony Orchestra archives, the Medfield Historical Society, and scrapbooks at the Boston Public Library. Many of these clippings are not accompanied by the paper name, article title, date, page number, or author. A few other items, not properly identifiable, are located in the Library of Congress. In these cases the citation concludes with the location of the clipping or article according to the following abbreviations:

BPL Boston Public Library
BSO Boston Symphony Orchestra
LC Library of Congress
MHS Medfield Historical Society

NOTES ON SPELLING

Quotations from Loeffler's letters written in English follow the original spelling, capitalization, and punctuation exactly. Excerpts from letters written in German and French have been translated by this author, but brief German or French phrases within primarily English letters are quoted in the original language and translated within brackets.

The spelling "Löffler" is used for Loeffler's father and grandfather, and "Loeffler" for the composer (except in quotations), in accordance with their own practices.

PREFACE

1. *New York Herald Tribune,* 21 May 1935.
2. Philip Hale, *Boston Journal,* 9 January 1898.
3. *New York Herald Tribune,* 21 May 1935.
4. Olin Downes, "Henry Gilbert: Nonconformist," in *A Birthday Offering to CE,* ed. Gustave Reese (New York: G. Schirmer, 1943), p. 88.
5. Lawrence Gilman, "Seventy Years Now Bear Him Witness," *Boston Transcript,* 30 January 1931, 9.
6. Carl Engel, "Charles Martin Loeffler," *Musical Quarterly* (hereafter cited as *MQ*) 11 (July 1925): 313.
7. Ibid., 314.

8. Engel's notes from this interview survive and are here cited as Engel/-Loeffler interview notes.

9. Engel, "Loeffler," 312.

CHAPTER 1

1. Moses Smith, "Loeffler and His Music," 25 May 1935, BSO clipping.

2. Information provided by the Evangelisches Zentralarchiv in Berlin; her baptism date is there given as 13.5.1838, Dreifaltigkeitskirche.

3. CML to EF, 29 September 1904, from Homburg.

4. CML to RA, 16 May 1923.

5. Carl Engel, "View and Reviews," *MQ* 21 (1935): 371.

6. Olin Downes, "Originality in Composer's Art Means Sophistication, says Loeffler," *Musical America* (April 16, 1910): 3.

7. This information, located by the Evangelisches Zentralarchiv, is recorded in Otto Fischer, "Evangelischen Pfarrerbuch für die Mark Brandenburg," Band II/1, Seite 512. A baptismal record for this date, however, was not located at the Evangelisches Zentralarchiv. Fischer states that Konrad Löffler was relieved of his office in 1844, though Franz Brummer gives 1828 as Konrad Löffler's death date. It is certain that by 1857, when Karl Löffler married, both his parents had died.

8. Information provided by the Evangelisches Zentralarchiv in Berlin; his baptism date is there given as 21.11.1821, St. Gertraudten-Kirche.

9. Franz Brummer, *Lexikon der deutschen Dichter und Prosaisten vom Beginn des 19. Jahrhunderts bis zur Gegenwarte.* 6th ed. (Leipzig: P. Reclam Jun., 1913; rpt. Nendeln/Liechtenstein: Kraus Reprint, 1975).

10. CML to EF, 1 August 1884, from Paris, translated from French.

11. Brummer (*Lexikon*) lists the papers as "Monatsrosen" (founded 1851), "Novellen-flora" (1852), "Belletrist" (1856), and "Berliner Gerichtszeitung" (1858).

12. Karl Löffler and Peter von Papi-Balogh, *Die nordamerikanische Zuckerfabrikation aus Sorgo und Imphy* (Debreczin: Carl von Csathy, 1868).

13. Société Impériale d'acclimatation zu Paris, Société Impériale zoologique zu Marseilles, der Kaiserlichen Oesterreichischen Landwirthschafts-Gesellschaft zu Agram, der Reale Accademia di Agricoltura zu Turin, Herzoglichen Vereins Rassauischer Land- und Forstwirthe, and Märkischen öconomischen Gesellschaft.

14. CML to JJC, 25 June 1916, from Medfield, Houghton Library.

15. Karl Löffler, *Das Chinesische Zuckerrohr (Kao-lien)* (Braunschweig: Friedrich Vieweg und Sohn, 1859); idem, *Ueber die Runkelrübenzucker-Fabrikation Frankreichs* (Berlin: Theodor Thiele, 1863).

16. Some Confederate money, perhaps a souvenir of this trip, was part of the Loeffler Collection when transferred to the Library of Congress. Also during this trip, Löffler may have gotten the idea for writing *Der Geisterseher, oder: Die Mormonenbraut* (1869).

17. The academy, however, has no record (other than the advertisement) of Löffler's having ever been on their teaching staff.

18. The sister's death is mentioned in CML to CE, IV 1925.

19. The Russian period is given by Engel as prior to the Hungarian, but placing the Löfflers in Russia before 1868 conflicts with Martin's recollections and would make both Martin and Helene too young for their memories there. In addition, it was not listed among Dr. Löffler's qualifications published in 1868.

20. Charles Martin Loeffler, *Memories of My Childhood (Life in a Russian Village)* (New York: G. Schirmer, 1925).

21. Notes appended to letter from CE to HaS, 26 April 1943, from New York. Engel believed Helene to be in error and continued in his notes, "however, there exists a picture of Martin with a violin in his hand, taken at Naumberg; and that picture shows him as a boy of eleven or twelve, or somewhat older than he was when he is supposed to have taken up the study of the violin."

22. CML to EF, 29 September 1904, from Homburg.

23. While the lexicon dates Löffler's assumption of the directorship of the sugar factory at 1860, a friend of Loeffler's, Gustave Strube, who was not born until 1867, recalled meeting Martin Loeffler at nearby Ballenstedt while the family was domiciled at Magdeburg about 1877.

24. CML to EF, 23 June 1884, from Paris, translated from French.

25. Engel, "Loeffler," 315.

26. CML to CE, n.d. [1925].

27. CML to "Henry," n.d. [1889].

28. CML to EF, 14 May 1883, from Memphis, translated from French.

29. CML to EF, 23 June 1884, from Paris, translated from French.

30. CML to EF, 2 May 1884, from Paris, translated from French.

31. HL to CML, 5 November 1888, from Paris, translated from German.

CHAPTER 2

1. Engel/Loeffler interview notes.

2. Carl Engel remarked that Karl Löffler "apparently even composed music for some comedies that he wrote" ("Charles Martin Loeffler," in *Great Modern Composers,* ed. Oscar Thompson [New York: Dodd, Mead, 1941], p. 161). A libretto, entitled "Nacht und Tag, Weltlichen Oratorium," written by Dr. Löffler has survived, without music, among his son's manuscripts.

3. Typewritten note headed "As told to Mr. Engel by Mr. Sam Franko on April 7, 1937," LC.

4. A letter, dated June 1874, to Loeffler from Edmund Singer gives Loeffler information on a Professor Scholl at the Realschule in Berlin. Whether Loeffler seriously considered any other school but the Hochschule at this time is unknown. Also, a unique reference to Philip Rüfer as another of Loeffler's composition teachers appears in a biographical summary compiled in 1923 by the Society for the Publication of American Music. Rüfer was then a piano

teacher at Stern's Conservatory and Kullach's Conservatory; it is possible that Loeffler did come into contact with him at this time.

5. Sam Franko, *Chords and Dischords: Memoirs of an American Musician* (New York: Viking Press, 1938), p. 22.

6. Clayton Johns, *Reminiscences of a Musician* (Cambridge: Washburn & Thomas, 1929), pp. 35–36.

7. Franko, *Chords and Dischords,* pp. 19–20.

8. CML to CE, 25 July 1922.

9. Franko, *Chords and Dischords,* p. 20.

10. Francis Judd Cooke, interview with author, Lexington, 8 April 1984.

11. Engel/Franko note, 1937. The incident has not been dated; since Loeffler, Franko, and Bial lived contemporaneously both in Berlin and New York, it may belong to either period, though it is unlikely to belong to 1881.

12. Johns, *Reminiscences,* p. 18.

13. Louis Elson, *The History of American Music,* revised to 1925 by Arthur Elson (New York: Macmillan, 1925), p. 218.

14. Johns, *Reminiscences,* pp. 18–19.

15. Engel, "Views," 372.

16. CML to EF, 9 June 1884, from Paris.

17. Engel/Franko note.

18. Gustave Strube to CE, 20 April 1943, from Baltimore, LC.

19. CML to EF, 1 August 1884, from Paris, translated from French.

20. CML to GS, 14 August 1905.

21. Unsigned, "The Music of Charles Martin Loeffler," *Christian Science Monitor* (29 January 1910).

22. CML to EF, 9 May 1890, from Cincinnati, translated from French.

23. E. L. Winn, "Charles Martin Loeffler: A Sketch," *Musical Observer,* 1910.

24. Engel, "Views," 372.

25. CML to CE, 25 July 1922.

26. Elson, *The History of American Music,* p. 218.

27. Franko, *Chords and Dischords,* pp. 29–30, 31.

28. Engel wrote that Loeffler played two seasons with Pasdeloup, the second season coming after Loeffler's time with the Derwies orchestra; however, the dates of Loeffler's contract with Derwies and of his emigration make a second season at that time impossible.

29. CML to HS, 17 July 1931.

30. Georges Favre, *Un haut-lieu musical niçois au xixième siècle: La Villa Valrose (1870–1881)* (Paris: Editions A. et J. Picard, n.d. [1977]), p. 12. Although Derwies was often called "prince," Loeffler explained that his title was baron (CML to CE, 6 September 1924).

31. Interview with Victor Herbert in *New York Morning Telegraph* (13 December 1914), quoted in Edward N. Waters, *Victor Herbert: A Life in Music* (New York: Macmillan, 1955), p. 10.

32. Engel/Loeffler interview notes.

33. CML to HS, 17 July 1931.

34. In a letter to EF, 19 April 1884, from Paris, Loeffler wrote that he had already met Ysaÿe in Switzerland. Ysaÿe also performed as a soloist with Pasdeloup during Franko's time, when Loeffler may have heard him.

CHAPTER 3

1. Emigration records for 1881 give the figure of immigrants as 669,431, nearly one-third of whom came from Germany; 430 were listed as musicians. *Emigration and Immigration. Reports of the Consular Officers of the United States* (Washington, D.C.: Government Printing Office, 1887).

2. Drafted on a letter written to CML from Louis Fontaine, 12 July n.y., translated from French.

3. Sir George Henschel, *Musings and Memories of a Musician* (New York: Macmillan, 1919; rpt., New York: Da Capo Press, 1979), pp. 244–45.

4. Draft on Fontaine letter to CML.

5. Franko, *Chords and Dischords*, pp. 63, 62.

6. Walter Damrosch, "Charles Martin Loeffler," Commemorative Tributes, Academy Publication #88 (New York: American Academy of Arts and Letters, 1936), pp. 167–68.

7. Ibid., p. 168.

8. Franko, *Chords and Dischords*, p. 64.

9. Ibid., p. 62.

10. CML to CE, 6 September 1924.

11. Theodore Thomas, *A Musical Autobiography*, ed. George P. Upton (Chicago: A. C. McClurg , 1905; rpt., New York: Da Capo Press, 1964), pp. 89–90.

12. CML to CE, 31 March 1925.

13. Franko, *Chords and Dischords*, p. 66.

14. Loeffler was described as a cult figure in the *New York Morning Telegraph,* 15 January 1904, and in the obituary written by Olin Downes for the *New York Times,* 26 May 1935.

CHAPTER 4

1. Henschel, *Musings and Memories of a Musician*, pp. 248–49.

2. Arthur Foote, *An Autobiography* (Norwood, Mass.: Plimpton Press, 1946; rpt., New York: Da Capo Press, 1979), p. 40.

3. M. A. DeWolfe Howe, *A Partial (and not impartial) Centennial History of the Tavern Club 1884–1934* (Cambridge: Riverside Press, 1935), p. 98.

4. M. A. DeWolfe Howe, *The Boston Symphony Orchestra 1881–1931,* rev. ed. with John N. Burke (Boston: Houghton Mifflin, 1931), p. 3.

5. BSO contract, quoted in Henschel, *Musings and Memories of a Musician*, p. 280.

6. Franko, *Chords and Dischords*, p. 88.

7. Engel, "Loeffler," 318.

8. Engel, "Charles Martin Loeffler," in *Great Modern Composers*, p. 167.

E. B. Hill [in "Charles Martin Loeffler," *Modern Music* 13 (November-December 1935): 26] stated that "Higginson had such confidence [in Loeffler] that no contract existed between them." Later this may have been true, but in the early years there was a contract.

9. CML to SF, 31 December 1882, German, NYPL.

10. CML to ISG, Friday, n.d., from Boston.

11. CML to EF, Thursday [22 March 1883], translated from French.

12. CML to EF, 7 May 1883, from Cleveland, translated from French.

13. Olin Downes, "Charles Martin Loeffler," *New York Times* (26 May 1935), sec. 2, p. 5.

14. Daniel Gregory Mason, *The Dilemma of American Music, and Other Essays* (New York: Macmillan, 1928), p. 7.

15. Kay Swift, interview with author, New York, 23 October 1980.

16. Engel, "Loeffler," 314.

17. Heinrich Gebhard, *Reminiscences of a Boston Musician* (privately printed, n.p., n.d.), p. 3.

18. Frank Benson, "Charles Martin Loeffler," typescript memorial address, May 1936, Tavern Club.

19. Walter Damrosch, *My Musical Life* (New York: Charles Scribner's Sons, 1940), p. 168.

20. Damrosch, "Loeffler," pp. 171–72.

21. Downes, "Originality."

22. Gebhard, *Reminiscences of a Boston Musician*, p. 3.

23. Hill, "Loeffler," 27.

24. Benson, "Charles Martin Loeffler."

25. Clara Kathleen Rogers, *The Story of Two Lives: Home, Friends, and Travels* (Norwood, Mass.: Plimpton Press, 1932), pp. 49–50.

26. CML to GrS, 8 April 1906.

27. Cooke interview.

28. Rubinstein's *Ocean* Symphony, CML to ISG, 10 April 1898; Clayton Johns, CML to EF, dimanche [12 May] 1889, from St. Louis.

29. CML to EF, 7 May 1883, from Cleveland, translated from French.

30. Engel, "Views," 371.

31. CML to EF, 12 January 1893, from New York, translated from French.

32. Eichheim, untitled score for violin and piano, 1894, LC.

33. EF to HuL, n.d. [1884].

34. CML to EF, 22 May 1884, from Paris, 14 May 1883, from Memphis, both translated from French.

35. CML to EF, 27 April 1883, from Baltimore, translated from German.

36. The itinerary, including dates where given in Loeffler's letters, included: Baltimore (26–28 April), Pittsburgh (30 April, 1–2 May), Bradford, Pa. (3 May), Buffalo (4 May), Erie (5 May), Cleveland (7–8 May), Columbus (9–10 May), Louisville (11–12 May), Memphis (14–15 May), Nashville (16 May), Cincinnati (17 May), St Louis (18–20 May), Kansas City (21–23 May), Keokuk (24–25 May), Cedar Rapids (26 May), St. Paul (28, 30 May), Minneapolis (29, 31 May), Waterloo (1 June), San Francisco (7–13 June), Salt

Lake (15–16 June), Denver (19–23 June), Topeka, Leavenworth, St. Joseph, Lincoln, Omaha, Fort Dodge, Des Moines, Rock Island, Burlington, and Chicago.

37. CML to EF, 14 May 1883, translated from French.

38. CML to EF, 27 April 1883.

39. CML to CE, n.d. [1925].

40. CML to EF, 25 May 1883, from Keokuk, translated from French.

41. CML to EF, 27 April 1883.

42. CML to EF, 7 May 1883, from Cleveland, translated from French.

43. CML to EF, 14 May 1883.

44. CML to EF, 7 May 1883.

45. CML to EF, 14 May 1883.

46. CML to EF, 25 May 1883.

47. CML to EF, 7 May 1883, 14 May 1883.

48. CML to EF, 7 May 1883.

49. CML to EF, 17 May 1883, from Nashville, translated from German.

50. CML to EF, 7 May 1883.

51. "Music of Loeffler," *Christian Science Monitor*.

52. Heinrich Gebhard, interview with Herbert Colvin, Boston, 8 August 1956.

CHAPTER 5

1. *Boston Traveller,* 19 November 1883, p. 2.

2. *Boston Morning Journal,* 19 November 1883, p. 3.

3. *Boston Daily Advertiser,* 19 November 1883, p. 5.

4. *Boston Evening Transcript,* 19 November 1883, p. 1.

5. Hill, "Loeffler," 26.

6. Gebhard, *Reminiscences of a Boston Musician,* p. 3.

7. *Boston Transcript,* 22 December 1884, p. 4.

8. *Boston Transcript,* 14 November 1887, p. 1.

9. *Boston Gazette,* 24 November 1888.

10. *Boston Journal,* 10 February 1890.

11. *Boston Gazette,* 26 February 1893.

12. William F. Apthorp, *Boston Transcript,* 30 November 1885, p. 1.

13. Apthorp, *Boston Transcript,* 19 February 1894.

14. *Boston Sunday Herald,* 26 February 1893, 18 February 1894.

15. *Boston Sunday Globe,* 6 January 1895, 10 January 1897; *Boston Traveller,* [November] 1885, BSO/BPL clipping; *Boston Sunday Globe,* 9 January 1898.

16. Winn, "Charles Martin Loeffler," p. 24.

17. *Boston Post,* 26 March 1889.

18. *Boston Transcript,* 14 November 1887, p. 1.

19. CML to EF, 9 May 1890.

20. Walter Muir Whitehall, *Museum of Fine Arts: A Centennial History,* 2 vols. (Cambridge: Belknap Press of Harvard University Press, 1970), 1:52.

21. EF to HuL, 22 January 1884.

22. Unidentified LC clipping.

23. CML to EF, 2 May 1884, from Paris, translated from French.

24. CML to EF, 11 April 1884, from Paris, translated from French.

25. CML to EF, 19 April 1884, from Paris, translated from French.

26. Ibid., translated from German.

27. Ibid., translated from French.

28. Ibid., translated from French and German.

29. CML to EF, 2 May 1884, translated from French.

30. Moszkowski inscribed a photograph of himself to Ch. Löffler-Tornov, 1879.

31. CML to EF, 2 May 1884.

32. Ibid.

33. Ibid.

34. Christine Merrick Ayars, *Contributions to the Art of Music in America by the Industries of Boston 1640 to 1936* (New York: H. W. Wilson, 1937), p. 201.

35. CML to EF, 13 May 1884, from Homburg, translated from French.

36. CML to EF, 9 June 1884, from Paris, translated from French and German.

37. CML to EF, 23 June, from Paris, translated from French.

38. CML to EF, 2 July 1884, from Paris, translated from French.

39. CML to EF, 21 July 1884, from Paris, translated from French.

40. CML to EF, 19 April 1884, 2 May 1884, 21 July 1884.

41. CML to EF, 1 August 1884, from Paris, translated from French.

42. Ibid.

43. CML to EF, 10 August 1884, from Paris, translated from French.

44. CML to CE, 25 July 1922.

45. CML to EF, 1 August 1884.

46. Ibid.

CHAPTER 6

1. Henschel, *Musings and Memories of a Musician,* p. 291.

2. Wilhelm Gericke, quoted in Howe, *BSO,* pp. 62–63.

3. Ibid, p. 63.

4. Franko, *Chords and Dischords,* p. 87.

5. Quoted in Howe, *BSO,* p. 63.

6. CML to EF, 9 June 1884, from Paris, translated from French.

7. CML to ISG, 27 January 1895, 26 January 1895.

8. HL to CML, 9.8.24 from Homburg, translated from French.

9. CML to EF, Vendredi soir [20 February 1885], n.p., translated from French.

10. CML to EF, Mardi soir [17 March 1885] n.p., translated from French.

11. CML to EF, 20 February 1885, translated from French.

12. *Boston Daily Advertiser,* 22 December 1884, p. 4; *Boston Evening Transcript,* 22 December 1884, p. 4.

13. HuL to CML, 12 February 1885, from Paris, translated from French.

14. *Boston Gazette,* 22 March 1885.

15. CML to AS, 27 May 1923.

16. Notes from the Engel/Loeffler interview contain the information that Loeffler studied with Léonard during the summer of 1885 as well as 1884. No documentation of a trip to Europe during this summer has appeared.

17. CML to EF, 27 June 1885.

18. Gericke, quoted in Howe, *BSO,* p. 60.

19. Franko, *Chords and Dischords,* p. 87.

20. Gericke, quoted in Howe, *BSO,* p. 64.

21. *Boston Transcript,* 30 November 1885, p. 1; *Boston Sunday Herald,* 29 November 1885, p. 10.

22. Quoted in Howe, *BSO,* p. 63.

23. Johns, *Reminiscences,* pp. 72, 68–69.

24. J. J. Chapman, quoted in Helen Howe, *The Gentle Americans 1864–1960: Biography of a Breed* (New York: Harper & Row, Publishers, 1965), p. 254.

25. CML to EF, 7 April 1886, from Springfield, 8 April from Providence, 10 April from Philadelphia, all translated from French.

26. EF to CML, 16 April 1886, from Boston, 12 April, 19 April, all translated from French.

27. CML to EF, 10 April 1886.

28. Gericke, quoted in Howe, *BSO,* pp. 65, 66.

29. *Boston Gazette,* n.d., BPL clipping; *Boston Courier,* 12 December 1886; *Boston Daily Advertiser,* 13 December 1886.

30. CML to EF, 16 April 1887, from Philadelphia, translated from French.

31. CML to EF, 14 April 1887, from Philadelphia, translated from French.

32. CML to EF, 15 July 1887, from Homburg, translated from French.

33. CML to EF, 27 July 1887, from Homburg, translated from French.

34. Ibid.

35. *Boston Gazette,* n.d., BPL clipping; *Boston Post,* n.d., BPL clipping.

36. CML to EC, quoted in Evan Charteris, *John Sargent* (New York: Charles Scribner's Sons, 1927), p. 147.

37. CML to JSS, 18 March 1921, Richard Ormond Collection.

38. CML to ISG, Mon 27th, n.y.

39. Johns, *Reminiscences,* pp. 65–66.

40. CML to ISG, 10 August 1898.

41. Johns, *Reminiscences,* p. 44.

42. Rogers, *The Story of Two Lives,* p. 49.

43. Ibid., p. 218.

44. Ibid., p. 36.

45. Johns, *Reminiscences,* pp. 55–56; the Paderewski story is also in Rogers, *The Story of Two Lives.*

46. CML to EF, 29 June 1888 or 1889, from Newburyport, translated from French.

47. *Boston Transcript,* 24 November 1888; *Boston Herald,* 24 November 1888; *Boston Traveller,* 24 November 1888.

48. CML to EF, 11 December, 12 December 1888, from Philadelphia, both translated from French.

49. CML to EF, Mercredi [27 April] 1892, from Baltimore.

50. CML to EF, Mardi [12 March] 1889, from New York, 15 March 1889, from Philadelphia, both translated from French.

51. CML to EF, Mardi V [7 May] 1889, from Chicago, translated from French; the resolution of the case is not given in Loeffler's letters.

52. Ibid.

53. CML to EF, 9 May 1889, from Milwaukee, Samedi [11 May] 1889, from St. Louis, Dimanche [12 May] 1889, from St. Louis, all translated from French.

54. CML to EF, Samedi [11 May] 1889.

55. CML to EF, Mercredi [8 May] 1889, from Chicago, translated from French.

56. CML to EF, 2d IV [2 May] 1889, from Buffalo, 9 May 1889, from Milwaukee, both translated from French.

57. CML to EF, Jeudi [16 May] 1889, from Pittsburgh, translated from French.

58. Ibid.

59. CML to EF, Vendredi [17 May] 1889, from Washington, translated from French.

60. Higginson, quoted in Howe, *BSO,* p. 62.

61. Gericke, quoted in Rogers, *The Story of Two Lives,* pp. 72–73.

CHAPTER 7

1. CML to EF, 2 IV [May] 1889, from Buffalo, translated from French.

2. DB to ISG, April 1888, from Boston.

3. Edward Weeks, ed., *The Tavern Club at Seventy-Five 1934–1959: A Medley* (Cambridge: Riverside Press, 1959), p. 144.

4. CML to EF, Dimanche [12 May] 1889, from St. Louis, translated from French.

5. DB to ISG, 23 July, 31 July 1889; DB to ISG, n.d., all from Medfield.

6. DB to ISG, n.d.

7. DB to ISG, 23 July 1889.

8. DB to ISG, 31 July 1889.

9. CML to EF, Jeudi matin [16 July] 1886, from Gloucester.

10. CML to EF, Jeudi 1888, from Washington, translated from French.

11. CML to EF, Jeudi soir [4 October], from Malden, 9 May 1890, from Cincinnati.

12. Rogers, *The Story of Two Lives,* pp. 248–49.

13. Nikisch, quoted in Howe, *BSO,* p. 91.

14. Rogers, *The Story of Two Lives,* p. 74.

15. *Gazette,* 9 February 1890; *Beacon,* 8 February 1890.

16. CML to EF, 1890, from Philadelphia, translated from French.

17. CML to EF, 9 May 1890, from Cincinnati, translated from French.

18. CML to EF, Jeudi 1888, from Washington, translated from French.

19. CML to EF, Vendredi 1890, from Richmond, translated from German.

20. CML to EF, n.d. 1890, translated from German, with the exception of the Dwight quotation written in English.

21. CML to EF, Dimanche soir [11 May] 1890, from Minneapolis.

22. Ibid.

23. CML to ISG, 1 September 1890, from Wayland.

24. Rogers, *The Story of Two Lives,* pp. 83–84.

25. CML to ISG, 1 September 1890.

26. Ibid.

27. CML to EF, Mercredi [12 November] 1890, from Philadelphia, translated from French.

28. CML to EF, [24 April 1891], from Southborough, translated from French.

29. CML to EF, Jeudi [13 August 1891], from Portsmouth, translated from French.

30. CML to EF, 9 May 1890, and Engel/Loeffler interview notes.

CHAPTER 8

1. H. Earle Johnson, *Symphony Hall, Boston* (Boston: Little, Brown, 1950), p. 37.

2. Edwin [*sic*] Burlingame Hill, "Musical Boston in the Gay Nineties: Halcyon Days at Harvard," *Etude* 67 (January 1949): 9.

3. Olin Downes, *New York Times* obituary.

4. Philip Hale, 9 January 1898, *Boston Journal.*

5. *Beacon,* 28 November 1891; *Boston Journal,* 23 November 1891.

6. *Boston Transcript,* 23 November 1891; *Beacon,* 28 November 1891; *Boston Home Journal,* 28 November 1891.

7. *Boston Gazette,* 29 November 1891; *Boston Courier,* 22 November 1891; *Musical Herald,* January 1892.

8. Elson, *History,* p. 217.

9. *Boston Sunday Herald,* 22 November 1891.

10. *Boston Post,* 4 January 1892; Philip Hale, *Boston Journal,* 4 January 1892.

11. CML to EF, Mercredi [27 April] 1892, from Baltimore.

12. *Boston Post,* 13 April 1892; *Boston Transcript,* 14 April 1892, p. 5.

13. *Boston Herald,* 13 April 1892.

14. Hale, *Boston Journal,* 13 April 1892, p. 5.

15. "Music of Loeffler," *Christian Science Monitor.*

16. CML to EF, 12 January 1893 from New York, translated from French.

17. CML to EF, Friday noon [10 February 1893], from New York, translated from French.

18. L. Elson, *Boston Daily Advertiser,* 28 February 1893; *Boston Transcript,* 28 February 1893, p. 5.

19. *Boston Journal,* 28 February 1893, p. 8.

20. CML to EF, n.d. "Friday noon" [10 February 1893]. Internal evidence suggests this undated letter was written before the Boston performance on the 27th; however, record of another performance has not been found.

21. *Boston Transcript,* 27 February 1893; *Beacon,* 4 March; *Boston Herald,* 26 February; *Boston Daily Advertiser,* 27 February; *Courier,* 26 February.

22. CML to EF, Samedi 1893, from Louisville, translated from French.

23. CML to EF, Mardi 1893, Chicago, translated from French.

24. Ibid.

25. Ibid.

26. Emil Paur, quoted in Howe, *BSO,* p. 100.

27. CML to ISG, 1894, from London.

28. CML to ISG, Wed. n.d., from Medfield.

29. *Boston Courier,* 4 February 1894.

30. *Boston Sunday Herald,* 4 February 1894; *Courier,* 4 February 1894.

31. *Musical and Dramatic World,* 10 February 1894.

32. *Boston Transcript,* 5 February 1894.

33. L. Elson, *Boston Daily Advertiser,* 5 February 1894.

34. Alfred H. Meyer, "Loeffler at Seventy Finds All Music Good," *Musical America* (January 25, 1931): 5.

35. *Boston Sunday Herald,* 18 February; *Boston Sunday Globe,* 18 February; *Courier,* 18 February; *Boston Transcript,* 19 February; *Boston Sunday Herald,* 18 February; *Boston Transcript,* 19 February 1894.

CHAPTER 9

1. CML to EF, [3 June] 1894, from London.

2. Ibid.

3. Ibid.

4. CML to EF, 15 June 1894.

5. CML to EF, 3 June 1894.

6. CML to EF, 10 June [1894], from Liège.

7. CML to EF, 15 June [1894] translated from French. Besides Hasselmann, Felix Godefroid is know to have been one of Helene's teachers.

8. CML to EF, 9 July 1894, from Paris, translated from French.

9. Ibid. The orchestration is given in CML to EF, 5 July 1894.

10. CML to EF, 5 July 1894, translated from French.

11. CML to EF, 9 July 1894.

12. Rogers, *The Story of Two Lives,* p. 249.

13. CML to EF, [15 July 1894], translated from French.

14. CML to EF, 20 June 1894, from Enghien, translated from French except the last sentence, which was written in English.

15. Lawrence Gilman, "The Music of Charles Martin Loeffler," *The Musician* 6 (October 1904): 1.

16. *New York Sun,* 15 January 1904.

17. "Music of Loeffler," *Christian Science Monitor.*

18. Downes, "Originality."

19. H.T.P., *Boston Evening Transcript,* 14 December 1906, p.13.

20. Hill, "Loeffler," 29.

21. Lawrence Gilman, "The Music of Loeffler," *North American Review* 193 (1911): 50–51.

22. CML to ISG, 10 August 1898, from Medfield.

23. *Boston Transcript,* 5 February 1894.

24. Downes, "Originality."

25. Philip Hale, *Boston Journal,* 4 February 1894; *New York Times,* 15 December 1899.

26. Arthur Shepherd, "'Papa' Goetschius in Retrospect," *The Musical Quarterly* 30 (July 1944): 308.

27. *New York Times,* 8 February 1895.

28. Loeffler used opus numbers inconsistently. A list of opus numbers in Loeffler's hand, dating from about 1901, is given in the right column. A list gleaned from numbers written on compositions is given to the left.

Opus	Opus
1 Divertimento pour violon	1 Sextet
	2 Quintet
3 Psalm 137	3 Veillées
	4 Divertimento
5 Quatre poèmes	5 viola songs
6 La mort de Tintagiles	6 Tintagiles
	7 L'archet
	8 Rapsodies
9 La villanelle du Diable	9 Bonne chanson
10 Quatre mélodies	10 Kahn songs
	11 Villanelle
	12 Poème paien
14 A Pagan Poem	[listed but not numbered]:
15 Four Poems	cello concerto
24 La mort de Tintagiles	2 saxophone pieces
(on 1 source)	romances
26 L'archet	octet [crossed off]

29. Philip Hale, *Musical Courier,* 9 January 1895, 26–27, 23 February 1898.

30. CML to ISG, 27 January 1895.

31. *Post,* 6 January 1895; *Boston Daily Advertiser,* 7 January 1895.

32. *Boston Sunday Herald,* 6 January 1895; *Boston Traveller,* 11 January 1897.

33. CML to ISG, 27 January 1895.

34. *Boston Gazette,* 10 January 1897; *Boston Transcript,* 11 January 1897.

35. CML to ISG, 27 January 1895.

36. CML to EF, [22 October 1904], from Homburg.

37. CML to ISG, 27 January 1895.

38. *New York Herald,* 8 February 1895.

39. CML to RA, n.d.

40. *Boston Daily Advertiser,* 19 February 1895; *Boston Transcript,* 19 February 1895, p. 5; *Courier,* BSO clipping.

41. Paul Rosenfeld, *Musical Portraits: An Interpretation of Twenty Modern Composers* (New York: Harcourt, Brace and Howe, 1920), pp. 257, 258, 261, 263, 264.

42. David Ewen, "Charles Martin Loeffler: 1861–1935," *The Chesterian* 16:122 (July-August 1935): 151–52.

43. Philip Hale, *New York Musical Courier,* 13 January 1897.

44. Gilman, "Music of Loeffler," *NA Review,* p. 50.

45. *New York Sun,* 13 January 1904.

46. Engel, "Loeffler," 325–26.

47. C. L. Capen, *Boston Journal,* 13 February 1897.

48. Apthorp, *Boston Transcript,* 15 February 1897.

49. CML to CE, 1 March 1925, from Medfield.

50. *Transcript,* 1 December 1897, p. 5; Philip Hale, "Music in Boston," *Musical Courier,* 8 December 1897, p. 26; "Themes and Topics in the Musical World," *New York Times,* 17 December 1899, 20:2.

51. Loeffler, quoted in Gilman's notes to New York Philharmonic program 1933.

52. "Town Topics" New York, 28 February 1901; Louis Elson, *Boston Daily Advertiser,* 10 January 1898.

53. Philip Hale, *Boston Journal,* 9 January 1898.

54. Cooke, interview with author.

55. *Boston Sunday Herald,* 9 January 1898.

56. Elson, *Boston Daily Advertiser,* 10 January 1898.

57. *Boston Courier,* 9 January 1898.

58. *Boston Sunday Herald,* 9 January 1898; *Boston Post,* 9 January 1898.

59. HEK, *New York Daily Tribune,* 1906; Elson, *Boston Daily Advertiser,* 10 January 1898.

60. Hale, quoted in Engel, "Loeffler," 320.

61. *Boston Herald,* 20 March 1898.

62. CML to ISG, 10 August 1898.

63. Elson, *Boston Daily Advertiser,* 27 November 1898; Apthorp, *Boston Transcript,* 27 November 1898.

64. RRG, "Music and Drama: Heinrich Gebhard's Concert," *Boston Transcript,* 15 March 1905.

65. [Lawrence Gilman], "Some Remarkable Songs," *Harpers Weekly* 48 (16 January 1904): 109.

CHAPTER 10

1. CML to EF, 17 May 1900, from the Columbia, translated in part from French.

2. CML to EF, 1 July 1900, from Homburg, translated from French.

3. CML to EF, [30 May 1900], from London.

4. Ibid.

5. CML to EF, 6 June 1900, from Homburg, translated from French.

6. CML to EF, 14 June 1900, from Homburg, translated from French.

7. CML to EF, 16 June 1900, from Homburg, translated from French

8. Lawrence Gilman, *Phases of Modern Music* (New York: Harper & Brothers, 1904), p. 65.

9. CML to EF, 14 June, 16 June 1900.

10. CML to EF, 22 July 1900, from London, translated from French.

11. CML to EF, 1 July 1900, translated from French.

12. Howe, *BSO,* p. 111.

13. Engel, "Loeffler," 326.

14. *Boston Transcript,* 30 January 1901, p. 18.

15. Philip Hale, "An Olla-Podrida," *Boston Sunday Journal,* Supplement 1.

16. *Boston Transcript,* 30 January 1901.

17. *Boston Herald,* 5 February 1902; Louis Elson, *Boston Daily Advertiser,* 5 February 1902.

18. *Boston Herald,* 5 February 1902; RRG, *Boston Transcript* [February 1902].

19. *Boston Journal* [February 1902].

20. RRG, *Boston Transcript,* 17 December 1901, p. 12; *Boston Journal,* 17 December 1901, p. 3.

21. Lawrence Gilman made reference to *The Sermon on the Mount* as though complete in 1911, but the only surviving manuscript is unfinished.

22. CML to WD, 28 March 1920.

23. RRG, *Boston Transcript,* 14 April 1902.

24. CML to ISG, n.d. Wed. [1902], from Dover.

25. Downes, "Originality."

26. Gebhard, *Reminiscences of a Boston Musician,* p. 3.

27. Ibid., pp. 10, 4–5. According to CML to ISG [1902] from Dover, the composition was finished in 1902.

28. CML to ISG, 1 January 1902. The year should be 1903.

29. Quoted in Louise Hall Tharp, *Mrs. Jack* (Boston: Little, Brown , 1965), p. 241.

30. CML to ISG, 4 January 1903.

31. Gebhard, *Reminiscences of a Boston Musician,* p. 5.

32. HG to ISG, 13 April 1905.

33. CML to ISG, 28 IV 1903.

34. *The World,* 16 January 1903.

35. CML to EF, Jeudi matin [6 November 1902], translated from French.

36. CML to EF, n.d., from New York, translated from French.

37. CML to WiG, 3d IV [4 May] 1903.

38. *Morning Telegraph,* 15 January 1904.

39. CML to ISG, Thursday [1904] from Boston.

40. Ibid.

41. CML to Rudolf Schirmer, Tuesday [26 July 1904], from Dover; Schirmer's reply is not known.

42. CML to EF, 8 October 1904, from Homburg.

43. CML to EF, 22 October 1904, from Homburg.

44. CML to EF, 8 October 1904.

45. EF to CML, 8 September, 21 September 1904, from Dover.

46. EF to CML, 8 September, 1904.

47. CML to EF, 20 September 1904, from Berlin.

48. EF to CML, 12 September 1904, from Dover.

49. CML to EF, 9 November 1904, from Paris, 29 September 1904, from Homburg.

CHAPTER 11

1. CML to GrS, 25 August 1904, from Dover.

2. CML to ISG, 10 August 1898, from Medfield.

3. CML to EF, 17 September 1904, from Homburg.

4. CML to EF, 20 September 1904, from Berlin.

5. CML to EF, 29 September 1904, from Homburg.

6. CML to EF, 20 September 1904.

7. CML to EF, 29 September 1904.

8. CML to ISG, 28 October 1904, from Homburg.

9. CML to EF, 20 September 1904.

10. CML to EF, 29 September 1904.

11. Ibid.

12. Ibid.

13. CML to EF, 8 October 1904, from Homburg.

14. Ibid.

15. Ibid.

16. CML to EF, 22 October 1904, from Homburg.

17. CML to ISG, 28 October 1904.

18. CML to EF, 22 October 1904.

19. Ibid.

20. CML to ISG, 28 October 1904.

21. CML to EF, 22 October 1904.

22. Ibid.

23. Ibid.

24. CML to EF, 31 October 1904, from Paris.

25. CML to EF, 8 October, 31 October 1904.

26. Downes, "Originality," 1910; "Music of Loeffler," *Christian Science Monitor;* Meyer, "Loeffler at Seventy."

27. CML to EF, 22 October 1904.

28. CML to GS, 15 March [1905], from Vienna.

29. Ibid.

30. CML to EF, 29 November 1904, from Paris.

31. Margaret Chanler, *Memory Makes Music* (New York: Stephan-Paul Publishers, 1948), p. 122.

32. CML to GrS, 17 January 1912.

33. CML to GS, 15 November 1904, from Paris.

34. CML to EF, 9 November 1904, from Paris.

35. Ibid.

36. CML to GS, 12 June 1906.

37. CML to EF, 9 November 1904, translated from French.

38. CML to ISG, 28 October 1904.

39. CML to GS, 15 November 1904.

40. CML to GrS, 8 January 1905, from Homburg.

41. CML to EF, 21 November [1904], from Paris.

42. CML to EF, 9 November 1904, 21 November [1904].

43. CML to EF, 9 November 1904.

44. CML to EF, 21 November 1904.

45. Ibid.

46. CML to GrS, 1 October 1906, from Medfield.

47. CML to EF, 29 November 1904.

48. CML to EF, 21 November 1904.

49. "Music of Loeffler," *Christian Science Monitor.*

50. CML to EF, 29 November 1904.

51. Downes, "Originality."

52. CML to EF, 29 November 1904.

53. Ibid.

54. CML to WD, 16 July 1905.

55. CML to EF, 12 December 1904, n.p.

56. CML to GrS, 8 January 1905, to EF, 3 May [1905], from Paris, to GrS, 6 October 1929.

57. CML to EF, 22 October 1904.

58. EY to Mme Chausson, 18 October 1904, from Bruxelles, copy made by CML.

59. CML to EF, 9 November 1904.

60. CML to EF, 12 December 1904.

61. CML to WD, 28 August 1907.

62. CML to GrS, 8 January 1905.

63. Ibid.

64. CML to EF, 21 November 1904.

65. Damrosch, "Loeffler," pp. 172–73.
66. Downes, "Originality."
67. Alexander Steinert, telephone interview with author, New York, 23 October 1980.
68. CML to GrS, 29 V 1912.
69. CML to ESC, 30 December 1925.
70. CML to HS, 4 September 1931.
71. Winn, "Charles Martin Loeffler," p. 25.
72. CML to GS, 25 August 1904.
73. CML to EF, 15 February 1905, from Berlin.
74. CML to EF, 3 May 1905.
75. CML to EF, 15 February 1905, from Berlin.
76. ChE to CML, 4 August 1905.
77. EF to CML, 14 November 1904.
78. CML to EF, 29 November 1904.
79. CML to EF, 8 October 1904.
80. CML to GrS, 25 August 1904.
81. CML to EF, 3 May 1905.
82. CML to EF, 3 May 1905.

CHAPTER 12

1. CML to GrS, 16 December 1906.
2. Gilman, "Copy of Philharmonic Symphony Broadcast" (Sunday, April 14, 1935), p. 3.
3. CML to OS, 5 April 1923, quoted in Reese, *A Birthday Offering to CE,* p. 158.
4. Meyer, "Loeffler at Seventy."
5. Downes, "Career."
6. "Music of Loeffler," *Christian Science Monitor.*
7. Lawrence Gilman, "Mr. Loeffler's Music," *Harper's Weekly* 50 (3 February 1906): 168.
8. Engel, "Loeffler," 313; Philip Hale, "Charles Martin Loeffler," Boston Music Company Bulletin (New York: G. Schirmer, Inc., n.d. [1931]), p. 5.
9. Gilman, "Music of Loeffler," *NA Review,* p. 57.
10. Mason, *Dilemma,* p. 7.
11. Hill, "Loeffler," 30.
12. CML to GrS, Tuesday [28 November 1905].
13. D. G. Mason, *Music in My Time, and Other Reminiscences* (New York: Macmillan, 1938), p. 78.
14. CML to WD, 14 October [1905], NYPL.
15. CML to WD, 23 January 1910.
16. ChE to CML, 17 October 1906.
17. The titles Loeffler gave at this time to Grace Schirmer were "The Host of the Air," "The Hosting of the Sidhe," and "The Travail of Passion," the third of which is mentioned nowhere but in this letter, 1 October 1906.

18. EF to ISG, 1 September [1906].

19. *Boston Transcript,* unidentified clipping, MHS.

20. EF to ISG, 1 September [1906].

21. CML to GrS, 9 December 1906.

22. *Boston Journal,* 25 November 1907; HTP, *Boston Transcript,* 23 November 1907.

23. Philip Hale, *Boston Herald,* 24 November 1907; Lawrence Gilman, "An Orchestral Master Work," *Harper's Weekly* 51 (7 December 1907): 1810.

24. Gebhard, *Reminiscences of a Boston Musician,* p. 6.

25. D.L.L., "Loeffler's Ardent Boston Champion," *Musical America* (12 February 1910): 9.

26. *Christian Science Monitor.*

27. Linton Martin clipping.

28. Nominating papers, American Academy files.

29. CML to GrS, 9 December 1906, 17 January 1907.

30. Medfield interview, unidentified MHS clipping.

31. CML to GrS, 9 December 1906.

32. CML described *Poème mystique* to GrS, 24 March 1907, and mentioned the carol to GrS, 21 December 1907.

33. CML to GrS, 8 July 1908.

34. CML to GrS, 26 August 1908.

35. *Boston Herald,* 9 April 1909, p. 9.

36. Unidentified clipping in Hale scrapbooks, BPL.

37. Gebhard, *Reminiscences of a Boston Musician,* pp. 12–13. Gebhard gives 1911 as the date, but the abbey guest book cannot confirm this and no record of a 1911 visit by Loeffler to Europe exists.

38. CML to GrS, 14 June 1909, from Frankfurt am Main.

39. CML to ISG, 26 January 1923.

40. CML to GrS, 29 V 1912.

41. CML to EF, 25 May 1883, from Keokuk, and 14 May 1883, from Memphis, both translated from French.

42. CML to ISG, 12 June 1909, from Frankfurt.

43. CML to WD, 23 January 1910.

44. Engel, "Views," 370–71.

CHAPTER 13

1. Nellie F. Walton, "Remodeling a Massachusetts Farmhouse," *American Homes and Gardens,* August 1914, 262. The article was rewritten as a chapter in Mary H. Northend, *Remodeled Farmhouses* (Boston: Little, Brown, 1915).

2. CML to ISG, Tuesday, n.d.

3. Ibid.

4. CML to EF, 30 May 1900, from London, translated from French (part was originally written in English).

5. CML to EF, 9 November [1904], from Paris.

6. CML to EF, Thursday [29 November 1924], from Cleveland.

7. WmD to CE, 9 July 1935.

8. Gebhard, *Reminiscences of a Boston Musician,* p. 3.

9. CML to DH, n.d., MHS.

10. CML to GrS, 8 January 1905, from Homburg.

11. Frank Benson, memorial address, TC.

12. Engel, "Views," 373–75.

13. CML to WD, 28 January 1920.

14. EF to ISG, 5 August n.y.

15. Medfield interview, MHS.

16. CML to Alexander Steinert, 27 May 1923, NYPL.

17. Winn, "Charles Martin Loeffler," pp. 24, 25.

18. Engel, "Views," 373.

19. Grace Deeran, conversation with author, 1981.

20. HS to author, 8 August 1981.

21. SG to author, 23 August 1981.

22. Irene Forte, interview with author, West Newton, 3 June 1983.

23. Damrosch, "Loeffler," p. 175.

24. Gebhard, *Reminiscences of a Boston Musician,* p. 9.

25. Eleanor Diemer to the author, 22 January 1981.

26. Marian Lawrence Peabody, *To Be Young Was Very Heaven* (Boston: Houghton Mifflin, 1967), p. 73.

27. Benson, Memorial address, TC.

28. Gebhard, *Reminiscences of a Boston Musician,* pp. 4, 11–12.

29. CML to AL, 6 November 1917.

30. CML to CE, 21 December 1924.

31. CML to AL, 23 February 1919.

32. AL to CML, 1 October 1918.

33. Engel, "Loeffler," 327.

34. Ibid, pp. 327–28.

CHAPTER 14

1. Henry Russell, *The Passing Show* (Boston: Little, Brown, 1926), p. 157.

2. CML to GrS, 21 December 1907.

3. CML to ISG, 24 November 1910.

4. CML to ISG, Friday, n.d.

5. Isabel Parker Semler, *Horatio Parker: A Memoir for His Grandchildren Compiled from Letters and Papers* (New York: G. P. Putnam's Sons, 1942), pp. 229–30.

6. WD to Cravath, 14 April 1911, NYPL.

7. WD to CML, 14 April 1911.

8. Quoted in Elizabeth A. Sharp, *William Sharp (Fiona MacLeod): A Memoir* (London: William Heinemann, 1910), p. 390.

9. CML to WD, 2 March 1913.

10. CML to ISG, 22 May 1912.

11. CML to WD, Sunday, n.d.

12. CML to ISG, 28 XII 1912.

13. CML to ISG, 28 October 1904, from Homburg.

14. EF to ISG, 1 September [1906], Medfield.

15. CML to ISG, 21 February 1920.

16. Gilman, "Music of Loeffler," *NA Review,* p. 53.

17. *Gazette de Lausanne et Journal Suisse,* 2 Juin 1910, p. 2, translated from French.

18. PG to CML, 15 October 1914.

19. *Sun,* 15 January 1913.

20. Gebhard, *Reminiscences of a Boston Musician,* p. 10.

CHAPTER 15

1. CML to GrS, 1 April 1918.

2. AC to CML, 15 September 1914.

3. CML to AL, 6 November 1914.

4. CML to WD, n.d.

5. CML to ISG, 6 January 1914.

6. Meyer, "Loeffler at Seventy."

7. Lawrence Gilman, "A Pilgrimage to Quietude," *The North American Review* 204 (1916): 137.

8. Henry Gilbert, "The American Composer," *Musical Quarterly* 1 (1915): 174–75.

9. CML to AL, 19 May 1916.

10. Gilman, "Pilgrimage," p. 137.

11. LS to CML, 4 April 1923, quoted in Oliver Daniel, *Stokowski: A Counterpoint of View* (New York: Dodd, Mead, 1982), p. 224.

12. Olin Downes, *Boston Post,* 3 March 1917; HTP, *Boston Transcript,* 3 March 1917, both BSO clippings.

13. PC to CML, 9 January 1917, translated from French.

14. Unidentified clipping, MHS; Olin Downes, "Three Artists in One Concert," *Boston Sunday Post,* 25 March 1917, p. 32.

15. CML to CE, 31 March 1925.

16. EF to ISG, 1917.

17. Engel, "Loeffler," 327.

18. Gebhard, *Reminiscences of a Boston Musician,* p. 13.

19. CML to JJC, 10 Octobre 1917.

20. CML to ISG, 19 November 1919.

21. An analysis of this work by the author has been published in *American Music* 2/3 (Fall 1984): 66–83.

22. AB to CML, 14 September 1918, translated from French.

23. CML to AL, 31 March 1918; AL to CML, 24 September 1918.

24. CML to AL, 21 March 1918.

25. CML to HC, draft, n.d.[1918], translated from French.

26. CML to GrS, 1 April 1918.

27. CML to GrS, 9 December 1906.

28. CML to WD, 1 April 1913.

29. Cooke interview.

30. CML to HS, 4 September 1931.

31. CML to ISG, 11 January 1920, 17 November 1918.

32. Ibid.

33. CML to CE, 6 February 1917.

34. CML to ISG, 17 November 1918.

35. CML to ISG, 11 January 1920.

36. Ibid.

37. CML to JSS, 18 March 1921, Richard Ormond Collection.

38. GF to CML, 10 November 1921, from French.

39. VI to CML, 28 October 21, translated from French.

40. CML to AS, 27 May 1923, NYPL.

41. CML to WD, 3 Feburary 1920.

42. CML to WD, 28 March 1920.

43. CML to WD, CML to WD, 28 February 1920.

44. WD to CML, 13 March 1920.

45. CML to ISG, 17 IV 1920.

46. CML to CE, 6 September 1924.

CHAPTER 16

1. Quoted in Percy Lee Atherton, "Boston Days (1909–1922): Some Engeliana," in Reese, *A Birthday Offering to CE*, p. 32.

2. Ibid.

3. Mason, *Music in My Time*, p. 78.

4. PA to CML, 18 March 1917.

5. CC to CML, 6 March 1917, 16 December 1924.

6. FC to CML, 10 January 1902, 11 March 1920.

7. WD to CML, 25 January 1910.

8. HE to CML, 19 February 1925.

9. WG to CML, 3 November 1918.

10. EBH to CML, 4 March 1917.

11. BJL to CML, n.d.

12. DGM to CML, 25 October 1921, 17 March 1922.

13. ArS to CML, 11 November 1921.

14. AW to CML, 9 October 1914.

15. Walter Raymond Spalding, *Music at Harvard* (New York: Coward-McCann, Inc., 1935), p. 329.

16. Hill, "Loeffler," 31.

17. *New York Times,* 18 January 1921, 14:1.

18. *New York Times,* 24 June 1926, 8:1.

19. Charles Henry Meltzer, "How Music Should Be Helped in America," *Arts and Decoration* 12/5 (March 25, 1920): 321.

20. CML to ESC, 18 August 1918.

21. CML to ISG, 11 January 1920.

22. CML to ISG, 29 January 1920, n.d. Monday.

23. CML to WD, quoted in Damrosch, *Life,* pp. 150–51.

24. As recorded by Atherton, "Boston Days," p. 28.

25. CML to WG, 30 May 1919, NEC.

26. "Music of Loeffler," *Christian Science Monitor.*

27. Ibid.

28. "Composer of Musical Masterpieces," *Hampton's Magazine* 26 (January 1911): 120.

29. "Music of Loeffler," *Christian Science Monitor.*

30. Arthur Shepherd, quoted in Richard Loucks, *Arthur Shepherd: American Composer* (Provo, Utah: Brigham Young University Press, 1980), p. 12.

31. Deems Taylor, *Of Men and Music* (New York: Simon and Schuster, 1945), pp. 140–41.

32. CML to GrS, Tuesday [28 November 1905].

33. *Wa-Wan Press Monthly.*

34. Edward N. Waters, "The Wa-Wan Press," in Reese, *A Birthday Offering to CE,* p. 219.

35. AS to EW, 30 March 1943, quoted in Loucks, *Arthur Shepherd,* p. 12.

36. Arthur Shepherd, quoted in ibid., p. 12.

37. Steinert interview.

38. Swift interview.

39. Louise Varèse, *Varèse: A Looking-Glass Diary, Volume 1: 1883–1928* (New York: W. W. Norton , 1972), p. 140.

40. Aaron Copland, *Music and Imagination* (Cambridge: Harvard University Press, 1953), p. 102.

41. Lawrence Gilman, *Boston Transcript,* 30 January 1931.

42. CML to CE, 22 May 1926, 6 February 1917.

43. CML to ISG, 25 January 1920.

44. CML to ISG, 29 January 1920.

45. CML to ISG, 29 July 1920.

46. H. T. Parker, *Boston Evening Transcript,* 11 March 1922; Olin Downes, *Boston Post,* 11 March 1922.

47. Ibid.

48. CML to GrS, 26 March 1922.

49. A description of the catalog is to be found in CML to CE, 25 July 1922.

50. CML to CE, 22 May 1922; to ISG, 22 March 1921; to CE, 22 May 1922.

51. CML to FK, 6 July 1923, translated from German, NYPL.

52. CML to OS, 3 August 1923, quoted in Reese, *A Birthday Offering to CE,* p. 159.

53. Elizabeth Babcock, telephone interview with author, Concord, 20 January 1981.

54. CML to CE, 22 May 1922.

55. PM to CML, 12 June 1924, translated from French.

56. CML to ISG, 11 January; to RA, 31 January 1920.

57. HR to CML, 18 May 1924, translated from French.

58. HL to CML, 11.5.26, translated from French.

59. Taylor, *Of Men and Music,* pp. 137–39.

60. LWS to CML, 31 May 1924.

61. CML to ESC, 18 November 1924.

62. Ibid.

63. Lawrence Gilman, *New York Herald Tribune,* 20 December 1925.

64. CML to CE, IV 1925.

65. Richard Aldrich, "Open Washington's New Music Hall," *New York Times* (29 October 1925), p. 28.

66. CML to ESC, 30 December 1925.

67. CML to CE, 25 December 1925.

68. CML to SK, 16 March 1929, translated from French.

69. HL to CML, 12.9.27, translated from French.

70. CML to RA, 18 September 1924.

71. CML to RA, 22 September 1924.

72. Medfield residents remember Juilliard students boarding there.

73. CML to EF, 20 November 1924, from Cleveland.

74. CML to EF, 3 October 1925, from Barrytown, 12 October 1924, from New York.

75. CML to EF, 23 October 1924, from Chicago.

76. CML to WD, 16 July 1905, NYPL.

77. CML to EF, 27 V 1925, from Evanston.

78. CML to EF, 27 V 1925.

79. CML to EF, 26 May 1925, from Evanston, 27 May 1925.

80. CML to EF, 23 November 1925, from Chicago.

81. CML to EF, 25 November, 27 November 1924, both from Cleveland.

82. CML to CE, 9 November 1924, from Philadelphia; to EF, 6 March, from Philadelphia, 8 March 1927. These "March" 1927 letters were acutally written in April.

83. CML to EF, 8 March 1927.

84. Ibid.

85. CML to EF, 10 January 1930, from New York.

86. CML to EF, 8 October 1924, from New York, 4 November 1924, from Philadelphia.

87. CML to GrS, 8 August 1923.

88. CML to CE, 21 December 1924.

89. CML to RA, 18 September 1924.

90. St. Botolph Club, Constitution and By-Laws, Boston, 1978.

91. Harold Bauer, *His Book* (New York: W. W. Norton, 1948), p. 156.

92. CML to ISG, 9 December 1920.

93. CML to RA, 18 September 1924.

94. PF to CML, 24 March 1925.

95. CML to EC, quoted in Charteris, *John Sargent,* pp. 148–49.

96. CML to CE, 2 III 1926.

CHAPTER 17

1. CML to SG, 20 December 1925.
2. Swift interview.
3. Engel, "Views," 375.
4. CML to KSW, 17 April 1927.
5. EF to ISG, 3 January 1920.
6. CML to ISG, 29 January 1920.
7. CML, draft in LC.
8. CML to SG, 20 December 1925.
9. Swift interview.
10. Ibid.
11. CML to KSW, 17 April 1927.
12. CML to GG, 27 June 1927.
13. Gebhard/Colvin interview.
14. CML to GG, 27 June 1927.
15. CML to GG, 10 March 1928.
16. CML to GG, 20 December 1928.
17. Ibid.
18. CML to GG, 3 January 1932.
19. CML to GrS, 1 February 1932.
20. CML to CE, 19 June 1929.
21. John Erskine, "MacDowell at Columbia: Some Recollections," *MQ* 28 (October 1942): 400.
22. CML to ISG, March 1921.
23. CML to ESC, n.d.
24. CML to ESC, 10 April 1930.
25. Arthur Lourié, *Serge Koussevitzky and His Epoch,* trans. S. W. Pring (New York: Alfred A. Knopf, 1931), p. 224.
26. Meyer, "Loeffler at Seventy."
27. Loeffler, quoted in John Bird, *Percy Grainger* (London: Paul Elek, 1976), p. 157.
28. Downes, "Originality."
29. CML to EF, 8 March 1927.
30. Meyer, "Loeffler at Seventy."
31. CML to CE, 27 February 1927.
32. CML to CE, 22 May 1922.
33. CML to ESC, 9 November 1925.

CHAPTER 18

1. CML to GrS, 2 February 1930.
2. CML to CE, 27 February 1927.
3. Mrs. Joel Goldthwaite, telephone interview with author, Medfield, 1982.
4. CML to GMW, 27 December 1932.

5. CML to GMW, 27 June 1930.

6. CML to CE, 22 December 1929.

7. CML to NS, 27 February 1927.

8. Ibid.

9. The vibraharp, built by J. C. Deagan, is now owned by the Oberlin Conservatory of Music.

10. CML to APH, quoted in Adella Prentiss Hughes, *Music Is My Life* (Cleveland: World Publishing Company, 1947), p. 83.

11. Sent to CML by WG, 26 April 1934.

12. CML to HS, 4 September; to HR, 4 September 1931.

13. Text of cable quoted in the *New York Times,* April 2, 1933, 1:2.

14. CML to HK, 18 June 1930.

15. Grace Deeran, conversation with author.

16. Engel, "Views," 371–72.

17. William Dolan to CE, 25 August 1936.

18. Ewen, "Charles Martin Loeffler: 1861–1935"; Linton Martin, "Themes and Variations," *Philadelphia Inquirer* (26 May 1935); Olin Downes, *New York Times,* 26 May 1935.

19. W. J. Henderson, *New York Sun,* 25 May 1935.

20. Frank Benson, TC Memorial.

21. Engel, "Views," 368, 370, 375.

CHAPTER 19

1. Olin Downes, "Career of Charles Martin Loeffler: The Evolution of a Modern Master—His Sympathies with and Expression of His Age—His Distinguished and Solitary Art," *New York Times,* 8 February 1931, X, 8:1.

2. Lawrence Gilman, "Philharmonic Broadcast," p. 2.

3. CML to HB, 16 June 1919.

4. CML to CE, 10 May 1924.

5. Rosenfeld, *Portraits.*

6. Smith, "Loeffler and His Music."

7. For example, Copland, who dismissed Loeffler as an ivory tower composer (quoted in chapter 16), confessed to the author in correspondence that he did not know the music of Loeffler well enough to form a personal opinion.

8. Spalding, *Music,* p. 329.

9. Earl Luther Henry points up the danger of strict comparison of Loeffler to Debussy in his dissertation, "Impressionism in the Arts and Its Influence on Selected Works by Charles Martin Loeffler and Charles Tomlinson Griffes" (University of Cincinnati, 1976), by examining Loeffler's music via a point-by-point comparison with Debussy's and unjustly evaluating his style and his position as an Impressionist by how closely he duplicated Debussy's vocabulary and practice.

10. Unidentified Boston critic quoted in unsigned, "Hybrid Musician," *MD,* March 1961, pp. 164.

11. James Huneker, "The Seven Arts," *Puck* 67 (May 8, 1915): 10.

12. Loeffler, quoted in "Music of Loeffler," *Christian Science Monitor.*

13. Oscar Thompson, *New York Evening Post,* 13 February 1931.

14. Philip Hale, *Boston Journal,* 9 January 1898; Engel, "Loeffler," 313; Hill, "Loeffler," 31.

15. Henderson, *New York Sun,* 9 April 1934.

BIBLIOGRAPHY

Atherton, Percy Lee. "Boston Days (1909–1922): Some Engeliana." In *A Birthday Offering to CE*. Edited by Gustave Reese. New York: G. Schirmer, 1943, pp. 27–34.

Ayars, Christine Merrick. *Contributions to the Art of Music in America by the Industries of Boston 1640–1936*. New York: H. W. Wilson, 1937.

Bauer, Harold. *His Book*. New York: W. W. Norton, 1948.

Benson, Frank. "Charles Martin Loeffler." Typescript memorial address, May 1936, delivered to the Tavern Club, Boston, Tavern Club Archives.

Bird, John. *Percy Grainger*. London: Paul Elek, 1976.

Brummer, Franz. *Lexikon der deutschen Dichter und Prosaisten vom beginn des 19. Jahrhunderts bis zur Gegenwarte*. 6th ed. Leipzig: P. Reclam Jun., 1913. Reprint. Nendeln/Liechtenstein: Kraus Reprint, 1975.

Busoni, Ferrucio. *Letters to His Wife*. Translated by Rosamund Ley. London: Edward Arnold, 1938.

"C. M. T. Loeffler, Dean of American Composers, Dies," *New York Post*, 21 May 1935.

Carter, Morris. *Isabella Stewart Gardner and Fenway Court*. Boston: Houghton Mifflin, 1925.

Chanler, Margaret. *Memory Makes Music*. New York: Stephan-Paul, 1948.

Chapman, Victor. *Victor Chapman's Letters from France*. Memoir by John Jay Chapman. New York: Macmillan, 1917.

"Charles Loeffler, Composer, Is Dead," *New York Times*, 21 May 1935.

"Charles M. T. Loeffler, 74, Dies; Composer Ranked with Great," *New York Herald Tribune*, 21 May 1935.

Charteris, Evan. *John Sargent*. New York: Charles Scribner's Sons, 1927.

Cohen, Paul. "The Saxophone Music of Charles Martin Loeffler." *The Saxophone Symposium* 6/4 (Fall 1981): 10–17.

Colvin, Otis Herbert, Jr. "Charles Martin Loeffler: His Life and Works." 2 vols. Ph.D. dissertation, University of Rochester, Eastman School of Music, 1957.

"Composer of Musical Masterpieces," *Hampton's Magazine* 26 (January 1911): 120.

Cooke, George Willis. *John Sullivan Dwight: Brook-Farmer, Editor, and*

Critic of Music. Boston: Small, Maynard, 1898. Reprint. New York: Da Capo Press, 1969.

Coolidge, Arlen R. "Loeffler, Patrician of Music Passes," *Musical America,* 25 May 1935, p. 6.

Copland, Aaron. *Music and Imagination.* Cambridge: Harvard University Press, 1953.

Cowell, Henry, ed. *American Publishers on American Music: A Symposium.* New York: Frederick Ungar, 1933.

Damon, S. Foster. *Amy Lowell: A Chronicle, with Extracts from Her Correspondence.* Boston: Houghton Mifflin, 1935.

Damrosch, Walter. "Charles Martin Loeffler." Commemorative Tribute, Academy Publication no. 88. New York: American Academy of Arts and Letters, 1936.

———. *My Musical Life.* New York: Charles Scribner's Sons, 1940.

Daniel, Oliver. *Stokowski: A Counterpoint of View.* New York: Dodd, Mead, 1982.

Dowd, Aelred. "A Descriptive Catalog of the Loeffler Collection of the Library of Congress Music Division." M.S., Catholic University of America, 1959.

Downes, Olin. "Career of Charles Martin Loeffler: The Evolution of a Modern Master—His Sympathies with and Expression of His Age—His Distinguished and Solitary Art." *New York Times,* 8 February 1931, X, 8:1.

———. "Charles Martin Loeffler." *New York Times,* 26 May 1935, 2:5.

———. "Henry Gilbert: Nonconformist." In *A Birthday Offering to C E.* Edited by Gustave Reese. New York: G. Schirmer, 1943, pp. 88–94.

———. "Originality in Composer's Art Means Sophistication, Says Loeffler." *Musical America* (16 April 1910): 3.

Eaton, Quaintance. *The Boston Opera Company.* New York: Appleton-Century, 1965.

Elson, Louis C. *The History of American Music.* Revised to 1925 by Arthur Elson. New York: Macmillan, 1925.

Emigration and Immigration. Reports of the Consular Office of the United States. Washington, D.C.: Government Printing Office, 1887.

Engel, Carl. "Charles Martin Loeffler," In *Great Modern Composers.* Edited by Oscar Thompson. New York: Dodd, Mead, 1941, pp. 158–79.

———. "Charles Martin Loeffler." *Musical Quarterly* 11 (1925): 311–30.

———. "Loeffler, Charles Martin Tornov." *Corbett's Cyclopedic Survey of Chamber Music* (1963), 2:101–2.

———. "Views and Reviews." *Musical Quarterly* 10 (1924): 296–98.

———. "Views and Reviews." *Musical Quarterly* 21 (1935): 368–75.

Erskine, John. "MacDowell at Columbia: Some Recollections." *Musical Quarterly* 28 (October 1942): 395–405.

Ewen, David. "Charles Martin Loeffler: 1861–1935." *Chesterian* 16/122 (July-August 1935): 149–52.

Farwell, Arthur, and W. Dermot Darby, eds. *Music in America.* Vol. 4 of *The*

Art of Music Edited by D. G. Mason. New York: National Society of Music, 1935.

Favre, Georges. *Un haut-lieu musical niçois au xixe siècle: La villa Valrose (1870–1881).* Paris: Editions A. et J. Picard, n.d. [1977].

Foote, Arthur. *An Autobiography.* Norwood, Mass.: Plimpton Press, 1946. Reprint. New York: Da Capo Press, 1979.

————. "Thirty-Five Years in Boston." *Harvard Musical Review* 1/1 (October 1912): 9.

Franko, Sam. *Chords and Dischords: Memoirs of an American Musician.* New York: Viking Press, 1938.

"From the Correspondence of Charles Martin Loeffler." In *A Birthday Offering to C[arl] E[ngel].* Edited by Gustave Reese. New York: G. Schirmer, 1943.

Gardner, Samuel. "Reminiscences of Samuel Gardner: Playing in the Kneisel Quartet, 1914–15." *Journal of the Violin Society of America* 2/3 (Summer 1976): 20–29.

Gebhard, Heinrich. "Reminiscences of a Boston Musician." Privately printed, n.d.

Gilbert, Henry. "The American Composer." *Musical Quarterly* 1 (1915): 169–80.

Gilman, Lawrence. "Concerning Charles Martin Loeffler." *New Music Review* (December 1905): 572–74.

————. "Copy of Philharmonic Broadcast." Typescript. 4 April 1934.

————. *Edward MacDowell: A Study.* New York, 1908. Reprint. New York: Da Capo Press, 1969.

————. "Loeffler at Seventy." *New York Herald-Tribune,* 1 February 1931. Reprint. New York: G. Schirmer, [1931]. [bound with Hale].

————. "Maeterlinck in Music." *Harper's Weekly* (20 January 1906): 59.

————. "Mr. Loeffler's Music." *Harper's Weekly* 50 (3 February 1906): 168.

————. "The Music of Charles Martin Loeffler." *Musician* 9 (October 1904): 1–2.

————. "The Music of Loeffler." *North American Review* 193 (1911): 47–59.

————. *Nature in Music and Other Studies in the Tone-Poetry of Today.* New York: John Lane, 1914.

————. "An Orchestral Master Work." *Harper's Weekly* 51 (7 December 1907): 1810.

————. *Phases of Modern Music.* New York: Harper & Brothers, 1904.

————. "A Pilgrimage to Quietude." *North American Review* 204 (1916): 135–38.

————. "Seventy Years Now Bear Him Witness." *Boston Transcript,* 30 January 1931, p. 9.

Hale, Philip. "Charles Martin Loeffler." From Boston Music Company Bulletin. Reprint. New York: G. Schirmer Inc., [1931] [Bound with Gilman.]

Henderson, W. J. "Charles Martin Loeffler." *New York Sun,* 25 May 1935.

Henry, Earl Luther. "Impressionism in the Arts and Its Influence on Selected Works by Charles Martin Loeffler and Charles Tomlinson Griffes." Ph.D. dissertation, University of Cincinnati, 1976.

Henschel, Sir George. *Musings and Memories of a Musician.* New York: Macmillan, 1919. Reprint. New York: Da Capo Press, 1979.

Hill, Edward Burlingame. "Charles Martin Loeffler." *Modern Music* 13 (1935): 26–31.

———. *Modern French Music.* Boston: Houghton Mifflin, 1924.

———. "Musical Boston in the Gay Nineties: Halcyon Days at Harvard." *Etude* 67 (January 1949): 9, 53, 55.

Howard, John Tasker. *Our American Music.* 4th ed. New York: Thomas Y. Crowell, 1935.

———. *Our Contemporary Composers.* New York: Thomas Y. Crowell, 1941.

Howe, Helen. *The Gentle Americans, 1864–1960: Biography of a Breed.* New York: Harper & Row, 1965.

Howe, M. A. Dewolfe. *The Boston Symphony Orchestra 1881–1931.* Revised edition with John N. Burk. Boston: Houghton Mifflin, 1931.

———. *A Partial (and not impartial) Semi-Centennial History of the Tavern Club, 1884–1934.* Cambridge: Riverside Press, 1935.

Hughes, Adella Prentiss. *Music Is My Life.* Cleveland: World, 1947.

Huneker, James Gibbons. *Letters of James Gibbons Huneker.* Edited by Josephine Huneker. New York: Charles Scribner's Sons, 1922.

———. *The Philharmonic Society of New York and Its Twenty-Fifth Anniversary.* [New York: Philharmonic Society, 1917].

———. "The Seven Arts." *Puck* 77 (8 May 1915): 10.

Johns, Clayton. *Reminiscences of a Musician.* Cambridge: Washburn & Thomas, 1929.

Johnson, H. Earle. *Symphony Hall, Boston.* Boston: Little, Brown, 1950.

Knight, Ellen. "Charles Martin Loeffler and George Gershwin: A Forgotten Friendship." *American Music* 3/4 (Winter 1985): 452–59.

———. "The Evolution of Loeffler's 'Music for Four Stringed Instruments.'" *American Music* 2/3 (Fall 1984): 66–83.

L., D. L. "Loeffler's Ardent Boston Champion." *Musical America* (12 February 1910), p. 9.

L. R.,/P. M. "Les Musiciens des Etats-Unis et leurs rapports avec la France." *Le courier musical de France* 55 (1976): 91–95.

Lahee, Henry C. *Annals of Music in America.* Boston: Marshall Jones, 1922.

Leichentritt, Hugo. *Serge Koussevitzky: The Boston Symphony Orchestra and the New American Music.* Cambridge, Mass.: Harvard University Press, 1947.

Locke, Ralph P. "Charles Martin Loeffler: Composer at Court." *Fenway Court* (1974): 30–37.

Löffler, Karl. *Die chinesische Zuckerrohr (Kao-Lien).* Braunschweig: Friedrich Vieweg und Sohn, 1859.

———. *Die Lehre von der Landwirthschaft.* Berlin: Theodor Thiele, n.d.

———. *Ueber die Runkelrübenzucker-Fabrikation Frankreichs*. Berlin: Theodor Thiele, 1863.

Löffler, Karl, and Peter von Papi-Balogh. *Die nordamerikanische zuckerfabrikation aus Sorgo und Imphy und deren hohe Wichtigkeit für Deutschland, Ungarn und die Schweiz*. Debreczin: Carl von Csáthy jun., 1868.

Loucks, Richard. *Arthur Shepherd: American Composer*. Provo, Utah: Brigham Young University Press, 1980.

Lourié, Arthur. *Sergei Koussevitzky and His Epoch*. Translated by S. W. Pring. New York: Alfred A. Knopf, 1931.

Maisel, Edward M. *Charles T. Griffes: The Life of an American Composer*. New York: Alfred A. Knopf, 1943. Reprint. New York: Da Capo Press, 1972.

Martin, Linton. "Themes and Variations." *Philadelphia Inquirer*, 26 May 1935.

Mason, Daniel Gregory. *The Dilemma of American Music, and Other Essays*. New York: Macmillan, 1928.

———. *Music in My Time, and Other Reminiscences*. New York: Macmillan, 1938.

———. *Tune In, America: A Study of Our Coming Musical Independence*. New York: Alfred A. Knopf, 1931.

Meltzer, Charles Henry. "How Music Should be Helped in America." *Arts and Decoration*, 12/5 (25 March 1920): 320–21, 350.

Meyer, Alfred H. "Loeffler at Seventy Finds All Music Good." *Musical America* (25 January 1931): 5.

"The Music of Charles Martin Loeffler." *Christian Science Monitor* (29 January 1910).

Northend, Mary H. *Remodeled Farmhouses*. Boston: Little, Brown, 1915.

Peabody, Marian Lawrence. *To Be Young Was Very Heaven*. Boston: Houghton Mifflin, 1967.

Reese, Gustave, ed. *A Birthday Offering to C[arl] E[ngel]*. New York: G. Schirmer, 1943.

Rogers, Clara Kathleen. *The Story of Two Lives: Home, Friends, and Travels*. Norwood, Mass.: Plimpton Press, 1932.

Rosenfeld, Paul. *An Hour with American Music*. Philadelphia: J. B. Lippincott, 1929.

———. "The Music of Charles Martin Loeffler." *American Music Lover*. (April 1942): 267–71.

———. *Musical Portraits: Interpretation of Twenty Modern Composers*. New York: Harcourt, Brace and Howe, 1920.

———. "Taylor, Carpenter and Loeffler." *New Republic* 66 (1931): 128–29.

Russell, Henry. *The Passing Show*. Boston: Little, Brown, 1926.

Salazar, Adolfo. *Music in Our Time: Trends in Music since the Romantic Era*. Translated by Isabel Pope. New York: W. W. Norton, 1946.

Schonberg, Harold C. "The Father of the American String Quartets." *New York Times*, 12 September 1976, p. 21.

Schwager, Myron. "A Contribution to the Biography of Ernest Bloch: Letters at the University of Hartford." *Current Musicology* 28 (1979): 41–53.

Semler, Isabel Parker. *Horatio Parker: A Memoir for His Grandchildren Compiled from Letters and Papers*. New York: G. P. Putnam's Sons, 1942.

Sharp, Elizabeth A. *William Sharp (Fiona MacLeod): A Memoir*. London: William Heinemann, 1910.

Shepherd, Arthur. "'Papa' Goetschius in Retrospect." *Musical Quarterly* 30 (July 1944): 307–18.

Slonimsky, Nicolas. *Music since 1900*. 4th ed. New York: Charles Scribner's Sons, 1971.

Smith, Moses. "Loeffler and His Music." 25 May 1935. BSO clipping.

———. "The Strange Case of Charles Martin Loeffler." *American Music Lover* (March 1936): 357–58, 362.

Spalding, Walter Raymond. *Music at Harvard*. New York: Coward-McCann, 1935.

Taylor, Deems. *Of Men and Music*. New York: Simon and Schuster, 1945.

Tharp, Louise Hall. *Mrs. Jack*. Boston: Little, Brown, 1965.

Thomas, Theodore. *A Musical Autobiography*. Edited by George P. Upton. Chicago: A. C. McClurg, 1905. Reprint. New York: Da Capo Press, 1964.

Varese, Louise. *Varese: A Looking-Glass Diary, Vol. 1: 1883–1928*. New York: W. W. Norton, 1972.

Walton, Nellie F. "Remodeling a Massachusetts Farmhouse." *American Homes and Gardens* (August 1914): 262–66.

Waters, Edward N. *Victor Herbert: A Life in Music*. New York: Macmillan, 1955.

———. "The Wa-Wan Press." In *A Birthday Offering to C[arl] E[ngel]*. Edited by Gustave Reese. New York: G. Schirmer, 1943.

Weeks, Edward, ed. *The Tavern Club at Seventy-Five, 1934–1959: A Medley*. Cambridge: Riverside Press, 1959.

Whitehill, Walter Muir. *Museum of Fine Arts Boston: A Centennial History*. 2 vols. Cambridge, Mass.: Belknap Press of Harvard University Press, 1970.

Whitwell, David. *The Longy Club: A Professional Wind Ensemble in Boston (1900–1917)*. Northridge, Calif.: WINDS, 1988.

Winn, E. L. "Charles Martin Loeffler: A Sketch." *The Musical Observer— New York* 4/10 (1910): 24–25.

INDEX

BOOKS IN THE SERIES MUSIC IN AMERICAN LIFE

Bibliographical Handbook of American Music
D. W. Krummel

Goin' to Kansas City
Nathan W. Pearson, Jr.

"Susanna," "Jeanie," and "The Old Folks at Home": The Songs
of Stephen C. Foster from His Time to Ours
Second Edition
William W. Austin

Songprints: The Musical Experience of Five Shoshone Women
Judith Vander

"Happy in the Service of the Lord": Afro-American Gospel
Quartets in Memphis
Kip Lornell

Paul Hindemith in the United States
Luther Noss

"My Song Is My Weapon": People's Songs, American Communism,
and the Politics of Culture
Robbie Lieberman

Chosen Voices: The Story of the American Cantorate
Mark Slobin

Theodore Thomas: America's Conductor and Builder
of Orchestras, 1835–1905
Ezra Schabas

"The Whorehouse Bells Were Ringing" and
Other Songs Cowboys Sing
Guy Logsdon

Crazeology: The Autobiography of a Chicago Jazzman
Bud Freeman, as Told to Robert Wolf

Discoursing Sweet Music: Brass Bands and Community Life
in Turn-of-the-Century Pennsylvania
Kenneth Kreitner

Mormonism and Music: A History
Michael Hicks

Voices of the Jazz Age: Profiles of Eight Vintage Jazzmen
Chip Deffaa

Pickin' on Peachtree: A History of Country Music in Atlanta, Georgia
Wayne W. Daniel

Bitter Music: Collected Journals, Essays, Introductions, and Librettos
Harry Partch; edited by Thomas McGeary

Ethnic Music on Records: A Discography of Ethnic Recordings
Produced in the United States, 1893 to 1942
Richard K. Spottswood

Downhome Blues Lyrics: An Anthology from
the Post-World War II Era
Jeff Todd Titon

Ellington: The Early Years
Mark Tucker

Chicago Soul
Robert Pruter

That Half-Barbaric Twang: The Banjo in American Popular Culture
Karen Linn

Hot Man: The Life of Art Hodes
Art Hodes and Chadwick Hansen

The Erotic Muse: American Bawdy Songs
Second Edition
Ed Cray

Barrio Rhythm: Mexican American Music in Los Angeles
Steven Loza

The Creation of Jazz: Music, Race, and Culture in Urban America
Burton W. Peretti

Charles Martin Loeffler: A Life Apart in American Music
Ellen Knight